Hollywood Quarterly

Hollywood Quarterly

FILM CULTURE IN
POSTWAR AMERICA,
1945–1957

EDITED BY Eric Smoodin
AND Ann Martin

UNIVERSITY OF CALIFORNIA PRESS   BERKELEY   LOS ANGELES   LONDON

University of California Press
Berkeley and Los Angeles, California

University of California Press, Ltd.
London, England

© 2002 by the Regents of the University of
California

A Cataloging-in-Publication record is available
from the Library of Congress
ISBN 0-520-23273-9 (cloth)
ISBN 0-520-23274-7 (pbk.)

The paper used in this publication is both acid-free
and totally chlorine-free (TCF). It meets the minimum requirements of ANSI/NISO z39.48-1992
(R 1997) *(Permanence of Paper).* ♾

Contents

Acknowledgments · ix

Introduction: The *Hollywood Quarterly*, 1945–1957
Eric Smoodin · xi

1945 . . . . Editorial Statement · 1

1 THE AVANT-GARDE

1947–48 . . . . . Experimental Cinema in America, Part One: 1921–1941
Lewis Jacobs · 5

1948 . . . . Experimental Cinema in America, Part Two:
The Postwar Revival · *Lewis Jacobs* · 28

1949 . . . . The Avant-Garde Film Seen from Within
Hans Richter · 51

1950 . . . . Cinema 16: A Showcase for the Nonfiction Film
Amos Vogel · 57

2 ANIMATION

1946 . . . . Animation Learns a New Language
John Hubley and Zachary Schwartz · 63

1946 . . . . Music and the Animated Cartoon · *Chuck Jones* · 69

1953 . . . . Notes on Animated Sound · *Norman McLaren* · 77

1957 . . . . Mr. Magoo as Public Dream · *Milton J. Rosenberg* · 84

3 DOCUMENTARY

1946 . . . . Postwar Patterns · *John Grierson* · 91

1946 . . . . The Documentary and Hollywood · *Philip Dunne* · 100

1957 . . . . Time Flickers Out: Notes on the Passing of
the *March of Time* · *Raymond Fielding* · 109

4 RADIO

1946 . . . . *The Case of David Smith:* A Script, with Commentary
by Sam Moore, Franklin Fearing, and Cal Kuhl
Abraham Polonsky · 119

1948 . . . . Radio's Attraction for Housewives · *Ruth Palter* · 139

1955 . . . . A New Kind of Diplomacy · *Gene King* · 152

5 PRACTICE

1946 . . . . A Costume Problem: From Shot to Stage to Screen
Edith Head · 161

1947–48 . . . . . Performance under Pressure · *Alexander Knox* · 166

1950 . . . . Designing *The Heiress* · *Harry Horner* · 180

1951 . . . . The Limitations of Television · *Rudy Bretz* · 186

6 TELEVISION

1949 . . . . Hollywood in the Television Age · *Samuel Goldwyn* · 199

1949 . . . . You and Television
Lyman Bryson and Edward R. Murrow · 205

1951 . . . . Children's Television Habits and Preferences
May V. Seagoe · 209

1952 . . . . How to Look at Television · *T. W. Adorno* · 222

7 THE HOLLYWOOD PICTURE

1946 . . . . Why Wait for Posterity? · *Iris Barry* · 243

1946 . . . . Hollywood—Illusion and Reality
John Howard Lawson · 253

1946 . . . . Negro Stereotypes on the Screen
Leon H. Hardwick · 256

1947 . . . . Today's Hero: A Review · *John Houseman* · 259

1947–48 . . . . . An Exhibitor Begs for "B's" · *Arthur L. Mayer* · 263

1951 . . . . A Word of Caution for the Intelligent Consumer
of Motion Pictures · *Franklin Fearing* · 271

1951 . . . . There's Really No Business Like Show Business
          Jay E. Gordon · 283

1952 . . . . There's Still No Business Like It
          Jean Hersholt et al. · 293

1952 . . . . Hollywood's Foreign Correspondents
          Harva Kaaren Sprager · 300

          8 SCENES FROM ABROAD

1946 . . . . Advanced Training for Film Workers: Russia
          Jay Leyda · 311

1946 . . . . Advanced Training for Film Workers: France
          Charles Boyer · 322

1947 . . . . The Global Film · *Vsevolod Pudovkin* · 327

1950 . . . . The Postwar French Cinema · *Georges Sadoul* · 334

1956 . . . . When in Rome . . . · *Hugh Gray* · 345

          9 NOTES AND COMMUNICATIONS

1946 . . . . J'Accuse · *Pierre Descaves* · 357

1947 . . . . Je Confirme · *Robert Joseph* · 360

1947 . . . . The Cinémathèque Française · *Henri Langlois* · 362

1947 . . . . Jean Vigo · *Siegfried Kracauer* · 366

1952 . . . . Two Views of a Director—Billy Wilder
          Herbert G. Luft and Charles Brackett · 370

1955 . . . . Dialogue between the Moviegoing Public and a Witness
          for Jean Cocteau · *Raymond Jean* · 381

          Selected Names Index · 387

          Selected Titles Index · 391

Acknowledgments

FOR THEIR INVALUABLE ASSISTANCE with film stills, all thanks go to Nancy Goldman and Jason Sanders at the Pacific Film Archive. Frame enlargements and film stills are included by courtesy of the following: Pacific Film Archive, AFE, MCA/Universal Pictures, Paramount, Soyuzdetfilm, Universal International, and the War Activities Committee of the Motion Pictures Industry. We also want to express our gratitude to the contributors to this volume—they represent a larger group whose work is a testament to the adventurous minds and stalwart spirits of this early generation of film and media scholars.

Closer to home, much gratitude to our generous colleagues Monica McCormick, Mary Koon, David Gill, and Kate Toll at the University of California Press, who deftly assisted us through various administrative and production mazes with goodwill and good humor. And thanks also—for her irreplaceable help and fabulous entertainment value—to our intern, UC Berkeley film studies senior Heatha' Comden. Ernest Callenbach was as always a model of common sense and sensibility. Caren and Bob were models of patience and understanding; we are under no illusions that we could have managed without them.

ERIC SMOODIN
ANN MARTIN

Introduction:
The *Hollywood Quarterly*, 1945–1957

WRITING JUST AFTER the end of World War II, the editors of the *Holly-wood Quarterly* posed the following question: "What part will the motion picture and the radio play in the consolidation of the victory, in the crea-tion of new patterns of world culture and understanding?" Asked at the beginning of volume 1, number 1, this question, and the "Editorial State-ment" of which it was a part, made particular sense in 1945. Today, more than half a century later, we might ask what made this question plausible, and why did the editors' concerns about peace, education, and aesthetics coalesce around the movies? We need to know, then, why a journal dedi-cated to the serious study of film, radio, and, later, television might have made such good sense at the time, and how it attracted a collection of writers unmatched in North American film studies, before or since, for the heterogeneity of their intellectual and practical concerns.

The first issue of the *Hollywood Quarterly* appeared in October 1945. Number 1 cost $1.25, although a reader could buy a four-issue annual sub-scription for only $4.00.[1] The University of California Press published the journal, the daily activities of which were overseen by the members of a five-person editorial board, who were themselves guided by a number of advisers in motion pictures, music, radio, and technology.[2] Number 1 had major articles under five headings: Motion Pictures, Radio, the Sta-tus of the Writer (not surprising for a journal with several prominent screenwriters on its editorial board and advisory committees), Technol-ogy, and Problems of Communication (about veterans acclimating to

---

1. In 1946, as a special "Supplement to Volume One," the *Quarterly* produced a fifth issue for the only time in the journal's history; this was the *Annual Communications Bib-liography*, with listings of recent literature on film, radio, and music in film and radio, along with an article called "Hollywood's War Films, 1942–1944."

2. These advisers included a number of prominent Hollywood professionals: Orson Welles, Gregg Toland, Fritz Lang, Edward Dmytryk, and Vincent Price, among many others.

ERIC SMOODIN

peacetime). Throughout the journal's history, all issues followed the same general format, with sections, typically, on motion pictures and radio, and then special sections—on documentary, or animation, or the special problems of television. Around 1954, television replaced radio as a recurring heading, but the special sections continued, on Shakespeare in film, or foreign films, or the origins of film.

The editorial board changed and expanded over the years, and in 1951 the *Hollywood Quarterly* became the *Quarterly Review of Film, Radio, and Television.* (For the sake of simplicity, and because the original title seems to best capture the aims of the journal, we chose to use *Hollywood Quarterly* in the title of this collection to cover the entire 1945–57 period of publication.) The cover design changed as well, from Gothic script on a plain background, to starker contemporary lettering, and finally to a mid-century modern spectacle of technological and cultural progress: a ballet dancer, a radio microphone, and two men, seemingly in a western shoot-out setting, each image in what looks to be a small square television set or movie screen. But the format rarely varied (early on the journal shifted from a two-column to a one-column page), with each issue conforming to the same six-by-nine-inch format and running between 100 and 130 pages, and the price never changed.

The *Hollywood Quarterly*, and the *Quarterly Review of Film, Radio, and Television,* continues today, in a manner of speaking, as *Film Quarterly,* the name the journal took in 1958, when it was fully reorganized and markedly reconfigured in terms of content and form. This probably makes it the longest-running serious film journal in the country, as well as almost certainly the first significant, successful, and regularly published journal of its kind produced in the United States. But the *Hollywood Quarterly* did not simply spring fully grown from the brow of its editorial committee. There had been major film journals in the United States before the *Quarterly. Experimental Cinema* and *Cinema* both began a few years of publication in the United States in 1930, and while distribution information is difficult to come by, *Close Up* and *Sight and Sound* probably traveled from Great Britain to the United States during the Great Depression.[3] There also had been a pre-*Quarterly* history of serious film scholarship originating in high-toned general-interest journals published

3. For a discussion of the journal *Close Up,* see James Donald, Anne Friedberg, and Laura Marcus, eds., *Close Up, 1927–1933: Cinema and Modernism* (Princeton: Princeton University Press, 1998). The editors discuss *Experimental Cinema* and *Cinema* on page 26.

in the United States, such as *Survey Graphic*, or in journals that concentrated on live drama, like *Theatre Magazine*, or in such special-interest publications as *Scientific American*. Some of the movie critics for "respected" newspapers and magazines—Frank Nugent of the *New York Times*, for instance, or James Rorty in *The Nation*, or Barbara Deming in the *Partisan Review* and elsewhere—considered the historical and aesthetic aspects of the cinema in their reviews, and such publications as *Parents' Magazine* regularly included articles by psychologists and other experts on the effects of movies on kids.

Nevertheless, in part because there was no successful prewar American journal committed exclusively to the study of film and related media, the misconception persists that little intellectual attention was paid to the movies in the United States before the 1950s. But the *Hollywood Quarterly* actually appeared toward the end of an eclectic and fertile period of film scholarship, one that included not just isolated essays in journals and magazines, but significant book-length studies by university-based scholars, usually from the social sciences. We might, then, see the *Quarterly* as maintaining a tradition that can be traced at least as far back as Robert and Helen Lynd's famous study, *Middletown*, from 1929, and including the Payne Fund Studies, published throughout the 1930s; Margaret Farrand Thorp's still underappreciated *America at the Movies*, which Yale published in 1939; and, in something of the apotheosis of this movement, sociologist Leo Handel's *Hollywood Looks at Its Audience*, from 1950 and published by the University of Illinois Press.

The editors of the *Quarterly* were committed to hearing from a broad range of experts, and so sought practical as well as intellectual contributions from film industry professionals—directors, writers, and exhibitors, for instance. Even here, the editors consolidated a practice that had been in place for many years. Cameramen, writers, directors, and theater owners had frequently written about their jobs for a variety of audiences, in publications ranging from fan magazines to journals such as *American Cinematographer* to book-length studies.[4]

---

4. The contributions of studio workers to professional journals and other publications (such as Academy of Arts and Sciences "Technical Bulletins") are too numerous even to begin to mention them here. For an example from a fan magazine, see Walt Disney, "Exposing Mickey Mouse," in *Screen Book* (January 1934), 16–17, 68–69. For a book-length study, see, for example, theater manager Frank H. Ricketson's *The Management of Motion Picture Theatres* (New York: McGraw-Hill Book Company, Inc.), 1938.

Issues not fully related to film scholarship, some broad and some more narrowly focused, also help situate the goals of the *Quarterly*. To open their editorial statement, the editors explained that "the war, with its complex demands for indoctrination, propaganda, and specialized training, emphasized the social function of film and radio." And, indeed, the war marked the consolidation of a new class of experts, as psychiatrists, psychologists, and a variety of other social scientists became government workers, with many of them using the millions of enlisted men as experimental subjects in the development of a sort of utopian postwar liberal modernism. Film, or, more precisely, the possibility for film to influence and indoctrinate, played an absolutely pivotal role in this development. The government became a film producer on a large scale, but the films the government made were designed to propagandize rather than entertain. Frank Capra's *Why We Fight* series, made to transform men who until recently had been civilians into a cohesive military force, stands out as the most impressive of the period's mobilization of the movies, but for the government's scientific experts the effectiveness of the series extended well beyond the context of the war. If Capra's documentaries could make nineteen- and twenty-year-olds understand the need to go into battle against the Germans and Japanese, then other movies, after the war, might be used to teach citizens how not to be racist or hypernationalist.[5]

The people involved with the *Hollywood Quarterly*, many of whom had worked in the war effort, shared this belief in the utopian possibilities of film. They hoped that the journal might become a forum for advancing a politicized, socially responsible cinema, one freed from what their editorial statement called the "'pure entertainment' myth, which had served to camouflage the social irresponsibility and creative impotence of much of the material presented on the screen and over the air" both before and during the war.

Film needed to teach, to enlighten, to persuade. In their statement, the editors stressed not only their desire to understand the "aesthetic" princi-

5. For discussions of the uses of the *Why We Fight* films, as well as of the wartime contributions of a variety of social scientists, see Carl I. Hovland, Arthur A. Lumsdaine, and Fred D. Sheffield, *Experiments on Mass Communication*, volume 3 (Princeton: Princeton University Press, 1949); Ron Robin, *The Barbed-Wire College: Reeducating German POWs in the United States during World War II* (Princeton: Princeton University Press, 1995); and Ellen Herman, *The Romance of American Psychology: Political Culture in the Age of Experts* (Berkeley: University of California Press, 1995).

ples of film and other media, but also their "social" and "educational" possibilities. In so saying, the editors aligned themselves not just with the social science of the war, but also with the film education movement, one of the significant developments in film studies from at least the previous twenty years, and one that had flourished particularly since the 1930s. This movement stressed the pedagogical possibilities of movies, even those churned out by Hollywood.

During the depression, hundreds of junior high and high schools instructed their students in film appreciation, typically as units in English classes.[6] Certainly, this curriculum had at least something to do with keeping bored kids occupied as they learned how to evaluate movies that they had seen in local theaters. But film educators—the teachers and social scientists who carefully planned curricula or wrote the textbooks that helped to organize film study principles—also understood the objectives of progressive education. They hoped to use the movies, both the best examples and the worst, to teach students about the effects of racism, class inequality, and war. These extraordinarily New Dealish efforts—on the part of film educators in the 1930s and government social scientists studying enlisted men during the war—had more or less disappeared by the postwar period, but their lessons were not lost on the *Hollywood Quarterly* editors, even the most moderate of whom were avid New Deal supporters, and all of whom believed in the promise of an enlightened, liberal future emerging from the chaos of a global war.

What late-1940s film studies had begun to lose, with the collapse of so much New Deal enthusiasm, it had gained in university attention to the cinema. Robert Gessner, for example, had taught a class in film history and aesthetics at New York University as early as 1938, and during the 1930s and early 1940s, for a variety of reasons, American studies began to flourish on college and university campuses. The faculty finally had started to include scholars whose connection to elite culture was somewhat tenuous, and whose main interests were more regional, vernacular, and popular—Jews, for instance, and a variety of leftists, and those who

6. For a full analysis of secondary-school film instruction, see Lea Jacobs, "Reformers and Spectators: The Film Education Movement in the Thirties," *Camera Obscura* 22 (January 1990), 29–49. Also during this period, the Catholic Church organized its own system of film education, marked not so much by the progressivism of the junior high and high school programs, but rather by a determination to teach children to resist the alleged evil of so many Hollywood movies.

had attended state universities rather than private institutions. The emer-
gence of vast state systems of university education in Wisconsin, California, and elsewhere also led to a determination to study the regional, and
to examine the ideological connection between artistic production and
the project of building the nation. The movies seemed the perfect match
for these interests (although not quite as much as literature by Twain or
Whitman or Stowe, among others). Responding to this enthusiasm for
corporate, popular art, the *Hollywood Quarterly*, while still championing
the European art cinema, took American movies very seriously, not just
as sociological artifacts but as aesthetic objects. Such seriousness might
not have been possible just fifteen years earlier, before both the entrance
of film studies into the secondary-school and university curriculum and
the extraordinary American studies movement of the World War II era.
In *Hollywood Quarterly*, then, with the journal's determination to study
and to educate, we can see the direct result of a recent history of linking
film to the classroom, to effective, enlightened liberal citizenship, and to
considerations of national character.

The *Hollywood Quarterly* also developed from a more immediate history, and from a more specific political instance. In October 1943, a group
of scholars at the University of California, Los Angeles, along with the
Hollywood Writers' Mobilization, sponsored the Writers' Congress on
the UCLA campus. The mobilization itself had been formed just after the
United States entered World War II, in order to assist in the war effort.[7]
Embodying the Popular Front sensibility of the war period, its members
ranged from the liberal Paramount producer Kenneth Macgowan to the
hard-line Communist screenwriter John Howard Lawson. In other words,
the entire spectrum of the Hollywood left supported the movement, with
the congress itself marking the formation of a significant coalition between university intelligentsia and movie studio intellectuals.

Even more specifically, the congress provided the opportunity for social
scientists, such as UCLA's Franklin Fearing, who specialized in the effects
of mass communication, to meet with Hollywood workers who believed
strongly in the possibility of an aesthetically informed, leftist commercial
cinema. This naturally raised the ire and concern of the Tenney Commit-

7. August Frugé, *A Skeptic among Scholars: August Frugé on University Publishing*
(Berkeley: University of California Press, 1993), page 157.

tee, the California senate's equivalent of the House Un-American Activities Committee, and the FBI, which kept careful tabs on the mobilization and many of the participants in the congress. The leaders of the Writers' Congress, then, were subject to the kind of anti-Semitic, anti-leftist persecution that would come to mark the blacklist era. But the congress, really, was nothing if not eclectic; fifteen hundred took part, including the dependably right-wing, at least mildly anti-Semitic, and unwaveringly anti-Communist Walt Disney.

The participants in the congress seem to have been bound by a sort of utopian, one-world-style belief in the power of the arts to promote national solidarity and global unity. In a surveillance report, the FBI noted that the congress passed a resolution advocating the "creation of [a] Department of Arts and Letters by [the] U.S. Government," while still other resolutions called for "a cultural and educational congress to meet in Central or South America in the near future, the development of cultural relations between the United Nations, and the establishment of a Continuations Committee of the Congress to explore possibilities of [a] National Congress on [the] problems of war and the post-war period." This was the promise of the mid-1940s, that a useful coalition might be formed between artists and intellectuals, one inspired by the left, but that might include even the likes of Walt Disney, whose visits to and films about Central and South America during the period made him at least initially sympathetic to many of the congress's internationalist goals.[8]

On a more modest scale, the congress initiated some publishing projects. The first, from 1944, simply collected and presented much that took place at that first gathering, as its title would indicate: *Writers' Congress: Proceedings* (published by the University of California Press). But the congress also proposed something that would appear more regularly, and that might keep stressing and refining the belief in the benefits of combining the arts with the social sciences: the *Hollywood Quarterly*. The name itself marked the unusual partnership of the congress. As former University of California Press director August Frugé noted, "*Hollywood*

---

8. The description of the Writers' Congress can be found in the file that the FBI maintained on Walt Disney. See document no. 100–5377, "League of American Writers."

for the profession, *Quarterly* for academia."⁹ The Hollywood Writers'
Mobilization and the University of California cosponsored the journal,
with the mobilization appointing two editorial board members and the
provost at UCLA appointing two others, with then–UC Press director
Samuel Farquhar acting as the fifth member.

Kenneth Macgowan and John Howard Lawson were the first editors
chosen by the mobilization (although Lawson soon resigned, after HUAC
began to persecute him). They were joined by Franklin Fearing and
Franklin Rolfe of UCLA, and also by Farquhar. At least in part a victim
of McCarthy-era cold war politics, the mobilization disbanded in 1947.
For a few months, a group called the *Hollywood Quarterly* Associates went
into business with the university to publish the journal, but by late 1947
the University of California became the sole sponsor. The Press had the
good sense to maintain the journal's Hollywood connection, and in 1949
half of an expanded eight-person board still worked in the movies—writers James Hilton, John Collier, and Abraham Polonsky, and actor-director
Irving Pichel. According to Frugé, it really was assistant editor Sylvia Jarrico who did most of the work for the board, but as another casualty of
the cold war, she left her position rather than take the newly imposed
University of California loyalty oath (her husband, screenwriter Paul Jarrico, would be a victim of the Hollywood blacklist).

During those early years, the *Quarterly* survived a 1946 investigation by
the Tenney Committee, and then a 1950 attack by *Red Channels,* the
"bible of the graylist," which concerned itself with Communist infiltra-
tion of the broadcast industry.¹⁰ There were, as well, internal struggles,
difficult to reconstruct now but that resulted—depending on whose
story one believes, the editorial board's or the Press's—either in the *Quarterly* falling a year behind in its publication schedule during 1948–49 or
in a temporary suspension of publication.¹¹ Subscriptions peaked for the

9. Frugé, *A Skeptic among Scholars,* page 158. For information on the history of the
Quarterly, we are indebted to Frugé's book, and in particular chapter 2, "Hollywood
and Berkeley: Getting into the Film Business," pages 157–166.

10. See Patrick McGilligan and Paul Buhle, *Tender Comrades: A Backstory of the Hollywood Blacklist* (New York: St. Martin's Griffon, 1999), page 318.

11. Ellen R. Seacoat, the manager of the University Periodicals Department, mentioned the suspension of publication in a memo on 28 May 1954 to the editors of the
Quarterly. In a 28 October 1954 memo, editorial committee chair Robert Usinger insisted there had been no suspension, only a delay in publication. (All correspondence
cited in this introduction is housed at the University of California Press in Berkeley.)

very first 1945 issue at about fifteen hundred, but a year later they had diminished to about twelve hundred, and then shrank to a little over seven hundred after the disputed delay/suspension. Until 1954, the last period for which numbers are available, subscriptions hovered between five hundred and seven hundred, with about two out of every three copies going to libraries or other institutions, and the rest to individuals.[12]

Of course, declining subscription rates concerned both the editorial board and the Press. Board members worried that the very name *Hollywood Quarterly* "undoubtedly worked to [the journal's] disadvantage so far as subscribers were concerned, since it seemed to imply that the prime consideration . . . was the Hollywood film industry."[13] As a result, the board considered changing the title to something that would make explicit the journal's combination of aesthetics and social science. The first choice was *Arts and Communication Quarterly,* but after further consultation between the board and the Press, yet another title finally was decided upon, one that emphasized media rather than methodology: The *Quarterly Review of Film, Radio, and Television,* appearing for the first time in 1951, on volume 6.

For their part, officials at the Press viewed the subscription problem largely in terms of content, and in ways that reflected many of the developments in film studies as a discipline during the 1950s. It was precisely during that period that film studies in the academy became less of a social science practice and much more one associated with the humanities. The reasons for this shift remain unclear but may have had something to do with the diversification of English departments of the era and the shifting interest of sociologists and psychologists from film to television. In any event, in a 1954 memo to Press director Frugé, periodicals manager Ellen Seacoat worried precisely about a kind of disciplinary unpredictability built into the journal. "I feel frustrated," she wrote, adding, "Who is sufficiently interested in all or most of these subjects [covered by the *Quarterly*] to pay for a subscription?" Seacoat wondered whether "the

12. See the Seacoat memo for subscription information. For information about institutional and individual subscriptions, see "Quarterly Review of Film, Radio, & TV: Facts and Figures on Subscriptions and Costs," University of California Press memo, 31 January 1955.

13. See Usinger's memo for information regarding the board's reaction to declining subscriptions.

person primarily interested in social science articles [would] be willing to pay for the other types of articles in which he is not particularly interested?" She then commended the direction of recent issues, and particularly volume 8, with their "heavy emphasis on Shakespeare and literature as brought to the public through mass media," which apparently convinced many readers teaching in universities and other schools to think of the journal "as an exciting adjunct to the teaching of English and related subjects." Seacoat was concerned, however, that the articles in volume 9 reverted to the social science form of previous volumes, thereby losing the readers that had only just been gained.[14]

Frugé himself worried about the continued influence of the social sciences in the journal, lamenting that, after the 1951 name change, the *Quarterly* "continued for another six years, running gradually down—or so I seem to remember—as the emphasis became more sociological and less cinematic."[15] In this narrative, the *Quarterly* stood out as a dinosaur, as a throwback to a depression-era and wartime interest in the social function of the cinema. By the late 1950s, it seemed much more obvious, and even desirable, that the movies could enlighten through aesthetic uplift rather than liberal pedagogy.

The Press did what it could to promote the *Quarterly*. Volume 8, for instance, featured Frankfurt School theorist Theodor Adorno's "How to Look at Television" (reproduced in this collection), and the Press understood that this was a scholarly event of some moment. A publicity release announced the article, something difficult to imagine today for any theoretical essay about spectatorship. But subscription rates seemed not to receive any boost and, according to Frugé, declined to about three hundred by 1957.[16] The *Quarterly*, clearly, had come to something of a crisis.

Frugé has written that he "braced [himself] for trouble with the editorial board." But Kenneth Macgowan, the board chair at the time, understood that the *Quarterly* was no longer economically viable. The other ed-

14. Ellen Seacoat, memo to August Frugé, regarding "*Quarterly* statement of purposes and principles," 3 November 1954.

15. Frugé, *A Skeptic among Scholars*, page 161.

16. For a discussion of the promotion of Adorno's essay, see Seacoat's memo to Frugé, 3 November 1954. Frugé discusses the subscription decline in *A Skeptic among Scholars*, page 160.

itors agreed, and so, in Frugé's words, "the old *Quarterly* died with neither a bang nor a whimper but with a shrug of the shoulders."[17] Even after its demise, however, at least for a while, the *Quarterly* maintained its
University of California subsidy. Rather than allowing that to revert to
the state, Frugé organized another journal, *Film Quarterly* (with Ernest
Callenbach as editor), modeled very much on the British *Sight and Sound*
and the French *Cahiers du cinéma*—that is, according to Frugé, "devoted
to film as an art and not as communication."[18] In American film studies
this as much as anything marked the disciplinary shift, placing cinema
scholarship firmly within the realm of the humanities, where, for better
and for worse, and despite a recent interest in social science methodologies, it still remains.

For its entire life the *Hollywood Quarterly* steadfastly held to the leftist
utopianism of the founding UCLA Writers' Congress and the immediate
postwar period, with its determination to mix essays by intellectuals with
those by Hollywood filmmakers, its belief in building a more peaceful,
tolerant global culture through better films, and its assertion of the high
quality of at least some American movies (although modernists that they
were, few contributors would have questioned the superiority of *Bicycle
Thieves* or *Grand Illusion*). The *Quarterly* maintained an interest in not
just film, but all of the major entertainment media, and in issue after issue insisted on the importance of both "aesthetic" and "sociological"
methodologies for studying popular culture.

In selecting the articles for this collection, we have tried to preserve the
journal's progressive beliefs as well as its intellectual and aesthetic standards. In the spirit of the *Quarterly,* we have put together special sections
on animation, the avant-garde, and documentary to go along with a representative sampling of articles about feature-length narrative films. We
also have collected articles on radio and television, reflecting the contents
of just about every issue of the *Quarterly.* Each issue devoted a few pages
to short dispatches in a "communications" section, and we have done the
same, with some commentary reflecting the journal's interest in directors,
here on Jean Vigo, Billy Wilder, and Jean Cocteau, and also a dispatch
from Henri Langlois on the Cinémathèque Française and a contretemps

17. Both citations come from Frugé, *A Skeptic among Scholars,* page 160.
18. Ibid., page 161.

between Pierre Descaves and French filmmaker Sacha Guitry on the latter's alleged collaboration with the Nazis during World War II.[19]

The *Quarterly* was a place for Hollywood workers to write about their craft and also to practice it, and so the journal featured the occasional publication of scripts. In this collection, we have reproduced Abraham Polonsky's radio play (which was in fact produced), *The Case of David Smith*. And in keeping with the *Quarterly*'s emphasis on the links between media production and education, we have also provided the commentary that followed.

This interest in practice extended to all aspects of media work. In fact, it was the *Quarterly*'s concern with labor issues that probably served best to separate it from the film journals that followed, journals that tended to focus attention on the finished product rather than on its making. As a result, we have devoted a section to these practical aspects of filmmaking—acting, set design, and fashion, for instance—and have scattered articles in other sections, notably by Georges Sadoul and Charles Boyer, about the less glamorous aspects of film work.

We have tried to achieve something of the style of the *Quarterly,* a kind of attention to the literary as well as to the purely academic—this was, after all, a journal on which some of the finest American writers from the midcentury served as editors and contributors. So along with a "just the facts" presentation, with sections on animation, practice, and other clearly labeled areas, we have called a section on American filmmaking "The Hollywood Picture," and on European, "Scenes from Abroad." Despite their interest in literary and aesthetic detail, and as if to maintain the journal's academic seriousness, the editors rarely made use of photographs and other images. We have in each case reproduced those few original illustrations—the photos accompanying Lewis Jacobs's two-part series on experimental cinema in America, Edith Head's fashion designs, and Chuck Jones's scientific squiggles—but in keeping with the expectations of modern film scholarship, we have also added some photographs wherever it seemed appropriate and feasible. For each essay's contributor's

---

19. According to Alan Williams, Guitry "profited handsomely and ostentatiously from his films and plays of the Occupation . . . and he had flagrantly socialized with high German officials. But he had apparently done no more than this," and so the government's case against him eventually was dismissed. See Williams, *Republic of Images: A History of French Filmmaking* (Cambridge: Harvard University Press, 1992), page 273.

note, we have chosen to use the description that appeared at the time of publication, rather than add any retrospective discussion of the career of an Iris Barry or Abraham Polonsky.

Finally, we have attempted to reproduce something of the astonishing eclecticism of the journal, with its interest in high art and housewives, with the heavy seriousness of John Howard Lawson coupled with the humor and good nature of Hugh Gray. Mostly, though, we have tried to give a sense of the full range of journal contributors. It surely says something about the values of the *Quarterly* that writers ranged from Samuel Goldwyn to Theodor Adorno, from Edith Head to Vsevolod Pudovkin. Exhibitors and existentialists shared the pages of the *Quarterly,* and that probably more than anything else speaks to the extraordinary moment in film and media studies that the journal captured and helped to create.

Hollywood Quarterly

FROM VOL. 1, NO. 1, OCTOBER 1945

Editorial Statement

THE WAR, WITH ITS COMPLEX demands for indoctrination, propaganda, and specialized training, emphasized the social function of film and radio. One of the first casualties of the conflict was the "pure entertainment" myth, which had served to camouflage the social irresponsibility and creative impotence of much of the material presented on the screen and over the air.

The motion picture and the radio reflected the anxieties and hopes of the long crisis, and reported the tumult and prayer that marked the day of victory. What part will the motion picture and the radio play in the consolidation of the victory, in the creation of new patterns of world culture and understanding?

The editors of the *Hollywood Quarterly* are not so incautious as to attempt an answer to this question. Rather, the purpose of the magazine will be to seek an answer by presenting the record of research and exploration in motion pictures and radio in order to provide a basis for evaluation of economic, social, aesthetic, educational, and technological trends. The first issue of the *Hollywood Quarterly* is necessarily experimental: the scope of subject matter, and the stimulating but somewhat unsystematic diversity of style and viewpoint that characterizes the various articles, suggest the difficulty of selection and arrangement, and the lack of precedent even in limiting and defining the field of investigation. If a clearer understanding, not only of current techniques of the film and radio, but also of the social, educational, and aesthetic functions, is arrived at, the editors will feel that the *Quarterly* has justified itself indeed.

1 The Avant-Garde

Experimental Cinema in America

Part One: 1921–1941

Lewis Jacobs has contributed articles on the motion picture to two encyclopedias and to numerous magazines. His book *The Rise of the American Film* is now published in three languages. In Hollywood, aside from his own screen writing, he has taught screenplay technique to new contract writers at Columbia Studios and is now completing a book on the structure and art of the motion picture for Harcourt, Brace.

This article is the first half of an essay which is to appear in a forthcoming book, *The Experimental Film,* a collection of essays on the avant-garde cinema of America, Britain, France, Russia, and other countries, edited by Roger Manvell and published in England by the Grey Walls Press. Part Two: 1941–1947, will appear in the Spring, 1948, issue of the *Hollywood Quarterly* [pp. 28–50, this volume].

. . . . .

EXPERIMENTAL CINEMA in America has had little in common with the main stream of the motion picture industry.

Living a kind of private life of its own, its concern has been solely with motion pictures as a medium of artistic expression. This emphasis upon means rather than content not only endows experimental films with a value of their own but distinguishes them from all other commercial, documentary, educational, and amateur productions. Although its influence upon the current of film expression has been deeper than is generally realized, the movement has always been small, its members scattered, its productions sporadic and, for the most part, viewed by few.

In Europe the term for experimental efforts, "the avant-garde," has an intellectually creative connotation. But in America experimenters saw their work referred to as "amateur," an expression used not in a laudatory, but in a derogatory sense. Lack of regard became an active force, inhibiting and retarding productivity. In the effort to overcome outside disdain, experimental film makers in the United States tended to become cliquey and in-bred, often ignorant of the work of others with similar aims. There was little interplay and exchange of ideas and sharing of discoveries. But

with postwar developments in this field the old disparaging attitude has
been supplanted by a new regard and the experimental film maker has begun to be looked upon with respect. Today the word "amateur" is no
longer used; it has been dropped in favor of the word "experimenter."

The American experimental movement was born in a period of artistic
ferment in the motion picture world. During the decade 1921–1931,
sometimes called the "golden period of silent films," movies were attaining new heights in expression. Innovations in technique, content, and
structural forms were being introduced in films from Germany, France,
and Russia: *The Cabinet of Dr. Caligari, Waxworks, The Golem, Variety,
The Last Laugh, Le Ballet mécanique, Entr'acte, The Fall of the House of
Usher, Emak Bakia, The Italian Straw Hat, Thérèse Raquin, The Passion of
Joan of Arc, Potemkin, The End of St. Petersburg, Ten Days That Shook the
World, The Man with the Camera, Arsenal, Fragment of an Empire, Soil.*

The "foreign invasion," as it came to be called, enlarged the aesthetic
horizons of American movie makers, critics, and writers, and fostered native ambitions. Intellectuals hitherto indifferent or hostile now began to
look upon the cinema as a new art form. Books, essays, articles, and even
special film magazines appeared which extolled the medium's potentialities and predicted a brilliant future. Film guilds, film societies, film forums,
and special art theaters devoted to showing "the unusual, the experimental, the artistic film" sprang up, so that by the end of the decade the film
as a new art form was not only widely recognized but inspired wide enthusiasm for production. Young artists, photographers, poets, novelists,
dancers, architects, eager to explore the rich terrain of movie expression,
learned how to handle a camera and with the most meager resources attempted to produce pictures of their own. The expense proved so great
that most of the efforts were abortive; in others, the technique was not
equal to the imagination; and in still others, the ideas were not fully
formed, but fragmentary and improvisational, depending upon the moment's inspiration. Consequently, while there was a great deal of activity
and talk, hardly any experimental films were completed. It was not until
the main current of foreign pictures had waned—around 1928—that experimental cinema in America really got under way.

Two films were finished in the early 'twenties, however, which stand out
as landmarks in American experiment: *Mannahatta* (1921) and *Twenty-
four Dollar Island* (1925). Both showed an independence of approach and

probed an aspect of film expression that had not been explored by the film makers from abroad.

Mannahatta was a collaborative effort of Charles Sheeler, the modern painter, and Paul Strand, photographer and disciple of Alfred Steiglitz. Their film, one reel in length, attempted to express New York through its essential characteristics—power and beauty, movement and excitement. The title was taken from a poem by Walt Whitman, and excerpts from the poem were used as subtitles.

In technique the film was simple and direct, avoiding all the so-called "tricks" of photography and setting. In a sense it was the forerunner of the documentary school which rose in the United States in the middle 1930's. *Mannahatta* revealed a discerning eye and a disciplined camera. Selected angle shots achieved quasi-abstract compositions: a Staten Island ferryboat makes its way into the South Ferry pier; crowds of commuters are suddenly released into the streets of lower Manhattan; an ocean liner is aided by tugboats at the docks; pencil-like office buildings stretch upward into limitless space; minute restless crowds of people throng deep, narrow, skyscraper canyons; silvery smoke and steam rise plumelike against filtered skies; massive shadows and sharp sunlight form geometric patterns. The picture's emphasis upon visual pattern within the real world was an innovation for the times and resulted in a striking new impression of New York.

Mannahatta was presented as a "short" on the program of several large theaters in New York City, but by and large it went unseen. In Paris, where it appeared as evidence of American modernism on a Dadaist program which included music by Erik Satie and poems by Guillaume Apollinaire, it received something of an ovation. In the late 1920's the film was shown around New York at private gatherings and in some of the first art theaters. Its influence, however, was felt more in still photography, then making an upsurge as an art form, than in the field of experimental films.

Twenty-four Dollar Island, employing the same approach as *Mannahatta* and having much in common with it, was Robert Flaherty's picture of New York City and its harbor. The director had already established a style of his own and a reputation with such pictures as *Nanook of the North* and *Moana.* In those films his major interest lay in documenting the lives and manners of primitive people. In *Twenty-four Dollar Island,* people were irrelevant. Flaherty conceived the film as "a camera poem, a sort of architectural lyric where people will be used only incidentally as part of the background."

Flaherty's camera, like that of Strand and Sheeler, sought the metropolitan spirit in silhouettes of buildings against the sky, deep narrow skyscraper canyons, sweeping spans of bridges, the flurry of pressing crowds, the reeling of subway lights. Flaherty also emphasized the semiabstract pictorial values of the city: foreshortened viewpoints, patterns of mass and line, the contrast of sunlight and shadow. The result, as the director himself said, was "not a film of human beings, but of skyscrapers which they had erected, completely dwarfing humanity itself."

What particularly appealed to Flaherty was the opportunity to use telephoto lenses. Fascinated by the longer-focus lens, he made shots from the top of nearly every skyscraper in Manhattan. "I shot New York buildings from the East River bridges, from the ferries and from the Jersey shore looking up to the peaks of Manhattan. The effects obtained with my long-focus lenses amazed me. I remember shooting from the roof of the Telephone Building across the Jersey shore with an eight-inch lens and, even at that distance, obtaining a stereoscopic effect that seemed magical. It was like drawing a veil from the beyond, revealing life scarcely visible to the naked eye."

Despite the uniqueness of the film and Flaherty's reputation, *Twenty-four Dollar Island* had a very restricted release. Its treatment by New York's largest theater, the Roxy, foreshadowed somewhat the later vandalism to be practiced by others upon Eisenstein's *Romance sentimentale* and *Que viva México*. After cutting down *Twenty-four Dollar Island* from two reels to one, the Roxy directors used the picture as a background projection for one of their lavishly staged dance routines called *The Sidewalks of New York*.

Apart from these two early efforts the main current of American experimental films began to appear in 1928. The first ones showed the influence of the expressionistic style of the German film, *The Cabinet of Dr. Caligari*. Expressionism not only appealed to the ideological temper of the time, but suited the technical resources of the motion picture novitiates as well. Lack of money and experience had to be offset by ingenuity and fearlessness. "Effects" became a chief goal. The camera and its devices, the setting, and any object at hand that could be manipulated for an effect were exploited toward achieving a striking expression. Native experimenters emphasized technique above everything else. Content was secondary, or so neglected as to become the merest statement. One of the first serious motion picture critics, Gilbert Seldes, writing in the *New Republic,* March 6, 1929, pointed out that the experimental film makers "are opposed to naturalism; they have no stars; they are over-influenced by *Caligari;* they want to give their complete picture without the aid of any medium except the camera and projector."

The first experimental film in this country to show the influence of the expressionistic technique was the one-reel *The Life and Death of 9413 — A Hollywood Extra.* Made in the early part of 1928, this film cost less than a hundred dollars and aroused so much interest and discussion that Film Booking Office, a major distribution agency, contracted to distribute it through their exchanges, booking it into seven hundred theaters here and abroad.

A Hollywood Extra (the shortened title) was written and directed by Robert Florey, a former European film journalist and assistant director, and designed and photographed by Slavko Vorkapich, a painter with an intense desire to make poetic films. It was produced at night in Vorkapich's kitchen out of odds and ends — paper cubes, cigar boxes, tin cans, moving and reflected lights (from a single 400-watt bulb), an erector set, cardboard figures — and a great deal of ingenuity. Its style, broad and impressionistic, disclosed a remarkable selectivity and resourcefulness in the use of props, painting, camera, and editing.

In content, *A Hollywood Extra* was a simple satirical fantasy highlighting the dreams of glory of a Mr. Jones, a would-be star. A letter of recommendation gets Mr. Jones to a Hollywood casting director. There Mr. Jones is changed from an individual into a number, 9413, which is placed in bold ciphers upon his forehead. Thereafter he begins to talk the gibberish of Hollywood, consisting of slight variations of "bah-bah-bah-bah . . ."

Meanwhile, handsome Number 15, formerly Mr. Blank, is being screen-tested for a feature part. He pronounces "bah-bah-bah" facing front, profile left, profile right. The executives approve with enthusiastic "bah-bahs."

Subsequently, the preview of Number 15's picture is a great success. A star is painted on his forehead and his "bah-bahs" become assertive and haughty.

But Number 9413 is less fortunate. In his strenuous attempt to climb the stairway to success the only recognition he receives is "nbah-nbah-

nbah"—no casting today. From visions of heavy bankrolls, night clubs, glamour, and fanfare his dreams shrink to: "Pork and Beans—15 cents."

Clutching the telephone out of which issue the repeated "nbahs" of the casting director, Number 9413 sinks to the floor and dies of starvation. But the picture ends on a happy note ("as all Hollywood pictures must end"). Number 9413 ascends to heaven. There an angel wipes the number off his forehead and he becomes human again.

Something of the film's quality can be seen in the description by Herman Weinberg (*Movie Makers,* January, 1929): "The hysteria and excitement centering around an opening-night performance . . . was quickly shown by photographing a skyscraper (cardboard miniatures) with an extremely mobile camera, swinging it up and down, and from side to side, past a battery of hissing arclights, over the theater façade and down to the arriving motor vehicles. To portray the mental anguish of the extra, Florey and Vorkapich cut grotesque strips of paper into the shape of gnarled, malignant-looking trees, silhouetted them against a background made up of moving shadows, and set them in motion with an electric fan."

Following *A Hollywood Extra,* Robert Florey made two other experimental fantasies: *The Loves of Zero* and *Johann the Coffin Maker.* Both films, also produced at a minimum cost, employed stylized backgrounds, costumes, and acting derived from *Caligari.*

The Loves of Zero was the better of the two, with a number of shots quite fanciful and inventive. Noteworthy were the split-screen close-ups of Zero, showing his face split into two different-sized parts, and the multiple-exposure views of Machine Street, the upper portion of the screen full of revolving machinery dominating the lower portion, which showed the tiny figure of Zero walking home.

Despite their shortcomings and their flagrant mirroring of German expressionism, these first experimental attempts were significant. Their low cost, their high inventive potential, their independence of studio crafts and staff, vividly brought home the fact that the medium was within anyone's reach. One did not have to spend a fortune or be a European or Hollywood "genius" to explore the artistic possibilities of movie making.

Appearing about the same time, but more ambitious in scope, was the six-reel experimental film *The Last Moment.* Produced in "sympathetic collaboration" by Paul Fejos, director, Leon Shamroy, cameraman, and Otto Matieson, the leading actor, this picture (also not studio-made) was

Synchronization (1934), by Joseph Shillinger and Lewis Jacobs;
drawings by Mary Ellen Bute

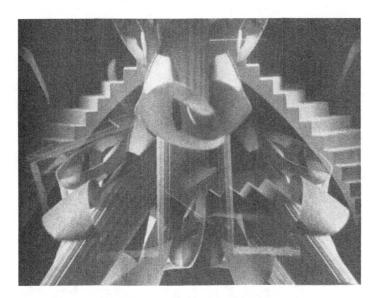

Evening Star (1937), by Mary Ellen Bute and Ted Nemeth;
score: Wagner's *Evening Star,* sung by Reinald Werrenrath

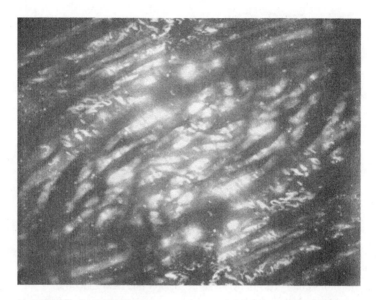

H_2O (1929), by Ralph Steiner

Parabola (1938), by Rutherford Boyd, Mary Ellen Bute,
and Ted Nemeth

The Last Moment (1928), by Paul Fejos, with Leon Shamroy
and Otto Matieson

Lot in Sodom (1933–34), by James Sibley Watson
and Melville Webber

A Hollywood Extra (1928), by Robert Florey and Slavko Vorkapich

Dawn to Dawn (1934), by Joseph Berne;
screenplay by Seymour Stern

saturated with artifice and effects gleaned from a careful study of the décor, lighting, and camera treatment of such German pictures as *Waxworks, Variety,* and *The Last Laugh*. Made up of innumerable brief, kaleidoscopic scenes, it was a vigorous manifestation of the expressionistic style.

The story was a "study in subjectivity," based on the theory that at the critical moment before a person loses consciousness he may see a panorama of pictures summarizing the memories of a lifetime. The film opens with a shot of troubled water. A struggling figure is seen. A hand reaches up "as if in entreaty." A man is drowning. This scene is followed by a sequence of rapid shots: the head of a Pierrot, faces of women, flashing headlights, spinning wheels, a star shower, an explosion, climaxed by a shot of a child's picture book.

From the book the camera flashes back to summarize the drowning man's life: impressions of school days, a fond mother, an unsympathetic father, a birthday party, reading Shakespeare, a first visit to the theater, the boy scrawling love notes, an adolescent affair with a carnival dancer, quarreling at home, leaving for the city, stowing away on a ship, being manhandled by a drunken captain, stumbling into a tavern, acting to amuse a circle of revelers, reeling in drunken stupor and run over by a car, attended by a sympathetic nurse, winning a reputation as an actor, marrying, quarreling, divorcing, gambling, acting, attending his mother's funeral, enlisting in the army, the battlefront. No attempt was made to probe into these actions; they were given as a series of narrative impressions.

The concluding portions of the film were told in the same impressionistic manner. The soldier returns to civilian life and resumes his acting career, falls in love with his leading lady, marries her, is informed of her accidental death, becomes distraught, and is finally impelled to suicide. Wearing his Pierrot costume, the actor wades out into the lake at night.

Now the camera repeats the opening summary: the troubled waters, the faces, the lights, the wheels, the star shower, the explosion. The outstretched hand gradually sinks from view. A few bubbles rise to the surface. The film ends.

In many respects the story was superficial and melodramatic, with moments of bathos. But the faults were overcome by freshness of treatment, conception, and technique, making the film a singular and arresting experiment.

This camera work of Leon Shamroy, then an unknown American photographer, was compared favorably with the best work of the European camera stylists. "*The Last Moment* is composed of a series of camera tricks, camera angles, and various motion picture devices which for completeness and novelty have never before been equaled upon the screen," wrote Tamar Lane in the *Film Mercury*, November 11, 1927. "Such remarkable camera work is achieved here as has never been surpassed—German films included," said Irene Thirer in the New York *Daily News*, March 12, 1928.

But *The Last Moment* had more than superior camera craftsmanship. For America it was a radical departure in structure, deliberately ignoring dramatic conventions of storytelling and striving for a cinematic form of narrative. Instead of subduing the camera for use solely as a recording device, the director boldly emphasized the camera's role and utilized all its narrative devices. The significant use of dissolves, multiple exposures, irises, mobility, and split screen created a style which, though indebted to the Germans, was better integrated in visual movement and rhythm and overshadowed the shallowness of the picture's content.

Exhibited in many theaters throughout the country, *The Last Moment* aroused more widespread critical attention than any other American picture of the year. Most of it was as favorable as that of John S. Cohen, Jr., in the New York *Sun*, March 3, 1928: "One of the most stimulating experiments in movie history . . . *The Last Moment* is a remarkable cinema projection of an arresting idea—and almost worthy of the misused designation of being a landmark in movie history."

More eclectic than previous American experiments was *The Tell-tale Heart*, directed by Charles Klein. It set out to capture the horror and insanity of Poe's story in a manner that was boldly imitative of *Caligari*. Like the German film, the foundation of the American's style lay in its décor. Angular flats, painted shadows, oblique windows and doors, and zigzag designs distorted perspective and increased the sense of space. But opposed to the expressionistic architecture were the early nineteenth-century costumes, the realistic acting, and the lighting, sometimes realistic, sometimes stylized.

Although poorly integrated and lacking the distinctive style of *Caligari*, *The Tell-tale Heart* had flavor. Even borrowed ideas and rhetorical effects were a refreshing experience, and the use of a Poe story was itself novel. Moreover, the general level of production was of so professional a standard that Clifford Howard in *Close Up*, August, 1928, wrote: "*The Tell-tale Heart* is perhaps the most finished production of its kind that has yet come out of Hollywood proper."

Soon after *The Tell-tale Heart,* a second film based on a story by Poe appeared, *The Fall of the House of Usher.* Poe's stories were to appeal more and more to the experimental and amateur film makers. Poe's stories not only were short and in the public domain, but depended more upon atmosphere and setting than upon characterization. What particularly kindled the imagination of the experimenter was the haunting, evocative atmosphere which brought to mind similar values in memorable German pictures which, like *Caligari,* had made a deep impression. Even to novitiates Poe's stories were so obviously visual that they seemed almost made to order for the imaginative cameraman and designer.

The Fall of the House of Usher was directed and photographed by James Sibley Watson, with continuity and setting by Melville Webber. Almost a year in the making although only two reels in length, the production strove to make the spectator feel whatever was "grotesque, strange, fearful and morbid in Poe's work."

Unlike the previous "Caligarized" Poe story, *The Fall of the House of Usher* displayed an original approach to its material and an imaginative and intense use of the means of expressionism which gave the picture a distinctive quality, setting it apart from the experimental films of the day. From the very opening—a horseman descending a plain obscured by white puffs of smoke—mystery and unreality are stressed. Images sinister and startling follow one upon the other. A dinner is served by disembodied hands in black rubber gloves. The cover of a dish is removed before one of the diners and on it is revealed the symbol of death. The visitor to the house of Usher loses his identity and becomes a hat, bouncing around rather miserably, "an intruder made uncomfortable by singular events that a hat might understand as well as a man."

The climax—the collapse of the house of Usher—is touched with grandeur and nightmarish terror. Lady Usher emerges from her incarceration with the dust of decay upon her, toiling up endless stairs from the tomb where she has been buried alive, and topples over the body of her demented brother. Then, in a kind of visual metaphor, the form of the sister covering the brother "crumbles and disintegrates like the stones of the house and mingles with its ashy particles in utter annihilation," wrote Shelley Hamilton in the *National Board of Review Magazine,* January, 1929.

The distinctive style of the picture was achieved by a technique which showed the makers' assimilation of the values of *Destiny, Nibelungen,* and *Waxworks.* The various influences, however, were never literally followed, but were integrated with the film makers' own feeling and imagination so that a new form emerged. Watson and Webber's contribution consisted in the use of light on wall board instead of painted sets, optical distortion through prisms, and unique multiple exposures and dissolves to create atmospheric effects that were neither realistic nor stylized and yet were both. Characters were also transformed to seem shadowy, almost phantom-like, moving in a tenuous, spectral world. The entire film had a saturated, gelatinous quality that rendered the unreal and evocative mood of Poe's story with corresponding vivid unreality.

Unfortunately the picture was marred by amateurish acting and ineffective stylized make-up and gestures. Nevertheless it was an outstanding and important independent effort, acclaimed by Harry Alan Potamkin in *Close Up,* December, 1929, as an "excellent achievement in physical materials."

In sharp opposition to the expressionistic approach and treatment was the work of another group of experimenters who appeared at this time. They looked for inspiration to the French films of Clair, Feyder, Cavalcanti, Leger, and Deslaw. Their approach was direct, their treatment naturalistic.

Perhaps the foremost practitioner in this field because of his work in still photography was Ralph Steiner, the New York photographer. Almost ascetic in repudiation of everything that might be called a device or a stunt, his pictures were "devoid of multiple exposures, use of the negative, distortion, truncation by angle, etc.," for the reason, he stated, "that simple content of the cinema medium has been far from conclusively exploited."

Here was a working creed that deliberately avoided effects in order to concentrate on subject matter. H_2O (1929), *Surf and Seaweed* (1930), and *Mechanical Principles* (1930) were produced with the straightforward vision and economy of means that characterized Steiner's still photography. Yet, curiously enough, these pictures in spite of their "straight photography" gave less evidence of concern for content than, say, *The Fall of the House of Usher,* which employed all the "tricks" of cinema. As a matter of fact the content in the Steiner films was hardly of any importance, certainly without social or human values, and was offered solely as a means of showing an ordinary object in a fresh way. Limited to this visual experience, the films' chief interest lay in honest and skilled photography and decorative appeal.

Steiner's first effort, H_2O, was a study of reflections on water, and won the $500 *Photoplay* award for the best amateur film of 1929. "I was interested in seeing how much material could be gotten by trying to see water in a new way," Steiner said, "rather than by doing things to it with the camera." Yet to get the water reflections enlarged and the abstract patterns of shadows, Steiner shot much of the film with 6- and 12-inch lenses. Although it was true that nothing was done to the water with the camera, it was also true that if Steiner had not used large-focus lenses he would not have seen the water in a new way. (The point is a quibbling one, for devices, like words, are determined by their associations in a larger unity. A device that may be integral to one film may be an affectation in another.) H_2O proved to be a series of smooth and lustrous abstract moving patterns of light and shade, "so amazingly effective" wrote Alexander Bakshy in *The Nation,* April 1, 1931, "that it made up for the lack of dynamic unity in the picture as a whole."

Surf and Seaweed captured the restless movement of surf, tides, and weeds with the same sharpness and precision of camerawork. *Mechanical Principles* portrayed the small demonstration models of gears, shafts, and eccentrics in action, at one point evoking a sort of whimsical humor by the comic antics of a shaft which kept "grasping a helpless bolt by the head."

Essentially, all three films were abstractions. Their concentrated, close-up style of photography made for an intensity and pictorial unity that were still novel. They represented somewhat refined, streamlined versions of *Le Ballet mécanique* (although without that historic film's percussive impact or dynamic treatment) and proved striking additions to the growing roster of American experimental works.

Another devotee of French films, Lewis Jacobs, together with Jo Gercon and Hershell Louis, all of Philadelphia, made a short experiment in 1930 called *Mobile Composition.* Although abstract in title, the film was realistic, the story of a developing love affair between a boy and girl who are thrust together for half an hour in a friend's studio.

The psychological treatment stemmed from the technique used by Feyder in *Thérèse Raquin.* Significant details, contrast lighting, double exposures, and large close-ups depicted the growing strain of disturbed emotions. In one of the scenes, in which the boy and girl were dancing together, the camera assumed a subjective viewpoint and showed the spinning walls and moving objects of the studio as seen by the boy, emphasizing a specific statuette to suggest the boy's inner disturbance.

Later, this scene cut to a dance rhythm stimulated Jo Gercon and Hershell Louis to do an entire film from a subjective viewpoint in an attempt at "intensiveness as against progression." The same story line was used, but instead of photographing the action of the boy and girl the camera showed who they were, where they went, what they saw and did, solely by objects. That film was called *The Story of a Nobody* (1930).

The film's structure was based on the sonata form in music, divided into three movements, the mutations of tempo in each movement—moderately quick, slow, very quick—captioned in analogy to music. It used freely such cinematic devices as the split screen, multiple exposures, masks, different camera speeds, mobile camera, reverse motion, etc. In one scene a telephone fills the center of the screen; on both sides of it, counterimages making up the subject of the telephone conversation alternate. The spectator knows what the boy and girl are talking about without ever seeing or hearing them. "Motion *within* the screen as differing from motion *across* the screen," pointed out Harry Alan Potamkin in *Close Up*, February, 1930, ". . . the most important American film I have seen since my return [from Europe]."

The spirit of the time changed, and as American experimenters grew more familiar with their medium they turned further away from the expressionism of the Germans and the naturalism of the French to the heightened realism of the Russians. The impact of Russian films and their artistic credo, summed up in the word "montage," was so shattering that they wiped out the aesthetic standards of their predecessors and ushered in new criteria. The principle of montage as presented in the films and writings of Eisenstein, Pudovkin, and especially Vertov, became by 1931 the aesthetic guide for most experimental film makers in the United States.

Among the first films to show the influence of Soviet technique was a short made by Charles Vidor called *The Spy* (1931–1932), adapted from Ambrose Bierce's story, *An Occurrence at Owl Creek Bridge*. *The Spy*, like *The Last Moment*, revealed the thoughts of a doomed man. But unlike the earlier film, which used a flashback technique *The Spy* used a *flash forward*. It depicted not the recollections of the events of a past life, but the thoughts of the immediate present, projected as if they were taking place in reality instead of in the mind of the doomed man.

The picture opens with the spy (Nicholas Bela) walking between the ranks of a firing squad. Everything seems quite casual, except for a slight tenseness in the face of the spy. We see the preparations for the hanging. A bayonet is driven into the masonry, the rope is fastened, the command is given, the drums begin to roll, the commanding officer orders the drummer boy to turn his face away from the scene, the noose is placed, the victim climbs to the bridge parapet. Now the drumbeats are intercut with the spy's beating chest. Suddenly there is a shot of a mother and child. At this point the unexpected occurs. The noose seems to break and the condemned man falls into the river. He quickly recovers and begins to swim away in an effort to escape. The soldiers go after him, shooting and missing, pursuing him through the woods until it appears that the spy has escaped. At the moment of his realization that he is free, the film cuts back to the bridge. The spy is suspended from the parapet where he has been hanged. He is dead.

The escape was only a flash forward of a dying man's last thoughts, a kind of wish fulfillment. The conclusion, true to Bierce's theme, offered a grim touch of irony.

In style *The Spy* was highly realistic. There were no camera tricks, no effects. The actors, who were nonprofessional, used no make-up. The sets were not painted flats nor studio backgrounds, but actual locations. The impact depended entirely upon straightforward cutting and mounting and showed that the director had a deep regard for Soviet technique.

Other experimental films in these years derived from the theories of Dziga Vertov and his Kino-Eye Productions. Vertov's advocation of pictures without professional actors, without stories, and without artificial scenery had great appeal to the numerous independent film makers who lacked experience with actors and story construction. These experimenters eagerly embraced the Russian's manifesto which said: "The news film is the foundation of film art." The camera must surprise life. Pictures should not be composed chronologically or dramatically, but thematically. They should be based on such themes as work, play, sports, rest, and other manifestations of daily life.

The pursuit of Vertov's dogmas led to a flock of "ciné poems" and "city symphonies." Notable efforts in this direction included John Hoffman's

Prelude to Spring, Herman Weinberg's *Autumn Fire* and *A City Symphony,* Emlen Etting's *Oramunde* and *Laureate,* Irving Browning's *City of Contrasts,* Jay Leyda's *A Bronx Morning,* Leslie Thatcher's *Another Day,* Seymour Stern's *Land of the Sun,* Lyn Riggs' *A Day in Santa Fe,* Mike Seibert's *Breakwater,* Henwar Rodakiewicz's *The Barge, Portrait of a Young Man,* and *Faces of New England,* and Lewis Jacobs' *Footnote to Fact.*

These films were mainly factual—descriptive of persons, places, and activities, or emphasizing human interest and ideas. Some were commentaries. All strove for perfection of visual values. Photography was carefully composed and filtered. Images were cut for tempo and rhythm and arranged in thematic order.

Other films strove to compose sagacious pictorial comments in a more satirical vein on a number of current topics. *Mr. Motorboat's Last Stand,* by John Flory and Theodore Huff, which won the League award for 1933, was a comedy of the depression. In a mixed style of realism and fantasy it told a story of an unemployed Negro (Leonard Motorboat Stirrup) who lives in an automobile graveyard and sells apples on a near-by street corner. Being of an imaginative sort, Mr. Motorboat pretends that he rides to work in a vehicle which was once an elegant car but which now stands battered and wheelless and serves as his home. The fantasy proceeds with Mr. Motorboat making a sum of money that he then uses as bait (literally and figuratively) for fishing in Wall Street. Soon he becomes phenomenally rich, only to lose everything suddenly in the financial collapse. With the shattering of his prosperity he awakens from his fantasy to discover that his apple stand has been smashed by a competitor. Called the "best experimental film of the year" by *Movie Makers,* December, 1933, the picture was a neat achievement in photography, cutting, and social criticism.

Another commentary on contemporary conditions was *Pie in the Sky* by Elia Kazan, Molly Day Thatcher, Irving Lerner, and Ralph Steiner. Improvization was the motivating element in this experiment, which sought to point out that, although things may not be right in this world, they would be in the next.

The people responsible for *Pie in the Sky*—filmically and socially alert—chose a city dump as a source of inspiration. There they discovered the remains of a Christmas celebration: a mangy tree, several almost petrified holly wreaths, broken whisky bottles, and some rather germy gadgets. The Group Theater–trained Elia Kazan began to improvise. The tree evoked memories of his early Greek Orthodox background. He began to perform a portion of the Greek Orthodox ceremonial. The other members of the group "caught on," extracting from the rubbish piles a seductive dressmaker's dummy, a collapsible baby-tub, some metal castings that served as haloes, the wrecked remains of a car, and a worn-out sign which read: "Welfare Dep't." With these objects they reacted to Kazan's improvisation and developed a situation on the theme that everything was going to be hunky-dory in the hereafter.

Pie in the Sky was not entirely successful. Its improvisational method accounted for both its weakness and its strength. Structurally and thematically it was shaky; yet its impact was fresh and at moments extraordinary. Its real value lay in the fact that it opened up a novel method of film making with wide possibilities, unfortunately not explored since.

Two other experiments sought to make amusing pointed statements by a use of montage. *Commercial Medley* by Lewis Jacobs poked fun at Hollywood's advertisements of "Coming Attractions" and its penchant for exaggeration by juxtaposing and mounting current advertising trailers. *Even as You and I* by Roger Barlow, LeRoy Robbins, and Harry Hay was an extravagant burlesque on surrealism.

Just when montage as a theory of film making was becoming firmly established, it was suddenly challenged by the invention of sound pictures. Experimental film makers, like all others, were thrown into confusion. Endless controversy raged around whether montage was finished, whether sound was a genuine contribution to film art, whether sound was merely a commercial expedient to bolster fallen box-office receipts, whether sound would soon disappear.

Strangely enough, most experimental film workers were against sound at first. They felt lost, let down. The core of their disapproval lay in fear and uncertainty about the changes the addition of the new element would make. Artistically, talking pictures seemed to upset whatever theories they had learned. Practically, the greatly increased cost of sound forced most experimenters to give up their cinematic activity.

There were some, however, who quickly displayed a sensitive adjustment to the introduction of sound. The first and probably the most distinguished experimental sound film of the period was *Lot in Sodom* (1933–1934), made by Watson and Webber, the producers of *The Fall of the House of Usher*. It told the Old Testament story of "that wicked city of the plain, upon which God sent destruction and the saving of God's man, Lot," almost completely in terms of homosexuality and the subconscious. The directors avoided literal statement and relied upon a rhythmical arrangement of symbols rather than chronological reconstruction of events. The picture proved a scintillating study, full of subtle imagery, of sensual pleasure and corruption. A specially composed score by Louis Siegel incorporated music closely and logically into the story's emotional values.

Lot in Sodom used a technique similar to that of *The Fall of the House of Usher*, but far more skillfully and resourcefully. It drew upon all the means of camera, lenses, multiple exposure, distortions, dissolves, and editing to achieve a beauty of mobile images, of dazzling light and shade, of melting rhythms, with an intensity of feeling that approached poetry. Its brilliant array of diaphanous shots and scenes—smoking plains, undulating curtains, waving candle flames, glistening flowers, voluptuous faces, sensual bodies, frenzied orgies—were so smoothly synthesized on the screen that the elements of each composition seemed to melt and flow into one another with extraordinary iridescence.

Outstanding for its splendor and intense poetry was the sequence of the daughter's pregnancy and giving birth. I quote from Herman Weinberg's review in *Close Up*, September, 1933: "I cannot impart how the sudden burst of buds to recall full bloom, disclosing the poignantly lyrical beauty of their stamens, as Lot's daughter lets drop her robe disclosing her naked loveliness, gets across so well the idea of reproduction. Her body floats in turbulent water during her travail, everything is immersed in rushing water until it calms down, the body rises above the gentle ripples, and now the water drops gently (in slow motion—three-quarters of the film seems to have been shot in slow motion) from the fingers. A child is born."

Suffused with majesty and serenity, this sequence can only be compared to the magnificent night passages in Dovzhenko's *Soil*. Like that Soviet film, the American was a luminous contribution to the realm of lyric cinema.

The second experimental sound film of note was *Dawn to Dawn* (1934), directed by Joseph Berne. The screenplay, written by Seymour Stern, was based on a story reminiscent of the work of Sherwood Anderson. A lonesome girl lives on an isolated farm, seeing no one but her father, who has been brutalized by poverty and illness. One day, into the house comes a wandering farm hand applying for a job. During the afternoon the girl and the farm hand fall in love and plan to leave together the next morning. That night the father, sensing what has happened and afraid to lose his daughter, drives the farm hand off the property. At dawn the father has a stroke and dies. The girl is left more alone than ever.

The subject differed from that of the usual experimental film, as from the sunshine-and-sugar romances of the commercial cinema. What it offered was sincerity instead of synthetic emotion. The actors wore no make-up. The girl (Julie Haydon, later to become a star) was a farm girl with neither artificial eyelashes, painted lips, glistening nails, nor picturesque smudges. All the drabness and pastoral beauty of farm life were photographed by actually going to a farm. There was an honesty of treatment, of detail and texture, far above the usual picture-postcard depictions. The musical score by Cameron McPherson, producer of the film, used Debussy-like passages to "corroborate both the pastoral and the erotic qualities" of the story.

The picture was weakest in dialogue. This was neither well written nor well spoken and seemed quite at odds with the photographic realism of the film. Nevertheless, *Dawn to Dawn* displayed such a real feeling for the subject and the medium that it moved Eric Knight, critic for the Philadelphia *Public Ledger* (March 18, 1936) to write: "I am tempted to call *Dawn to Dawn* one of the most remarkable attempts in independent cinematography in America."

Other films continued to be made, but only two used sound. *Broken Earth* by Roman Freulich and Clarence Muse combined music and song in a glorification of the "spiritually minded Negro." *Underground Printer,* directed by Thomas Bouchard and photographed by Lewis Jacobs, presented a political satire in "monodance" drama featuring the dancer, John Bovingdon, utilizing speech, sound effects, and stylized movements.

Two other silent films were made at this time: *Synchronization,* by Joseph Schillinger and Lewis Jacobs, with drawings by Mary Ellen Bute, illustrated the principles of rhythm in motion; *Olvera Street,* by Mike Seibert, was a tense dramatization of the aftermath of a flirtation between two Spanish street vendors.

By 1935 the economic depression was so widespread that all efforts at artistic experiment seemed pointless. Interest centered now on social conditions. A new kind of film making took hold: the documentary. Under dire economic distress aesthetic rebellion gave way to social rebellion. Practically all the former experimental film makers were absorbed in the American documentary film movement, which rapidly became a potent force in motion picture progress.

One team continued to make pictures under the old credo but with the addition of sound—Mary Ellen Bute, designer, and Ted Nemeth, cameraman. These two welded light, color, movement, and music into abstract films which they called "visual symphonies." Their aim was to "bring to the eyes a combination of visual forms unfolding along with the thematic development and rhythmic cadences of music."

Their films, three in black and white—*Anitra's Dance* (1936), *Evening Star* (1937), *Parabola* (1938)—and three in color—*Tocatta and Fugue* (1940), *Tarantella* (1941), and *Sport Spools* (1941)—were all composed upon mathematical formulae, depicting in ever changing lights and shadows, growing lines and forms, deepening colors and tones, the tumbling, racing impressions evoked by the musical accompaniment. Their compositions were synchronized sound and image following a chromatic scale or in counterpoint.

At first glance, the Bute-Nemeth pictures seemed like an echo of the former German pioneer, Oscar Fischinger, one of the first to experiment with the problems of abstract motion and sound. Actually, they were variations on Fischinger's method, but less rigid in their patterns and choice of objects, tactile in their forms; more sensuous in their use of light and color rhythms, more concerned with the problems of depth, more concerned with music complimenting rather than corresponding to the visuals.

The difference in quality between the Bute-Nemeth pictures and Fischinger's came largely from a difference in technique. Fischinger worked with two-dimensional animated drawings; Bute and Nemeth used any three-dimensional substance at hand: ping-pong balls, paper cutouts, sculptured models, cellophane, rhinestones, buttons, all the odds and ends picked up at the five and ten cent store. Fischinger used flat lighting on flat surfaces; Bute and Nemeth employed ingenious lighting and camera effects by shooting through long-focus lenses, prisms, distorting mirrors, ice cubes, etc. Both utilized a schematic process of composition. Fischinger worked out his own method. Bute and Nemeth used Schillinger's mathematical system of composition as the basis for the visual and aural continuities and their interrelationship.

Along with their strangely beautiful pictorial effects and their sur-prising rhythmic patterns, the Bute-Nemeth "visual symphonies" often included effective theatrical patterns such as comedy, suspense, pathos, and drama in the action of the objects, which lifted the films above the usual abstract films and made them interesting experiments in a new experience.

Experimental Cinema in America
Part Two: The Postwar Revival

WHEN AMERICA ENTERED the war the experimental film went into limbo, but with the war's end there was a sharp and unexpected outburst of interest and activity in experimental movies in all parts of the United States. Behind this phenomenal postwar revival were two forces that had been set in motion during the war years. The first was the circulation of programs from the Film Library of the Museum of Modern Art, at a nominal cost, to nonprofit groups. The Museum's collection of pictures and its program notes on the history, art, and traditions of cinema went to hundreds of colleges, universities, museums, film-appreciation groups, and study groups. These widespread exhibitions, as well as the Museum of Modern Art's own showings in its theater in New York City, exerted a major influence in preparing the way for broader appreciation and production of experimental films.

The second force was the entirely new and heightened prestige that film acquired through its service to the war effort. New, vast audiences saw ideological, documentary, educational, and training subjects for the first time and developed a taste for experimental and noncommercial techniques. Moreover, thousands of film makers were developed in the various branches of service. Many of these, having learned to handle motion picture and sound apparatus, have begun to use their skills to seek out, through their own experiments, the artistic potentialities of the medium.

As the result of these two forces, groups fostering art in cinema have appeared in various parts of the country. One of the most active is headed by Frank Stauffacher and Richard Foster in San Francisco. With the assistance of the staff of the San Francisco Museum of Art they were actually the first in this country to assemble, document, and exhibit on a large scale a series of strictly avant-garde films. The spirited response to the series resulted in the publication of a symposium on the art of avant-garde films, together with program notes and references, called *Art in Cinema*. This book, a nonprofit publication, is a notable contribution to the growing body of serious film literature in this country.

Among others advancing the cause of experimental films are Paul Ballard, who organized innumerable avant-garde film showings throughout Southern California, and the Creative Film Associates and the People's Educational Center, both of Los Angeles and equally energetic on the behalf of creative cinema.

To Maya Deren goes the credit for being the first since the end of the war to inject a fresh note into experimental-film production. Her four pictures—all short, all silent, all in black and white—have been consistently individual and striking. Moreover, she has the organizational ability to assure that film groups, museums, schools, and little theaters see her efforts, and the writing skill to express her ideas and credos in magazine articles, books, and pamphlets which are well circulated. She is today, therefore, one of the better-known film experimenters.

Meshes of the Afternoon (1943), Maya Deren's first picture, was made in collaboration with Alexander Hammid (co-director with Herbert Kline of the documentary films *Crisis, Lights Out in Europe,* and *Forgotten Village*). It attempted to show the way in which an apparently simple and casual occurrence develops subsconciously into a critical emotional experience. A girl (acted by Miss Deren herself) comes home one afternoon and falls asleep. In a dream she sees herself returning home, tortured by loneliness and frustration and impulsively committing suicide. The story has a double climax, in which it appears that the imagined—the dream— has become the real

The film utilizes nonactors—Miss Deren and Alexander Hammid— and the setting is their actual home. The photography is direct and objective, although the intent is to evoke a mood. In this respect the film is not completely successful. It skips from objectivity to subjectivity without transitions or preparation and is often confusing. But in the process of unreeling its own meshes, despite some symbols borrowed from Cocteau's *Blood of a Poet,* the picture attests a unique gift for the medium. Sensitivity and cinematic awareness are expressed in the cutting, the camera angles, and the feeling for pace and movement.

Her second film, *At Land* (1944), an independent effort, starts at a lonely beach upon which the waves, moving in reverse, deposit a sleeping girl (Miss Deren). She slowly awakens, climbs a dead tree trunk—her face innocent and expectant, as though she were seeing the world for the first time—and arrives at a banquet. There, completely ignored by the diners, she crawls along the length of the dining table to a chess game, snatches the queen, and sees it fall into a hole. She follows it down a precipitous slope to a rock formation where the queen is washed away to sea.

Writing about her intentions in this film, Miss Deren said, "It presents a relativistic universe . . . in which the problem of the individual, as the sole continuous element, is to relate herself to a fluid, apparently incoherent, universe. It is in a sense a mythological voyage of the twentieth century."

Fraught with complexities of ideas and symbols, the film's major cinematic value lay in its fresh contiguities of shots, achieved through the technique of beginning a movement in one place and concluding it in another. Thus real time and space were destroyed. In their place was created a cinematic time-space which enabled unrelated persons, places, and objects to be related and brought into a harmony of new meaning and form much in the same way as a poem might achieve its effects through diverse associations or allegory.

The cinematic conception underlying *At Land* was further exploited and more simply pointed in the short film that followed: *A Study in Choreography for the Camera* (1945). This picture, featuring the dancer Talley Beatty, opens with a slow pan of a birch-tree forest. In the distance the figure of a dancer is discovered; while the camera continues its circular pan, the dancer is seen again and again, but each time closer to the camera and in successive stages of movement. Finally, the dancer is revealed in close-up. As he whirls away (still in the woods), there is a cut on his movement, which completes itself in the next shot as he lands in the Metropolitan Museum's Egyptian Hall. There he begins a pirouette; another cut, and he completes the movement in an apartment. Another leap, another cut, and this time he continues the movement on a high cliff overlooking a river. The next leap is done in close-up with the movement of actual flight carried far beyond its natural duration by slow motion, thus gaining the effect of the dancer's soaring nonhumanly through space. The effect was not carried out quite fully, but it was an exciting and stimulating demonstration of what could be done in manipulating space and time and motion.

Dispensing with the limitations of form (in actual space and time) upon choreography for the stage, the film achieved a new choreography based upon the temporal and spatial resources of the camera and the cutting process. It was a new kind of film dance, indigenous to the medium and novel to the screen. John Martin, dance critic for the New York *Times,* called it "the beginnings of a virtually new art of 'chorecinema' in which the dance and the camera collaborate on the creation of a single new work of art."

Ritual in Transfigured Time (1946), Miss Deren's next effort, illustrated, in her words, "a critical metamorphosis, the changing of a widow into a bride. Its process, however, is not narrative or dramatic, but choreographic. The attempt here is to create a dance film, not only out of filmic time and space relations, but also out of nondance elements. Except for the two leading performers, Rita Christiani and Frank Westbrook, none of the performers are dancers, and save for a final sequence the actual movements are not dance movements."

The dance quality is best expressed in the heart of the picture, a party scene. The party is treated as a choreographic pattern of movements. Conversational pauses and gestures are eliminated, leaving only a constantly moving group of smiling, socially anxious people striving to reach one another in a continuous ebb and flow of motion.

Miss Deren calls her picture a ritual. She bases the concept upon the fact that, "anthropologically speaking, a ritual is a form which depersonalizes by use of masks, voluminous garments, group movements, etc., and in so doing fuses all elements into a transcendant tribal power towards the achievement of some extraordinary grace . . . usually reserved for . . . some inversion towards life; the passage from sterile winter into fertile spring, mortality into immortality, the child-son into the man-father."

Such a change—"a critical metamorphosis"—takes place at the conclusion of the picture. After a dance duet which culminates the party, one of the dancers, whose role resembles that of a high priest, terrifies the widow when he changes from a man into a statue. As she flees, he becomes a man again, pursuing her. Now the widow, in the black clothes seen at the opening, becomes, by means of another cinematic device— using the negative—a bride in a white gown. Upon a close-up of her metamorphosis the film abruptly ends. In its intensity and complexity *Ritual in Transfigured Time* is an unusual accomplishment, as well as a further advance in power over Miss Deren's previous uncommon efforts.

Less concerned with cinematic form and more with human conflict are the pictures of Kenneth Anger. *Escape Episode* (1946) begins with a boy and girl parting at the edge of the sea. As the girl walks away she is watched by a woman from a plaster castle. The castle turns out to be a spiritualist's temple; the woman, a medium and the girl's aunt. Both dominate and twist the girl's life until she is in despair. Finally, in a gesture of defiance, the girl invites the boy to the castle. The aunt, informed by spirits, becomes enraged and threatens divine retribution. The girl is frustrated, becomes bitter, and resolves to escape.

The quality of the film is unique and shows an extreme sensitivity to personal relationships. But because the thoughts, feelings, and ideas of the film maker are beyond his command of the medium, the effect is often fumbling and incomplete; the film's parts are superior to the whole.

Fireworks (1947), however, which deals with the neurosis of a homosexual, an "outcast" who dreams he is tracked down by some of his own group and brutally beaten, has none of the uncertainties of Anger's other film. Here, despite the difficulties of "forbidden" subject matter, the film's intensity of imagery, the strength and precision of its shots and continuity, produce an effect of imaginativeness and daring honesty which on the screen is startling. Ordinary objects—ornaments, a Roman candle, a Christmas tree—take on extraordinary vitality when Anger uses them suddenly, arbitrarily, with almost explosive force, as symbols of the neurosis which springs from an "ill-starred sense of the grandeur of catastrophe." The objectivity of the style captures the incipient violence and perversion vividly, and the film becomes a frank and deliberate expression of personality. Consequently the film has a rare individuality which no literal summary of its qualities can communicate.

Closely related in spirit and technique to Anger's *Fireworks* is Curtis Harrington's *Fragment of Seeking* (1946–1947). This film has for its theme the torture of adolescent self-love. A young man (acted by the film maker himself), troubled by the nature of his narcissism, yet all the time curiously aware of the presence of girls, is seen returning home. The long corridors, the courtyard surrounded by walls, and the cell-like room suggest a prison. The boy, not quite understanding his agony, throws himself on his cot in despair. Suddenly he rouses himself, to discover that a girl has entered his room. In a violent gesture of defiance he responds to her invitation. But at the moment of embracing her he is struck by a revulsion of feeling. He pushes her away, only to discover that she is not a girl but a leering skeleton with blond tresses. He stares incredulously, then runs or rather whirls away in horror to another room, where, seeing himself, he is made to face the realization of his own nature. The film's structure has a singular simplicity. Unity and totality of effect make it comparable to some of the stories by Poe. Through overtones, suggestions, and relations between its images it expresses with complete clarity and forthrightness a critical personal experience, leaving the spectator moved by the revelation.

In the same vein but less concrete is *The Potted Psalm* (1947) by Sidney Peterson and James Broughton. This picture is the result of a dozen scripts, each discarded for another, written over a period of three months during the actual shooting of thousands of feet of film which eventually were cut down to less than three reels, of 148 parts.

The ambiguity of the film's production process is reflected on the screen. What might have been an intense experience for the spectator remains an unresolved experiment by the film makers in a "new method to resolve both myth and allegory." "The replacement of observation by intuition . . . of an analysis by synthesis and of reality by symbolism," to quote the film makers, unfortunately results in intellectualizing to the point of abstraction.

Pictorially, the film is striking and stirs the imagination. Structurally, it has little cinematic cohesion. Shot after shot is polished, arresting symbol, but there is insufficient interaction and hardly any progression that adds up to organic form. As a consequence, the ornamental imagery— the "field of dry grass to the city, to the grave marked 'Mother' and made specific by the accident of a crawling caterpillar, to the form of a spiral, thence to a tattered palm and a bust of a male on a tomb"—exciting as it is in itself, emerges in isolation as arabesque.

Like the films of Deren, Anger, and Harrington, *The Potted Psalm* does not attempt fiction, but expresses a self-revelation. Like the other films, its methods are still quite new to the medium.

In spite of minor technical faults, occasional lack of structural incisiveness, and an overabundance of sexual symbols, this group of film makers has moved boldly away from the eclecticism of the prewar experimental film. Their films show little or no influence from the European avant-garde. They are attempting to create symbolic images—*feeling images*— and to thus increase the efficacy of film language itself. Strictly a fresh contribution, it may be christened with a phrase taken from Maya Deren (*New Directions No. 9*, 1946): "The great art expressions will come later, as they always have; and they will be dedicated, again, to the *agony* and *experience* rather than the incident." The "agony-and-experience film" sums up succinctly the work of this group.

Fundamentally, the films, although executed under diverse circumstances, reveal many qualities in common. First, properly, there is a real concern for the integrity of the film as a whole. Then, there is a unanimity of approach: an objective style to portray a subjective conflict. There is no story or plot in the conventional sense; no interest in locality as such—backgrounds are placeless although manifestly the action of the films takes place at a beach, in a house, a room, the countryside, or the streets. For the most part the action is in the immediate present, the *now*, with a great proportion of the total action taking place in the mind of the chief character. The films exploit dream analysis, not unlike the works of some of the more advanced younger writers.

In the main, the "agony-and-experience" films constitute personal statements concerned exclusively with the doings and feelings of the film makers themselves. In none of the films does the film maker assume an omniscient attitude. The camera is nearly always upon the film maker himself—Maya Deren, Kenneth Anger, Curtis Harrington—or upon his filmic representatives or symbols. Yet the central characters are not specific individuals, but abstract or generalized types. In becoming acquainted with the types the spectator apprehends areas of maladjustment.

The problem of adjustment is at the thematic core of all the films in this group. Sometimes it applies to sexual morality and the conflict of adolescent self-love and homosexuality; sometimes it applies to racial or other social tensions. In portraying psychological disturbances the film makers are striving for an extension of imaginative as well as objective reality that promises a rich, new, filmic development.

Another group of experimental film makers, since the war's end, are carrying on the nonobjective school of abstract film design. To this group the medium is not only an instrument, but an end in itself. They seek to employ abstract images, color, and rhythm, as experiences in themselves, apart from their power to express thoughts or ideas. They are exclusively concerned with so organizing shapes, forms, and colors in movement that out of their relationships comes an emotional experience. Their aim is to manipulate images not for meaning, but for plastic beauty. They have their roots in the Eggling-Richter-Ruttman European experiments of the early 'twenties, the first attempts to create relationships between plastic forms in movement.

The most sophisticated and accomplished member of the nonobjective school is Oscar Fischinger, already referred to.[1] Formerly a disciple of Walter Ruttman, the outstanding pre-Hitler German experimenter, and a leader in the European avant-garde, Fischinger, in America for the past ten years, has been working steadily on the problems of design, movement, color, and sound. Believing that "the creative artist of the highest level always works at his best alone," his aim has been "to produce only for the highest ideals—not thinking in terms of money or sensations or to please the masses."

In addition to a color sequence for Disney based on Bach's *Toccata and Fugue* that was ultimately eliminated from the released version of *Fantasia,* Fischinger has made three other color pictures in this country: *Allegretto,* an abstraction based on jazz; *Optical Poem,* based on Liszt's *Second Hungarian Rhapsody,* for Metro-Goldwyn-Mayer; and *An American March,* based on Sousa's *Stars and Stripes Forever.*

Fischinger calls his pictures "absolute film studies." All represent the flood of feeling created through music in cinematic terms, by color and graphic design welded together in patterns of rhythmic movement. He manipulates the simplest kinds of shapes—the square, the circle, the triangle—along a curve of changing emotional patterns suggested by the music and based upon the laws of musical form. Thus he creates a unique structural form of his own in which can be sensed rocket flights, subtly molded curves, delicate gradations, as well as tight, pure, classical shapeliness. All are composed in complex movement with myriad minute variations and with superb technical control. One of the few original film makers, Fischinger represents the first rank of cinematic expression in the nonobjective school.

Like Fischinger, John and James Whitney are keenly interested in the problems of abstract color, movement, and sound. However, they feel that the image structure should dictate or inspire the sound structure, or both should be reached simultaneously and have a common creative ori-

1. In "Experimental Cinema in America, Part I" [pp. 5–27, this volume].

gin. Therefore, instead of translating previously composed music into some visual equivalent, they have extended their work into the field of sound and of sound composition. A special technique has resulted after five years of constant experimentation.

Beginning with conventional methods of animation, the Whitney brothers evolved a process which permits unlimited control of images and a new kind of sound track. First, they compose a thematic design in a black-and-white sketch. Then, using an optical printer, pantograph, and color filters, they develop the sketch cinematically in movement and color. Multiple exposures, enlarging, reducing, and inverting enable them to achieve an infinite variety of compositions in time and space.

Their sound is entirely synthetic, a product of their own ingenuity. Twelve pendulums of various lengths are connected by means of steel wires to an optical wedge in a recording box. This wedge is caused to oscillate over a light slit by the movement of the swinging pendulums, which can be operated separately, together, or in selected combinations. The frequency of the pendulums can be "tuned" or adjusted to a full range of audio frequencies. Their motion, greatly reduced in size, is recorded on motion picture film as a pattern which, in the sound projector, generates tone. Both image and sound can easily be varied and controlled.

Thus far the Whitneys have produced five short films, which they call "exercises," conceived as "rehearsals for a species of audiovisual performances." All are nonrepresentational, made up of geometric shapes, flat and contrasting in color, poster-like in pattern, moving on the surface of the screen or in perspective by shifting, interlacing, interlocking and intersecting, fluent and alive in changing waves of color. The sound rises and falls, advancing and receding in beats and tones with the formally designed moving images.

Cold and formal in structure, the Whitneys' exercises are warm and diverting in effect. As distinctive experiments in an independent cinematic idiom they offer possibilities within the abstract film that have still to be explored. They suggest opportunities for more complex and plastic ensembles that can be endowed with power and richness.

A more intuitive approach to nonobjective expression is manifested in the fragmentary color films of Douglas Crockwell: *Fantasmagoria, The Chase,* and *Glenn Falls Sequence.* These pictures might be called "moving paintings." Shape, color, and action of changing abstract forms are deliberately improvised. Full of vagaries, they are worked into a situation and out of it by the feeling and imagination of the film maker at the moment of composition, motivated solely by the "play and hazard of raw material."

Crockwell's technique is an extension of the methods of animation. His first efforts, the *Fantasmagoria* series, were made with an overhead camera and the surface of a piece of glass upon which oil colors were spread in meaningless fashion. The colors were animated with stop motion. As the work progressed, colors were added, removed, and otherwise manipulated by razor blades, brushes or fingers, as whim dictated. In a later picture, *The Chase,* nondrying oils were mixed with the colors, other glass levels were added, and—which was most important—the painting surface was shifted to the underside of the glass. This last gave a finished appearance to the paint in all stages. In *Glenn Falls Sequence,* his most recent effort, air brush and pantograph were used, and motion was given to the various glass panels. Also, a new method of photography was introduced—shooting along the incident rays of the light source. This eliminated superfluous shadows in the lower glass levels.

The distinguishing trait of Crockwell's pictures is their spontaneity. Sensuous in color, fluid in composition, the abstractions occasionally move into action that is dramatic or humorous, the more so for its unexpectedness.

Markedly different in approach, technique, and style from the pictures of the other nonobjectivists is the film by Sara Arledge called *Introspection.* The original plan called for a dance film based on the theme of the "unfolding of a dance pattern in the conscious mind of the dancer." Technical difficulties and lack of funds made it necessary to present the work as a series of loosely connected technical and aesthetic experiments.

In the words of Miss Arledge, "effective planning of a dance film has little in common with stage choreography. . . . The effective movements of a dancer in film are not necessarily those most satisfactory on the stage." No recognizable patterns of dance choreography are seen in this picture. There are none of the contiguities of shots indicated in the dance experiment by Maya Deren; nor are any of the various methods of animation used. Instead, disembodied parts of dancers are seen moving freely in black space. Dancers wear tights blacked out except for particular parts— the hand, arm, shoulder, torso, or the entire body—which are specially colored and form a moving and rhythmic three-dimensional design of

House of Cards (1947), by Joseph Vogel

Ritual in Transfigured Time (1946), by Maya Deren

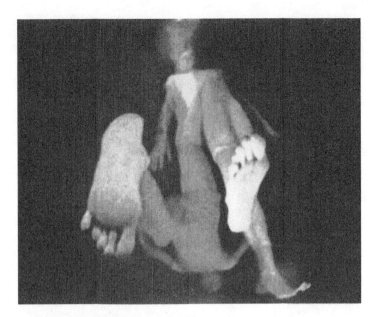

Introspection (1941), by Sara Arledge

Dreams That Money Can Buy (1947), by Hans Richter

The Cage (1947), by Sidney Peterson; production by
Workshop Twenty, California School of Fine Arts

Forest Murmurs (1941),
by Slavko Vorkapich

semi-abstract shapes. The problem created by the screen's reducing the dancer to a two-dimensional figure was overcome by ingenious use of wide-angle lens, a convex reflecting surface, special lighting effects, slow motion, and multiple exposures.

The result is a kind of abstraction, a completely new visual experience especially heightened when two or three colored forms are juxtaposed in multiple exposure. The use of color is striking and unlike color in any other experiment thus far. Although episodic and incomplete, *Introspection* is original in style. Its departure in technique suggests new directions in unconventional and abstract cinema.

These experiments in nonobjective films reveal the rich possibilities for the most part still unexplored in this field. Their development will come about through a constantly increasing command over more varied forms and plastic means. As structural design becomes more and more paramount, color more sensuous and complex, movement and sound more firmly knit into the continuity, simple decoration will give way to deeper aspects of film form.

A third group of experimentalists at work today aim at the exact opposite of the nonobjective school. They attempt to deal not with subjective experiments, but with objective reality. Unlike the documentary film makers, they seek to make personal observations and comments on people, nature, or the world around them. Concern for aesthetic values is uppermost. While the subjects in themselves may be slight, they are given importance by the form and dramatic intensity of expression and the perception of the film maker.

The most widely known of the group, because of his "montages," is Slavko Vorkapich. Ever since he collaborated on *A Hollywood Extra*[2] back in 1928, Vorkapich has been interested in film as an artistic medium of expression. In his fifteen years of working in Hollywood studios he has tried repeatedly, but without success, to get persons in the industry to finance experiments.

Independently he has made two shorts—pictorial interpretations of Wagner's *Forest Murmurs* and Mendelssohn's *Fingal's Cave* (in collabo-

2. The section on *A Hollywood Extra* in "Experimental Cinema in America," Part I, failed to note that in addition to co-directing the film with Robert Florey, Slavko Vorkapich designed, photographed, and edited it. The close-ups were shot by Gregg Toland, today one of Hollywood's outstanding cameramen.

ration with John Hoffman). *Forest Murmurs* was bought by Metro-Goldwyn-Mayer, but was withheld as "too artistic for general release." Both films express a poet's love for nature and a film maker's regard for cinematic expression. Extraordinary camerawork captures a multitude of intimate impressions of the forest and sea. Animals, birds, trees, water, mist, sky—the essence and flavor of natural phenomena is captured in striking visual sequences the structural form of which blends rhythmically with that of the symphonic music. In the rich interplay of the two forms to increase emotion and intensity of sensation Vorkapich's talent for agile cinematic expression and his poetic vision are revealed.

Somewhat similar in its feeling for nature and form is *Storm Warning*, photographed and directed by Paul Burnford. This picture is a dramatization of weather and the forecasting of a storm that sweeps across the United States. Made as a two-reeler, it was purchased by Metro-Goldwyn-Mayer and distributed, after reëditing, as two separate one-reel pictures.

The intact version of *Storm Warning* testifies to a discerning eye for significant detail, high skill in photography, and an individual sense of cinematic construction. From the opening sequence, which shows the inadequacy of primitive man to cope with weather, the picture comes alive. It proceeds with beautiful and expressive shots of people at work, of wind, of rain, snow, clouds, rivers, ships, streets—the tenderness and the turbulence of weather in its effects on modern man. The whole is made highly dramatic through selective camera angles and camera movements cut for continuous flow and varied rhythms.

The highlight of the picture is the approaching storm and its climax. This begins with a feeling of apprehension. We see leaves, paper, windmills, and trees blowing in the wind, each shot moving progressively faster, all movement in the same direction, creating a feeling of mounting intensity. Then, just before the storm breaks, a forecaster pencils in the storm line on a weather map. There is a huge close-up of the forecaster's black pencil approaching the lens. The black pencil quickly dissolves into a black storm cloud moving at the same relative speed in the same direction, out of which flashes a streak of lightning.

The climax of the storm is reached when a girl on a city street is caught in a blizzard. Her hair is violently blown. She covers her head to protect herself from the wind. This movement is an upward one. And from this point onward no more persons appear, but only nature in all its violence. The succeeding shots are of the sea crashing against a stone wall in upward movements, progressively quicker, and as each wave breaks it fills more and more of the screen until the last wave obliterates everything from view. When the last wave crashes into the camera, the upward movements which the spectator has come to expect are now suddenly abandoned, and the final three shots of the sequence—a burst of lightning, trees violently blowing, and furiously swirling water—move respectively downward, horizontally, and circularly. The sudden contrast to the upward movement intensifies the excitement. Furthermore, each of the shots becomes progressively darker, so that when the storm reaches its highest pitch there is almost a natural fade-out.

Immediately following is a fade-in on the quiet aftermath. In extreme contrast to the violent movement and darkness of the preceding shots, the screen now shows an ice-covered telegraph pole, sparkling with the sunlight's reflected rays like a star. This is followed by white, scintillating shots of ice-covered trees that sway with a gentle motion in the breeze. The scenes take on added beauty by the juxtaposition of extreme contrasts.

Throughout, the music accentuates the emotion. At the climax of the storm the music and the natural sound effects rage against each other, clashing, fighting for power. But in the storm's aftermath, all natural sounds cease and the music becomes only background, so soft that it is scarcely heard, as delicate and crystal-like as the ice-covered trees.

The picture is forceful and moving. The spectator seems actually to participate in what is taking place on the screen and is swept along on a rising tide of emotion. The extraordinary facility and command of expression that permeate *Storm Warning* make it a notable contribution to experimental cinema.

Another film maker experimenting in this field of observation and comment is Lewis Jacobs. *Tree Trunk to Head* was a study of Chaim Gross, the modern sculptor, at work in his studio carving a head out of the trunk of a tree. The personality of the sculptor, his mannerisms, his characteristic method of work, and his technique are intimately disclosed—a sort of candid-camera study. Dramatic form and cinematic structure give the presentation excitement, humor, and interest.

The basic structural element of the film is movement. The shots and the action within the shots are all treated as modifications of movement and aspects of movement. The introduction, which deals with inanimate objects—finished works of Gross' sculpture—is given movement by a series of pans and tilts. These camera movements are repeated in various directions to create a pattern of motion. The sizes and shapes of the sculpture in these shots are likewise arranged and edited in patterns of increasing and diminishing progression, to create a sense of motion.

The climax of this sequence presents a series of statues with highly polished waxed surfaces. Unlike those which precede them, they are given no camera movement, but achieve movement through a progression of diminishing scale and tempo. The first statue fills the entire screen frame; the second, four-fifths; the third, three-quarters; and so on down the scale until the final statue—a figurine about the size of a hand—stands at the very bottom of the screen. These shots are all cut progressively shorter, so that the effect is a speeding downward movement to the bottom of the screen. Suddenly the final shot of the sequence looms up, covering the entire screen frame. In contrast to the glistening statues we have just seen, this is a massive, dull tree trunk slowly revolving to reveal a bark of rough, corrugated texture and implying in effect that all those shiny smooth works of art originated from this crude, dead piece of wood.

From the tree trunk the camera pans slowly to the right to include the sculptor at work behind it on a preliminary drawing for a portrait. Posing for him is his model. This begins the body of the film, which, in contrast to the introduction, is made up of static shots treated as part of a design in movement by leaving the action within each shot uncompleted. Each shot is cut on a point of action and continued in the next shot. No shot is held beyond its single point in an effort to instill a lively internal tempo.

A subsidiary design of movement is made up from combinations of sizes and shapes of the subject matter. It is achieved through repetition, progression, or contrast of close-ups, medium shots, and long shots of the sculptor at work. A third design is based upon the direction of the action within the shots in terms of patterns of down, up, to the left or to the right. Sometimes these are contrasted or repeated, depending on the nature of the sculptor's activity. By strict regard for tempo in these intermediary designs the over-all structure maintains a fluid, rhythmic integration.

Sunday Beach, another film by Lewis Jacobs, tells the story of how people spend their Sunday on the beach—any public beach. The camera observes families, adolescents, children, and the lonely ones arriving in battered cars, in buses, and on foot, setting up their little islands of umbrellas and blankets, undressing and removing their outer garments, relaxing, bathing, reading, eating, gambling, playing, lovemaking, sleeping, quarreling, and returning home, to leave the beach empty again at the end of the day.

The picture was photographed without the subjects' being aware of the camera. By the use of long-focus lenses—four, six, and twelve inches— and other subterfuges of candid-camera photography it was possible to capture the fleeting honesty of unobserved activity. The effect of the unposed and realistic detail is revealing and often moving.

Since the subject matter could at no point be staged or controlled— had to be stolen, so to speak—a formal design as originally planned could not be executed without eliminating many happy accidents of natural behavior. The preliminary plan had to be adjusted to allow the material itself to dictate the structure. The aim then was so to cut the picture that the underlying structural design would be integrated with the spontaneity of the subject and the intervention of the film maker would not be apparent.

Like the nonobjective film makers, this group of what might be called "realists" are essentially formalists. But, unlike the former, they are striving for a convincing reality in which the means are not the end, but the process by which human values are projected. What is essential in that process is that it should have individuality and should express the film maker's perception of the world in which he lives.

Thomas Bouchard is a film maker who follows none of the tendencies yet defined. He has been working independently, with all the difficulties of restricted space and income, since about 1938. His first experiments in film (influenced by his work in still photography) dealt with the contemporary dance. His purpose was not to film the narration of the dance, but to catch those movements at which the dancer has lost awareness of routine and measure and the camera is able to seize the essential details of expression, movement, and gesture.

The subjects of Bouchard's four dance films are: *The Shakers,* based on the primitive American theme of religious ecstasy, by Doris Humphrey and Charles Weidman and their group; the Flamenco dancers, Rosario and Antonio; the "queen of gypsy dancers," Carmen Amaya; and Hanya Holm's *Golden Fleece.*

A versatile and sensitive photographer, Bouchard shows a feeling for picturesque composition, expressive movement, and a preference for deep, acid colors. His films show none of the sense for "chorecinema" expressed in Maya Deren's *A Study in Choreography for the Dancer*, nor the awareness of abstract distortion for the sake of design apparent in Sara Arledge's *Introspection*, but indicate rather a natural sensitiveness and a productive camera. Essentially, his pictures are reproductions of dance choreography, not filmic re-creations. His search is not for an individual filmic conception, but for a rendering of fleeting movement.

More recently, Bouchard has turned to painters and painting for subjects of his films. *The New Realism of Fernand Léger* and *Jean Helion— One Artist at Work* are his latest efforts. The Léger film has a commentary by the artist himself and music by Edgar Varese. The intention of this film is to give an account of the new painting that Léger did while in America and to show its place in the development of modern art. It is experimental in its personal approach. Léger is shown leisurely gathering materials and ideas for his canvases as he wanders in the streets of New York and the countryside of New Hampshire. Then he is shown at work, revealing his method of abstraction as he draws and paints his impressions of the motifs he has found.

The Helion film follows a similar approach, with the painter as his own narrator and a score by Stanley Bates. Like the Léger film, it is relaxed and intimate, done in the style of the photo story.

In these, as in the dance films, the medium serves mainly as a recording instrument. Bouchard's camera has a distinctive rhetoric, but it is the rhetoric of still photography.

Looming up significantly, and now in the final stages of editing or scoring, are pictures by Hans Richter,[3] Joseph Vogel, and Chester Kessler. These films might be classified as examples of a combined subjective-objective style. They deal with facets of both the outer and the inner life and rely upon the contents of the inward stream of consciousness—a source more and more used for the material of experimental film makers.

The most ambitious production is the feature-length color film, *Dreams That Money Can Buy*, directed by Hans Richter, the famous European avant-garde film pioneer. In production for almost two years, the picture will be a "documentation of what modern artists feel." In addition to

3. Released.

Richter, five artists—Max Ernst, Fernand Léger, Marcel Duchamp, Man Ray, and Alexander Calder—contributed five "scenarios" for five separate sequences. Richter supplied the framework which ties all the material together.

The picture tells the story of seven persons who come to a heavenly psychiatrist to escape the terrible struggle for survival. The psychiatrist looks into their eyes and sees the images of their dreams, then sends them back in "satisfying doubt" of whether the inner world is not just as real as the outer one, and more satisfying.

Each of the visions in the inner eye is a color sequence directed after suggestions, drawings, and objects of the five artists. Man Ray contributed an original script. Léger contributed a version of American folklore: the love story of two window manikins; it is accompanied by the lyrics of John Latouche. A drawing by Max Ernst inspired the story of the "passion and desire of a young man listening to the dreams of a young girl." Paul Bowles wrote the music, and Ernst supplied a stream-of-consciousness monologue. Marcel Duchamp contributed his color records and a "life animation" of his famous painting, *Nude Descending a Staircase*. John Cage did the music. Man Ray's story is a satire on movies and movie audiences, in which the audience imitates the action on the screen. Darius Milhaud wrote the score. Alexander Calder's mobiles are treated as a "ballet in the universe." Music by Edgar Varese accompanies it. Richter's own sequence, the last in the film, tells a Narcissus story of a man who meets his alter ego, discovers that his real face is blue, and becomes an outcast from society.

The total budget for *Dreams That Money Can Buy* was less than fifteen thousand dollars, less than the cost of a Hollywood-produced black-and-white one-reel "short." Artist and movie maker, Richter feels that the lack of great sums of money is a challenge to the ingenuity of the film maker. "If you have no money," he says, "you have time—and there is nothing you cannot do with time and effort."

A second picture in the offing is *House of Cards* by Joseph Vogel, a modern painter. This film attempts to delineate the thin thread of reality that maintains the precarious balance of sanity in a modern, high-pressure world. Vogel has called it "a reflection in the tarnished mirror held up by our daily press."

"I realized," Vogel said, "that the very nature of the story called for a departure from conventional approach. I felt that the picture must assume a style of its own, determined by its imagery, its stylized action and acting, and a kind of stream-of-consciousness autopsy performed on the brain of its principal character."

So deliberately free an approach afforded Vogel the opportunity of creating pictorial elements out of his experience as a painter and graphic artist. His own lithographs serve as settings for a number of backgrounds. Aided by John and James Whitney, the nonobjective film makers, he devised a masking technique in conjunction with the optical printer to integrate lithographs with live action into an architectural whole.

A third picture nearing completion is Chester Kessler's *Plague Summer,* an animated cartoon film adapted from Kenneth Patchen's novel, *The Journal of Albion Moonlight.* It is a record of a journey of six allegorical characters through landscapes brutalized by war and "the chronicle of an inner voyage through the mental climate of a sensitive artist in the war-torn summer of 1940."

The drawings for this film made by Kessler share nothing in common with the typical bam-wham cartoons. They are original illustrations drawn with extraordinary imagination. Sensitive to screen shape, space, tone, and design, Kessler makes the commonplace fantastic by juxtaposing its elements and relating them to unlikely locales, achieving a subjective transformation of its appearances.

In addition to these almost completed films there are others in various stages of productions. Except for *Horror Dream* by Sidney Peterson, with an original score by John Cage, they are nonobjective experiments: *Absolute Films 2, 3, 4* by Harry Smith, *Transmutation* by Jordan Belson, *Meta* by Robert Howard, and *Suite 12* by Harold McCormick and Albert Hoflich.

Perhaps the most encouraging signs that the experimental film has gained a new enhanced status are the financial aids granted to film makers by two major foundations in the fields of art and science. In 1946 the John Simon Guggenheim Memorial Foundation awarded a grant (approximately $2,500) for further experimental film work to Maya Deren. The same year, the Whitney brothers received a grant from the Solomon Guggenheim Foundation. In 1947, the Whitneys received a second grant from the John Simon Guggenheim Memorial Foundation.

By its contributions and accomplishments the experimental film has had and will continue to have an effect on motion picture progress and on the appreciation of motion pictures as a medium of expression. Many of those who have begun as experimental film makers have gone on to make their contribution in other fields of film work. The horizon of Hollywood film makers has been broadened and they have often incorporated ideas gleaned from experimental efforts. But even more than this, some experimental films must be considered as works of art in their own right. Despite shortcomings and crudities, they have assumed more and not less importance with the passage of time. All over the country, in colleges, universities, and museums, experimental films, old and new, are being revived and exhibited over and over again. Such exhibitions create new audiences, stimulate criticism, and inspire productions.

Today, a new spirit of independence, originality, and experiment in film making has begun to assert itself. The old European avant-garde influence and technique can still be seen, but many have begun to reach out for more indigenous forms and styles. The films are compelling in terms of their own standards and aims and each beats the drum for the experimenter's right to self-expression. The future for experimental films is more promising than ever before.

The Avant-Garde Film
Seen from Within

Hans Richter, painter and film producer, directs the Institute of Film Techniques of the City College of New York. In 1921, as a painter chiefly interested in the musical interrelationship of forms, he produced the first abstract film, *Rhythm 21*. In addition to his subsequent experimental films, he has produced documentaries and features in Germany, France, Switzerland, Austria, Holland, and the United States. His most recent film, the color feature *Dreams That Money Can Buy* (1947), is to be followed by *Minotaur, the Story of the Labyrinth,* now in preparation.

. . . . .

TWENTY YEARS AGO most documentary films, like those made by Ivens, Vigo, Vertov, and Grierson, were shown as avant-garde films on avant-garde programs. Today the documentary film is a respected, well-defined category in the film industry alongside the fictional entertainment film.

It is time, I think, to introduce the experimental film as a third, legitimate if nonrespected, category, quite distinct from the other two. It has its own philosophy, its own audience, and, I feel, its necessary place in our twentieth-century society. These claims may be more difficult to prove than similar ones for the documentary or the fictional film, but even a partial failure would be a partial success in view of the current confusion about what the experimental film is and what its goals are.

It does not matter what name one chooses to give a thing so long as all agree on its meaning, but it seems that the new name for avant-garde [1]— experimental—signifies an attempt to make this movement "behave," to make it more "responsible," to give it a more "down-to-earth" reason for being. The freedom of the artist? Yes, but within limits! Experiments? Yes, but for a practical purpose!

What purpose? To invent new techniques, forms, gadgets, tricks, and

1. The term avant-garde was applied in the 'twenties to the work of independent film artists interested in film as a visual art.

[51]

methods that might become useful in furthering the film industry. What else *could* be the justification of an experimental film?

There are, however, considerations that make the wisdom of this too facile rationalization questionable. Certainly there are, among other things, techniques, forms, gadgets, tricks, and methods that have been found or developed by the avant-garde. But these concomitants are no more the essence of the avant-garde than the complex chemical processes in the growth of a plant are the essence of a flower. It is a misunderstanding to think that the technical means that the avant-garde used in order to grow reveal its meaning. It is rather the uninhibited use of creative energies, inherent in every human being, that gives the avant-garde meaning and justification: the freedom of the artist—an obvious contradiction to the necessities of the film industry with its social, financial, and other responsibilities.

The fact that Bonwit-Teller uses Dali's style or even Dali himself, and that Macy's uses Mondrianesque, Arpesque, or Picassoid patterns in their show windows proves nothing, neither for nor against Bonwit-Teller or Macy's, nor for or against Dali, Mondrian, Arp, or Picasso. The relationship between Macy's and Picasso is slightly more than accidental. It is, moreover, in my opinion, exactly the relationship between the film industry and the avant-garde. I cannot see, for instance, that anything was proved when Dali was invited to make a sequence in surrealist fashion for *Spellbound* except the considerable public-relations talent of the producer. The film industry fulfills an important social function by satisfying the desires of human beings who are unsatisfied in life, by offering significant if childish dreams. The avant-garde expresses the visions, the dreams, the playfulness, or the whims (it all depends on how you look at it) of the artist.

No eternal standards or rules for measuring the usefulness of art and the artist can ever be found. Respect for them, however, undoubtedly goes back to the time of the cavemen, when one of them decided to decorate the cave of his tribe. Since that time, art and the artist have been regarded with a certain awe in every society. Picasso, Mondrian, and Dali still profit from the reputation of that first whimsical caveman. They still draw upon his credit (to the horror of some members of the "tribes" of today who wish that the original caveman were back).

No one would try to judge art from the point of view of window dressing alone. One would still allow for the original "magic," one would still concede to the artist the right to rule freely in the realm of his vision. Why not reserve this right for the experimental film as well? To measure it with any other, more practical, standard of values is just as sensible as it is to measure the beauty of a woman with a tape measure.

The origin and development of avant-garde films make a special point of the freedom of the artist (and may suggest, also, why there are no swimming pools in it for their makers).

1. *Orchestration of motion,* the dynamic joy of movement, fascinated and inspired the futurist painters: in 1912, Duchamp's *Nude Descending a Staircase,* Picabia's *Boxing.* They discovered "dynamism" and "simultaneity." But movement on a canvas remains, by the nature of the canvas, more or less analytical. Viking Eggeling's scrolls, and my own (1919), contained step-by-step transformations of abstract forms which embodied a substantial continuity. They implied real movement. This implication was so forceful that it thrust us toward using film instead of canvas (1921: *Diagonal Symphony* and *Rhythm 21*).

The fascination with abstract movement has been sustained over a period of nearly thirty years: Ruttman, Duchamp, Fischinger, Brugière, Len Lye, McLaren, Grant, Crockwell, the Whitney brothers. Nowhere, except in some hundred feet of Disney's *Fantasia,* and earlier in some fifty feet of Lang's *The Niebelungen* (1929), has it found a place in the productions of the film industry.

2. "To create the rhythm of common objects in space and time, to present them in their *plastic beauty,* seems to me worth while" (Fernand Léger). Not the "plastic beauty" of Greta or Marlene but of details of ordinary kitchenware (Léger), a dancing collar (Man Ray), the nondimensional reflections of a crystal (Chomette-Beaumont). Delluc called it, in 1912, "photogenic" beauty. It penetrated the arts, literature, music, dance, but evaporated before the practical eyes of the film industry. As a technical achievement it was just not tangible enough; as a philosophy or an aesthetic of modern art it was too far removed from the patent-leather dream world which it should have served.

3. Another contribution that the avant-garde film offered was "distortion" or "dissection" of a movement or a form. The desire of the early cubists to dissect the object and to rebuild it in terms of painting instead of nature, was reflected on the screen (which is also a canvas). Did the artists who distorted and dissected familiar objects wish to give a kind of distance to our conventional perception of these objects and thus a new

aspect to our surroundings in general? Man Ray shot through mottled glass; Cavalcanti printed through monk's cloth; Chomette-Beaumont used multiple exposure; Germaine Dulac used distorting lenses; I turned the camera sideways.

None of these poetic "denaturalizations" was copyrighted; nevertheless they were left untouched by the industry. Of course, in a regular feature they would have disturbed the "expectations" to which the industry has conditioned the general audience everywhere in the world. To develop these "expectations" the industry has spent hundreds of millions until they have become major sociological factors, giving the audience the easiest way to self-identification. And that's why people go to the movies: to forget themselves; don't they?

4. There is finally surrealism, a descendant of the more revolutionary dadaism, loaded with an appeal that reaches even practical minds: sex, as seen by Freud, and the subconscious. Its intention is not to "explain" subconscious phenomena but to project them in the virgin state of the original dream. It seeks to re-create the subconscious, using the original material of the subconscious and its own methods.

Man Ray's *Emak Bakia* (1926), my *Film Study* (1926), Germaine Dulac's *Seashell and Clergyman* (1928: forerunner of Maya Deren's films)— they all used the associative method to express the experience of dreams and subconscious happenings. Luis Bunuel found a new synthesis in *An Andalusian Dog* (1929), a violently emotional, strongly Freudian film, surpassed in violence only by his last surrealist feature film, *The Golden Age* (1930); Jean Cocteau's milder *Blood of a Poet* (1929) accepted as subject matter, in addition to sex, other experiences, for instance, the lifetime shock to a sensitive boy of being hit in the eye by an icy snowball; the "Narcissus" sequence in *Dreams That Money Can Buy* (1947) follows Jung rather than Freud when Narcissus falls suddenly out of love with Narcissus and has to face his true self.

It is a mistake to feel that these new filmic studies in the realm of the subconscious should have been welcome gifts to an industry that, for sociological and other reasons, cannot afford to take more than an occasional step away from love and sex. True, Hedy Lamarr and Ingrid Bergman were made up as psychoanalysts; in *Lost Weekend* and *The Snakepit* psychological themes were treated more sincerely, but without breaking away in the least from conventional storytelling, in which all respect goes to the rational, to logic and chronology, and none to the irrational. In the industry's "psychological" films the irrational is treated, at least by implication, as a kind of mental measles that healthy people, unlike drunkards and the insane, don't have. The unpredictable and irrational qualities of the surrealist films, of the experimental film as a whole, were unadaptable and unsuitable to the film industry. From the point of view of the industry the experimental film is a failure.

Social significance and the experimental film.—If the avant-garde film has not influenced the industry, if it is not really an "experimental laboratory," what can be its practical value? It is difficult to answer—because there is no right answer to a wrong question.

The greatest creative power of an individual has not always been found to have practical value for society as a whole, at least in the judgment of his contemporaries. Should we rule out creative expressions that cannot be traced for their collective worth? Potentates and dictators have periodically forbidden "modern art." But art, modern or otherwise, survives against all "rational" resistance.

Nobody really knows enough about the ways and channels through which new or even old experiences are integrated into our general behavior. There is more than an even chance that we learn as much through unchanneled and unexpected observations and experiences as through college curricula or, to talk in terms of the motion picture, through standard, obvious, and rationalistic storytelling. Also, nobody knows what will become valuable tomorrow. It is more than conceivable that in suppressing the "un-understandable" experiences of today we might rob ourselves of new experiences *altogether*. Who will predict, for instance, what the discovery of the atom or of the subconscious, to mention only two that are already in the public's mind, will mean in terms of emotional experiences? Would it not be wise to tolerate and even respect "experiment" in films, as an acknowledgment of our fallibility?

It might be not only wiser, but unavoidable. The "experimental" is part of life and no new generation goes along with the reasonable and useful alone. It seeks the unexplained, which cannot be "produced" but has to be "found," "created" by one or another individual. In any society in which the individual is respected, the counterplay of society and the individual and the tensions between them should be considered a healthy sign—even on the screen.

The answer to the question, What is the function of the avant-garde film? must, in my opinion, be: the same as the function of all arts—to integrate new experiences emotionally, or to express visions which life has withheld from us, or however the analyst of the social function of art chooses to define it.

Experimental and industrial film production are not different steps toward the same goal. They are different processes to reach different goals. Whatever they do in the way of influencing each other is accidental. This, at least, is my personal opinion, hardened by the experience of twenty-eight years with the experimental film.

On occasion, film production becomes destandardized, decentralized, deindustrialized; single groups may make single films loaded with the enthusiasm and the experiences of their makers. If one of these makers has the magic of an artist, a rather wide integration of experiments (individual experiences) into film production may take place, as it did, for instance, in Grierson's *Night Mail.* There are also the rare seconds in film history: at the beginning of great psychological or sociological crises, for example, the Russian film directly after the Russian Revolution and the Italian film now after the liberation from a tyrant. (Thus, a *Potemkin* and *Paisan* were created.) At such times, the desires and ideas of the individual may become practically identical with those of society; all the free creative energies will then flow together with the aims of the collective. But except at such rare occasions the needs of the individual and of society are just as much identical as they are different, whatever else we might wish for the sake of mankind.

As to experimental film, I think that the more sharply the contradictory features are designed and the less assimilation of them, the better. For the film industry it will mean a healthy thorn in the flesh; for the experimental film maker it will mean diving into himself instead of working for a tide pool to dive into; for the audience it will mean a chance to choose between remaining in delightful indolence or switching over to active, intelligent collaboration; and the critic might learn not to try so hard to find potatoes where flowers are offered.

In the end we may discover that the independent growth of an experimental film will be not only useful but essential to society, a healthy rebellion against a too complete domestication. I should not worry about *who* gets *what* out of experimental film, as long as it is made with love and conviction. Life will take care of that.

Cinema 16: A Showcase for the Nonfiction Film

NEW YORKERS NO LONGER have to be school children, "shut-ins," or club members in order to see documentary films. Cinema 16, at first an ambitious dream to create a permanent showcase for 16-mm. documentary and experimental films, has today become very much a reality. More than 3,000 persons crowded into New York's modern Central Needle Trades Auditorium to see one of Cinema 16's shows. Radio stations and magazines carried announcements, and the *New York Times* alone printed releases in three different sections of one Sunday issue.

Organized on a shoestring by people with more enthusiasm than experience, Cinema 16 has validated its original contentions: first, that there were scores of superior nonfiction films gathering dust on film-library shelves; and second, that there were large potential audiences eager to see them.

Cinema 16 offers films that comment on the state of man, his world, and his crises, either by means of realistic documentation or through experimental techniques. It "glorifies" nonfiction. It finds excitement in the life of ants, Hindustan music, microbiology, aboriginal life. It hails a film that is a work of art, but will not hesitate to present a film that is important only because of its subject matter. Its avant-garde films comment on the tensions and psychological insecurity of modern existence or are significant expressions of modern art. Its social documentaries stimulate rather than stifle discussion and controversy.

Incorporated as an educational, nonprofit, membership society, it has, since its inception in October, 1947, presented more than eighty films. They include Julian Huxley's *Monkey into Man*, Grierson's *Night Mail*, *Lamentation* (a dance study of Martha Graham), Rotha's *The World Is Rich*, Eisenstein's *Death Day*, the Canadian *Feeling of Rejection*, *Seeds of Destiny*, Ferno's *And So They Live*, *Boundary Lines* (International Film

Foundation), and such films as *Crystallization*, Lester's *On Time and Light, Neurosis and Alcohol* (PCR). The films *Maillol* and *Henry Moore* are examples of the art films shown.

Among the experimental films are *Un Chien andalou*, Peterson's *The Potted Psalm*, color abstractions by Francis Lee and Douglas Crockwell, Markopoulos' *Psyche*, the Whitney brothers' *Abstract Film Exercises* with synthetic sound, *Fragment of Seeking* (Harrington), and *House of Cards* (Joseph Vogel). Freed from customary censorship restrictions as a result of its status as a membership organization, Cinema 16 has shown Liam O'Flaherty's controversial *The Puritan* and Hackenschmied's *Private Life of a Cat*, both of which are barred from public showing.

Originally, Cinema 16 presented its films to the general public at the Provincetown Playhouse. Its first twenty performances were sold out; for four months, four performances a week were regularly presented. More than 14,000 people attended. Financial and censorship problems led to the incorporation of Cinema 16 as a film society. Starting with 150 members, the society now has more than 2,200 members and continues to grow. Each member sees one two-hour program a month, consisting of four or five films (usually a social documentary, a scientific, an animated, an experimental, and a "special interest" film). Members are also entitled to free guest tickets and discounts on film books and equipment. Yearly membership is $10, $17 for husband and wife, $8 for students or groups. Performances are held at the Barbizon Plaza Theatre, the Hunter College Playhouse, and the Central Needle Trades Auditorium.

The founders of Cinema 16 included Amos Vogel as executive secretary, Marcia Vogel in charge of organization and membership, Renee Avery, Robert Delson, and David E. Diener. The work of the organization is carried on by three full-time employees and the many volunteers without whom such a project can never succeed. In spite of its success, financial problems continue. Costs of promotion and advertising are almost prohibitive, suitable and reasonably priced auditoriums difficult to find. Patient recruiting activities, mailings, and publicity work consume a disproportionate amount of time and money.

The benefits of this full-scale, professionally conducted showcase for the 16-mm. industry have been both direct and immediate. Often for the first time, members of the general public are becoming aware of the very existence of films of this type. Program notes and Cinema 16's information service refer them to producers and distributors. Press releases, special previews for the press, and reviews further increase public awareness. Professional, rather than slipshod projection, with new arc equipment (in an auditorium seating 1,600!), gives evidence that 16-mm. projection can be as satisfactory as 35-mm. Representatives of social, labor, teacher, and parent organizations using films in their programs belong to Cinema 16 and thus see important new releases. Hundreds of letters ask for advice on film sources and programming. More and more, Cinema 16 is becoming a clearinghouse for information on documentary films now available in the United States.

Present plans call for a further expansion of membership and increases in membership privileges. Expansion to other metropolitan centers is indicated, and specialized screenings for clubs, unions, and children are being planned.

Increasingly, the nonfiction film is coming into its own in the United States. The work started by the British film societies, the comprehensive and important activities of New York's Museum of Modern Art, and the screenings of San Francisco's Art in Cinema and other societies are now bearing fruit. As the only showcase devoted to the exclusive and regular presentation of such films, Cinema 16 has already made its own modest contribution to the future of the nonfiction film in the United States.

2 Animation

FROM VOL. 1, NO. 4, JULY 1946

John Hubley
Zachary Schwartz

Animation Learns a New Language

John Hubley is a director of cartoons at United Productions. He has worked as art director and director of Disney Studios, at Columbia, and in the First Motion Picture Unit of the Army Air Forces.

Zachary Schwartz was one of three organizers of United Productions, where he is now a director. He has worked on Disney productions and on wartime training films. He is now preparing a training film for State Department personnel.

. . . . .

SELECT ANY TWO ANIMALS, grind together, and stir into a plot. Add prat-falls, head and body blows, and slide whistle effects to taste. Garnish with Brooklyn accents. Slice into 600-foot lengths and release.

This was the standard recipe for the animated cartoon. That is, it was standard until Hollywood's fantasy makers were presented the task of teaching people how to fight.

Six months before America entered World War II, the animated motion picture industry of Hollywood was engaged in the production of the following films:

 1 Feature-length cartoon about a deer
16 Short subjects about a duck
12 Short subjects about rabbits
 7 Short subjects of a cat chasing a mouse
 5 Short subjects with pigs
 3 Short subjects with a demented woodpecker
10 Short subjects with assorted animals
 1 Short technical subject on the process of flush riveting.

Since that time, the lone educational short, dubbed by the industry a "nuts and bolts" film, has been augmented by hundreds of thousands of feet of animated educational film. Because of wartime necessity, pigs and bunnies have collided with nuts and bolts.

Sudden change from peace to war presented to government agencies, the military services, and industrial organizations a fundamental problem. This was the necessity of teaching millions of people an understanding of objective information with which they were essentially unfamiliar. The thinking and mechanical skills of millions had either to be changed or developed. And fast. Thinking, that is, and understanding regarding international policies, the nature of the enemy, coöperative safety measures, the fight against disease, price control, taxes, motor skills involving the thousands of tactical details of warfare for fighting men, and the hundreds of new methods for unskilled workers.

Thus it also became necessary for the craftsman-animators of the motion picture industry to analyze and reëvaluate their medium; for visual education, or more specifically the motion picture, bore the burden of this tremendous orientation program. Previously, animation usage in the educational film had been singularly undeveloped. While the theatrical cartoon developed an ability to emphasize and exaggerate for comedy purposes, and perfected the techniques of dramatization, "nuts and bolts" animation remained static. It consisted of rigid charts, diagrams, mechanical operations, maps, and labels. Unlike its Hollywood counterpart, it contained no humor, no personalized or intensified image, no emotional impact, no imaginative association of ideas to enable one to retain its content.

It presented cold facts, and left its audiences in the same state. But because of the urgency of the war situation; because of the varied specialized groups to be taught; because of the attitudes to be formed or converted, new and more effective means were necessary. The collision of these two animation methods occurred because of the need to present objective information in human terms.

Film units in the Armed Forces, and many professional studios producing educational films of infinitely varied subjects, soon discovered that, within the medium of film, animation provided the *only* means of portraying many complex aspects of a complex society. Through animated drawings artists were able to visualize areas of life and thought which photography was incapable of showing.

Psychological tests and reaction studies conducted by the military indicate an exceptional popularity and response to animated technical and orientation films. The Signal Corps found that the reaction to the animated

"Snafu series" was greater than the reaction to any of the live-action films. The Air Forces Psychological Test Film Unit undertook a study of how much was learned through use of an animated training film as compared with how much through oral and written instruction on the same subject matter. The superiority of the film, both for learning and retention, was particularly clear *when full use was made of the unique possibilities inherent in the medium.*[1]

What are these unique factors? To understand them we must examine the basic difference between animation and photographed action.

Now a *single* drawing, especially the cartoon, has always been capable of expressing a great many ideas. A drawing of a man, for instance, can glorify him or ridicule him. Further, it can emphasize aspects of his physical form and subdue or eliminate others. It can combine ideas, such as a human face on a locomotive, an animal in a tuxedo, a skeleton with a cloak and scythe, etc. It can represent a specific object (a portrait, a landscape, a still life). Or it can represent a symbol of *all* men, *all* trees; the drawing of Uncle Sam representing America; the eye representing sight; the skull representing death: the single image can represent the *general* idea. The part can be interpreted as a symbol for the *whole.*

Thus a drawing's range of expression, its area of vision, is wider than that of the photograph, since the camera records but a particular aspect of reality in a single perspective from a fixed position. In short, while the film records what we *see,* the drawing can record also what we *know.* The photograph records a *specific* object; the drawing *represents* an object, specific or general.

Animated drawings are a series of single images drawn in the progressive stages of a motion, which, when photographed on film and projected, create a visual symbol of that motion. In this lies the significant element that creates the possibility of a new visual language.

Our *general* idea, our broadest observations of reality, can be visualized in terms of the personal emotional appeal of the *specific* idea. What does this mean in terms of the *communication* of ideas? It means that the mental process which the individual scientist has undergone to achieve a greater understanding of nature can now be *visualized* for millions of people.

1. Results are published in *Research Bulletin 45-14,* Psychological Test Film Unit, AAF Western Flying Training Command.

For example, a scientist deduces that by grafting two plants a seed is produced that will bring forth a new type of plant. He then proves his deduction by experimentation and comparison. We can *see* the result. We can see the original plants; we can *see* the seed. But we only *understand* the *process* by means of a language whereby the scientist explains the development to us. He may use words, and is thereby limited to audio images. Or he may photograph the specific parts of his experiment in motion pictures and, by assembling the parts in conjunction with words, produce a segmentary progression of the process. Or, by using stop action or other camera devices, he may photograph the growing plant itself.

But were he to translate the process into animation, he could represent, by means of the *dynamic* graphic symbol, the entire process, each stage or degree of development; the entire growth, from the grafting, through the semination of the seed, to the resultant plant. This quality of compression, of *continuous* change in terms of visual images, supplies the scientist with a simple language and a means of representing his own process of observation to millions.

Since the artist controls the image of a drawing, he also has the ability to change its shape or form. He is able to change a tree to a stone, an egg to a chicken, in one continuous movement. And he can compress a process that would by nature take centuries, or days, into minutes, or seconds. Or he may extend a rapid movement, such as the release of atomic energy, from split seconds to minutes, that it may be more carefully observed. These aspects of natural movement, and simultaneous conflicts of opposite movements, such as physical action and reaction, positive and negative electricity, processes we *know*, we can now *see*.

We must be clear that the effectiveness of live-action photography is by no means reduced by animation. It is only necessary to understand photography's functions and capabilities in relation to animation. This may be stated as an ability to represent a *specific* aspect of reality in very real terms. We can photograph reality. Or we can create a synthesis of reality, and record it.

For instance, we may see the subtle shades of expression on the face of a resistance leader before a fascist firing squad. This may be actual (documentary) or enacted. We see his bodily aspect, his clothes, his hands, the barren wall behind him, the distance between the man and the guns, the sky, the trembling, the blood. Dramatically, we are made to feel the relationship between the victim and the firing squad, the emotional conflict, the tension, the fear, the hatred. We can understand these emotions because we have experienced similar emotions. The specific situation is the focal point that gives us the clue to the general situation. We see this victim of fascism shot, and we gain a better understanding of the general nature of fascism.

With animation, this process is reversed. Instead of an implied understanding resulting from the vicarious experience of a specific situation, animation represents the *general* idea directly. The audience experiences an understanding of the whole situation.

Dynamic symbols, images representing whole ideas, the flags, the skulls, the cartoon characters, can explain the nature of fascism in terms of its economic roots, the forces behind it, the necessity for its policies of aggression, its historical roots, its political structure. The dynamics of changing symbols—ballots turning into guns, books to poison, plowshares to swords, children changing to soldiers, soldiers to graves— can carry a visual potency as clear as the growth of a seed into a plant. Our understanding of the process as a whole is experienced directly and immediately.

The significance of the animated film as a means of communication is best realized in terms of its flexibility and scope of expression. It places no limitations upon ideas; the graphic representation grows out of the idea. The broadest abstract theory may be treated in a factual manner and made interesting, clear, and memorable through the use of movement and sound. All degrees of the general and particular are within its normal scope because anything that the brain can conceive can be expressed through the symbol. For instance, the subject might demand an extremely impressive statement of reality. It might then be advisable to use a combination of photography and animation, the photography to state the facts of outward appearance and the animation to illustrate the inner construction, or comments upon the subject, or to suggest emotional reactions of the subject. This kind of treatment creates a super-reality in which we are conscious of many aspects simultaneously.

In animation, the artist and writer have at their command all the traditional means of graphic expression and the new means which grew out of moving symbols and sound. One of these is the concept of explanation through change from an object as it is to the thing it signifies. For instance, in explaining the function of the liver the picture changes from a liver to a recognizable sugar bowl filled with cubes of sugar. The cubes hop out into the blood stream and bob away into the circulatory system. Or, we might wish to give graphic expression to an emotional reaction. One person is being protected by another, and for a moment the protector animates up into a proud knight and charger. We hear the clank of metal and stamp of horse's hoofs for just an instant, and then the whole image animates down again into its original form. Another example of this is the picturization of certain words in dialogue to stress a particular idea. A person is being taught a difficult mechanical technique involving rapid manipulation of buttons and levers, etc. He protests, "What do you think I am—an octopus?" At the moment the word is spoken the character changes to an octopus and then back again so quickly that the observer has just gotten a fleeting impression of the picture of the word. These examples indicate the kind of picture solution that can be evolved from an idea no matter how abstract.

We have found that the medium of animation has become a new language. It is no longer the vaudeville world of pigs and bunnies. Nor is it the mechanical diagram, the photographed charts of the old "training film." It has encompassed the whole field of visual images, including the photograph. We have found that line, shape, color, and symbols in movement can represent the essence of an idea, can express it humorously, with force, with clarity. The method is only dependent upon the idea to be expressed. And a suitable form can be found for any idea.

Music and the Animated Cartoon*

Chuck Jones has worked in animated cartoons for fifteen years. He is now a director of cartoons at Warner Brothers Studios, where he has participated in some experimental and pioneering work.

. . . . .

THE ANIMATED CARTOON, in its mature form, can be the most facile and
elastic form of graphic art. Since the first Cro-Magnon Picasso hacked
etchings on his cave wall every artist has longingly sought the ideal medium — one that would contain within its structure color, light, expanse,
and movement. The animated cartoon can supply these needs. It knows
no bounds in form or scope. It can approach an absolute in technical realism and it can reach the absolute in abstraction. It can bridge the two
without taking a deep breath. The technical problems present in live action, when it tends toward the unreal or fantastic, are simply not present
to the animator. The transition of Dr. Jekyll to Mr. Hyde is workaday
routine to the animator. He can do it and add three pink elephants to the
transition. He can do it while stifling a yawn. In fact, he frequently does.
A red ant can grow to a golden elephant under his hand, a flying horse re-
cede to a black pearl. He can create thunderstorms, tidal waves, flying
carpets, talking hornets, dancing orchids, all with credibility, all with no
technical obstructions.

Yet in spite of these potentialities the animated cartoon has been se-
verely restricted in its growth. Its use as an educational device is a comparatively recent development, stimulated by wartime needs. Culturally,
the animated cartoon is in the toddling stage, as it is politically. It has
made few profound statements about anything. Like all other motion
pictures, it is dependent on a wide and highly diversified audience ap-

*Author's Note: The title of this article may be misleading, as it implies an easy skill
and familiarity with both the animated cartoon *and* music. It is rather an animation cartoonist discussing some of the potentialities of his medium with the musician.

proval—the thing known in some quarters as "box office," and "box office" in terms of animated cartoons is judged almost wholly by the degree
of audible audience reaction. The appreciative chuckle, the pleased cluck,
does not add up—in animation circles—to good "box office." This has
resulted in a wave of reaction throughout the industry against the type of
cartoons known as "Rembrandts"; that is, any type of cartoon except
those based on the "boff" or belly laugh. One producer asked his artists
to use lots of purple in the backgrounds because, as he put it, "purple is a
funny color." Well, I think G-flat is a funny note. I mention these instances, not because I am unsympathetic with the producer's viewpoint or
wish to suggest that the imperative pressures of the box office can be dis-
regarded, but because I believe that a deeper understanding of the aesthetic and cultural possibilities of the medium can serve to broaden its usage and increase its popularity. My purpose here is the appraisal of one of
these possibilities—the function of music in relation to the cartoon.

All cartoons use music as an integral element in their format. Nearly all
cartoons use it badly, confining it as they do to the hackneyed, the time-
worn, the proverbial. The average cartoon musician was a theater organ-
ist during the silent era and so *William Tell* takes quite a beating in the
average cartoon. For some reason, many cartoon musicians are more concerned with exact synchronization or "mickey-mousing" than with the
originality of their contribution or the variety of their arrangement. To be
sure, many of the cartoons as they reach the musician are something less
than inspirational, but most of them, even the best, gain less than they
should from his contribution. I have seen a good cartoon ruined by a
deadly score. If you can visualize *Death and Transfiguration* as a theme to
Peter Rabbit, you get the idea. Nor is this a diatribe against the practicing
musicians in the cartoon field; many are excellent and conscientious
artists (among them Carl Stalling, Warner Bros.; Scott Bradley, MGM;
Frank Churchill, Paul Smith, Larry Morey, and others for the Disney features and shorts), but many tend to underrate the medium and to disregard its musical potentialities.

Here are two examples of what I believe to be the nearly perfect wedding of music and graphics which occurs when the visual and auditory
impacts are simultaneous and almost equal. Both examples are from the
picture *Fantasia;* both are bits. One consumed about four seconds in the
Toccata and Fugue sequence. It pictured simply a ponderous, rocklike,

coffinlike mass that waddled into a murky background accompanied by a series of deep bass notes. I should not say "accompanied," because this Thing was the music: to my mind there was no separation; the fusion of the auditory and the visual was perfect. The second of my two instances represents, I believe, the happiest, most perfect single sequence ever done in animated cartoons, perhaps in motion pictures: the little mushroom dance from the *Nutcracker Suite*. Here was an instance of almost pure delight; again, an entrancing blend of the eye and the ear in which I found the music itself personified on the screen. There was a personal quality to these sequences, too, that was generally lacking throughout the rest of the film. It may be that if the makers of future *Fantasias* will be less concerned with the pageantry of their project and will search harder for the humanness of the music, we will have better films *and* better box office; for I believe that the mushroom dance has universal appeal, that it will go well in St. Jo and Walla Walla—as well as it will go in Hollywood or New York.

I am not going to attempt a general survey of the use, or misuse, of music in the cartoon of today. It is rather my purpose to suggest certain potentialities.

These potentialities may be classified in six rough categories: (1) Musical Education, (2) Television, (3) Program or Narrative, (4) Regional and Folklore, (5) Satire, (6) Abstract or Absolute.

1) MUSICAL EDUCATION. This is a wide and exciting field, one in which the cartoonist and musician must band together. Here the simple, strong diagrams of the cartoonist in conjunction with the sound track can do for a classroom of embryo musicians what only individual instruction could do before. I do not mean that we are going to have platoons of Bachs underfoot, but we can have a musically intelligent generation, a thing that has not been particularly feasible heretofore. But we must be guarded in our use of this new medium, because it will be quite possible to teach a thousand children the simultaneous rudiments of the glockenspiel—a result hardly to be desired. Therefore the musician must be there to direct the artist in what to teach and how to teach it; and he may be sure that the artist will do an exciting and interesting job of presentation. It is important at this time to remember that visual education has a head start on other educational methods in that we have a sympathetic audience to start with. The motion picture is widely known and widely appreciated. It is our responsibility to maintain this attitude, and we have

learned valuable lessons during the war in so doing. Education can be fun, it can be attractive, but only if we, as teachers, keep it so.

2) TELEVISION. The signature music of today's radio must be bolstered in tomorrow's television by some sort of visual image, something in the nature of MGM's lion, Warners' shield, and so on. Many educational programs will also use the cartoon, as will children's programs, comedy, and musical programs. The opportunities here hardly need elucidation; they are obvious. The points I shall stress in ensuing categories will of course apply to television as well, because the broadcasting of motion pictures will represent an important feature of television.

3) PROGRAM OR NARRATIVE. Here is another wide and tremendously provocative field for the animator and musician to explore together. Here we are free from the prejudice resulting from the visual interpretation of more abstract music.

Peter and the Wolf, Hänsel and Gretel, Don Quixote, among many others, are exciting possibilities. Richard Strauss' ballet, *Schlagobers (Whipped Cream),* about the nightmare of a cream-puff addict, seems to me to offer an enormous amount of fun. And consider two titles of Erik Satie's, *The Dreamy Fish* and *Airs to Make One Run,* parts of which, the composer noted, should be played "on yellow velvet," "dry as a cuckoo," "like a nightingale with a toothache." He must have seen us coming. *Rip Van Winkle, The Fire Bird.* The list is endless.

The animated cartoon medium is the logical medium vehicle for these, because, among all media, it lends the greatest credence to fantasy. And in this field the greatest delight is measured in the degree of credibility. The magic of the great juggler, of the trapeze artist, of Charlie McCarthy, of the storyteller, lies in his ability to convince you that the impossible is quite possible—nay, is logical; is, in fact, as the children say, "Reely!" The animated cartoon can match, enhance, make credible the melodic fantasy of the composer. Overlapping here a little bit, I believe that the educational system will one day demand a library for its public schools of just such painless introductions to classic and semiclassic music.

4) REGIONAL AND FOLKLORE. I believe that the animated cartoon has immense advantage in the exhibition of regional and national dances, songs, and cultures, because here we can combine the folk art with the folk dance. Straight cinematography covers this field to a certain extent, but seeing strange people in unusual costumes, dancing sarabands or tarantel-

las, gives us little insight into the thoughts of these people, their dreams, or their desires. But folk art does. It gives us a rich insight into the hopes and needs of a people. The pottery, furniture, and fabrics of any nationality suggest colorful fields for the artist. The bright blues, yellows, and reds used by the Scandinavian artisans in the creation of the jaunty figures which decorate their dish cupboards, ski shirts, and aprons would make a dancing, happy accompaniment to Grieg's *Norwegian Dances* or Stravinsky's *Norwegian Moods*. No live-action color camera could do for the West Indies what Covarrubias has done in painting. I have often thought that the *Habañera*, or even a group of Calypsos, against his silky greens, murky jungle yellows, and luminescently coppery islanders, would be a striking experiment. Javanese, Egyptian carvings can be brought to life to the sounds of their ancient rhythms and instruments.

Mosaics and tapestries have enchanting stories to tell—in fact, will become understandable to most of us only when they become more human. The run-of-the-mill tapestry contains about the same degree of credibility to me as a petrified salamander. I can't believe the salamander ever salamandered, and the tapestry looks about as human as a geological fault. We can do something about it if we will, and there are several reasons why we should—among them a personal one of my own concerning a seventeenth-century bucolic tapestry called "Apollo and the Muses." The thing is crowded with variously voluptuous and idiotically unconcerned ladies in déshabille, surrounding a handsome rube, dressed in a shirt, with a twenty-five-pound lyre poised lightly in his off hand. His other hand is daintily uplifted, preparatory to a downward strum. He apparently is a past master at his instrument because his head is upturned toward a sort of Stuka angel whose power dive has carried him within about three feet of our hero's face. This little monster is on the point of releasing a very lethal-looking arrow. For three hundred and forty years this scene has remained in a state of suspended animation, and I, for one, would like to unsuspend it—if only to determine whether our friend succeeds in finishing his piece or gets spitted. His girl friends may be unconcerned, but I am not.

5) SATIRE. Satire, as I use it here, is best exemplified in such cartoons as *The Band Concert* and one we made at Warners called *Rhapsody in Rivets*. I shall consider the latter because I am more familiar with it. Friz Freleng, who made the picture, seemed to have a complete disregard—per-

haps contempt—for the pomp, ceremony, and sacred concept of music. *Rhapsody in Rivets* took the second *Hungarian Rhapsody* of Franz Liszt and performed a nice job of first-degree premeditated murder. The visual theme was the construction of a building. The job foreman served as orchestra conductor, using the blueprints as a score. The riveting machines served as instruments. As I describe it, this may sound like the usual cornily gagged cartoon; I assure you that it was not. The music was not used as a background, but as the dictating factor in the actions of the characters. Thus, when the musical pace was *allegro* their actions became quick and lively; if the music moved to *prestissimo* they became frantic in their endeavor to keep up with it. It moved from there to *mysterioso, grave,* or *pianissimo;* in any case, the characters were dragged inexorably with it. It didn't take the audience long to appreciate what was happening. I can tell you they laughed. They split their stitches.

In this field of satire one factor constitutes a limitation of sorts: the piece selected should have a certain amount of familiarity, because this adds anticipatory enjoyment for the audience. Other than this the field is limited only by the imagination of the cartoonist and the satiric ability of the musician. They should "hoke" the number to the nicest degree of subtlety, the cartoonist going the composer one point better in his degree of shading, particularly in pace and arrangement. (Friz Freleng, who displays an unusual mastery of this sort of thing, seems to have a preference for Hungarians; because he later directed a take-off on the immortal *Three Little Pigs,* using as his theme the immortal Brahms *Hungarian Dances.*)

6) ABSTRACT OR ABSOLUTE. Here is the greatest field for controversy because here the composer does not define his intention; he does not tell us what he means, or what ax he is grinding. So we all form our own ideas, and when some lout comes along and presumes to interpret *his* way, we get all stuffy and hot under the collar, and resentful, and start muttering, ". . . where the devil does *he* get off, the big stuffed shirt." Rightfully, too. He has the right to think or say what he wants to, and ours is the right to disagree as vociferously as we will. Dorothy Thompson found *Fantasia* fascistic; she is entitled to that opinion, even though it was a little startling to the artists who made *Fantasia.*

I believe that the best solution to interpretation of abstract music is to go along with it; that is, to be abstract graphically. Audiences may read into your drawings the thing they've been visualizing all the time. I don't mean that you can throw a blob of ultramarine on the screen and hope thereby that the lady in the third row is going to find her dream prince, while the old gentleman in the right rear is mentally gulping flagons of sparkling mead. But there are some generally accepted symbols in art as in music. Just as the low note of a contrabassoon does not conjure in your mind "hummingbird," a single scarlet line does not, in drawing, say "elephant." These are definite things, yet it is possible to find abstract sounds and abstract images that are sympathetic. Here are two abstract shapes.

And here are two abstract words: "tackety" and "goloomb." The words become sounds when spoken, but they have no specific meanings. Yet it is simple to match the abstract words and sounds to the abstract shapes. The angular shape is obviously "tackety," and the curved one "goloomb."

Or, and now we are approaching music, take these two figures:

And take the two sounds: "ooooooooooomp" and "pooooooooooo-o-."

To go clear into music, which of these is the bassoon, and which is the harp?

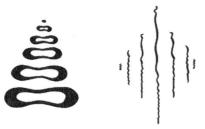

Andante thus becomes:

Abandon:

Crescendo could be thus:

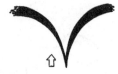

Diminuendo so:

These are static examples of what are mostly static sounds. The art of animation brings them to life, brings them fluidity and power; endows them, in short, with the qualities of music. The field of graphic symbols is a great but highly unexplored field. It will, I believe, prove an important one to the musician, and to any audience that is interested in satisfying the visual appetite, side by side with the auditory appetite.

An article of this kind can only be sketchy. We are dealing with a relatively new but immensely versatile and horizonless medium. The ideas suggested in this paper serve merely to suggest, or outline, a few possibilities from *one* viewpoint. Any imaginative person can easily elaborate on it. My sincere hope is that such people in the motion picture industry will see fit to do so. Only one serious danger confronts the animator: an underevaluation of his medium. If the motion picture producer, writer, or musician believes the end purpose of the animated cartoon to be the cartoon short of today, then it must follow that the end purpose of easel painting is the comic strip. The animated cartoon as an artistic, educational, and entertainment medium is in its infancy. Its maturity depends on you.

| Norman McLaren

Introduction by William Jordan

Notes on Animated Sound

Norman McLaren is currently in India on a film assignment for UNESCO, but will return to Ottawa, Canada, to resume his work with the Canadian Film Board. A pioneer in animation, McLaren composed and photographed music and sound effects from drawings in three notable films, *Love Your Neighbor, Now Is the Time,* and *Two Bagatelles.*

William Jordan, a member of the Theater Arts Department of the University of California, Los Angeles campus, introduces Mr. McLaren's description of his animated sound method with an explanation of normal sound recording.

. . . . .

In normal sound recording, the "live" voice, music, or noise, is collected by a microphone which converts these audible sound energies into corresponding, fluctuating electrical energy. This current is then carried through wires to the recording apparatus. After amplification, the electrical impulses actuate a light valve which produces on film emulsion a photographic image of the original sounds. Depending upon the kind of light valve used, the image may be either one of varying area—a saw-toothed pattern where black meets white—or one of varying density, which appears as strips of lightness or darkness. These photographic images of sound waves are recorded on a narrow strip near one edge of the film width, and are converted back to sound when the completed film is run through a sound projector. In other words, actual sounds are translated into energy, and the energy into light, which can be recorded on film as a pattern of light and dark. Because the animated sound techniques described in this article also produce patterns on film, animated and recorded live sound can be used in the same film. McLaren's Two Bagatelles *contains a section of recorded calliope music, and Maurice Blackburn, who composed and photographed music for* Twirligig *and* Phantasy, *used in the latter a combination of animated sound and saxophones.*

In the article which follows, Norman McLaren describes each step of his animated sound technique.

A SMALL LIBRARY OF several dozen cards, each containing black-and-white areas representing sound waves, replaced traditional musical instruments and noisemaking devices in the animated sound process developed at the National Film Board in Canada.

These drawings were photographed with the same kind of motion-picture camera as is normally used in the shooting of animated cartoons. In fact, they were shot in precisely the same way as the drawings of a cartoon; that is, one drawing is placed in front of the camera and one frame of film is taken. Then the first drawing is removed, replaced with another drawing, and the second frame of film taken; the drawing is changed again, the third frame taken, and so on.

The only difference from normal cartoon picture shooting is that the drawings are not of scenes from the visible world around us but are of sound waves, and they are not done on cards of motion-picture screen proportions but on long, narrow cards. These cards are photographed not on the area of the film occupied by the picture but to the left of it, on the narrow vertical strip normally reserved for the sound track.

When the film is developed and printed, and run on a sound projector, the photographed images of these black-and-white drawings are heard as either noise, sound effects, or music. It is therefore logical to call the kind of sound produced in this way "animated" sound, for it is made by the same method as animated pictures, and from a creative and artistic point of view it shares many of the peculiarities and possibilities of animated visuals. It could also be called "drawn" or "graphic" sound; in the past it has frequently been called "synthetic" sound, which is correct, but since "synthetic" sound also includes sound made by new electronic and electrical instruments which do not necessarily involve the use of motion-picture film, this is a more general term. "Animated" is by far the most precise term for the type of sound discussed in this article.

There are many possible ways of making animated sound, some of which were tried out as long ago as 1931. These notes deal only with the method we have been developing during the last few years at the National Film Board of Canada.

It would have been possible to make drawings of sound waves by recording "live" music sounds on film sound track, then tracing the resulting patterns from the track. However, to do this would be as pointless and creatively stultifying as to make animated cartoons by photographing live actors and tracing their outlines. Instead, in the films under discussion, a nonnaturalistic approach was taken, with no particular attempt to imitate natural sounds or traditional musical instruments. New kinds of sound waves were made by using simple and easily drawn shapes.

The drawings consist of a basic figure or simple shape that is repeated over and over to form a patterned band. The figure may be no more than a white line on a dark ground or a single gradation of tone from light to dark, but, by virtue of its identical repetition, it builds up into a series of sound waves having a definite tone color.

Each card in the library of drawings carries one such band of repeated patterns on an area one inch wide by twelve inches long. On some cards the basic figure is repeated only about four times within this area, and this, when photographed on one frame of film, will sound as a musical note of a fairly deep pitch (about two octaves below middle A). For mid-pitches there are from twenty to thirty repetitions of the basic figure on each card, and for very high-pitched notes as many as one hundred and twenty.

There is one card for each semitone of the chromatic scale, and in all, for the sound tracks of *Love Your Neighbour, Now Is the Time, Two Bagatelles, Twirligig,* and *Phantasy,* sixty such cards were used, covering a range of five octaves, from two octaves below middle A to three octaves above.

These sixty cards were labeled with the standard musical notation and arranged systematically in a small box to form a kind of keyboard.

When the music was being shot, the box was placed beside the camera so that the composer (who would also operate the camera), desiring a particular pitch, could select from the box the required card and place it in front of the camera.

To get notes of a very deep pitch, the music was shot twice as fast as finally desired; in the process of rerecording it was slowed down by half, and thus dropped one octave in pitch.

Because a *picture* camera takes film intermittently by the frameful (rather than running continuously as in the ordinary sound recording equipment) the sound track has a mosaic nature; in other words, it builds up out of small units each one twenty-fourth of a second long.[1]

---

1. The standard for projecting sound motion pictures is at the rate of twenty-four images per second.

If longer duration of a note is desired, several successive frames of the same card are shot, building up a sustained effect by a very rapid repetition of the same note, as in a mandolin or xylophone; for a very short note, just one frame or at most two frames suffice.

For rests and pauses a black card is photographed. Thus by photographing combinations of picture cards and black cards for varying lengths of time and at varying speeds, the composer controls both pitch and rhythm.

Before exposing the film, however, the composer has to determine the precise volume or dynamic level of the notes. This is one of the important new factors in animated music, for in the past dynamic markings have never been written into traditional music scoring with any degree of precision. The difference between forte and fortissimo, piano and pianissimo, for example, is relative, not exact.

In addition, the standard *pp, p, mf, f,* and *ff,* etc., indicating relative and approximate amounts of volume, are never applied to every single note in a score, and their final determining is left to the interpreting artist; but in creating animated music, the composer determines the precise dynamics of every note in the score. In other words, the composer must also be the interpretive artist.

To this end, twenty-four degrees of dynamic level were used (representing a decibel scale) and opposite each note in the score the number representing the desired dynamic level of that note was written.

For instance, 0, 1, and 2 represent three differing degrees of *ppp;* 9, 10, and 11, three shades of *mp;* 12, 13, and 14, three degrees of *mf;* 21, 22, and 23, three degrees of *fff;* 24 represents a *ffff.*

Subdivisions of these twenty-four degrees were constantly being used (particularly in crescendos and diminuendos), but were seldom written into the score. In local or rapid crescendos and diminuendos only the starting and finishing dynamic marks were written and the type of crescendos and diminuendos (such as "arithmetical" or "geometric") were indicated by a small sketch.

The volume was controlled sometimes by manipulating the shutter or diaphragm of the camera and so affecting the exposure (variable density control) but more often by covering up the one-inch-wide drawing until only a half or fourth or other fraction of its width was visible (variable area control). Whichever method was used, the calibration was in decibels, giving the composer complete control of dynamics.

The sound of a note, however, is affected not only by volume but by its attack, sustention, and decay, or tone contour. Not only did the composer have the last and precise word on dynamics but he was also forced to specify the exact tone contour of each note. This is important because the contouring of the note is more important than its basic tone quality in determining "instrumental" effect. In traditional musical sounds, for instance, a piano note has a very rapid attack, no period of sustention, but a long period of decay; its contour is like a mountain peak with one very steep side, and one gently sloping side. A typical organ note has an abrupt attack, a prolonged sustention, and a rapid decay; a contour rather like a plateau with a precipice at one side and a steep slope at the other. A tap on a wood block has a sudden attack, no sustention, and a very rapid decay. Wind instruments are capable of much less abrupt forms of attack than percussion instruments. A violin, like the human voice, is capable of almost any kind of attack, sustention, and decay.

By giving a particular contour to each note, the composer gave it what would traditionally be called its instrumental quality. In practice this was done by placing black masks of varying shapes in front of the selected pitch card bearing the drawing of the sound waves; in this way we obtained about six kinds of tone contour, some not possible by traditional instruments.

In *Love Your Neighbour* there was very considerable use of variable tone contouring, while in the other films only one percussive type of contour (wedge-shaped) predominated.

In the sound track of *Love Your Neighbour* the range and variety of sound effects and tone qualities were considerably enlarged by using several supplementary sets of drawings, some of which had rising and falling pitches for portamento and glissando effects. Some drawings, though simple to the eye and easy to prepare, had a complex sound-wave structure, rich in harmonics, thus giving very strident and harsh sound qualities.

For several simultaneous musical parts, either in harmony or counterpoint, three methods were used. In one, different drawings were superimposed on each other by several separate exposures. In another, the sound track was divided lengthwise into several parallel strips and the different drawings shot beside each other in each strip. The third was a method in which each musical part was shot on a separate film and the various parts mixed together during rerecording.

Animated sound produced by this method is normally completely "dry," or without resonance or echo. To achieve more resonance and add acoustic quality, two methods were used. The first, mainly for specific notes and localized or momentary effects, was done by shooting the same note in a rapid series of diminishing volumes (that is, the same drawing in smaller and smaller sizes); this simulates the natural effect of the sound waves bouncing back and forth from the walls of an instrument, room, hall, or cavern. The degree to which any particular note in the score can be placed in such an acoustical environment is controlled during shooting by the number and nature of diminishing replicas of the original drawing of that note.

To obtain the general or over-all acoustical environment, varying amounts of reverberation and echo were added, either electronically or acoustically during a rerecording.

To sum up the various features of animated sound as developed to date at the National Film Board of Canada:

The composer has control over pitch (to the nearest 1/10 of a tone), over dynamics (to at least 1 per cent of the total dynamic range), over rhythm and metric spacing (to the nearest 1/50 of a second). The control over "timbre" (tone contour and tone quality) is less flexible, but a variety of about a half dozen types of tone quality and tone contour are possible, which by cross combination give quite a range of "instrumental" effects.

Now that the initial research has been done it has sometimes been found more economical to make animated rather than live music, particularly for animated visuals. This is understandable if we consider the hours of rehearsal which musicians have to endure in order to match synchronously the visual action of a film. On the other hand, the composer of animated music, working slowly in increments of 1/24 of a second, can correlate his music with the most subtle visual movement. The differences both in cost, especially in terms of man-hours, and precision can be considerable. Subsequent changes and alterations to parts of the music can be made without the need to rephotograph the whole score, simply by reshooting the particular notes affected.

Although we consider the possibilities of animated sound still largely unexplored, and this particular method to be not only one of many but still far from perfect, we are already keenly aware of some of its salient features as a medium of expression.

It is free from the normal limitations affecting the human performance of musical instruments and from the usual laws of acoustics. For the musician, perhaps the most important point is that the shooting of the music is not carried on at the same speed as that at which it will finally be heard, but as slowly as desired, thus permitting the composer to plan precisely and to deliberate on the execution of the music as much as on the composing.

Mr. Magoo as Public Dream

Milton J. Rosenberg is an assistant professor of psychology at Yale, where he is also an associate in the Yale Communications Research Project. He has held consultant-ships with various organizations including the Naval War College and the National Conference of Christians and Jews. Most of Mr. Rosenberg's previous publications have been in psychological journals.

. . . . .

FROM THE TIME OF ITS introduction into America in the late thirties, the psychoanalytic approach to the study of mass entertainments has steadily won adherents and sometimes transformed them into partisans.

Its root proposition is now very well known: the contents of popular entertainments may be symbolically reduced and translated so as to provide a picture of the unconscious needs and fears of their audiences. Production workers, critics, and social scientists have, in the main, been willing to accept this proposition; to grant that entertainments are public and saleable dreams. But, in recent years, they have come to suspect that the content-analysis techniques that flow from this proposition are sometimes methodologically deficient.

At least two such failings have become sharply evident. One of these objections is based upon the fact that all the members of the national public do not consume mass entertainments with equal frequency or equal pleasure. If, for example, the movie-going audience is drawn largely from the ranks of adolescents and unmarried adults, must not the major themes of our films, if they reflect anybody's unconscious needs and fears, be more diagnostic of the immature rather than the mature members of our society?

Once we are persuaded that the audience that watches and enjoys any particular type of entertainment is a "biased" rather than a random sample of our population, we must accordingly develop hypotheses concerned with the psychological attributes of the particular social group in question. Thus, popular entertainments can be used in estimating national character only by examining and relating to each other whatever clues these entertainments reveal about various "subnational" characters.

A second and still more imperative objection hounds the entertainment analyst. He has begun to face up to the unsettling realization that even in orthodox Freudian theory it is not assumed that the unconscious meaning of a particular symbol will be the same in every respect for some ten million persons, each of whom has separately experienced that symbol.

One is still chilled to recall some of the grandiose *gaffes* that lie only a few years behind us. An excellent and well-remembered example was provided by Robert Warshow with regard to the scene in *The Best Years of Our Lives* in which the sailor's fiancee detaches his prosthetic arms. In insisting that this scene moved the audience because it gave externalization to the American male's wish for castration (and to the American female's desire to do the job), Warshow was, to say the least, applying psychoanalytic theory rather promiscuously.

I do not mean to suggest that, by way of remedy, we abandon the speculative search for unconscious symbolic meanings. Indeed, it seems to me a patent truth that without hypotheses about such unconscious meanings we cannot begin to conduct empirical investigations. However, there are more *parsimonious* ways of developing such hypotheses. By avoiding the concrete specification of fine shades of symbolic meaning—a pursuit appropriate only in the one-therapist, one-patient, one-couch situation—we may the more successfully highlight the shared meanings that exist in all or most of the consumers of the entertainment being analyzed.

It would be presumptuous to offer final rules for such an interpretive approach except that it can be pursued only by abandoning the *intricate details* of the psychoanalytic theory of dream symbolism. In its place may be employed interpretive categories limited to some small set of crucial human needs, anxiety arousers, and defense mechanisms.

The best way to make clear just what I have in mind is to offer, for illustrative purposes, a speculative analysis of a particular popular entertainment. For this purpose, let us examine the series of animated cartoons built around the adventures of that lovable, senescent daredevil-to-end-all daredevils—the very near-sighted Mr. Magoo.

Too little work has been done on the analysis of the latent meanings of comic entertainments. For this reason, and also because of the (untested) impression that Magoo is highly popular with adult and mature people, his has seemed to me a public dream whose analysis might well offer some useful hypotheses about the psychological viscissitudes of the lives of at least some contemporary Americans. Whatever interpretations are here developed must, of course, be taken as hypothetical constructions, which can have scientific value only to the extent that they make possible the formulation of researchable questions. But the purpose of the remainder of this paper is not to state such questions in their empirically verifiable form; rather, it is to illustrate a style of interpretation that, in my belief, is appropriate to getting at the generalizable latent meanings of mass entertainments. A second purpose is to offer, as an earnest of gratefulness for pleasure received, a psychologist's approximation of a fan letter for Magoo.

In general, humor has a lot to do with fear. The dissociated expression of a deep fear in a context that reduces that fear is one of the mechanisms of humor. This mechanism certainly figures in the Magoo cartoons. Frequently, humor has a lot to do also with hope, which is, after all, the reverse of fear. Hope too figures very prominently in the Magoo cartoons.

In all of his adventures, Mr. Magoo has been in a desperate situation. He is virtually blind, pitifully weak, and very small. He is handicapped also by a majestic inability to understand the dynamics of the world through which he stumbles. Yet every time we encounter him, he is face-to-face with malignant and inimical forces of both the animate and inanimate orders. Shysters, confidence men, and bandits try to do him in or to bleed him dry. His near-blindness inevitably carries him to a point just short of irredeemable destruction. He has teetered on girders, fallen down elevator shafts, had a wild leopard for a pet, played golf with a bear and tennis with a bull walrus. No man so ill-equipped and so endangered can possibly survive—except in the dream world of the animated cartoon.

By now we have seen enough Magoo cartoons to know the basic plot line; but we have not yet tired of his incredible good luck, and I do not think we will. The joke of Magoo's improbable survival will continue to amuse us because, behind the joke, there lies a reassurance that we all need. As we watch him we all *become* Magoo. He is a personification of a part, though only a part, of every man's inner image of himself. Our own feebleness, our own ineptitude, our own confusion are drawn out of unconsciousness and externalized for us in the dream image of Mr. Magoo. The dangers he faces symbolize the less dramatic dangers to which we all are sensitive in our own lives. Perhaps all ages have been ages of anxiety, but certainly ours is as full of fright as any other. The fear of war, the fear of loss of identity, the fear of boredom, the fear of isolation, the fear of our own impulses—all these are rearoused in us as Magoo faces his more concrete horrors.

But dreams, whether private or public, are wish-fulfilling; and it is Magoo's function to still our fears. This he does splendidly. If this monument to bumbling ineptitude and incapacity always comes through—not only having saved his skin, but with some gain to show for the experience— why then, we too may rest easy. The dangers we face are surmountable; nothing can touch us any more than it does Magoo. With him, we are inviolate.

This comic device for the arousal and reduction of anxiety through the evasion of physical threat is, of course, as old as slapstick comedy itself. Disney has used it effectively, as did such great comic heroes as Chaplin, Charlie Chase, Harold Lloyd, and W. C. Fields. But all of these heroes were at least partially responsible for their own escape from physical threat. To some degree, they earned their salvation. Fields had a certain low, illegitimate cunning. Harold Lloyd had inexhaustible reserves of energy. And even Chaplin the tramp had his wonderful physical grace, which was really a kind of athletic prowess.

On the other hand, Mr. Magoo's survival in the face of danger is inexplicable. It seems to us a sheer gratuity, totally unrelated to any source of power in the man himself. But is this true? *Is Magoo just plain lucky?* Or is there perhaps some secret power that he *does* possess, some obscure but trustworthy magic of his own devising? Is his survival a gift of inscrutable fate, or does he earn it?

Running through all the Magoo cartoons there is, I believe, a secret intimation that it is not fate that has saved Magoo but rather, that he has saved *himself.* How has he done this? Here the artists of UPA unconsciously voice a hope that lies deep and not fully known within each of us. Magoo has saved himself—and we may save ourselves—by complete allegiance to a set of social values and moral conceptions.

The values Magoo lives by are those of yesterday's self-made man. In comic guise, he is a personification of the verities of a social era contiguous with our own. He is American individualism in its purest moral form. With a directness that verges on quixotism, he wants what he wants when he wants it—but only because he is convinced that the *rules* of society justify his wants and have put him clearly "in the right." He speaks his mind always and expects as much from other men. He plays fair and expects to be treated fairly. His personality is compounded in equal parts of eccentric individuality, square shooting, get-up-and-go vigor, and classic persistence. Furthermore, he never questions the tenets of his existence; the honest word, strongly spoken, will always do the trick. A respect for tradition, exemplified in the Victorian clutter of his home or in the firm bond of the old school tie, supports him in his unquestioning belief in himself. And, ultimately, this belief in himself, rooted in his internal loyalty to a moral view of existence, keeps him whole and secure in the face of dangers that, because of his *faith* rather than his myopia, are not visibly real.

So the underlying serious and unconscious message of these cartoons is, as I see it, simply this: *to stand securely in an insecure world, a man must stand for something.* I do not believe that the artists behind Mr. Magoo are suggesting that we should stand, as he does, for primitive rugged individualism. For Magoo is, after all, treated by them with ridicule as well as love. What they are saying to us, and with us, is that individual man finds his fulfillment in commitment to purposes and truths that encompass more than himself.

For those who may be numbered among Mr. Magoo's loyal following (it would be interesting to know precisely who and how many they are), the appeal of these cartoons must be based in large part on the fact that they give expression to the hunger for a moral meaning in existence. Their unconscious recognition of the connection between Magoo's moral dedication and the near-miracle of his survival must certainly serve the members of his audience by reassuring them that the hunger for moral meaning is neither futile nor aberrant. Indeed, I am tempted to borrow some terms from David Riesman's lexicon and to suggest that Magoo may have his greatest appeal in the eyes of lonely "inner-directed" persons caught up in an increasingly "other-directed" round of existence.

3 Documentary

Postwar Patterns

The name of John Grierson is practically synonymous with the documentary film. He has been associated in the formation of the Empire Marketing Board Film Unit, the Empire Film Library, the Film Center, and British Documentary Film Center, and is a member of the Cinematograph Films Council. He has written many articles and essays on painting, educational theory, and the cinema. During the war he was General Manager of the Canadian Government Film Services and Government Films Commissioner.

. . . . .

THE POSSIBILITIES OF the documentary film have been defined and speculated upon a thousand times over, for years past. I am not going over the old ground, and for a very simple reason. The documentary must be considered in relation to the realities it tries to describe and illumine and dramatize. More than any other kind of film, it is most truly to be described in terms of what it does and of the themes with which it is preoccupied. Its interests today are necessarily different from those which shaped its manner and style in the 'thirties.

Perhaps I am assuming too much knowledge of this aspect of film work, on the part of my readers? Let me say then, briefly, that the documentary is the branch of film production which goes to the actual, and photographs it and edits it and shapes it. It attempts to give form and pattern to the complex of direct observation. Intimacy with the fact of the matter is therefore the distinguishing mark of the documentary; and it is not greatly important how this is achieved. Although *Grapes of Wrath* was a studio picture, some of us would not object to its being called a documentary picture, because in the reënactment little of Steinbeck's original and direct observation was lost. The studios did not, as they so often do, erect a barrier between the spectator and the actual. This time, their filter was permissive rather than preventive of reality.

In contrast, one might say that many films shot on location and face to face with the actual are much less documentary in the true sense than

Grapes of Wrath. For we can come directly at life and miss its significance and its reality by a mile. On a building at the Paris Exposition there was an inscription that said, in effect, "If you come with empty hands we can give you nothing, but if you come with gifts we will enrich you greatly." It is like that with documentary films. The presence of the actual does not make a documentary film, because what one does with the actual can be as meretricious and synthetic and phony as Hollywood at its worst. One has only to bring a silly eye to the actual and pick the wrong things to shoot. One has only to ask the wrong questions to photograph the wrong answers.

"Vision without understanding is empty," said Kant; and understanding without vision is blind. One may well take this as a special guide for one's approach to the documentary film. No branch of art has ever more deliberately tried to combine research with interpretation, or laid so much emphasis on the intellectual background of art. I represent, I suppose, the very strongest view in this regard. Certainly, so far as my own operations are concerned, I am convinced that the surest way to apprenticeship in documentary is a good degree in political science or economics. I have often been taken to task for this. I have been told that artists do not come out of libraries, and that, all too often, academic abilities are analytical, and exclusive of the aesthetic or creative powers. I answer that if you do not know what you are looking for you will not find it. It is true that there is no exercise of the imagination unless there is eagerness of heart, and no art unless there is affection. But I would say that eagerness of heart and warmth of affection will, by themselves, be only the poorest guides to the vast and difficult complex of realities in which we live today; that if they are not supported by understanding, they must inevitably break down in sentimentalism, pessimism, cynicism, and at last in nihilism, and that, in fact, we are seeing this self-destruction in every school of art that does not face up to the hard aesthetic law of Plato and later of Bergson: that it is only when the work has been analyzed and thought about and greatly labored over that the flame shoots up and the light kindles.

How warmth and affection and beauty may come to inhabit the edifices of truth, I hope I shall be able to indicate. I shall be content for the moment to assert that it is a basic tenet of documentary theory that the primary search is not for beauty, but for the fact of the matter, and that in the fact of the matter is the only path to beauty that will not soon wear down. I can best illustrate this distinction with all its many consequences in art and education by telling you about Robert Flaherty. The history of the documentary film so far as I personally have been concerned with it has derived in part from my own theoretical deviation from Flaherty; but I ought also to add that we have been the closest of friends for twenty years and that no difference of opinion has affected our complete dependence on each other. In the profoundest kind of way we live and prosper, each of us, by denouncing the other.

Flaherty's approach to documentary in *Nanook* and *Moana* in the early 'twenties was a naturalist's approach. He was in revolt against the synthetic dramas of Hollywood. He believed that the film camera was denying its destiny in shutting itself up inside the studios; that its destiny was to get about on the earth, and be the means of opening the end wall of the theater on the whole wide world. He added that we would find the truest film drama — that is to say, the drama truest to the film medium — not by imposing synthetic stories on fake or even real backgrounds, but by drawing real drama from real backgrounds. Thus his tale of the fight for food among Eskimos, and his tale of the tattoo as a test of manhood in the South Sea Islands. He added that the film was at its best when fronting the phenomena of nature; that there were no movements so fine in front of the camera as the movements and expressions that were spontaneous, or had been formed in affection for a craft, or worn smooth by tradition and ceremony. All this, of course, was very sensible and exercised an enormous influence on those of us who were thinking our way to the film of reality.

The influence of Flaherty's outlook was the greater because of the highly refined personal talent he brought to his observation. No eye was clearer, nor, for that matter, more innocent. He was by nature a poet in the manner of W. H. Davies. He could see things with great simplicity, and everything he touched found added grace at his hands. So far so good. In any estimate, Flaherty has been one of the greatest film teachers of our day, and not one of us but has been enriched by his example — and I shall add, but has been even more greatly enriched by failing to follow it.

I have said that Flaherty was innocent. He was all too innocent. His revolt was not just against the synthetics of Hollywood; there was at the same time a revolt more dangerous: against the very terms of our actual and present civilization. Flaherty's choice of themes was significant. It was primitive man in Labrador or primitive man in Samoa or primitive man in the Aran Islands, or primitive man in industry, or primitive man, in the significant person of romantic youth, taming elephants in India. Flaherty would be shocked all over again to hear me say so; for he would maintain, with his usual great distinction, that the beauties they enact are age-old beauties and therefore classical. I merely make the point that his people and his themes are noticeably distant from those which preoccupy the minds of mankind today, and that if they were not so notably distant Flaherty would make them so.

But there is a problem of the Eskimo that is all too close to our own problems, as our technological civilization marches northward in Asia and America and takes him in. His hunting grounds today are scientifically observed, and his economy is progressively planned. He is subjected to the white man's religion and the white man's justice and the white man's misunderstanding of polygamy. His clothes and his blankets most often come from Manchester, supplied by a department store in Winnipeg, which, incidentally, has the public health of the Eskimo on its conscience. Some hunt by motor boats, and some travel by air. They listen to fur prices over the radio, and are subjected to the fast operations of commercial opportunists flying in from New York. They operate tractors and bulldozers, and increasingly the northern lands, and with them the Eskimos who inhabit them, become part of our global concern.

Our contrary approach to documentary has been so different as to appear sometimes all too practical and all too materialistic and, in the sense of plain sailing, all too plain. We have not denied the fine first principles of Flaherty's, though, but rather have given them a different application. We have struck out, against every temptation, and not without a grim measure of self-discipline, against the attraction of both romance and commerce, to the here and now of our own society. We have sought not the residuum of the ancient beauties, but the beginnings of new ones in the somewhat unlikely milieu of the chaotic present. We have believed with persistence that the first and last place to find the drama of reality is in what men today are doing and thinking and planning and fighting for. We have indeed found our field of observation and the rough patterns of our work in the clash of forces inside our own metropolitan community.

I am speaking of the vast majority of documentary film makers: of the English school and the Canadian school, of creative workers in the United States like Lorens and Van Dyke, Jacoby, Steiner, Strand, Ivens, Ferno,

Huston, Kline, Hackensmidt, Van Dongen, Rodakiewicz, and of sponsors of great enlightenment like Arthur Mayer and Osgood Field. We are
all of us, first and foremost, observers of our time; students of the political and social realities, and artists only in that regard. It may be that we
exaggerate the political and social duty of documentary observation; we
are often accused of doing so. There is certainly nothing in our theory to
demand an avoidance of the play of natural phenomena: of day and night,
of the seasons of the year, of people in their more personal relationships,
of every *damnum fatale,* which, like fire, storm, and flood, cut across even
the best-ordered pattern of social thought. If we avoid them, as we tend
to do, it is, I am sure, lest weakness set in, and the social and political duty
tend to be forgotten. I, for one, regret sometimes the hard disciplines we
have set ourselves. On the other hand, documentary would not have been
the great and growing force that it is today if we had not imposed them.

Most of us are working with governments. As I write this article, Joris
Ivens is Film Officer for the Dutch East Indies, operating with a team
drawn from the Canadian government. Jean Painlevé is Film Officer of
the new French government. Basil Wright is head of the British government's film unit, and Arthur Elton is supervisor of the British government's production schedule. Stuart Legg is producing the *World in Action*
for Canada, and I myself am its Film Commissioner. Harry Watt is operating for the Australian government. Van Dyke, Jacoby, and many of
the other American documentary people are serving with the O.W.I. or
the armed forces. This is not simply as a result of the war, because, in fact,
nearly all documentary production in the past fifteen years has been
sponsored either by government or by industries. The excursions into
freedom from this relationship have been rare indeed, and the reason is
simple. Our theory of approach has, from the first, been related to the
needs of governments and peoples. On the one hand, we wanted to find
the patterns of the social processes; on the other hand, governments
wanted these patterns found and described and illumined and presented.
So, too, with the national associations and public utilities. They were interested in showing what they did in the world, interested in the fine
complex of their technological or economic or social stewardship. In each
was an opportunity for the documentary film to see and sort out one pattern or another in the social whole. Never, perhaps, did an aesthetic urge
find so logical or ready a sponsorship.

The line of development of the British documentary school will illustrate this as well as any other. It was initiated and encouraged by a British government which wanted to use the film as a means of communication between the various parts of the British Commonwealth. It wanted to describe how the various people lived, what they did, what they produced, and how well they produced it. They were soon interested in men's skills, and interested in men's researches and the results of them. We led them, step by step, deeper and deeper, to the subject matter of public import; to the web of modern communications, to the web of trade relationships, to the patterns of labor and organization in the technological society which they governed. There followed consideration of problems of public health, slum clearance, and town planning, of the improvement of educational and nutritional standards, of the development of local governments.

At every stage there were films to make—though this is to put it all too simply. Themes like these are not easy to handle, but mean first an understanding of how things work and who works them. At every turn we were concerned with the brave but difficult discovery of our own time. There is no wonder, therefore, that many of our first efforts with the new materials of observation were halting and confused. The surfaces were often apparently ugly and the system of their relationships difficult to discern. On the other hand, we had the assurance that in the film, with all its powers of juxtaposition, we had in our hands the only aesthetic instrument that could bring into relationship and order the complexes of a coöperative world. It was our promise that however difficult the theme might be, it could, through film, be brought to order and significance and therefore to beauty. It might not be the same kind of beauty as is to be found in lyric and idyl and epic, but perhaps another kind of beauty altogether, as different from the aesthetic patterns of the past as the patterns of Braque from those of Bellini. We took the view that we might be creating a visual order as radically different from the old as the mental order now being created by political and economic events. We felt that we might be reflecting the deep alteration in the categories of thought which a progressively coöperative society was establishing. In any case, we went step by step with the need on the part of governments for an explanation and understanding of what was going on in the world, and we found therein the source of both our economy and our aesthetic.

During the war we necessarily tended to preoccupy ourselves with the reporting of the armed forces, and some fine films have resulted, as, for example, *Memphis Belle* and *Target for Tonight*. But to the purist among us this has been a diversion only, necessary but not of final importance in the development of the documentary film. The war's largest significance has been in the searchlight it has directed upon the social structure, and in the constructive service it has prompted with respect to the social structure. The panoplies of war are of only passing significance and have, I think, no ultimate import except in the sight they give of the bravery of men. As before, all the best documentary work has been done on the deeper, more lasting levels of human effort. What remains, now that the war is over, is what we have done to describe the nature and the aspirations of the United Nations to each other, what has been done to describe the new spirit of unity at home and of international cooperation abroad. Our economic and political horizons have stretched remarkably, and our imaginations have been enriched past all computation during the five years of war. In many respects the documentary film has kept pace with this development, and it may even have done something to shed light on the process. In Canada, in the planning of our production, the recording of war has occupied only one department of our work. We have been concerned, like the citizens of other countries, with rehabilitation and reconstruction and the part we have to play in the comity of nations; with our duty to Bretton Woods and Dumbarton Oaks, UNRRA, ILO, and the other agencies of international coöperation. We, too, are under an obligation to replan our agriculture and our fisheries; we have to articulate anew our trade relationships. We are all too conscious that we have abundant material resources to discover and develop. We have the same deep sociological programs as other countries: the equalization of our economy to effect; new standards of nutrition and health to establish and maintain; new breaks to establish for education and the child; new measures of amenity to introduce to the industrial and the rural community alike.

You will understand me, therefore, when I say that we makers of documentary do not think so much of making films as of town planning and regional planning, community centers, country libraries, day nurseries, and larger school areas. Such are the subjects which our film makers think about; and they would regard it as the measure of their creative work that they should have done something to illumine the problems of their concern, and contributed something to their solution. I hope you are not disappointed if this all seems too mundane, and a far cry from the beauties of documentary which Flaherty envisaged. The film makers I know would be apt to say that there is nothing mundane or unbeautiful about the giving of beauty where little today exists. They would be apt to quote the slogan of the early American lumberjacks, and say that there is nothing more inspiring than letting light into the swamp; and they would be astonished if it were suggested that this is not a true basis of aesthetics. For myself, I will only say that I cannot think of any reality more pleasant, or better worth discovering. If you are concerned with service to your time, there is opportunity and to spare in such a conception of documentary. If you are concerned with education, there is surely no better way to serve it than to bring alive to the citizen the terms of the world in which he lives. He knows the better, then, the far reaches of his social self, however local it may immediately appear. He understands how common to all the world are his problems of housing and health and food and the rearing of children. He has in the film the seeing eye of his active and creative citizenship, firing his imagination where best it should be fired, in the terms of his basic and real interests.

I mentioned at the beginning that documentary could only be understood in its relation to the materials of reality which it brings into focus. Today the materials for its observation are extended enormously and in direct proportion to the increase in man's will to bring society to a state of order. We are facing a period of great changes in society, and a first prerequisite of these changes must be a deeper study of society's nature and society's problems, and a closer relationship and understanding between governments and peoples, peoples and governments. In both these developments the documentary film has the power to play an enormous part.

I hardly think you need worry too much about how the artist will come out in the process. I am constantly being told by sentimentalists and romanticists that art in the public service must inevitably lose its freedom. I have been told this for sixteen years, and can only register the fact that I have now been concerned with many hundreds of films and have never made them in any other way than the way I wanted them made. I am told that I have built up a coöperative approach to art which denies personal expression and therefore art itself, and I am told that where so much expert knowledge is involved there must inevitably be experts and that the artist's soul must stifle in contact with the academician and the bureaucrat. I can only say that no man, the artist least of all, can be free from the reality in which he lives, or avoid the duty of bringing it to such order as is within his power and his talents. Only at his peril will he try to escape from it, for he cannot easily take creative root elsewhere, in the isolation of the distant, or the isolation of the past, or the isolation of his own fancy. So far as documentary films go, the reality I have sketched is the only one I know and the only one in which an artist can find honest work to do. I have no complaint if some think they see greener pastures on the high hills, but I have never known any that found them. I am a cold and Calvinistic observer who believes that they do not exist.

By the very conditions of that reality, we are concerned not with a personal work, but with a public work. We are not concerned with personal expression in the old, private sense: we are concerned, each man, with whatever contribution can be made to a difficult and complex work for which many varieties of talent are needed. It is, of very necessity, coöperative, and no one, technician or creative worker so-called, is more important than his neighbor. I believe that the individual is not less rich in his life and his expression for entering such a coöperative, but vastly richer. I believe it simply as Plato believed it. In the last resort, I would point to the fact that our theory of documentary has worked. It has trained and inspired hundreds of creative workers, and very few who have once adopted it have abandoned it. The doctrine has spread to many countries, and wherever it has gone it has, by some inner alchemy, commanded the loyalty of young and eager men, and entered into the service of the common people and the progress of mankind. It has been responsible now for thousands of films. They have together and cumulatively set their mark on education; they have inspired the public service and the service of the public; they have put an instrument of progressive understanding and progressive citizenship into the hands of labor and management alike. Few of the films have been great, perhaps, and not all have been notable, but, again, by some inner law of documentary itself, they have almost always been authentic and honest. It would be a wonder if, in the presence of the living forces of our time, and the drama of man's needs, sacrifices, efforts, and achievements, they had not sometimes found the materials of beauty. I am sure they have.

The Documentary and Hollywood

During the war Philip Dunne was Chief of Production of the Motion Picture Bureau, OWI, Overseas Branch. He is at present a member of the Executive Board of the Screen Writers Guild, and a member of the Board of Governors, Academy of Motion Picture Arts and Sciences. Author of *How Green Was My Valley,* he is now working on *The Late George Apley.*

.....

ALMOST EVERYTHING that needs to be said about the documentary per se, analytically or historically, has already been said by such well-qualified professionals as John Grierson, Raymond Spottiswoode, and Paul Rotha (three Britishers; none of the able American documentarians has yet taken time out to write the book that needs to be written about the American documentary). Indeed, an able analysis of the documentary by Mr. Grierson appears elsewhere in this issue [pp. 91–99, this volume]. However, I do feel that I may be permitted to describe the appearance of the documentary to a fairly typical Hollywood picturemaker thrown suddenly into the field and into close association with professionals in the medium. This association, a creature of the war, is one I profoundly hope will continue into the peace. Hollywood picturemakers have much to learn from the documentarians, and vice versa. Both groups have suffered from inbreeding.

I learned about documentaries the hard way: in the process of directing the production activities of Robert Riskin's OWI Overseas Motion Picture Bureau. My associates, and teachers, were all veterans of the American documentary movement, such men as Willard van Dyke, Irving Lerner, Alexander Hackenschmied, Sidney Meyers, Irving Jacoby, Roger Barlow, and Henwar Rodakiewicz.

I should guess that most of these names are unknown to a majority of Hollywood picturemakers. They will continue to be unknown as long as some in Hollywood persist in looking on the documentary as a poor relation of "The Industry"; as long as so many in that "Industry" continue to consider the typical documentarian a long-haired crank, his mind cluttered with impracticalities.

So far from being impractical, most established documentarians can take a camera apart, cut their own negative, and perform a hundred other useful little chores which would flabbergast the average Hollywood writer, director, or producer. All documentarians are unit managers in the Hollywood sense, and nothing could be more practical than that. They manage their own crews in the field, forage for their production materials, and bring in exposed film at a cost per foot which would appear visionary to a Gower Street independent.

Why, then, the allegation of impracticality? I venture to think it is because the documentarian insists that his film must nurture an idea. We have recently listened on the radio to various influential Hollywood personalities to whom ideas seem to be anathema. I believe that it is in these quarters that we are most likely to find contempt for the documentary; and precisely in these quarters that we will find the kind of thinking, and the kind of picturemaking, which instill a reciprocal contempt for "The Industry" in the mind of the average documentarian.

The gap between the two media is not so wide that it cannot be bridged.

It is difficult to set down in category the salient features of the documentary as opposed to what we may as well call the entertainment film. (I use the phrase with the warning that the reader should not infer that a documentary is by definition not entertaining.) The documentarian, like his fellow craftsman in the entertainment field, is not bound by iron regulation or custom. By its very nature the documentary is experimental and inventive. Contrary to the general impression, it may even employ actors. It may deal in fantasy or fact. It may or may not possess a plot. But most documentaries have one thing in common: each springs from a definite need; each is conceived as an idea-weapon to strike a blow for whatever cause the originator has in mind. In the broadest sense the documentary is almost always, therefore, an instrument of propaganda. And in this we can make the first major distinction between the documentary and entertainment media.

Every film we made for the Overseas Branch of the OWI was built round a central idea: to make friends for America. Pare Lorentz made *The River* to awaken the people to the dangers of industrial and agricultural negligence, and to point to the antidotes. Kline and Hackenschmied's *Crisis* was a powerful protest against the assassination of Czechoslovakia's independence. On the other side, Leni Riefenstahl's *Triumph of the Will*, so valuable a source of Nazi material to all the American war-film agencies, was produced expressly to reunite the Party behind Hitler after his murder of Ernst Roehm and associates on the "Night of the Long Knives."

At this point, I should like to make a distinction between the two types of documentary: the "factual film," and what we might call the "true documentary."

The factual film is a legitimate descendant of the newsreel, often with a strong strain of the old-fashioned travelogue in its ancestry. But the factual film is not, like the newsreel, limited to mere reportorial coverage of a particular event at a particular time. It is, like all documentaries, built round an idea, a point which the producer tries to make. To make this point, he uses old newsreels, animations, reënacted scenes, blending all, by careful construction and tempo, into a homogeneous document. The needs of war stimulated the growth of the factual film as in a hothouse. In 1942 such films began to appear in feature length. That factual films can be both instructive and gripping (entertaining, in the broad sense) has been amply proved by the justly admired series produced by Colonel Frank Capra's unit. The Capra films are classics of their kind.

But the factual film is not the realm of the true documentarian, although many individuals with documentary experience have contributed to its development. The technique of the factual film in this country has been dictated largely by the needs of war. The producers of such films, recruited mostly from Hollywood studios and the newsreels, learned their techniques as they worked, shaped their product to the needs of the times, and gave them the mood dictated by the emotions of a world at war. Most of these men will return to their normal occupations with the coming of peace. It is extremely doubtful if the form they created—the emotional propaganda film—will survive in theatrical feature length the times which gave it birth. But there is no question that it has played an important and significant role in the winning of the war.

There remains the "true documentary," a permanent fixture in the film world, and potentially of as great importance as the purely entertainment film. In the hands of a hardy and devoted few the documentary flourished in Europe and, more obscurely, in America before the war. During the war it was subjected to the same sort of forcing process as that experienced by the factual film, but not to the same degree. In these postwar times, as nontheatrical outlets for distribution increase, and as theater audiences begin to demand—as I am sure they will—programs on a higher intellectual level, the documentary should retain its wartime growth and become an important factor in the education and entertainment of the public. Its influence on the entertainment film may well become profound.

The true documentary is usually limited in pictorial scope, though the idea it espouses may be as large as the idea of democracy itself. To express its idea, it will make use of a convenient microcosm, a homogeneous setting and cast of characters through which the idea can be advanced.

The true documentary, unlike the factual film, makes little use of stock material. It strives for uniformity in quality and mood and, like the entertainment film, achieves it by shooting original material to express its central idea. Since budgets perforce are meager, production planning is not impressive from the Hollywood point of view.

The simplicity of production arrangements marks the second essential difference between the documentary and entertainment films. The typical documentary is filmed in a natural setting, exterior and interior, and uses actual personalities selected on the scene to play its parts. A comparatively small crew, by Hollywood standards, handles the shooting. In our OWI operation, the standard crew consisted of eight men: director, cameraman, unit manager, two assistant cameramen, electrician and assistant, and a driver-helper. Standard equipment was a station wagon and a light truck, a moderate number of lights, a Mitchell camera, and an Eyemo. At our operational peak in the summer of 1944, we had five such units in the field. In three years of operation OWI shot film in more than thirty of the forty-eight states.

The mechanics of field production of this sort dictate sharp variations from typical Hollywood techniques. Nine documentaries out of ten are location pictures. All shooting is done in the field, sometimes thousands of miles from home; retakes after a preview are therefore almost always out of the question. To maintain good quality under constantly varying atmospheric conditions requires much time and patience.

Working with nonprofessional performers also consumes much time. It is his ability to work with such performers that distinguishes the documentary director: He must be able to "cast," from among an average group of villagers or steelworkers or students, the exact type called for in the script—or to change the script if he finds a better type. Acting ability cannot be assumed; indeed, the opposite is true. He must be careful not to select the born ham, the man or woman who once played in local amateur theatricals (and who is certain to push himself forward). He must possess a monumental patience; the ability to wait till the farmer's self-consciousness passes, for the golden moment when the child forgets the camera and grows really interested in the nesting bird. He must be both psychologist and politician. He cannot, like his Hollywood confrere, fall back on a combination of good acting and good writing. His responsibility—and his opportunity—are as great as that of the Hollywood director before the advent of sound forced him to follow his script, not to lead it. And, like that vanished genius of the early Hollywood scene, the documentary director should be above all a writer, wielding the camera instead of the pen.

The conditions under which documentaries are shot dictate other variations from Hollywood techniques. The best documentary photography is sharper, more realistic, less glossy and high-lighted than the Hollywood article. Make-up is almost unknown. The film editor has a great deal more freedom than in Hollywood. He is less concerned with the careful "geography" of the typical Hollywood scene, more concerned with making a story point by an adroit cut. A documentary editor thinks nothing of moving actors in time or space by direct cuts instead of by the traditional Hollywood dissolve. (In this, the heritage of the newsreel is evident.) In general, editors in this field, working with what is usually silent film, have more freedom than their Hollywood confreres. In documentary practice a film editor is also in effect a writer, using a moviola instead of a typewriter. Give a good documentary editor an idea and he will express it for you in film: pictorial image, mood, and tempo. His function is more often creative than editorial.

As a quid pro quo, the documentary writer has an important semieditorial function: the writing of the narration, a common feature of documentary films, though somewhat rarer in Hollywood. Its importance to the documentary, particularly to the silent film, cannot be overestimated. Many a weak documentary has been given a semblance of life by an inspired commentary; many a strong one has been marred by wooden or insipid words. Narration should add something to the image, not merely explain it. If the image needs explanation, the writer and director have not done their work properly (and this is also a good working rule in Holly-wood). The best narration is simple, sparse, often poetic. Its tempo should be in close synchronization with the tempo of the film. In the best doc-umentary practice, the writer of the narration is encouraged to suggest changes in the editing of the film. Words and image can thus be dove-tailed and emerge, not as a mere illustrated lecture, nor as a reel of film with spoken comments, but as an artistic entity.

Similarly with the music. The composer of a documentary score is not required, as is too often the Hollywood practice, to lay out so many feet of music against so many feet of film. He is encouraged to participate, to become a part of the editorial team. Documentaries are often recut and rewritten to meet the requirements of the composer. His ideas are always heard with respect. It is thus no accident that many of the best American composers have done some of their most striking work for the documentary.

This brings us to another significant difference between the documen-tary and the entertainment film. In Hollywood, the contribution of each craftsman to a given picture is fairly well understood. We can assume that the writer wrote the script, that the director shot it with usually minor alterations, and that the editor put the film together, all supervised by the producer. There is a sharp differentiation of function between the various crafts. Only in comparatively rare instances do we find individuals who combine two or more of these functions. Very rarely is there any serious overstepping of craft lines. At its best, this differentiation leads to that happy collaboration of all crafts which makes for fine pictures; at its worst, it leads to the sort of assembly-line production once in vogue at several major studios, though now, happily, on its way to the ash heap.

Such differentiation is the exception rather than the rule in the docu-mentary field. Writer-directors, editor-directors, writer-editors, and indi-viduals who can write, direct, and edit their own films are common. There is also a constant interchange of functions. It is nothing unusual to find a writer filling in at the camera, a director cutting film, or an editor writing scripts.

Documentary films are usually far more flexible than the typical Holly-wood product. In part, of course, this arises from the fact that most docu-mentaries are shot silent. (Recutting was the rule rather than the exception in Hollywood's silent days.) But this quality is also inherent in the uncertain nature of the documentary, based, as it often is, on things still happening. Our film on the San Francisco Conference had to be revised from day to day. A Navy camera crew went out on the new *Yorktown* to shoot the "life and death of a carrier." After two years she was still afloat, and thus, happily, *The Fighting Lady* was deprived of its original ending. Also happily, the first Battle of the Philippine Sea provided a more than satisfactory substitute. There are admittedly extreme cases, but many documentaries must be turned inside out, either while still in production or in the cutting room.

For this and other reasons, documentary scripts are usually simple affairs, allowing the director plenty of leeway for substitution or invention in the field. They are notably devoid of "situations," melodrama, or suspense developed from plot devices, or from intricate interrelations between characters.

In the first place, such situations are usually beyond the abilities of nonprofessional performers. In the second place, they are not consonant with the characteristic goal of the documentary: to drive across an idea. This does not mean that the documentary need lack suspense, or even the "menace" for which the fabled producer so plaintively cried. The documentary "menace" is there, but he doesn't wear striped pants or whiskers, or carry a whip. He is the unseen enemy in John Huston's *The Battle of San Pietro;* in *Fighting Lady,* the pink tracers floating up from the hostile atoll; he is the starboard engine sputtering and the ground fog in Britain's magnificent *Target for Tonight;* he may be as intangible as the gray loneliness of the English housewife in *They Also Serve,* as tangible as the dreadful specter of flood and erosion in *Valley of the Tennessee.*

For the same rules hold true for documentary as for entertainment films: the audience must be *for* one thing, *against* something else. The documentary must have a "pulling" interest. The script, simple as it usually is, strives to enhance this interest. Thus the best documentary, like the best entertainment film, has suspense, light and shade, honest dramatic motivation throughout.

As I have said above, it is the fashion in some Hollywood quarters to deride the documentary as pedantic, undramatic, and "arty." I have even heard the documentarians accused by one producer (who should know better) of trying to drive audiences out of the theaters.

The Battle of San Pietro (1945), by John Huston

The charge of "artiness" cannot be wholly denied, but it should be leveled not against the medium per se but only against those few producers who have so indulged their aestheticism. The other charges are more serious since they imply that no film dealing in truth can ever hope to win public acceptance; and this, of course, is a matter of the very first importance to the producer of entertainment films.

Yet many of Hollywood's finest pictures have dealt with material usually considered to be purely documentary. The menace in *Fury* was not the cruelty of individuals, but the psychotic hatred of a mob; *The Grapes of Wrath* pointed out the evils of selfishness and economic troglodytism: the theme of *Citizen Kane* was the well-worn aphorism that absolute power corrupts absolutely; and in *Wilson* we saw a great man destroyed, not by one whiskered senator, but by the ignorance and indifference of a nation. This fine film also pleaded powerfully for its cause in the best documentary tradition. *Zola* and *Juarez*, among many others, also had something very definite to say.

Several producers of Hollywood pictures have begun to grasp the enormous responsibility and the opportunity facing the industry in the critical years ahead. Their ideas are winning acceptance. The trend is obviously toward greater realism, toward a more frequent selection of factual American themes, toward the theory that motion pictures should not only entertain and make money, but should also give expression to the American and democratic ideals: to "the truth" as we, the citizens of democracy, accept it. The industry is preparing to do its part in the fight for human freedom, tolerance, and dignity. This preparation should be not only spiritual but technical. Hollywood can and should prove to its own satisfaction that truth is not only stranger, but stronger, than fiction. It can do this best by closely observing the methods, and sometimes absorbing the personnel, of the documentary field. After all, the words, "truthful" and "documentary" are nearly synonymous.

Citizen Kane. RKO Radio, 1941. Director, Orson Welles. Original screenplay, Herman J. Mankiewicz and Orson Welles.

Crisis. Mayer-Burstyn, 1939. Director, Herbert Kline. Commentary, Vincent Sheean.

The Fighting Lady. Fox, 1944. Director, S. Sylvan Simon. Narration, John S. Martin and Eugene Ling.

Fury. MGM, 1936. Director, Fritz Lang. Original story, Norman Krasna. Screenplay, Bartlett Cormack and Fritz Lang.

The Grapes of Wrath. Fox, 1939. Director, John Ford. Novel, John Steinbeck. Screenplay, Nunnally Johnson.

Juarez. WB, First Nat'l, 1939. Director, William Dieterle. Adapted from play *Juarez and Maximilian* by Franz Werfel and novel *The Phantom Crown* by Bertita Harding. Screenplay, John Huston, Aeneas MacKenzie, and Wolfgang Reinhardt.

San Pietro. U.S.A. Signal Corps Campaign Report, 1945. Narration, Maj. John Huston.

The Life of Emile Zola. WB, First Nat'l, 1937. Director, William Dieterle. Original screen story, Heinz Herald and Geza Herczeg. Screenplay, Norman Reilly Raine, Heinz Herald, and Geza Herczeg.

The River. U.S. Govt, 1937. Written and directed by Pare Lorentz.

Target for Tonight. Crown Film Unit, B.M.I., 1941. Director and supervisor of narrative, Henry Watt.

They Also Serve. B.M.O.I., 1942. Producer, Ruby Grierson.

Wilson. Fox, 1944. Director, Henry King. Original screenplay, Lamar Trotti.

Valley of the Tennessee. O.W.I., Overseas, 1945. Director, Alexander Hackenschmied. Writer, May Sarton.

Time Flickers Out: Notes on the Passing of the *March of Time*

Raymond Fielding is an educational motion-picture writer and director. He recently produced, in Japan, the award-winning documentary *The Honorable Mountain*. His latest publication is *The Wills of the Presidents* (Oceana, 1957). The following is one of a series of articles based upon Mr. Fielding's recently completed historical study of the *March of Time*.

. . . . .

IN THE SPRING OF 1935, a brilliantly conceived informational film series burst upon the American motion-picture scene, startling journalists and political observers and shattering the complacent calm of Hollywood's film colony. Entitled the *March of Time*, the series was designed to explore the contemporary American and international scene. Many people believed that it was also deliberately designed to provoke controversy. Certainly few film critics, friendly or not, expected it to survive more than a few months.

Sixteen years and over 160 issues later, in the fall of 1951, this ubiquitous, impudent, omniscient film series ceased theatrical production and disappeared from motion-picture screens. For many people, the silence was deafening. Missed were the crisis-packed sepulchral tones of Westbrook Van Voorhis, the fast-paced ingenious editing, the dramatic pronouncements ex cathedra, and the other unique trademarks familiar to an audience of several millions throughout the world.

Bosley Crowther best expressed the shock and regret that film devotees, critics, and the average citizen felt when *Time* announced withdrawal of this significant series:

> ... more than a sentimental sadness over the passing of a cinematic friend will
> be felt by those toilers in the vineyards who have sweat blood over documen-
> tary films. For to them, no matter how they may have snickered at the series'
> recognized conventional form, the *March of Time* has stood up as a symbol

of real accomplishment in the "pictorial journalism" field. Out of the turbulent Nineteen Thirties, out of those restless years of social change and evolution and growing tension in the world, it emerged with all the eagerness and confidence of the new journalistic approach, pacing off with the fruitful innovators and waving the aspirants on.[1]

Today, six years after the series' demise, it seems high time to perform a critical autopsy, through which the agents of death may be revealed for the edification of other surviving "idea-film" producers who aspire to theatrical release.

Considering the film's high prestige value to Time, Incorporated, and the obvious efforts of the parent firm to salvage and perpetuate the series, it seems reasonable to assume that financial failure lay behind its withdrawal rather than *Time's* displeasure with its own handiwork.

If we are to understand this failure, then, we must first examine the motion-picture industry through which the film was released. It is an industry in which short subjects have never enjoyed a financially secure position; a business in which even the traditional newsreel and the ever popular cartoon have generally failed to return their investments.[2] Indeed, if the full-length feature film had sprung full-blown from the early, pre-1910 studios, the short subject might never have appeared at all. As it happened, of course, the shorts came first—comedies, melodramas, travelogues, westerns—a potpourri of ten-minute turns that flooded the theaters and established an audience taste for program variety.

The status of the short subject began to change shortly after 1912, following the successful introduction of the full-length feature film. As the popularity of the feature increased, that of the short declined. By 1920, the short had become the poor relation of a prosperous film industry, block-booked as a "filler" and designed to divert motion-picture audiences in much the same manner as the late nineteenth-century film had served as an intermission between stage variety acts. Such then was the position of the common short when the *March of Time* made its bow in 1935: a necessary distribution evil, subsidized by the major producers and

1. "Time Marches Off," New York *Times*, July 15, 1951, II, 1.
2. For a detailed discussion of the financial problems of newsreel production and distribution, see Peter Baechlin and Maurice Muller-Strauss, *Newsreels Across the World* (Paris: UNESCO, 1952), 16 ff.

packaged with income-producing features. Lacking promotion and publicity, the occasional pre-*March of Time* information film found its way to its intended audience less through design than accident.

That the independently produced *March of Time* should have ultimately failed under such circumstances seems less remarkable than that it managed to survive beyond the first year of release. It had what was, until then, possibly the largest short-subject budget in the history of the industry—in excess of $900,000 per year.[3] Only an independent producer with the tenacity and financial resources of Time, Incorporated, could have sustained such a series until its audience had been built and its distribution and promotion organized along precedent-setting lines. Such a budget, spawned during the lean years of the depression, could only increase with the passing of time. During and subsequent to World War II, the cost of labor and material rose greatly and so presumably did the film's budget. Finally, in the late 1940's, in common with the rest of the film industry, its profits disappeared as the ranks of its audience were attenuated by the electronic marvels of television—in all respects, an economic foe so formidable that continued theatrical production became impractical. *Time*'s motion-picture compeers weathered the storm with 3-D adventures and wide-screen extravaganzas. But the *March of Time* was selling ideas—they were wide in scope, but hardly competition for the talking puppet, the tousled wrestler, and the dancing beer cans.

Despite such formidable economic problems, however, it would seem premature to equate the *March of Time*'s failure merely in terms of high cost and industry recession. The passing of the series may be considered roughly analogous to the recent disappearance from newsstands of two of this country's oldest and most popular magazines. In both cases, financial failure may quite possibly be traced back to atypical audience response or unintentionally aggravated audience apathy.

In its halcyon days, the *March of Time* enjoyed the devotion and regular attendance of over twenty million people a month in 9,000 theaters in the United States alone.[4] As its producers immodestly but accurately proclaimed, the film played in more theaters than did any other regular motion-picture series. Yet, this audience had been built during the period

3. *Four Hours a Year* (New York: Time, Inc., 1936), 17.
4. *Nation,* May 1, 1937, 501; and Baechlin and Muller-Strauss, *op. cit.,* 67 and 90.

from 1935 to 1941 and was maintained only throughout the war. These were the golden years of the *March of Time:* years of wrath, years of crisis, conflict, and uncertainty—an atmosphere in which the *March of Time,* with its air of Jovian omniscience, could thrive and grow in stature, from an experimental newsreel to a powerful cinematic oracle.

With the closing of the war in 1945, movie audiences turned gratefully from crisis-packed, politico-military films to lighter, peacetime fare. The *March of Time* found itself for the first time unable to interest audiences in "clouds no bigger than a man's hand." Concomitantly, the quality of *MOT* editions declined as writers and directors relied more and more on conventionalized staging and editing.

Earlier, with the outbreak of hostilities in 1941, disorganization began to threaten the production group. Some of the technicians on *Time's* staff were absorbed into the Armed Forces and the government agencies. Distribution of the series was removed from the hands of RKO in 1942 and given to Twentieth Century-Fox. And, in the same year, Louis de Rochemont, father and guiding spirit of the *March of Time,* left the organization to join Twentieth Century-Fox as a feature-film producer. Though control of production remained in the able hands of director Richard de Rochemont and *Time* president Roy Larsen, Louis de Rochemont's talents must have been sorely missed.

Finally, and most fatally, the style and format of the *March of Time* had scarcely varied from the day it opened shop until the day it closed its doors. In 1935, its innovations had had an electrifying effect upon other film makers, infusing the documentary movement with new vitality and popularizing the "idea-film" for theatrical audiences. Indeed, it has been said that the *March of Time* founded a new school of documentary film production. John Grierson, leader of the British documentarians, acknowledged as much when he stated that he had been obliged to "dramatize public information." [5] If the *March of Time's* originality had been a growing, changing thing, if it had inspired more emulation than it did imitation, it might have survived the familiarity that breeds net losses at the box office. Back in 1935 Alistair Cooke had cautioned film makers against "witless imitation" of the *March of Time.* [6] Grierson unintention-

5. Jean Benoit-Levy, *The Art of the Motion Picture* (New York: Coward-McCann, 1946), 107.
6. *The Listener,* November 20, 1935, 931.

ally echoed Cooke's warning, prophesying that "it will soon be called by
a dozen names—Window on the World, World Eye, Brave New World,
and what not."[7] Subsequent years brought a rash of the expected copies,
most of them very poor. Their producers appropriated *March of Time*
style and format but obviously lacked the brilliance, experience, and resources of the originator.

That the *March of Time* had considerable influence on other documentary films cannot be denied. The extent of its influence on newsreels,
however, remains moot. In 1936, critic Andrew Buchanan enthusiastically
found

> signs that news films will ultimately be made which shall be so intelligent, ab-
> sorbingly interesting and completely different . . . that, in time . . . we shall
> go to see a news-reel with the same thrill we experience when about to view a
> production by Grierson, Pudovkin or Rotha. The most significant of such
> signs is "The March of Time."[8]

Today, however, as we view the current output of the newsreel factories,
we are forced to conclude that Buchanan's enthusiasm was premature. Of
course, the *March of Time*, which considered itself an interpretive "magazine of the screen," usually did its best to disassociate itself from the more
common name of "newsreel." Only when dealing with various censor
boards, to whom newsreels were sacrosanct, and in fighting the demands
of the Screen Actors Guild for union actors in the film's staged sequences,
did the *March of Time* appear to embrace the term.[9]

Whatever the *March of Time*'s faults may have been—and there were
many—it was always direct, positive, and self-confident. Such qualities,
when found in a news film, should be counted as virtues. The therapeu-
tic value of the firm and knowing statements was not lost on fearful audiences. The movie patron, even when finding *Time*'s solutions inadequate,
was at least impressed with the earth-shaking self-confidence with which
they had been presented. *Time* generously shared its executive omniscience with its public, momentarily lifting viewers out of the crises that
surrounded them and allowing them to view the confusion with revealing perspective. Even when *Time* declined to attempt a solution, its audi-

7. *Grierson on Documentary* (New York: Harcourt, Brace and Company, 1947), 161.
8. *The Art of Film Production* (London: Sir I. Pitman and Sons, Ltd., 1936), 72.
9. New York *Times*, October 12, 1946, 8; and January 8, 1947, 28.

ence rarely felt cheated. No matter how dreadful the conditions exposed, no matter how terrifying the consequences predicted, *Time*'s very act of examination seemed somehow as good as a bona fide solution. The knowledge that *MOT* was "doing" a subject was, in itself, reassuring: it meant that lively debate and public awareness of the issues would follow.

Withdrawal of the *March of Time* from movie theaters in 1951 brought this colorful era of motion-picture journalism to an abrupt end. As indicated earlier, the series' death was probably long overdue. Only a few of the postwar issues sparkled with the same vitality, originality, and brilliance that had characterized the prewar product. *Time*'s order to cease production came as cinematic euthanasia for this once-dynamic giant of the documentary field that had fallen on poorer days of mass production and formula fabrication.

Will the *March of Time* or a successor again appear on the American scene? Probably not, unless some happy circumstance brings such dynamic talents as de Rochemont and Larsen and the munificent patronage of a Luce together again, along with the less happy circumstance of accompanying economic and military crises. Even given such a rare combination of talent, capital and catalyst again, there is some doubt whether there is still a place for the *March of Time* in the American scene. Certainly, political and military crises still remain, but the dogged faith of the 1930's appears to have given way to fatalism in the 1950's. In the past, the appeal of the *March of Time* lay largely in the implied assumption that problems *could* be solved and that answers *would* be forthcoming. There is some question whether the *March of Time*'s dynamic pronouncements would have any meaning today for a citizenry that questions its own power to control the atom and command its own destiny.

To some extent, the *March of Time* may also be considered a victim of prosperity—an anachronism in an age of plenty. The pressing economic problems, the hunger, and the anger of the 1930's have disappeared, and with them the need for the film's reassuring predictions. The "Voice of Time," with its message of hope, can no longer be heard above the rush and rumble of the automatic dishwasher, the garbage disposal unit, and the power lawn mower. The public does not need the *March of Time*, or if it does, is not aware of it.

Nor should we look to the television screen for its reappearance. The powers of video, inordinately sensitive to the political protests of vocal minorities, eschew the intentionally controversial film series. Sponsors understandably hesitate to underwrite programs calculated to arouse and possibly alienate portions of their audience. Furthermore, either from preference or conditioning, television viewers appear to reject the unseen, off-stage narrator in favor of the "News Personality"—a flesh and blood visitor to their living rooms whom they can recognize and admire or criticize.

The unusually powerful and compelling off-stage voice which narrated the *March of Time* was that of Westbrook Van Voorhis. Curiously, this "Voice of Time" had no distinct personality characteristics with which members of the audience could identify either themselves or their neighbors. As such, it was a difficult voice to question or attack. Like many of *Time's* pronouncements, it appeared to speak with the weight of some omniscient power behind it. Today, in television, the sentential voice of Edward R. Murrow, with its "voice of doom" inflection, comes closest to approximating the unseen presence of Van Voorhis. The omniscient voice remains, but is now revealed to have mortal form and substance. Lacking the visual anonymity of Van Voorhis, Murrow and other such commentators become highly vulnerable targets for politically irritated segments of the television audience.

And so, with a backward glance and a ruffle of drums, *Time* marches off to the film vaults, perhaps to be reincarnated under a different name for another troubled generation, or perhaps, instead, simply to mingle its nitrate dust with that of other forgotten films. The "Voice of the Tomb," home at last, echoes through the crowded corridors of the film vault, its insistent dictum providing a grim reminder for those who court the public's taste: Time . . . Marches On!

4 Radio

Abraham Polonsky

The Case of David Smith*

Before coming to Hollywood, Abraham Polonsky lived in New York, where he taught English at the College of the City of New York and wrote for the radio. He is now a writer at Paramount, where he has been working on *The Paris Story*.

. . . . .

Introductory Note | Sam Moore

Sam Moore has been writing for radio since 1931, and is currently writing *The Great Gildersleeve* in collaboration with John Whedon. He is president of the Radio Writers' Guild.

THE PROJECT WHICH eventually became the radio program *Reunion U.S.A.* resulted from a series of seminars conducted by the Hollywood Writers Mobilization, in 1944, on the general problems of adjustment which would have to be faced by soldiers and civilians alike when the process of demobilization should begin on a mass scale. Discussions led by psychologists, psychiatrists, social workers, army officers and enlisted men, with participation from radio and screen writers and directors, led to the conclusion that these problems were so complex and of such importance as to warrant an attempt to present them, or at least some phases of them, to the civilian population. Radio seemed the logical medium to use in this attempt, because it could reach a mass audience quickly and conveniently, avoiding the necessary production delays (and expense) of a comprehensive film program.

This educational project was the more urgent because of the wide publicity given, late in the war, to the special problems of the psychoneurotic

*This script, for one of the series of programs entitled *Reunion U.S.A.*, was broadcast, November 5, 1945, over the network of the American Broadcasting Company (originating at Station KECA, Los Angeles, 7:30 to 8:00 P.M. P.S.T.). The music for the entire series of *Reunion U.S.A.* was composed and directed by Basil Adlam.

soldier. The dramatic possibilities of a returned soldier suffering from deeply buried fears, guilt feelings, and so on, appealed to writers of fiction whose only solution of the difficulty, all too often, was the love and "understanding" of a pretty girl. That formula was so popular, indeed, that the entire nation was receiving the impression that most of our returning soldiers would not be psychologically "normal."

The Mobilization's series of seminars brought out the true facts, and demonstrated the danger of this overemphasis on the question of the psychoneurotic. The general conclusions of the seminars, broadly stated, were that the mere fact of spatial and temporal separation between the two enormous groups of civilians and soldiers would necessarily bring about psychological changes in both, but most soldiers would return to their homes completely normal, though often much more mature than before their army experience, and with a changed point of view toward many questions of individual and social behavior. The writers for these programs were committed to write within this framework.

A prospectus for a radio program presenting this point of view in a series of dramatic stories was drawn up in the spring of 1945 and submitted to the War Department, the O.W.I., the Veterans Administration, and various radio networks. The project was vigorously approved by all the government agencies, and network time was obtained from the American Broadcasting Company.

Reunion U.S.A. represents a technical experiment in radio education in that the documentary form developed by Norman Corwin and others was rejected in favor of the traditional radio dramatic form. Following the presentation of each play there was a two- or three-minute commentary by an expert, usually a psychologist, in which the major point of the story was stated in simple terms. In the eighteen plays presented, all the stories concerned ordinary people, faced with problems which, if not exactly "ordinary," were rapidly becoming statistically probable. I believe that the success of the series, as determined by its audience popularity, proves the correctness of this decision on the question of form.

The program had the benefit of very little publicity, almost no advertising, and also lacked another useful adjunct to the quick building of a large radio audience—a continuing "name" star. In spite of these obstacles, *Reunion U.S.A.* quickly gathered a listening audience of some ten million people, and was at one time among the five most popular programs on the entire American network.

Among the specific problems treated were the veteran's paramount anxiety about a job, his desire to continue his education, his adjustment to a wife unwilling to give up her employment and return to the drudgery of the kitchen, his changed attitude toward political and social questions, his awareness of the world and America's position in it, and his wish, resulting from that awareness, to participate in community activities as an adult citizen. The plays varied widely in content and treatment: some of them were closely packed with social and philosophical implications; others were relatively superficial in their handling of simpler themes. There was no observable correlation between the complexity of treatment and the size of the listening audience, which steadily increased.

One is tempted to the conclusion that, contrary to the general supposition, there is a large audience which is anxious to hear dramatic programs in which an attempt is made to deal with problems having a real basis in the life of America today. Perhaps the radio audience is not a horde of twelve-year-old mentalities breathlessly awaiting the wolf jokes, the childish love stories of adapted movies, the slow-motion "problem" dramas presented by the soap manufacturers. *Reunion U.S.A.* had something to say. The program's only asset was the fact of its serious mission to reach millions with information and a small quantity of very tentative advice. But the millions, struggling against the difficulties and dislocations of war, and seeing clearly the approaching dangers of the peace, listened eagerly. The lesson should be clear to writers, network program directors, and advertisers.

The Script

Cast

WRANGLE	Bill Johnstone
MYERS	John Lund
LAPHAM	Paul McVey
FLECK	Howard Duff
MINERVA	Peg La Centra
MAN	Paul McVey
WOMAN	Lynn Whitney
DAVID	Paul Theodore
NURSE	Lynn Whitney

FATHER . . . . Eddie Walker

DOG . . . . Earl Keen

HUMBER . . . . Ken Peters

VOICE . . . . Howard Duff

TANA . . . . Sidney

ANNOUNCER: *(On dead air)* Thousands of men are being discharged from the Armed Forces of the United States every month . . . and they are coming home!

MUSIC: *Intro to main title theme. . . . Fade for:*

ANNOUNCER: Reunion U.S.A.

MUSIC: *Theme—main title*

ANNOUNCER: 'Reunion U.S.A.' is a series of half-hour dramas on the theme of the soldier's return from war, presented by the American Broadcasting Company in coöperation with the Hollywood Writers Mobilization.

MUSIC: *Up and fade for:*

ANNOUNCER: Tonight's play stars John Lund. It is written by Abraham Polonsky and directed by Cal Kuhl. The title, 'The Case of David Smith.'

MUSIC: *Up and segue to theme for story*

. . . . .

MUSIC: *Drums and trumpets to an unresolved rhythm and chord, and out*

WRANGLE: Captain Myers?

MYERS: Sir?

WRANGLE: You may be seated.

MYERS: Thank you, sir. *(Narrative voice, introspective: designated by brackets).* [So this is Wrangle, Colonel Wrangle, and his two assistants. I admit the situation with my neat obedience. My briefcase rests upon my knees, my shoes are shined, my uniform pressed. Yes, my face and attitude are careful with respect for rank and authority.]

WRANGLE: Ready, gentlemen?

LAPHAM: Yes, Colonel Wrangle.

SOUND: *Pencil tapping on desk*

LAPHAM: I'm sure I had lead in this pencil.

FLECK: Here's a pencil, Lapham.

LAPHAM: Thanks, Fleck.

SOUND: *Tapping of pencil*

LAPHAM: It can't have just disappeared.

WRANGLE: Are these files duplicates, Captain Myers?

MYERS: Yes, sir.

SOUND: *The little rigmarole of papers, files, and ash trays as the men make ready while Myers continues to speak*

MYERS: [This is Wrangle, a beefy man with restless eyes: Wrangle, who completed his classification of the human race in 1924 and regards all subsequent history as unmitigated gall. To his left is Major Lapham, not a practicing psychiatrist like Wrangle, but a popularizer. You've seen his books advertised in Sunday book supplements, and on the back covers of pulp magazines: 'The Psychiatry of Everyday Life,' and then a splash of red letters shrieking: ARE YOU INSANE? *(Pause)* The futility of making them understand is apparent.]

WRANGLE: Captain Myers?

MYERS: Sir?

WRANGLE: We're sitting as an informal board on the Smith case. Frankly, I have no strong opinions. And I'm sure Majors Lapham and Fleck are in the same boat.

MYERS: [I smile again to show my eagerness to coöperate. I know Wrangle wants this curious Smith case closed: Let's have no new reasons for new disasters! I smile at Lapham. He examines his mechanical pencil while he thinks of book sales on drug counters and in department stores. Now for Major Fleck, whoever he is. I want him to think I'm intelligent but not forward. We are colleagues but not equals. This smile is familiar among professionals, more subtle than that of the Mona Lisa. *(Pause)* No. This is a different kind of man. Fleck? Fleck? Who is Fleck? I suddenly remember a few papers in obscure journals, some careful studies, a handful of insights. Fleck. Perhaps Fleck can understand the whole horror of this Smith case. This man may listen, think. I unlock my briefcase

SOUND: *Unlocking briefcase*

and take out my personal file on Smith, leaving the letter in its gray envelope safe in the leather pocket. Perhaps the letter can be read, if Fleck is anything at all. But later.] I'll be glad to tell you anything you want to know, gentlemen.

WRANGLE: Thank you, captain. It seems from a first glance that we have an extreme but typical melancholia.

MYERS: [His restless black eyes dart aimless, typical glances, looking through life for typical patterns. The man is hopeless.] There is evidence to that effect, sir.

WRANGLE: What do you think, Lapham?

LAPHAM: I agree. I agree completely. A very sad case, one of those dreary prices for victory. Very. The three years Lieutenant Smith spent in the Japanese prison camps definitely unhinged him. But definitely.

WRANGLE: Undoubtedly, but there must be probable genetic patterns. What do you think, Fleck?

MYERS: [I look at Fleck, who blinks his heavy-lidded eyes most innocently. Does he care to know? Will he try?]

FLECK: I should like to hear Captain Myers' observations. *(Pause)* Perhaps there's something we can learn.

MYERS: [This is a man.]

WRANGLE: You may proceed, Captain Myers.

MYERS: [I slowly open the file of the strange case of Lt. David Smith, Army of the United States. Whatever hopelessness I carried into the room is still with me. The affair is so complex, the need to understand so grave. Fleck is my man. I shall talk to him, and to him alone. The other two have buried the corpse.] Lieutenant David Smith, admitted October 12 – 0500. Weight, 152, ten pounds below normal. Pulse, 72; blood pressure, 126. Basal metabolism, minus 3. Walked stiffly, obeyed instructions, apparently unable to speak. Generally apathetic . . . depressed. I examined him quite carefully. His body bore healed scars from outrageous acts of violence inflicted on him during his three years' captivity. The left hand, for instance, though healed, was completely crushed and useless, the bones having been broken in the wrists and fingers, the nerves atrophied. As I learned later, the Japanese had done this with a light hammer after tying Smith's hand to a wooden block and beating it repeatedly.

LAPHAM: *(Involuntarily)* The savages.

MYERS: Smith appeared to be in the first stages of some enormous psychological shock.

WRANGLE: Delayed, no doubt. A mass recall.

LAPHAM: A sudden realization of all he had gone through.

WRANGLE: It's quite common.

(Pause: painful)

FLECK: Will you continue, Captain?

MYERS: Thank you. I had Smith put to bed, sent for his records, and interviewed his wife on the following morning. You have the summary of our remarks there before you.

WRANGLE: Mrs. Minerva Smith?

SOUND: *Rustling of papers*

MYERS: Yes, sir. [I remember that interview with Mrs. Minerva Smith most distinctly. It was the first sign of the deeper meaning in her husband's case. She sat in the barred sunlight that came through the Venetian blinds.]

SOUND: *A lawn mower off, by spells*

MYERS: [Someone was mowing the grass outside. She was pretty, placid, pained, a middle-class matron at twenty-two. She wore white washable gloves, carried a black purse that matched her dress, black and appropriate for the sad occasion. Her legs were modestly quiet and uncrossed, her hat just so on her upswept hair. But she felt hurt; let down, I suppose.]

MINERVA: The way I feel, doctor . . . *(a false half laugh)* . . . or should I call you Captain? It doesn't seem right. I've been waiting so long.

MYERS: I realize that. How did your husband act when he first came home?

MINERVA: That's just it. He seemed so ready to be happy.

MYERS: Affectionate?

MINERVA: *(primly)* Pardon?

MYERS: I mean just generally.

MINERVA: Oh, yes. David is an affectionate man. I'm an affectionate woman myself.

MYERS: [Here she smiled at me, inviting my deep sympathy. I was deeply sympathetic.] When did he first begin to act strangely?

MINERVA: From the very first, in a way. He wanted to read all the papers and magazines of the last three years. He listened to news broadcasts all the time. I mean, doctor, after all . . . here we were, reunited, after so long. You'd think he'd be sick of the whole past. And then, he didn't seem particularly anxious to meet our friends again, people who had worried day and night over his safety for years.

MYERS: Did he tell you why?

MINERVA: No, Doctor, although after his visit to his father I finally did arrange a party.

SOUND: *Party noises fading in. Glasses, voices, etc.*

MAN: David, you know the Japs better than we do. Do you think they'll want to pull a Pearl Harbor first chance they get?

MINERVA: Oh, please . . . We can't be living in the past the rest of our lives.

WOMAN: Minerva's right. Let's *not* talk politics. We can leave that to the government. Tell us, David, how did your first ice cream soda taste? Here in town, I mean.

DAVID: You really want to know?

WOMAN: *(Loudly)* Everybody quiet. Quiet!

SOUND: *Party noises down*

WOMAN: David is going to make his first public statement on his first ice cream soda in town.

SOUND: *Laughter, silence*

WOMAN: How *did* it taste?

DAVID: Bitter.

SOUND: *Voices up cross-fade to Minerva*

MINERVA: People just stared, Doctor. We felt . . . I felt . . . that he hated us.

MYERS: [Her smooth cheeks shook. The whole thing was so uncomfortable.] Tell me, Mrs. Smith, was there anything in your husband's past, any frustration, any unhealthy attitude towards people or life—anything you remember that might help us?

MINERVA: No. No. David was quite normal—except, of course, you know he was studying to be an anthropologist. He wanted to go off and live with primitive peoples, stuff like that. I used to think it was so romantic . . .

MYERS: Anything else?

MINERVA: Nothing really . . . perhaps . . . well, when he was in college he used to belong to an organization—I forget its name, but it was antiwar. He hated war. He comes from a family of Quakers. But it wasn't very serious because, when war came, he volunteered. You know that? He's a volunteer.

MYERS: Yes, I know. *(Pause)* Would you like to see your husband now?

MINERVA: *(Pause)* Is he the same?

MYERS: I'm afraid so.

MINERVA: Well . . . *(hesitates)* . . . no, I think not. It's all so unfair. I've waited so long. *(Pause)* I'm like all the other normal people in the world. I say let the dead past bury its dead.

MYERS: [She stood there, hesitating, not daring to say what she meant—that she wished he were dead. And I politely showed her out and went to see my patient. Signs, portents, meanings already floated above his martyred head.] No change, nurse?

NURSE: No, Doctor. I raised him to a sitting position about ten minutes ago and he hasn't moved once.

MYERS: [Smith faced the wall, resting limply in his bed against the pillows. His eyes were closed. Twenty-six years old, but he looked fifty, his hair gray, his temples hollow, the ache of creeping death upon him.] Smith! Smith, can you hear me? [His eyelids slowly opened and glazed eyes stared ahead. The glance was inward on the unfathomable horror which he alone knew, which he, alone of us all, possessed.] Smith! Smith! [His eyes closed again. That was all.] What do the tests show, Nurse?

NURSE: Nothing, sir. Absolutely nothing.

MYERS: [I knew then as I know now that the inner need of this man could be touched only through the mind. I simply had to get to him, to Smith, the human being aware of himself. This body, this dying vegetable in the bed, had no meaning for him any more. We could feed it.]

NURSE: By tube, sir. He took some nourishment.

MYERS: [We could wash it, watch it, measure it. But we couldn't release it from some deep vision, some deep abstraction which the mind possessed. *This* was living death, a renunciation. *(Pause)* I tried to get to everyone who had known him.]

WRANGLE: I see the reports here, Captain.

MYERS: Yes, sir. But, as you can see, no one seemed to mean anything to Smith, not even his father.

WRANGLE: Stephen Smith?

MYERS: Yes, sir. [I'm being so careful with these men. Perhaps the violent significance of Smith's case will echo in their ears. Wrangle palps the papers. Lapham draws girls with curly hair. Fleck looks at me. Very well, let us stare at each other, Major Fleck. If you wish to recognize the guilt, you must share it.]

WRANGLE: The father was Mr. Stephen Smith, a retired farmer from Linville.

MYERS: Yes, sir. He came to the hospital. You have the gist of our remarks in the report before you. [The gist, yes. The father was an old man, for David had been a late son. The father seemed remote from life, wifeless and now to be childless.] You say he came to visit you, Mr. Smith?

FATHER: Why, yes, Doctor. It was supposed to be for a week, but David only stayed one night. We didn't seem to have much to say to each other.

MYERS: Why do you think he came?

FATHER: Filial duty, I suppose. He was always a good boy. But in the morning he was up and on his way.

MYERS: Yes?

FATHER: We hadn't really said anything to each other, Doctor. I don't know what it was he expected of me. I'm old and I'm tired. David was always queer. He wanted to be a missionary in China like his grandfather, but he soon got over that when he grew up. I don't believe in running all over the earth changing things. What does it matter, anyway?

MYERS: Did he say anything that I should know?

FATHER: Well, in a way. It was about seven and he was dressed to leave.

SOUND: *Dog barking, off*

FATHER: The dog kept barking outside, remembering him. . . . Going, David?

DAVID: Yes.

FATHER: I thought you were going to stay a few days.

DAVID: What for? What's the use of it? *(Pause)* What's the use of you?

SOUND: *Steps going to door. Door opens. Dog barking in, loudly. Door slams*

FATHER: You hear, Doctor. He said that to me. What's the use of me? What did he want?

MYERS: [And then at last we stood in David's hospital room, the father, the nurse, and myself. David was stretched out flat on the bed, breathing lightly, wasting away.]

FATHER: Looks bad. Some tropical disease?

MYERS: No. Something mental, I think.

FATHER: Well, that's it. He used to be a fine young man, and now look at him, older than me. Do you think it was worth while—for him, I mean—all the war and the prison camp, and such?

MYERS: Was it worth while for you?

FATHER: I don't know.

MYERS: [He stood there, the father. And then he walked over to the bed, gently bent down, and kissed his son's forehead.]

FATHER: *(Clears throat)* I keep wondering, Doctor, if we're not entitled to another Flood . . .

MYERS: [It got so I used to spend hours in Smith's room, just looking at him, wondering. The thing grew on me until I began to feel that this wasn't a 'case'; this was myself, my own responsibility. It was a nightmare—to be burdened and overwhelmed with the sense that somehow the meaning of my own life was bound into the apathetic hulk upon the bed, that wasting flesh, those cheeks sinking beneath the bone.] Smith! David! Can you hear me? Open your eyes! [But by now they no longer opened, and we all knew this was the dying. I felt it was my duty—it had become my sole duty—to make this man open his lips again, to speak, to say the thing that tormented him, for it was an unspeakable torment that had magnetized his brain into silence. Nothing of the world outside, not the wind at morning, nor the faces of men, mattered. He was alone with himself. *(Pause)* I wonder do these men before me seek to understand. They turn the pages of the file. They glance at one another. And Fleck . . . does he find a glimmer? He dreams away behind half-closed lids. Wrangle coughs upon his ignorance.]

SOUND: *Wrangle coughs*

WRANGLE: There are mysteries, Captain Myers. You did your best. Is there anything else you want to say?

MYERS: [Anything else I want to say? Shall I shout it at you? Must the dead spring from their graves with banners and trumpets?] There was, sir, the interview I had with the rescuing officer—

WRANGLE: John Humber, Lieutenant Senior Grade, United States Naval Reserve?

MYERS: Yes, sir. [Humber popped in on me. He was brisk and in his middle thirties, an affable advertising man turned warrior.]

HUMBER: How do you do, Captain? I received your note.

MYERS: Sorry to bother you.

HUMBER: Not at all. Not at all. How's Smith?

MYERS: Would you like to see him? [Humber gave me a quick, suspicious look. Was this a responsibility? Then his blue eyes found golden glints. He smiled.]

HUMBER: Why not? I brought him back into the world; a kind of second birth, you know . . .

MYERS: Yes. This way, please. [Humber looked at me as if I had breached an inviolate law of social decency when he stared at the human skeleton in the bed.]

HUMBER: *(In wonder)* But that's the way he looked when I first saw him. You know we rushed the camp, and Smith was lying in the dirt, a bloody bruise on his cheek where some Jap animal had just kicked him. What's wrong?

MYERS: We don't know. That's why I asked you over. I thought perhaps you might know. It's psychological.

HUMBER: Poor chap. He had the devil of a time. Three years of it, and the worst, the very worst.

MYERS: Did you talk to him?

HUMBER: A little. I found him lying in the dirt in the hot sun. The Japs wouldn't let any of the other prisoners go near him or help. This Smith was a devil. He never gave up for a moment, the other prisoners told me. He knew . . .

MYERS: He knew what?

HUMBER: I don't know how to say it exactly . . . but . . . he felt, he knew, that to live on, to endure, to defy them guaranteed the faith and honor of those back at home. He was a man of honor. *(Pause)* Anyway . . . There was a little shooting . . .

SOUND: *A burst of shots, off. A few lone ones*

HUMBER: This way, men. Lively!

SOUND: *Feet on dirt, etc.*

HUMBER: Who's this?

VOICE: Smith, sir. Lieutenant Smith.

HUMBER: Is he dead?

VOICE: No, sir.

HUMBER: Smith! Hello there, Smith! You're free! We're here! We've returned!

SMITH: *(Weakly)* Hello.

HUMBER: Take it easy, old man. *(Calls)* Stretcher here!

SMITH: I'm all right.

HUMBER: You'll be all right.

SOUND: *Stretcher bearers, etc.*

HUMBER: Easy there, men. In with him.

SMITH: Lieutenant?

HUMBER: Just take it easy, old man. You'll be eating ice cream sodas in your own town before long. It's over.

SMITH: Have you got a gun?

HUMBER: None of that, old man. You'll make it.

SMITH: I just want to feel a gun again.

SOUND: *Voices up briefly, and out*

HUMBER: Well, I handed him my forty-five. I don't know why. He asked for it. This skeleton, this devilish living scarecrow of a man. You could see the blood pumping through his veins, he was so thin . . . covered with sores . . . a sight . . . a blasted revolting sight! Imagine, Captain, an American, and they had treated him this way! And off the stretcher went, and Smith sitting up in it, fondling the gun. The Jap commandant was standing there, stiffly, with his men all lined up, damned proper and full of protocol all of a sudden. The stretcher stopped in front of him; and Smith, he sat there. Then he pointed the gun . . .

SOUND: *Two shots. Pause. Three shots. Two shots. A long pause. A final shot*
MYERS: He killed him?
HUMBER: God, yes. Smashed him up and dropped the gun and began to cry. And look at him! This man had guts, Captain. What is it?
MYERS: I don't know. I don't think we'll have time to find out.
HUMBER: Dying?
MYERS: Yes.
HUMBER: Well, it's too bad. *(Sighs)* After living through three years of prison camp. *(Pause)* I have to be going.
MYERS: Thanks a lot.
HUMBER: Nothing at all.
MYERS: [He turned back for a last look, shook his short-cropped blond head.]
HUMBER: Anyway, he got back at them. He got one. You know, this is strictly off the record, Captain. It's not *comme il faut.*
MYERS: I know. [In a way, I do. A symbolic act, the punishment of the guilty. Not so much revenge as justice. I wanted Smith to talk, to say a word. What had suddenly overwhelmed him back here in the United States, suddenly found a focus and invited this living death on a hospital bed? *(Pause)* I look at the advisory board—Wrangle, Lapham, and Fleck. Fleck's eyes are on me.]
FLECK: Tell me, Captain Myers . . .
MYERS: Yes, Major Fleck?
FLECK: I know we can't actually separate causes, but, essentially, do you think it was the experience of the war or the experience of the peace that shocked him?
MYERS: [This is crucial. I have the letter in my briefcase. Wrangle's quick eyes scurry like mice. Lapham yawns.] All I know, sir, is what Smith finally said.

WRANGLE: You mean he spoke?

MYERS: Finally, Colonel Wrangle. It was after I interviewed Sergeant Tana, the man who infiltrated the enemy territory with Lieutenant Smith. You know their mission was to go in behind the lines to raise and organize guerrilla bands against the Japanese, Smith being a little familiar with the language, an anthropologist of sorts. Tana was a Filipino, educated here, a fine man. He came in to see me the day Smith spoke. [Fleck is watching me closely. I think he begins to understand, because I can see that same film of sickness in his eyes. He begins to see the whole point of the case of David Smith.] The way Tana put it was simple.

TANA: You understand, Captain, we went in to get these people to fight. But people don't fight for nothing. And Smith, my lieutenant, was an honest man. I don't know what his orders were, his authority to speak, but he told them: You fight to be free. I'm an American. And you'll be free. My government sent me. That's what my lieutenant said to them.

MYERS: They believed him?

TANA: Yes, even though for a native to be caught by the Japanese meant not easy death. There are certain tortures I need not describe. Your manhood goes quickly. The nerves have no conscience, no idealistic slogans. They shatter. But all the natives knew the meaning. You see, this was their jungle. I mean the native, as we Americans call them. It was theirs to have, to keep, to be their very own. So my lieutenant said it. He said it again and again and again. Then he was captured. We fought on with some success until the war was over. Then the colony was re-established, all with due order and a little shooting. I have myself a certain sense of guilt; but then, I'm a native myself. Here is the letter from Smith.

MYERS: What letter?

TANA: He mailed it to me a month ago. I picked it up at my home in San Francisco. I'm a native. I don't have very great expectations. But then, Smith made the promises, he being the officer, not me. If my lieutenant reaches consciousness, tell him for me, I forgive. Of course, I forgive! I have more faith in history. We cannot be defeated forever. One must have the experience of the disaster in such affairs. Good-bye.

MYERS: Good-bye. [He was out with a quick step, a brown little man, wiry and tough. That night I spoke to Smith, and Smith answered. It was close to midnight, and the nurse and I sat there looking at our patient. He was pretty much gone, breathing heavily. I took his hand and bent close to his ear.] Smith . . . David . . . *(whispering)* David. Can you hear me? I just spoke to Sergeant Tana. [A profound shudder moved through his body.]

NURSE: Doctor, his pulse is faster.

MYERS: [I took my stethescope and listened.]

SOUND: *The clink of the earpieces. Then the beating of the heart on mike. This will grow faster as it continues under.*

MYERS: David, *(excitement grows)* listen to me! I spoke to Tana. Tana! You hear? Tana! He says he forgives. Tana! Tana!

SOUND: *The heartbeat is faster, and now the tympani will take up the beat most delicately*

NURSE: *(agitated)* Doctor!

MYERS: [Smith's body began to tremble. His breath came faster.]

SOUND: *Smith breathing heavily*

MYERS: [My ears seemed to be at the end of long antennae probing into the tremors of Smith's mind. There were earthquakes of consciousness stirring within that body.] Smith! Tana! He was here. He said he forgives! [It was like someone rising from the dead; as if the tiny almost extinguished light of sensibility had begun to burn again; as if warmth were seeping into the brain. His body twitched, the muscles loose and dissolute with energy. The habits of conscious living had been dormant so long. Sweat broke out on his brow.] David, can you hear me? David. Tana. Listen to me. Tana. He forgives! [And then his eyes opened . . . a glaze-fixed light. He seemed to struggle to sit up.] Help him, Nurse.

NURSE: I am. [She raised him slowly, and those eyes stared and stared.]

MYERS: David, Tana was here. He forgives.

SOUND: *Heart and music, now! The rhythm coming up*

MYERS: [I could sense the long shift, the immense focus of his mind. He seemed to come out of the fog. He fought his way into the daylight world again, and then consciousness fluttered in his eyes. He looked at me . . . at the room. Realization blazed, darkened with sin and horror, with immense guilt. He shrieked.]

DAVID: I want . . . I want . . .

MYERS: David!

DAVID: I want simple justice!

SOUND: *A crescendo of beat continues for a few seconds. Then profound silence—pause*

MYERS: [Then he quite simply died.]

WRANGLE: *(Pause)* Most extraordinary. That was all?

MYERS: Yes, sir.

LAPHAM: "I want simple justice," he said.

MYERS: Yes, Major Lapham.

WRANGLE: Extraordinary. Most extraordinary. A peculiar fixation.

MYERS: Yes, sir.

WRANGLE: That was all?

MYERS: Yes, sir.

WRANGLE: You have the letter?

MYERS: *(Pause)* [I look at Fleck. His eyes are closed. He opens them and slowly nods, with contempt almost. I open the briefcase and take out the letter.] Shall I read it, sir?

WRANGLE: Yes, of course. Does it throw any light on the case?

MYERS: This is it, sir. [I unfold the letter.]

SOUND: *Paper*

MYERS: [Fleck wants it. Very well. Let him live with the meaning, too. These others won't understand.] Dear Tana—I believed in the promise I made them, the promise of freedom. Who is going to keep it, and when? Please forgive me. David Smith.

WRANGLE: That's all?

MYERS: That's all, Colonel Wrangle.

WRANGLE: Extraordinary. Well, Captain, you did your best.

MYERS: Thank you, sir.

WRANGLE: Gentlemen, what do you say? Can we consider the case closed?

SOUND: *Resolve here the unresolved chord.*

. . . . .

ANNOUNCER: And now, for a comment on tonight's play, we present Franklin Fearing, Professor of Psychology in the University of California, Los Angeles. Doctor Fearing.

Commentary*

FEARING: This is not a story of a soldier who became psychoneurotic because of experiences in the war. Let us be clear on this point. It is a story

---

*This commentary was specially written for the broadcast by Professor Fearing, who also served as psychological consultant for the series.

of what happens when a soldier returns and looks at civilian life and tries, as he must, to find some meaning in the world that he now confronts. He has endured pain, anxiety, and fatigue. He may have been injured physically. He has discovered that he could face death and inflict it. These unimagined and unimaginable experiences have left their mark. They have not necessarily impaired his capacity to live happily and participate effectively in a world at peace. But he cannot possibly see that world as he saw it before he went to war. He now seeks some evidence that the world of civilians in which he finds himself understands, if only faintly, the reasons for which the war was fought and the price which must be paid for peace. If, instead, he finds a complacent willingness to return to the past or glib talk about our enemies in the next war, he will retreat in horror and revulsion. The mental sickness of David Smith was not caused by the war. It occurred when he was unable to find the answers to his simple questions. It was caused by what he found in the peace.

Director's Notes | Cal Kuhl

Cal Kuhl has been producing and directing commercial radio programs for the past fifteen years.

The four officers, Wrangle, Lapham, Fleck, and Myers, meet to dispose of the Smith case. What they actually say to each other totals less than one-tenth of what we hear, and is made up of short snatches of dialogue spotted throughout the other nine-tenths of the dialogue, action, narration, and introspection. Nevertheless, the unity, conflict, and climax of the play are lost unless throughout the play the listener is constantly aware of these four men facing each other, disposing of the Smith case. In the production, therefore, some auditory means of stamping this picture on the mind of the listener was a special requirement. The employment of any of the obvious mechanical devices such as music, a filter, or an echo chamber, whenever the four were speaking, to make them and the scene immediately identifiable and memorable, would, aside from being unworthy of the script, destroy the realism the play demanded and deserved. Instead, when these four spoke to one another, their positions relative to the microphone were slightly distant as compared with normal, and the lines were slightly projected in delivery, more nearly as if the actors were on the stage of a small theater. To heighten the resulting effect, the reading of the lines by these four was purposely stylized, markedly deliberate, brusque, military, formal. This acoustical perspective and dimension, this convention of the Wrangle-Lapham-Fleck-Myers scenes, was of course reserved for them alone. Whatever the means, it is obvious that some convention must be established so that this set scene in the play stays with the listener, either in the foreground or the background, and stays there despite the demands made upon the listener by the story itself as told by Myers.

Myers, aside from what he says to his colleagues, has three main functions. He unfolds the story, sometimes in straight narration, sometimes in narration leading into and out of a flashback; he is introspective in recall, as when he reports to the listener what he thought and felt at the time when the incident he is describing took place; and he is introspective in the present, as when he describes and analyzes the psychic score of Wrangle, Lapham, Fleck, and himself, sitting informally on the Smith case.

It is evident that if the listener is to be given a reasonable chance of orienting himself to Myers in each of these three functions, a convention must be established with respect to Myers when he is not talking with his colleagues. It is equally evident that this convention must be as unrestricted as possible if the actor is to have a reasonable chance of playing the part. He needs all the latitude possible, short of confusing the listener, to do a good job as Myers. The situation could be described as shifting back and forth between two locations.

In the scenes involving the board (Wrangle, Lapham, Fleck, and Myers) the listener is in the room overhearing the conversation; the other nine-tenths of the time the listener is in Myers' mind. In the board scenes the microphone is on the table; the rest of the time, the microphone is in Myers' head between his ears. The problem is how to make this clear to the listener in such a way that there is a minimum loss of realism and a maximum awareness of where we are at a given moment. Here, again, any use of filters, or the like, is ruled out for the same reasons as given above with respect to the board scenes. The convention for Myers was a decidedly closer than normal distance whenever he was interviewing someone—Smith's wife, Smith's father, and the others. Myers' closer than normal position necessitated not only the absence of any projection in delivery of the lines, but markedly less volume and inflection than in normal living-room conversation. Otherwise the delivery was completely informal, in contrast to the stylized Wrangle-Lapham-Fleck-Myers delivery. The sharpness of the contrast between Myers when talking to his colleagues and Myers when talking about them was heightened by a generally rapid tempo on his part whenever he was introspective in the present. Otherwise his tempo in the closer than normal position was the one called for by the lines and situations themselves. In the scenes where Myers is interviewing someone who knew Smith, the distance from the microphone, the voice volume, the tempo were normal. Thus, in general, the various levels (of the board, of Myers narrating, Myers introspective in recall, Myers introspective in the present) which are implicit in the script call for a similar auditory characterization in terms of acoustic perspective and dimension. These conventions or auditory characterizations are entirely aside from the "characterization" in the usual sense, given by the actor.

There remains yet one more overall consideration. Once these conventions are established and the play develops, the listener becomes aware of the parallel struggles of Myers: one, the jockeying with his colleagues, the desperation of his unspoken appeal to Fleck; and the other, the realization of the answer to the Smith case in Myers' own mind and the kinetic compulsion within him to wrest the articulation of that answer from the speechless Smith. By the time Myers (and the listener) gets through with the interview with Tana, the conventions are established, the tension is approaching the maximum, and all that remains is the fearsome indictment or question from Smith himself, who until now, in Myers' personal experience, has been only spoken of, but has never spoken. How, with the four auditory conventions already established, and the tension of the drama itself at practically peak level, is the subject of the previous twenty-five minutes of build-up to be introduced? Nor merely be introduced, but made equal to the build-up?

Any musical portrayal of the heartbeat and the labored breathing would not only be false, but would present a mechanical difficulty in terms of dynamics. (If the heartbeat music tops Myers as the heartbeat should, the climax that Myers has been building up to ever since the play began is ruined, irrespective of the kind of music.) The breathing, suiting itself to Myers' words, can be synchronized with the normal minute hiatuses of Myers' lines, and the shifting that Myers has to do from analyses and description to exhorting Smith, and back again. In dynamic level it can be on a par with Myers. But the heartbeat must dominate, and in perspective it must be unique. If the microphone in this scene is in Myers' head, the heart must be *in* the microphone! Tympani clearly could not have this presence in perspective, and aside from other considerations a contact microphone on a willing chest would still leave unsolved the necessity of gradually increasing the tempo of the heartbeat. A mechanical heartbeat, courtesy of the sound technician, alone can dominate the scene without detracting from Myers' climax and Smith's last utterance. The few moments the heart continues to beat after Smith's final word make possible the amplification of the beat to the maximum volume permitted by broadcasting standards. The abrupt and profound silence sets the stage for the final scene.

Reunion, U.S.A.: American Broadcasting Company, Monday, 7:30–8:00 P.M., P.W.T. Written and produced by the Hollywood Writers Mobilization. Writers: Abraham L. Polonsky; Pauline and Leo Townsend; John Whedon; Ranald MacDougall and Sam Moore; Jerome Epstein; Leon Meadow; Milton Merlin; Carlton Moss and Sylvia Richards; Aaron Reuben; Louis Solomon and Harold Buchman; Dwight Hauser; Janet and Philip Stevenson; David Hertz.

Ruth Palter

Radio's Attraction for Housewives

Ruth Palter, formerly a research assistant at the Bureau of Applied Social Research, Columbia University, is at present a graduate student at the University of Chicago, Department of Sociology, engaged in research on intergroup relations.

. . . . .

WHAT DOES IT MEAN when urban housewives say about the radio: "I don't know what I'd do without it"; "We'd be lost without it . . . be sort of miserable"; "If that radio was to go bad tonight I'd pay $200 to get a new one tomorrow morning. I wouldn't stay here a minute longer than I'd have to without it"? What does it mean in terms of human behavior? And more specifically, what does it mean in terms of urban problems of loneliness, boredom, and passivity? Although communication research provides data about the content of the media and the opinions and buying habits of the audience, we still know very little about the general psychological importance of print, radio, and film to their users.

In an attempt to explore this problem, we undertook a reconnaissance study which had as its research goal the discovery of some hypotheses and suggestions useful as guides to more detailed and precise future researches.*

It seemed advisable to limit the study to a few women who did a great deal of radio listening, avoiding the problem of representative sampling of all radio listeners. We used four factors as guides to the selection of respondents: women, white, lower middle class, had the radio on three or more hours a day. We selected from the U.S. Census of 1940 an area in south-side Chicago that contains a large number of white American-born families, the fathers being predominantly the breadwinners in skilled and semiskilled work, and the majority having no more than a grammar school

---

*I should like to express my gratitude to Mr. Bernard Berelson and Mr. Louis Wirth, whose helpful guidance made this study possible.

education. The median rental figure of the area provided a rough check on the economic status of the neighborhood. Women who said that they had the radio on three or more hours a day were chosen from a particular block within the area. During the fall of 1946 we completed twenty-two interviews, each lasting a little more than an hour. Although a schedule guide was used, the interviews were kept as informal as possible in order to encourage the women to talk freely of their radio experiences. Notes were taken infrequently, and only when the interviewer felt that writing would not disturb rapport.

We were interested in investigating two broad areas: the depth of radio attraction, and the possible psychological reasons for the attraction. To get some idea of the emotional hold of the radio we asked questions about missing the radio if it were not available (broken or being repaired), about preferences for other kinds of enjoyment (movies, magazines, etc.), radio-listening habit patterns, and the results of the interruption of these patterns. To get at the reasons for radio attractiveness we asked about listening to the radio with family and friends, awareness or ignorance of radio content (even though the person was "listening"), doing housework with the radio on, and listening to the radio when feeling "blue," happy, upset, etc. All we can do is illustrate each of these areas by quotations, suggest hypotheses based on the data, and indicate where the data are insufficient; the study affords no proofs.

Part I. Radio Attractiveness

"I tell you, the only time it isn't on is when I'm out of the house . . ."

Past researches leave us with no doubts about the number of hours a day that housewives listen to the radio and the tremendous importance they attach to listening.[1] And yet, even having this knowledge, we are still unable to appreciate the actual degree of radio attractiveness and of dependence on the radio. Although we were using three hours a day as an index to listening, not one of the women interviewed listened less than five hours a day, the mean listening hours a day being slightly more than

1. Cf. Francis Holter, "Radio among the Unemployed," *Journal of Applied Psychology,* Vol. 23 (February, 1939), pp. 163–169, for discussion of dependence on radio and desire to keep radio in spite of all financial difficulties.

eight. But how significant is this if we know that each of the respondents goes to the movies at least once a week, and that half of them read at least three magazines regularly (mostly the big weeklies)?[2] Obviously, these women don't depend solely on the radio for commercial entertainment. Our data, however, indicate that radio listening is in a class by itself, not comparable to the other means of entertainment. One indication of the depth of radio attraction can be seen in the statements about the omnipresence of the radio in the home. Most of the homes had more than one radio, so that wherever the housewife happened to be, she could listen; where there was only one radio, it was moved about from room to room with the housewife.

"We have one radio—but we move it all around; wherever we are, the radio is!"

"Oh, I always can hear it. I have two in my bedroom, and my husband has one in his bedroom, and we have one in the kitchen and one in here (the dining room) and one in the sitting room. And when I go inside to make the beds I just turn it on in there, and when I go back I switch it on out here."

Reactions to being without the radio while it was being repaired or out of service are another indication of the depth of its attractiveness.[3]

(When it was being repaired) "I went downstairs to my Aunt's to listen to my favorite programs. I used to say, 'Gosh, I wish I had the radio.'"

A housewife fifty-six years old, with two years of high school education, the wife of a railroad switchman, and president of a women's auxiliary, said:

"My husband gets up at about 10 A.M.—he's a night worker—and from then till the time I go to bed the radio is going. . . . I want to tell you, honey, if it wasn't for the radio I don't know what I'd do."

When asked if the radio had ever been broken, a rather haggard Irish housewife—her husband, also, a night worker—with two small children remarked:

"Yeah, once it broke. I almost went nuts! It makes the night so much longer, you know. I just sat around and acted dumb. I went over to my

2. Bimodal on magazine reading: approximately half the women read no magazines regularly, the other half at least three.

3. Bernard Berelson, "What Missing the Newspaper Means," a forthcoming publication. Mr. Berelson analyzes the emotional aspect of missing the daily newspaper.

sister-in-law's the whole time it was being fixed. I didn't want to stay in the house that way. I didn't stay home one night."

Another forceful statement of dependence on radio:

[Ever without it?] "Only when it has to be repaired. Then we listen at my brother's. This summer we were away in the country but we didn't like it because we missed the radio. And we had lots of entertainment—and still we needed the radio."

Even at the mention of being without the radio something akin to desperation is temporarily felt. Radio attraction can be estimated by determining the ease with which other media or forms of entertainment are substituted for it, and whether these substitutes bring as much or more satisfaction. Every housewife who answered this question indicated that nothing would "really" take the place of the radio.

"I would be ruined! I guess I'd make my piano be my radio. But you know, when you come to think of it, I have to work around, and I couldn't do that."

"I'd go to the picture show every night, that's what I'd do. I'd be so lost I wouldn't know what to do if I didn't have that company every day."

"God! I'd be lost without it. I'd try to get another one first thing. I'd go next door and listen to my neighbor's."

When confronted with the reflection that, after all, some women did manage to survive without radios, including all of their own mothers and grandmothers, these housewives were quite amazed.

[What do you think women did before they had radios?] "Well, to tell you the truth, I don't know. I just can't imagine what they done. I can remember when I was a girl we didn't have radios—but I don't know how they got on. I don't know how they got by in those days."

In point of fact, the radio appears so overwhelmingly fascinating that it interferes with work, and must be avoided.

[Do you listen to the radio when you do your housework?] "Not all the time. It slows me up when I want to listen and I should be working."

[Do you work better or not when the radio is on?] "No, that's just it— if you have the radio on, you just put down the mop and start listening. You never can get your work done; don't you think so? I just drop everything and listen. And I have so much to do with the washin' and cookin' I can't be listening to the radio of a morning."

Radio listening is not passively accepted; it is actively sought, and sometimes consciously denied. Future research might fruitfully investigate cases of deliberate denial of pleasure.

Women listen to the radio all day; they feel lost without it; they find no adequate substitute for it. It seems clear that the radio is essential to feelings of well-being and contentment. We are faced with the task of explaining why the radio, of all the media, is uniquely and unquestioningly desired. We will discuss some of the possible psychological bases for this intense bond between radio and housewife.

Part II. Psychological Reasons for Attractiveness

[*a. Reliever of the monotony of housework.*] "It takes the drudge out of it . . . just helps out."

Women have always had housework to do, and have always had much more to do than they have today. It would seem that the quantity of the work has decreased without affecting the general work habits and attitudes of housewives. Our respondents feel that housework is a day-long burden, relieved only by the presence of the radio. Most of them know that they are using the radio as an antidote to boredom.

"I like to iron and bake while it's on—you don't even mind it—because you think about the stories, or something."

"Oh, the ironing goes much faster. You don't have to put your mind to it—you don't have to think about it if you have the radio on, so it goes faster."

"I don't know what I'd do if I couldn't listen. I can always get more done if the radio's on—it breaks the monotony and I don't even think about what I'm doing. I just keep working till I'm finished, and I hardly know it's done."

However, this is an obvious point. The significance of listening to the radio to forget the housework is that dependence on the radio is so strong that housework is adjusted to listening. Here is a crucial problem for future research. We believe that the important aspect of this question is not whether the radio "takes the drudge" out of housework, but whether the whole routine of the day's work depends on the radio schedule. Two suggestive responses support the latter.

"I get up and do sewing on Saturday, you know. I don't miss any of them stories then, because they don't go on on Saturday."

"When I'm using the washing machine I get up and do it by 8 A.M. because I can't have it going with the radio—so if I get the wash done early I can listen and it doesn't bother me none."

[*b. Preserver of family unity.*] "If we didn't have it, we wouldn't have a family."

Entertainment is expensive, self-interests and initiative are rare, and excitement and stimulation infrequent. The housewife feels shut in all day, with only the trip to the corner store and an occasional chat with a neighbor to widen the horizon. Having the radio brings her closer to her husband's world and compensates in part for her chores.

"If a woman has the radio it gives her a happier frame of mind. She ain't stuck in the ol' house. When her husband comes home—you feel you got part of the world in your house."

Few of these women belong to clubs. Outside of the radio, there isn't anything "neutral" to talk about to their husbands.

"My husband likes the same things I do. He listens to the football and baseball in the day. But I don't mind that even. And if he misses one [serial] I tell him what happened—or he'll ask me what happened, or what did Walter Winchell say on Sunday—and I'll tell him. Or what happened to so and so. And then he'll say, 'Oh, for God's sake, we have to wait till next Monday to find out!' He keeps up with them just the same as I do. . . . We love to talk about the stories and he likes the same ones I do, so it's nice."

We suggest that the radio serves as a cohesive agent, preserving family harmony in the absence of other common interests and pursuits. Having answered that the radio didn't reduce her worries because she didn't have any since her husband's recent return from armed service, a young woman said:

"God! I'd be lost without it. . . . I really couldn't sit and talk night after night—you'd get bored stiff. . . . If you didn't have the radio and you just had to sit all night and twiddle your thumbs and sit and look at each other, you'd go nuts!"

These quotes illustrate one of the important roles the radio has in establishing family unity: it prevents both husband and wife from sitting and wondering what to talk about; it gives them something to do which is easily accessible and never provocative.

"It kind of gives us something to do for part of the evening. . . . My brother-in-law comes up to listen to the *Inner Sanctum* and football games and fights with us—or we go down to my aunt's to listen with them."

The radio gets the members of the family together without their having to depend on their own talents for amusement.

But the radio can also create family friction when one spouse is a more rabid listener than the other. There seems to be evidence that the spouse who wants to listen will not be deterred, despite the antagonism created. One young woman, obviously having had many battles over the radio with her husband, responded immediately when asked if she and her husband ever argued over the radio:

"He don't listen, he reads! I get so mad. He's such a bookworm—he never wants to listen. He just thinks it's a waste of time to listen to them things, and I love them. I want him to listen with me, but he just makes a lot of noise. Then sometimes he makes believe he's listening—you know, he imitates me by the radio, and I could kill him. It 'gets' me. [What do you do?] I listen anyway. If he wants to read I shut the door on him."

A woman who uses the radio to relieve the monotony of housework, but less fanatic than most, says this about the radio and her husband:

"Well, to tell you the truth, sometimes I get annoyed at all the chatter—just empty chatter. I say, 'Why don't you talk to me once in a while. You don't see me all day and then at night you just sit there and listen to the radio.' It gets me mad. [What do you do?] I just go out and visit, that's all."

How widespread this friction over the radio is cannot be determined from our data. It would seem that the radio is far more important as a unifier of the family than as a disrupter.

Our data on children's listening and their quarrels over the radio is too meager to support any conclusions. This area might yield extremely interesting information about the use of the radio by parents to control children and to prevent fights among them.

[*c. Reliever of worries.*] "You can't do two things, worry and listen."

Half the women interviewed said definitely that listening to the radio "helped" them because they found they worried less when they listened, or didn't worry at all.

"I think when you just sit down and the house is still you just sit and think—but if you can listen to them programs it's better. I know I'm happier at night than I am during the day—when I put the kids to bed and I can just put on the radio. And it makes you stop worrying, you know. . . . If I could stay up till 2 A.M I'd have the radio blaring. . . . When I sit and listen I forget all the worries I have. I don't have to bother with the family or talking, I just can relax and listen."

Asked when they particularly liked to listen to the radio, not one of the women said she preferred to listen when she felt happy; almost all said they liked to listen when they felt "blue." What "blue" means was never made explicit, yet radio listening seemed to soothe and narcotize. We have only one comparison of the radio with the other media.

"It really relaxes me. If you're listening you don't think about things on your mind. [Is it different when you read?] Well, when you're reading you have your own troubles. You have to concentrate more when you're listening. [I'm not quite sure I understand what you mean. If you can think more when you listen to the radio, then you worry more.] Yeah, I guess that's right! I never thought about it that way. But reading is different. [In what way?] I just think the radio is more relaxing—for me anyway. I don't have to bother with it. I just leave it on and I can work around. I guess that sounds funny. . . ."

And again:

"Sometimes it is soothing. It's good for relaxing and thinking, just to have nice, soft music on."

[d. Reliever of loneliness.] "It's nice to have company. But if you don't, it's nice to have the radio."

This was said by a woman who probably was completely unaware of the fact that she had hit upon one of the most significant reasons for radio's attraction: the failure of friendships. Much has been written in the social sciences about the importance of the break from small communities and the enforced isolation of the modern urban housewife.

". . . friends nowadays they just ain't the same. Seems like they look out for theirselves. With me working—they used to come over most every day—but now I don't see 'em at all."

"It's [the radio] something to have with you when you're alone. In this house everyone is for themselves, so you can't make no friends."

It would be important to know just how much of the housewife's day is actually spent alone. Although the radio does, no doubt, help to pass the time when no one is around the house, the respondents insist that listening is more pleasurable when no one is at home. Almost all the women agreed that the radio was company for them. We quote a few typical statements.

"It breaks the stillness of it, being here alone. I mean, it takes the place of people."

"When my husband Joe's out at 2 P.M., I depend on the radio for company. I never get lonesome when it's on."

"You feel less lonesome. The house is not alone."

". . . oh, I tell you, it's company to me—someone with me all the time in the house. Just like conversation on when I can hear it."

"When my husband and sister go out bowling and I'm alone, I turn it on. The time doesn't drag so much—you have some action and sound with you. The radio takes the place of someone in the house."

The radio is spoken to, cajoled, scolded with apparently little self-consciousness. It has become so much a part of the household that using it as another person—in fact, speaking of it as "company" and as "someone in the house"—is neither strange nor unexpected.

And yet we might be hard pressed to explain such statements as the result solely of urban loneliness. Why is it that the housewife can speak of the radio as a person in the house? Why can she believe she is carrying on a "real" conversation when she talks back to the radio? We are forced to consider "loneliness listening" as merely a part of a more comprehensive reason for listening, that is, as the need for fantasy escape.

The mirrored void.—"Escape" is a word that has become part of the scholastic's equipment—a word that Hollywood capitalized on without explicitly stating its claims, and now takes the liberty to exploit openly—a word, and a policy, that has made the big fan magazines sell millions of copies. It is a word, however, which when used technically still carries much meaning for the psychologist. We usually think of fantasy escape as one way of resolving tensions and conflicts (usually unconscious) resulting from unfulfilled goals or from conflicts between goals. Such mechanisms of defense as denial, projection, repression, reaction formation, isolation, and regression work to prevent the tension or conflict, which may be harmful to the individual, from incapacitating him. It might be helpful to think of radio listening as one of the more obvious methods of dealing with the unmanageable conflicts of modern life.

Let us examine more closely the peculiar nature of radio listening.

When the respondents were asked when they preferred to listen to the radio—alone? or with others?—almost all preferred to listen alone, as was
indicated above. Yet we know they repeatedly said that the radio "broke
the gloom" of being alone. These answers don't seem to add up to the
same thing. As a matter of fact, it seems likely that listening alone is not
only desirable, but necessary, to preserve the aura of reality surrounding
the radio. It is almost as though the radio were life, and life itself the unpleasant interlude from Friday to Monday,[4] and any other time when the
radio is not available. For example, a young girl with a high school education, keeping house for her father and brother, says:

"Yeah, then I don't have to talk to no one around. I can just think about
places I've been, what happened at the time, and who I was with. The
music makes me recall the past."

People around interfere with the dreamlike state achievable when the
radio can be listened to in isolation from the household milieu:

"Sometimes it bothers me [to have others around], depending on what
was on. [What do you mean?] Well, if it's one of them stories and someone comes in at the wrong time and bothers me I get sore—I like to have
it quiet and listen. Then I *really* like it."

". . . you know them things that continues from day to day, it's hard to
say what's going on or what's going to happen next time if you don't listen to it. I can't stand no talkin' while I'm listenin'."

[If someone should happen to phone while you're listening what do
you usually do?] "I just say, 'Kid, I'm listening to so-and-so, will you call
me back or I'll call you back.' I hate to have someone come in in the
middle of one of the good stories. But if there's music on and someone
phones up I just turn it down, I don't turn it off."

[Do you enjoy the radio more when you're alone or with others?] "When
I'm alone. Naturally when you're with others they start to talk and they
interrupt your listening ways."

If, as Geoffrey Gorer suggested,[5] the radio were simply subliminal
noise, then anything that happened to be on would be suitable, as long as

4. For a detailed discussion of daytime serial listening see Herta Hertzog, "What
Do We Really Know about Daytime Serial Listeners?" *Radio Research 1942–43* (New
York, 1944).
5. Geoffrey Gorer, "Certain Hypotheses with Regard to Movies and Radio" (1939).

it provided a background of noise. This thesis does not seem to be supported by our data. The housewife listens for her favorite programs, following these with an earnestness of belief that forbids conversation with people around, and insists upon concentration on the radio life, shutting off the life in her own home. One of the housewives gave us a clue to the dream world which the radio weaves:

"I'll tell you one thing, it spoils it if they publish their pictures. We got a picture of Ma Perkins as a middle-aged woman, and she's a young girl. You like to picture an older lady, and that goes and spoils it all."

Spoils what? Spoils the seriousness of the stories, spoils the closeness to the characters, spoils the chances for maintaining the fantasy.[6] Just as having people around sharpens the differences between the desired world and the world as it exists for these women, so do any "true" revelations about the players. Reality must be preserved—the reality of the fantasy—inane, turgid, melodramatic.

Radio people are considered to be more attractive as personal friends than the everyday people one is forced to associate with. With little affection, loyalty, and support provided by friends and family, it is small wonder that the Kate Smiths and Pepper Youngs attain such popularity.[7] Radio people are good, kind, helpful, straightforward, understanding, romantic. They are wholly desirable as friends, and to be envied.

"They're all so sweet and I love them [her family], but naturally if I had my choice I'd like to have them like *my people on the radio*."

". . . Some of the ones I like, they have better dispositions than the friends . . . as a radio group there are some lovely families—like Pepper Young's family. How they get along! Ain't it wonderful? Wouldn't ya like to know them people, though, so nice . . . [Rather have people on the radio as friends?] Well, I guess the people in the radio have better dispositions. Friends are so unpredictable. You can never tell whether they're for you or not. But radio people are reliable."

"Oh, she's nice—Stella Dallas. [Are your friends as nice, or nicer?] Oh yeah, nice, but she's *really* nice."

They're nice, exciting, reliable. Perhaps we are dealing here with one of the ways in which American housewives deny dissatisfactions and disap-

6. Thomas Whiteside, "Life Can be Terrible," *New Republic,* July 14, 1947.
7. Robert K. Merton, *Mass Persuasion* (New York, 1946).

pointments in their own lives and find compensation in the lives of their radio friends. So alluring do these fictions become that some women are not even embarrassed to say that they prefer radio people to their own families. A thirty-year-old housewife, a grammar school graduate, whose husband is a grocery-store clerk and who has three young children, says:

"Well, my husband, he works in the store all day and he comes home and you never know what to expect. He flies off the handle all the time. You can't blame him — he has to put up with the women all day long. But he's always flying off. [Who would you like him to be like?] Well, like Tom Righter. [Why is that?] He's so understanding and tender. Of course he flies off the handle once in a while, but that's understandable. My husband is so unpredictable. You never know what he'll like or not."

With this perspective before us, it is not difficult to imagine the role these radio characters play as dispensers of advice and guidance. We have much valuable information on this subject from the work done by Hertzog[8] and Merton.[9] We need only add that our data support their conclusions that life is made more comfortable, more bearable, more intelligible, through the homespun, well-meant advice of one's favorite radio figure.

Respondents referred frequently to the Pepper Young philosophy of life as being particularly helpful to them — the "let things take care of themselves" philosophy. We see here a reflection of the urban dilemma: there are too many confusions and difficulties to cope with; there is no one who can be trusted to turn to; there is easy and stimulating gratification through the vicarious living-out of the fictitious adventures of radio heroes. The advice that these radio characters give in no way changes the status quo; it tries rather to force harmony into it by recommending acceptance of it.

Unfortunately, we had too few data on listening to the radio with friends and in social gatherings to form any comparative hypotheses. It may be that in this capacity the radio can be a potential source of friendmaking. Whether or not the desire to listen alone accompanies all programs at all times we cannot determine from our data. One thing seems apparent: the radio often operates to protect and preserve isolation — an isolation that is strongly desired.

8. Herta Hertzog, *op. cit.*
9. Robert K. Merton, *op. cit.*

Conclusion.—We have tried to indicate some of the reasons why the radio is so attractive to housewives. We have briefly mentioned its importance as a relief from housework boredom, a family unifier, a protector from worry and loneliness, and, finally, a fantasy escape and a defense against dissatisfactions.

It has been said that radio listening is like a habit. If, however, we think of habit in the more technical sense, as meaning the half-conscious repetition of an act in response to a given stimulus, we see that our data do not support such a hypothesis. Listening is definitely conscious, in two ways: it is deliberately sought and consciously desired.

But a question is raised for future research. Our data indicated that there might be a difference between listening to "talk" programs and listening to music. Perhaps listening to music is, in the manner of a habit, an automatic half-conscious response, as well as a response to a desire for subliminal background noise.

Future research will also have to investigate the unexplored area of the personality characteristics of the radio audience as well as of avowed non-listeners. What kind of people listen to what kind of programs and establish what kind of relationships with the radio characters? Routine personality checklists have proved rather unsatisfactory. Until we are prepared to discuss the personal and general psychological motives for radio listening we shall not be able to understand its importance with respect to other types of human behavior.

A New Kind of Diplomacy

Gene (Eugene H.) King is Program Manager of *The Voice of America,* the radio service of the U.S. Information Agency. His more than 20 years' experience in radio has been with several independent stations, two commercial networks, and the U.S. government's information program in Europe. Mr. King has also lectured at Harvard, New York University, and Columbia School of Journalism; and he has been a member of the faculty of Boston University. The succeeding article was given as a talk by Mr. King last spring at the Institute for Education by Radio-Television, Columbus, Ohio, as part of a general evening session on "Some World-Wide Aspects of Broadcasting."

. . . . .

FOR A RADIO MAN, my present job on *The Voice of America* is just short of Heaven. "Short" because there are problems, to be sure. We practically always, for example, have budgetary troubles. *The Voice of America,* last year, had only a little over sixteen million dollars; when I add that with that we cover the world, what I mean by budgetary troubles is understandable. There are a number of industrial firms which spend twice that a year on advertising. All in all, private business in the United States spends nearly eight billion dollars a year on advertising, and a goodly percentage of it goes into radio and television.

Americans generally believe in advertising, but it took us a long time to appreciate that advertising had a place in our international relations. Assistant Secretary of State George Allen, former United States Ambassador to India, has called U.S. Information Agency activities "a new kind of diplomacy." He has pointed out that, in the past, diplomats dealt only with the officials of other countries. Now we know that widespread public understanding of our foreign policies and objectives is necessary to their success. President Eisenhower has put it this way:

> It isn't enough for us [the United States] to have sound policies, dedicated to goals of universal peace, freedom and progress. These policies must be made known to and understood by all peoples throughout the world.

"All peoples throughout the world" is a large order. Making United States policies "known to and understood by" these people is a considerable job. But it can be done. Modern communication techniques have given us the tools with which to do it.

I have, naturally, a slight bias in favor of radio; but honesty compels me to admit that there are areas where radio, today, is not the most effective communication technique. India, for example, has only about one million receiving sets. In a country of 370 million people, this situation reduces the effectiveness of radio. Those million receiving sets are important. We must not ignore them. But to reach the great masses in India, we have to supplement radio.

Radio, however, is our chief technique for penetrating the Curtains. For that reason about three fourths of *The Voice of America* broadcasts are beamed to the Communist orbit. Budgetwise, we spent about ten of our sixteen million dollars last year on these programs.

Last year, *The Voice of America* moved its studios from New York to Washington. The move was made under a Congressional directive, and created problems. But, organizationally, the new location is more efficient; and the psychological value of "This is Washington" is important. Our studios are now housed in a building just at the foot of Capitol Hill, in the very shadow of the great, gray Capitol dome.

The move from New York, which got under way in the spring, was completed November 1, 1954, without any interruption of the broadcasting schedule. This required some doing since we have more than 75 separate programs a day. Broadcasts are made in 38 different languages. The new layout has 14 studios; and, with that kind of a schedule, they are occupied almost continuously. It sounds like Babel in old Shinar or, at least, Bedlam; but it isn't. It is a very smooth working operation.

In addition to the studios, there are ten recording rooms with equipment to make 40 discs or tapes simultaneously, ten tape-editing booths, a recording control center, and the master control room. The rest of the nearly 100,000 square feet of space allotted to us is occupied by editorial offices, music and transcription libraries, and other offices required to keep *The Voice of America* in operation 24 hours a day.

To give a few more technical details, *The Voice of America* has a network of 78 transmitters, including 30 short-wave stations in the United States which are operated for us by private broadcasting companies. Overseas, the U.S. Information Agency owns and controls relay stations at Salonika, Tangier, Ceylon, Honolulu, Munich, the Philippines, and Okinawa. The last three—Munich, the Philippines, and Okinawa—have million-watt transmitters, the world's most powerful known broadcasting facilities.

Relay facilities overseas are also leased from the B.B.C. in England and from local broadcasters throughout Western Europe, Africa, the Middle East, and Asia. To combat "jamming," we have, in addition, a floating relay station in the U.S. Coast Guard Cutter "Courier," now stationed in the Mediterranean.

The Voice of America's daily program includes 30½ hours of direct broadcasts and 64 hours of repeat programs. To counter Soviet jamming, these are recorded at overseas relay bases and repeated on short-, medium-, and long-wave. Jamming is, of course, one of our problems. The Communists spend more on jamming than we do for the entire *Voice of America* operation.

We give the U.S.S.R. and the Soviet-controlled areas about 76½ hours daily. Despite all efforts to prevent, *The Voice of America* does get through. We have conclusive evidence of that. Josef Swiatlo, former head of the Communist secret service in Poland, tells us that *The Voice of America* is the most effective instrument employed by the free world in combating the spread of communism and in keeping hope alive in the hearts of the peoples behind the Curtains. He reports having attended sessions of the Polish secret police where the topics of discussion were *The Voice of America* and how to keep the Poles from listening. Nevertheless, according to his report, the broadcasts are heard; and they are effective. We have literally thousands of similar reports. Practically all escapees and defectors, in fact, report having listened. And that goes for the U.S.S.R. as well as Communist China and the satellites.

Generally speaking, the programs consist of news, news analyses and features, political commentaries, press reviews, round-table discussions, documentaries, and special events. The breakdown between news and the other programs is generally fifty-fifty. We have found that *The Voice of America* audiences, particularly behind the Curtains, are eager for news. They want to know what is happening in the world. They want facts and not propaganda.

Sometimes, of course, news and features can be included in the same broadcast. Recently, for example, we have noted that Communist diplomatic officials throughout the free world are making a concerted effort to spread the impression that the United States has a Curtain. A prospective traveler to the United States goes to the consular office of one of the satellite nations. The officer politely advises the would-be traveler not to let the American consul know that he is also applying for a U.S.S.R. visa. Then the Communist officer offers, ever so courteously, to give the required U.S.S.R. visa on a separate piece of paper. Or, he tells the applicant to come back after a visit to the United States consular office. All this is done very, very politely. The Communist consul is trying so hard to spare the traveler embarrassment.

On March 2, we answered the above in a broadcast. We just gave the facts: the number of Americans, about 500,000, who had applied for passports last year and the 378,000 Europeans who came to the United States during the same time. We posed a few questions about the number of Soviet citizens who had stepped from behind the Iron Curtain in the same period. We also asked about the number of visitors to the U.S.S.R., Communist China, and the satellites. Then, we included a few remarks about those who had left the Curtain countries without visas, having fled to freedom at the risk of their lives. This kind of program we would ordinarily term a feature, but it did have a news angle in light of the current Communist campaign.

To give another example, we recently had a lot of fun with an international quiz program. Daily, Monday through Friday, we directed a question at some particular Communist paper or radio station. On Saturdays, *The Voice of America* obligated itself to repeat the answers received. The program stretched over several weeks. We are still waiting for the first Communist reply. Of course, our questions were a bit ticklish to answer. One, directed to Radio Tirana and three Albanian newspapers, asked why bread in Albania was still rationed after ten years of Communist rule. Czechoslovakia was asked why the store shelves of the country were empty if Czech factories, as reported in the Communist press, were producing so much. The Communist silence is understandable.

Outside the Curtains, there is no difficulty about our audience. The letters that pour into each of the Agency's 210 posts in 79 countries bear witness to *The Voice of America's* appeal. A 15-year-old lad has written our Cairo post recently that he is poor and adds, "Of course, I do not have a radio." Because of his poverty and his youth, he cannot sit in cafés and listen. But he has found a way to hear *The Voice of America*. A neighbor in the adjoining apartment has a radio, and by placing his ear to the intervening wall he can hear. When our program in Arabic goes on the air, he is at his post, his ear against the wall. The programs have become his teacher. They are his contact with America—with, indeed, the outside world. He prays that they will be continued. "Do not forget," he ended his letter, "that I am listening behind the walls."

I have found that letter particularly moving. Throughout the world, there are many walls between the United States and other peoples—walls (as in this lad's case) of poverty, walls of prejudice, walls of ignorance, walls that we know as the Curtains. But they are not impenetrable, as this letter writer and many thousands of others bear witness.

The Voice of America coöperates, of course, with other Agency media in publicizing United States foreign policies. One major Agency project this past year has been President Eisenhower's proposal for world coöperation in the advancement of the peaceful use of atomic energy, which was first announced in his speech before the General Assembly of the United Nations, December 8, 1953. The President had not finished speaking before *The Voice of America* was on the air. The story was carried first in English and, later that day and the next, was repeated on all of our foreign-language broadcasts. It was given the most thorough follow-up of any story ever handled by any radio broadcasting service. We devoted program after program to developments; we still are, in fact; and we will continue to do so.

In addition, the Wireless File, a daily 7,000-word news bulletin of the Agency's Press and Publication division was transmitting the full text of the President's speech before he had left the United Nations rostrum. Our overseas posts were supplied with reprints of articles on the subject appearing in United States publications, roundups of editorial comment, special features, news pictures, leaflets, and pamphlets.

And the Motion Picture Division swung into line with full newsreel coverage and a series of special documentary films prepared either in our shop or by private producers. These films are now being shown throughout the world.

As a part of the coöperative effort, the libraries of our 157 information centers overseas and of the binational centers set up special shelves of books on the subject. Lectures were arranged by specialists sent abroad under the Department of State's Educational Exchange Program. Exhibits were opened to the public in a number of the larger cities: Rome, Brussels,

West Berlin, São Paulo, New Delhi, and Karachi. After weeks or sometimes months at their original stand, the exhibits went on tour of the smaller towns and provinces. The response has been magnificent. Over two million persons, for example, have already seen the Rome exhibit. The São Paulo exhibit is on permanent display in that city. Some 250,000 saw the Karachi show in its first few weeks.

Our Office of Private Coöperation has arranged for United States business firms to include highlights of the President's speech in their overseas correspondence. Other projects are under way by which American private individuals and groups—business, civic, religious, etc.—can coöperate in telling the "Atoms-for-Peace" story abroad.

In one way or another, we estimate over a billion persons this past year heard of the United States's proposal on the peaceful uses of atomic energy. Give us a little more time, and it will be "all peoples throughout the world."

The present U.S. Information Agency is just a little over two years old. It was created as of August 1, 1953, by President Eisenhower and was given independent status and complete responsibility for all United States non-military overseas information programs. These included those previously handled by the Department of State and the Mutual Security Agency.

The new Agency has benefited, of course, by the experience of its predecessors. We are convinced that now we have an organization that can handle the job. In the increased venom of Communist attacks on the program, we see evidence that we are handling it. World-wide, the Communists have recently stepped up their efforts, have been reorganizing their propaganda apparatus and have been pouring in increased funds. They recognize that they have a fight on their hands. The Communists have made propaganda a major weapon in the campaign for the establishment of a Communist world order. In 1953, it has been estimated, they poured over three billion dollars into the fight. This estimate is undoubtedly conservative, and we know that they are spending more now.

We do not propose to try to match them in the volume of their effort, but we think we are superior in determination. President Eisenhower is very insistent that we stick to truth, and we agree with him. But, the fight isn't going to be won overnight. I have heard the figures 40 to 50 years used. It could be so.

5 Practice

A Costume Problem
From Shop to Stage to Screen

One of the many myths of Hollywood is that the screen exaggerates all women's costumes. This has been true in some pictures—and still is. Not so many years ago one of our leading studios put its actresses into dresses of almost unimaginable extravagance. But the trend today is away from eccentricity of line and color, flounce and peplum, ruffle and jabot. Exaggeration of reality, which is necessary on the stage because of the distance that separates the audience and the actress, is absurd in terms of the close shot. The tendency today is to clothe actresses as if they were indeed playing characters and not themselves, and yet to be conscious of the points of design which agree with the physique and personality of the player. The Hollywood Quarterly *has asked a designer who is particularly successful in this—Edith Head, of Paramount—to explain in her own words and her own pictures just how a basic dress develops from the reality of life into the costumes of characters played by actresses. In order that the characterization in each dress may be emphasized, Miss Head has not sketched in the face of each different actress, but has given them all the same fashion-plate visage.*

THE EDITORS

A typical suit which could be bought in a store. This suit was not selected with any idea of its being photographed, or any attempt to bring out any characteristics in the wearer. It is a very average suit, and can be worn by the average woman.

A stage version of the same suit, using color contrast. The suit accessories are more stylized. However, this suit could still be worn by the average woman.

For Barbara Stanwyck in *Cry
Wolf!* A very simple version
of the original suit. She plays
a young geologist, so the suit
must be professional-looking.
Note use of a headband, since
Miss Stanwyck avoids hats as
much as possible.

For Veronica Lake in *The Blue
Dahlia*. Simple, boyish, and
"tweedy," to counteract the
feminine, little-girl look. Beret
and boy's tie are particularly
good with Miss Lake's long
hair and slender neck.

For Joan Fontaine in *The Af-fairs of Susan*. In this sequence, Miss Fontaine is supposed to look very smart, with a young sophistication. The fur peplum and muff are for smartness, and the stocking cap to keep her from looking too grown up. Dark cap to accentuate her blond hair. Light coat because the character is shot at in a park at dusk.

For Ingrid Bergman in *The Arch of Triumph*. Dark to em-phasize her coloring. Simple in line and detail for character. This suit must be as nonde-script as possible because of the nature of the story. The white collar is necessary for close-ups.

For Dorothy Lamour in *My Favorite Wife*. Light color to emphasize Miss Lamour's dark type. Hat and muff also emphasize the glamour of the character, mysterious and alluring. The draping of coat and skirt keep the suit from a too tailored look.

For Loretta Young in *The Perfect Marriage*. A molded suit with sable stole and sophisticated hat for character as a fashion editor. Note the exaggeration of the coat, and the addition of jeweled buttons. Eye veil and jeweled choker are very good for close-ups.

Performance under Pressure

Alexander Knox is an actor, playwright, novelist, and screenwriter. His last two films were *Indian Summer,* at RKO, which he co-authored and played in, and *Sign of the Ram,* at Columbia, both unreleased.

. . . . .

IN AN EARLIER ARTICLE in the *Hollywood Quarterly* I tried to prove that there is a difference between acting and behaving, that acting is richer than behaving, and that since acting in isolated moments has been caught on film there is no reason why it should not be caught more frequently in sustained performances. At this time I should like to deal with a few more of the facts and conditions in the motion picture industry in Hollywood which militate against acting, and to refer to one postwar development which seems to prove my point—my point being simply that I view with rather more alarm than some of my contemporaries certain obstacles which acting must hurdle before it can reach the public.

Like most people, I find a certain enjoyment in viewing things with alarm, and first, I hope you will indulge me in such oversimplifications and exaggerations as are bound to accompany the "viewing with alarm" type of trend spotting. Second, it is important to remember that the subject I am dealing with is very poorly documented—that the skills, moods, emotions, and personality exploitations that go to make up a performance are so evanescent that any discussion of them is likely to share that quality. And thirdly, you may be more sympathetic toward my conclusions if I am explicit about the point of view from which they arise.

You are probably familiar with Mr. Harley Granville-Barker's preface to *Hamlet,* the first few pages of which express this point of view expertly. Mr. Granville-Barker considers that the dramatist's master secret is to learn the right sort of material to give his actors: "Shakespeare learns to work in the living mediums of the actors and their acting. If the dramatist cannot work in it, clearly he is no dramatist at all. He soon sees, moreover, that it is the *essential thing* which no pageantry must be let over-shadow, nor mechanical tricks degrade." This conclusion was reached on the subject of *plays* written to be acted *without scenery,* and some people may find it difficult to see the connection between this comment and the film, which is frequently written to provide magnificent scenery for the minute speck of more-or-less decorative acting, like the fly on the wedding cake; but this is only one kind of film, and it is my belief that, as the me-dium develops, the actor will become—in a somewhat different way—as essential to it as he was to the theater. I think it is true that pageantry and mechanical tricks have received more attention from creative film makers than performances have done, and this is of course reasonable and natural in the present stage of development of the film.

In achieving a suspension of disbelief there have been, still are, and prob-ably always will be, two tendencies in technique, manifest in films wher-ever they are made—toward "actualism" and "stylization." In this connec-tion, of course, these words refer to techniques, not matter; to manner, not subject. Any manner can be used to deal with any subject, and the rights and wrongs of this or that relationship of manner and subject doesn't concern us here. It is obvious that all performing is to some extent stylization, and it is equally obvious that the more actualistic a film is in manner (whatever its matter), the more behaving it will require and the less acting. In this discussion, therefore, I am thinking mainly of those films the appeal of which is, at least in some degree, larger than life.

I have referred to the "creative film makers," and before we go any fur-ther I think it might be wise to make some effort to find out just who cre-ates what, when, and where. Film making is a curious mixture of critical and creative talents, and there seems to me to be an unnecessary amount of jealousy between different departments of film making which might be at least partly eliminated by a consideration of the critical and creative contributions.

Plato assumed quite simply that the creative state occurs when "the mind is no longer in a man," and that unless man has attained this state he is powerless as an artist. Herbert Read in *The Innocent Eye* makes the same point somewhat differently when he says, "It is the function of art to reconcile the contradictions inherent in our experience, but obviously the art which keeps to the canons of reason cannot make the necessary syntheses. Only the art which rises above conscious reality is adequate."

E. M. Forster calls it "dipping into the subconscious." If these quotations from experts indicate the truth about the creative state, it must be admitted (*a*) that talent is not creation, and (*b*) that the creative state is, to say the least, somewhat unusual. Unusual or not, it is the precise proportion of the product of this state that must give to any work whatever of freshness or excellence it may have. So it becomes increasingly curious to note the general feeling among moviemakers that their personal honor is being attacked when it is suggested that the creative element in movies is sometimes somewhat hard to find.

It is obvious that a cameraman may be creative when he conceives a shot and, to a lesser degree, when he executes it. It is obvious that a cutter may be creative when he hauls up from his subconscious a happy juxtaposition of two scenes. The writer is creative before and during his writing. The director, purely in his function as director, is creative when he conceives shots and when he executes them. From all this it is obvious that there is a great deal of overlapping. The overlapping is sometimes called "coöperation," but more often "interference," and it is interesting to note that the coöperation or the interference takes effect at one point—the set: the only place where the actor can be creative.

If we examine these overlapping functions closely, I think we may find that some of the so-called creative functions are not creative at all, but critical. It may be very helpful to separate these two tendencies rather carefully. E. M. Forster, in an address at the Harvard Symposium on Music, had many vital and illuminating things to say on the subject of criticism in relation to music, and I wish he could be persuaded to spend a little time separating the creative and critical functions in moviemaking. "Think before you speak is criticism's motto," he says; "Speak before you think, creation's." And, later in the essay, "If criticism strays from her central aesthetic quest, something happens, but not a work of art." "Criticism," he says, "can eliminate a particular defect, perhaps; to substitute merit is the difficulty."

With so much "coöperation" in films, defects are eliminated and lie writhing all along the path of progress, but I am not so sure that a merit automatically springs into being whenever a defect is dropped by the wayside.

Where the actor is concerned, acting merit certainly cannot be created in the cutting room, although it may seem to be, and although that grim chamber is eminently suited to the elimination of whatever almost anyone, from the wardrobe man to the producer, happens to consider a defect. So the actor must create when the cameraman has finished his arduous work of setting up a shot and is very anxious to get on to the next setup; when the director has just come back from telling the producer on the telephone that he is doing the best he can with the hams the budget has allowed him; and when the cutter sits on the outside of the circle sharpening his scissors. Incidentally, the writer is no help at this point, because he has just had a good line altered, first by the producer, rewritten by the director, and said incorrectly by the actor. The writer is aware that it is his business to write the words and the actor's business to say them, but he remembers certain passages in, for instance, Shakespeare, which from a casual reading would appear impossible to speak, yet when they are spoken by an accomplished actor have a totally unexpected brillance and power. Such a writer might wonder what would happen to a similar gem of *his* in a film script, and he might regret that the present studio technique is apt to encourage that kind of acting which hasn't time to spend on difficult concentrated speeches, and therefore that kind of writing which needs grunting, not speaking.

Mr. Granville-Barker spoke the truth when he said that Shakespeare "cut the coat to fit the cloth" or tempered the wind of his inspiration to the shorn lamb—the shorn lamb being the actor—but Shakespeare had the right to demand that the actor be capable of more than a smile and a grunt. For the actor, then, there are two places where defects can be eliminated, the set and the cutting room, and there is one place where merits can be created, the set. And it is here at this critical point that all the financial and mechanical and creative and critical forces in the industry are brought to bear, resulting frequently in a profusion of second-rate performances and ulcers.

The nature of the creative process among actors is one of those questions—like the best way to make coffee—which cannot be finally decided; but in the making of coffee there are certain fundamentals, water and coffee, without which good coffee has seldom been made, and in the making of a performance there are also certain fundamentals.

Preparation beforehand does not solve the problem. When an actor is studying a particular part in the theater, he has two important aids: the emotional sweep of the play, and the relationship, in both its subtle and its obvious aspects, between himself and his audience. He must still create the "illusion of the first time" and must behave as a human being. This behaving is very similar in process to a child's trying to behave. He must do a greater or less violence to his own personality for an end which he considers worth the effort. A child often finds direct and immediate advantages in behaving—peace of mind, absence of punishment, being liked, being admired. The actor's satisfaction in the film is not psychic, but monetary; it is not immediate; and certainly it is not direct.

Then, at the same time that he is behaving, he must have an attitude toward his behaving. In its crudest form this attitude may be a consciousness of the necessity to keep in key. In its more complicated forms it is a comment on the character in its relation to the story, just definite enough to be undetectable, but never absent. It is this comment which makes some performances, for the period of their duration and long afterward, seem more immediate, intimate, and affecting than the real people we meet and talk with. To gain the maximum effect in any dramatic presentation, the audience must seem to know the characters in the story far better than they know themselves. At any given moment, if the actor leaves his knowledge and understanding of the character out of his mind and his voice, there is a loss of richness.

In the two-hour playing time of a film, no author can tell everything about a complex character. We could watch a real situation in life for many more than two hours and fail to gain a real understanding of the people involved. An important difference between life and drama is simply this: that the significant details are crowded together in drama. These details are the bones to which the actor gives life. If he gives only the immediate, thin, literal meaning of the line, it isn't life at all, but a mechanical imitation; for an emotion without a comment, an emotion without an emoter, does not exist.

Sometimes, for the sake of the drama, it is necessary for the actor apparently to do just this—to create an emotion without an emoter, to wring all human elements from a line so that it is dry, brittle, and lifeless. This, too, the actor must do, and this the inferior actor cannot do. The inferior actor cannot help filling a line with the comment of his own personality, and if this personality happens to be vacuous or petty, the comment destroys part of what the writer tried to say and the vacuousness becomes more interesting to the audience than the character, and the spell of the drama is broken.

In my experience, the actor who is incapable of making the right kind of comment in a performance is apt to be incapable of refraining from making the wrong kind—and most bad performances spring from this cause.

If the personality of the actor is vivid and interesting and the part is written for its display, we have what is popularly known as personality acting, in which the comment is made in terms of the actor's own personality. Naturally, he does not say the lines or perform the gestures of a film in the way he privately behaves at home. Each line and each gesture is a bundle of impressions charged with years of experience in making his own personality clear to spectators and in captivating them with the personality thus presented. Personality acting is, in short, a sort of public wooing, bisexual, and therefore both polygamous and polyandrous.

This kind of acting is interesting and valuable both in theater and on film, and as long as suitable parts are provided they will be suitably played; but it is wise to remember that many of these actors are capable of another kind of acting which, to me, is more impressive as acting.

The heights of the profession are reached by actors who can play a number of different parts, behave the parts accurately, comment in the person of the imagined character, and play them all, not as if the parts were written for them, but as if they were created for the parts.

This is a subtle and curious art, requiring at its best a high degree of skill, and the precise degree of consciousness—how much you forget yourself in your part—is a matter of individual habit and technique. The actor may have dipped into his subconscious at home or anywhere, but on the set he must, even if slightly, dip again. He must also retain the active memory of all the preceding dips. Whatever the degree of consciousness, and whatever qualities of skill or nerve he may possess, the acting of a scene of any size and scope requires unusual concentration.

What are the conditions under which this act of creation is expected to take place?

You have been waiting for hours. Suddenly your waiting is ended. One second you were waiting. The next you are holding up production. The setup is made. You are ready. Set, props, furniture, lights, effects, sound, and camera are now waiting. You have a last flurry of doubt about remembering lines. It is somewhat warm under the lights. You can't see who is shouting at you. The cameraman creeps in and reminds you in a fatherly manner not to bend too far to the left on the turn. The sound man appears at your other side and reminds you to raise your voice on the speech where you drop your head. All this time the make-up man is patting you with puffs or swabbing the sweat from your forehead. Wardrobe runs in and peers at you, then explains that he had nervous prostration lest you were wearing the wrong tie. The prop man is messing around with the eggs you are about to eat. The gaffer puts a light meter against your left eye. *Speed. Action.* So you dip into your subconscious.

I was watching a popular star one day at a distance of about fifty feet. He had an enormously difficult scene to play and he was walking along muttering his words. An opera singer can practice aloud backstage. An actor, for some reason, mutters. This actor, who had received a deserved Oscar, made a timid gesture or so. An electrician in the gallery inquired in a friendly manner, "What'cha doin', bub, rehearsin'?"

On one occasion, and I admit it is somewhat exceptional, I had a four-page scene coming up. We began it. Seventeen times we began it, and each time there was a mechanical breakdown—arc noise, camera noise, dolly noise, light failure, or someone with several bronchial difficulties on the set. On the eighteenth take everything was perfect until the last sentence and the silence was heavy as fate, all animation, all breathing even, being suspended, waiting on my words.

I blew.

Since the last rehearsal we had been over the beginning of the scene seventeen times, the end not once.

These occasions are trying to a director. He is reasonable enough to know that it is not profitable to scold the arc for failing, the film for breaking, or the camera for being noisy, and it is considered bad discipline to scold the actor. But the actor who blows is conscious of not being scolded and, in time, he is apt to develop curious resentments against the mechanical gadgets which make his work possible and impossible at the same time. These resentments change to active distrust—no arc light has ever been fired because an actor blew, so why should he feel guilty when an arc splutters? Gradually he is convinced that the lights are purposely malignant, and the men in white coats pick him up in the back garden wearing heavy boots and trampling burnt-out mazdas.

I once visited a set where a parrot and a cat were performing. The assistant director, hoarse and frenetic, shouted, "Now this time when I say quiet I mean QUIET! Please, please remember we're working with animals!"

I have tried to indicate some phases of the creative process in an actor's performance and the conditions under which it is expected to proceed. If my impression is even partly correct, no general improvement in performances can be expected without, first, a keener recognition by production managers of those scenes the quality of which will depend largely on performances, and second, a willingness to discover ways and means of providing the actor with a somewhat more relaxed atmosphere and set of circumstances in which to work when such a scene is to be shot. There is no other solution to the problem except a little more time and this costs money.

In the cutting room the actor's creation—finished—fixed—irrevocable—is held up for approval or disapproval before the eyes of four or more functionaries whose boredom with the procedure can be assumed to be in direct relation to their creative frustration. Here is an anecdote which illustrates the extremes to which this frustration on one occasion led three persons: A well-known character actor was given an important line to say at a point where the writer, the director, and the producer required a laugh. They had given the line a great deal of thought and it was an excellent line. The actor, when the line was given him, recognized its quality but realized that in the situation, if he read it in the obvious way, part of the audience might be ahead of him, get the point on the third word, begin laughing, and prevent the rest of the audience from enjoying the joke by making it impossible for them to hear it. So the actor read the line in a manner which concealed its emotional implications until the necessary information had been imparted; the picture was cut and run and nobody in the audience laughed, and there were wild recriminations in the producer's office next day. The actor was called in to do a retake of the line. Before doing it, they ran the film so that he could see what was wrong. What was wrong was, quite simply, that in the cutting room a movement of the eyes which had occurred at the end of the line had been considered unnecessary and had been cut out. Three intelligent men thought the joke was in the words. Actually, the joke was in the gesture. What had happened, obviously, was that these three men in the projection room or the cutting room knew what was coming and, knowing it, failed to see it. They were not objective about what was happening on the screen; they were seeing preconceived notions, and in the interests of brevity they had ruined the joke. I do not believe it is possible for anyone to see the same scene done from ten different angles, repeated over and over again, and remain objective. If the scene has emotional tension, any unexpectedness in a given take is apt to be embarrassing, and, generally speaking, I think that a great many actors would agree with me when I suggest that of a given set of takes the probability is that a mediocre one will be chosen. Actually, I should be surprised if this were not so. Art by committee is criticism, not creation, and the conditions in a projection room are not always friendly even to good criticism.

To make it more difficult, most actors agree that when they see themselves in rushes they experience the emotion they felt at the time of the take, and find it impossible to be objective, and if anyone thought I had a solution to offer for this unfortunate state of affairs, I am sorry to disappoint them. The semidivine critical faculty will continue to be exercised in adverse circumstances, and the divine creative faculty will continue to be exercised under inhuman conditions. There is a slight hope that, with more time on the set, one of the forces inimical to performances will be to some extent controlled. More time on the set will make possible either an alteration in existing contractual arrangements, allowing for more flexibility on the part of both artists and producers, or a state of affairs permitting the fact of good performances to have greater interest to the public and therefore greater financial value to the producer.

Of course, there are many points which I have not time here even to mention. The selection of actors is important, and there is plenty of material elsewhere which proves how damaging the star system, for instance, is to the standards of acting.

There is the question of rehearsal periods before shooting begins. Repeated rehearsal seems to be increasing, and I have not spoken to a director or an actor who disapproves, although many do not think it solves the real problem.

There is the large question of the training of actors. Most studios now pay dramatic coaches comparatively small salaries, although they have sometimes done excellent work.

From this point of view alone, if I were a major producer, I would view with alarm the definite and steady decline in the number of theatrical productions in New York and the more frightening decline in the professional theater outside of New York. The amateur theater is only a slight mitigation, and the summer theaters not much more. When rehearsals are limited to a week or so, the actor learns little but facility, even if the director is good. In this connection it is interesting to note that of twenty actors receiving Academy Oscars during the past five years, sixteen were theater-trained. In the five British pictures which have received general acclaim in this country within the past two years, the eighteen stars and featured players have all been theater-trained.

Most of us, I suppose, have seen these five films: *Henry V, Brief Encounter, Great Expectations, Odd Man Out,* and *Thunder Rock.* They have been greeted with a concerted cantata of serious interest, and, for the most part, praise from critics which is unusual in the history of American film criticism. "British Film" as an entity has suddenly become important—a serious subject for conversation.

Some consider the British invasion a looming threat.[1] Others, like Mr. Goldwyn, say that it will stimulate us to greater efforts. Early in August, Mr. Harry Brand, the President of the Independent Exhibitors Association, stated in the *Hollywood Reporter* that the great motion picture industry in Hollywood need have no fear whatever of British films, because the American public, if we follow one simple procedure, will not go to see them, and the procedure which we must follow is to make films as good.

Can we? Let us consider these British films. There is obviously nothing startling about their subjects. Shakespeare has been attempted before; so has Dickens; *The Informer* was made a long time before *Odd Man Out;* marital tangles were popular in Hollywood before *Vacation from Marriage* or *Brief Encounter;* and a great variety of Hollywood fantasies preceded *Thunder Rock.*

It is equally obvious, from a list of fine Hollywood films which would probably include *Wuthering Heights, All Quiet on the Western Front,* and *Stagecoach,* that Hollywood has writers and directors as capable as any in Great Britain. Several of the actors in the British films I have mentioned have appeared in Hollywood films or are available for them. Hollywood has never been reluctant to import talented actors.

It seems to me that there are two interesting facts about British productions which may help to explain the quality of these films. The first fact is general and deals with the whole somewhat disorganized nature of the British industry. In Great Britain, in recent years, the creative people in

1. This paper was written prior to the imposition by the British Parliament of a heavy import duty on American films, and its repercussions in America.

the film industry seem to have been given a much more complete authority by Mr. Rank than by any major producer in Hollywood up to this
date, Second, the contractual obligations between producers and studio
owners, between producers and craft unions, between producers and actors, are so flexible in England that it is possible, without overpowering
financial loss, to stop production on a picture for a few days. This fact
alone is, in my opinion, of great importance to the industry, because on
it depends a kind of leisure on the set which is a necessary condition for
really good performances. In reading reviews of these pictures, most of us
were probably struck by the uniformity with which all the performances
were praised. One reason became clear when we saw Finlay Curray, the
convict of *Great Expectations,* doing a three-word bit in *Odd Man Out,* or
Robert Donat appearing for a minute in *Captain Boycott.* Undoubtedly,
there are many factors which must be investigated in explaining the excellence of these films, but very important among them is the whole fab-
ric of flawless performances so detailed, so careful, and so shrewd that even
the somewhat phony heroics of *This Happy Breed* were almost concealed
by them. Of course, the value of the performances is vastly increased by
the sensitivity of direction and the general excellence of dialogue. But that
is not the subject of this paper. It is important to note that the factor
which many actors feel is seriously lacking in Hollywood—time on the
set—is present in England.

I have heard two producers who have returned from England in the
past year after making a film complain bitterly about the English industry's amateur spirit and its inefficient system of film making. I am sure
these producers are not really more concerned about efficiency of manufacture than about quality of product, but it would seem that some of the
Hollywood efficiency they missed in England might with advantage be
applied to the problem of finding an economical means of providing a
little more time for acting when it is necessary. Personally, I do not think
it would require much more than two or three days added to the schedule of the average film, an added cost of twenty to seventy thousand dollars. This is a rather small figure when we think of the sets costing five
times as much that are built and never used.

The closeness of the British film industry to theatrical London has
often been mentioned as a reason for the general high level of performances in British films, and undoubtedly this has an effect; but it is also

Odd Man Out (1947), by Carol Reed, with James Mason (left)
and F. J. McCormick

necessary to remember that film schedules for people appearing in a play
in London have to be adjusted and readjusted to a degree that would persuade a Hollywood production manager to find another way of making a
living.

And if anyone thinks that the answer to what I have said about British
films is the simple statement that they have not made money, I believe he
is fooling himself dangerously. To be valid, any comparison between the
box office of British and of American films exhibited in the United States
must be objective enough to include three considerations: the quality of
the release, the budget for promotion, and the amount of money spent
(sometimes over a period of many years) publicizing the actors. If it is to
be valid, we must compare the gross of any British picture with the gross
of a Hollywood picture made with unpublicized actors, a low promotion
budget, and a poor release. A picture without a star is generally considered box-office suicide in Hollywood. If a comparison such as I have indicated were made by men who have access to the necessary information,
I have no doubt that they would be forced to the conclusion that quality
itself has value at the box office—a sentiment one is often urged to deny.

Inasmuch as the Hollywood film industry is an industry, the men in financial control must inevitably, out of the normal instincts of self-preservation, view this whole problem from a somewhat different standpoint than the creative artist. They must hover somewhere between two very definite points of view: that which says spend as much on quality as the traffic will bear, and that which says get by with the least the public will accept.

And please don't conclude that I am equating quality with costs. I am speaking of an industry in which one production technique seems to have come dangerously close to resulting in an automatic reduction in quality.

For certain types of scenes, most actors I have spoken to agree that generally they do not have enough rehearsal time, and, more important, they do not feel the interest and the quiet and the relaxation which can alone encourage the real act of creation.

Altogether, it seems to me that organization and efficiency, concentrating as they do on the one moment when the actor can be creative, have already passed the safety point, and that there is a remote possibility that Hollywood may, in an orderly and efficient manner, organize itself out of the film business.

When a man chooses a subject to make into a film, not because it interests him creatively but because he thinks it will make money, he is going to be timid about the way he makes the film. The enemy of creative effort in any art is the man who has so little faith in the validity of what he has to say that he, in terror, insures himself by saying it in an old and proved way. When one is either confident of the reception of what one has to say or careless of its nature, the method of expression is apt to be more daring, more exciting, and more effective. Ultimately, many of the difficulties of the creative branches of the film industry spring from an inherent contradiction implied in the classifications art and industry.

It is probable that both of these aspects are best served when the techniques are under the control of creative people. Eric Johnston, speaking before the United States Chamber of Commerce, urged the need for a new definition of capitalism. He said that capitalism should be considered a "competitive economic system designed for the enrichment of the many, and not to make a few men rich." I am sure that the film industry will "enrich the many" in more than one sense when its control is more largely in the hands of its creative men. The industry will serve the public best when it also serves its creators.

It is very doubtful that an undeviating adherence to factory methods of production will ever get the quality of performance that could be obtained in other ways. Only a man who is confident of what he has to say is relaxed enough to recognize new and surprising skills in any department. A good actor, finally, is an actor who can at one and the same time satisfy and surprise you. When a man is looking for clichés, he is too nervous to be satisfied by anything, and he certainly does not want to be surprised.

Granville-Barker emphasized the fact that Shakespeare wrote for actors. The writer and the director in certain kinds of film must fulfill the same function, and I feel that in British films recently they have fulfilled this function with great skill and with resultant profit. In my opinion, it is not an observation of minor importance that the creative men connected with the manufacture of recent British films seemed to value acting, to some extent at least, for its own sake, and it is no accident that it is the creative men, the men who have something to say, who *do* so value it. If Hollywood is right in being a little nervous about the British invasion, a study of conditions necessary to good performances might afford part of the remedy.

Designing *The Heiress*

Harry Horner, a graduate of Max Reinhardt's Theatrical Seminary in Vienna, came to America as a designer with Reinhardt fifteen years ago. He designed a dozen plays on Broadway, including *Lady in the Dark* and the Theater Guild's *The World We Make.* He also did set designs for the Metropolitan and San Francisco opera companies. He has designed and supervised the art work on such films as *Our Town, Little Foxes,* and *A Double Life,* and he recently won an Academy Award for his work on *The Heiress.* Currently Mr. Horner is making his debut as a director in the filming of *The World Inside.*

. . . . .

IT RARELY HAPPENS THAT the designer of a motion picture production has the opportunity of making his designs an integral part of the dramatic effect of the picture, but this opportunity was given to me in the production designs for the film *The Heiress.*

Many faithful Broadway theatergoers will remember the play, the story of Dr. Sloper, residing at No. 16, Washington Square North, in New York in the 1850's, and the tragedy of his daughter Catherine. Every reader of Henry James's novels will certainly remember the story, *Washington Square,* from which this play was taken.

In one of our first discussions William Wyler, the director of *The Heiress* (and of such other great character studies as *The Best Years of Our Lives* and *Wuthering Heights*), said to me: "Almost the entire picture plays in one house. It will depend a great deal upon the designs and the arrangements of the rooms in this house, upon the style in which the story is told—in other words, upon the conception of the designer—how convincing the characters will become, and therefore how successful the motion picture, *The Heiress,* will be."

How does the designer translate the style and conception of a story into a practical motion picture setting? It was not enough to be authentic in period and locale; deeper analyses of the lives of the characters in the play were necessary. It was essential to know as much about their backgrounds as if the designer had grown up with them, lived and visited with them, and even hired their servants for them. To search for the smallest characteristic habits became part of the creative function of design. Would the doctor, after arriving home from his professional calls, go immediately into his parlor and sit in his favorite chair to rest and smoke and read, or would he more probably join his daughter and other members of his family? A question like that determined the position of the parlor in relation to the house, and determined also the position of the chair in which he would sit in relation to the parlor. Would Catherine, the daughter, take her breakfast with her father, or would she eat separately, perhaps in her room upstairs? Those are examples of the many and challenging questions which influenced and shaped the creation on the drawing board.

The fact that there was only one important set, namely, the house on Washington Square, made it necessary that the house should have a personality of its own which, in different ways, would affect those inhabitants with whom the story deals and also would impress the character whose visit to the house plays so vital a part in the drama.

It was a challenge—to inject the house with a personality of its own. Very often, houses that have a memory of one kind or another attached to them are able to dominate the inhabitants and mold them with a definite force of their own. To Dr. Sloper the house on Washington Square bore the memory of his wife; to Catherine it represented the enclosure which became torture; for Catherine's lover the house became almost a lure, a very nearly human temptation, the possession of which he desired more than he desired Catherine.

How to design this house, how to keep it authentic and still make it come alive with its own soul and with the soul of its inhabitants, became the main task of the designer.

As a counterweight against any overcharacterization, I remembered Mr. Wyler's warning not to give the secrets of the story away in the designs. "The story may be a serious one," he said, "but this should not show in the designs of the house, since the structure could not know in advance what its inhabitants would do."

So I started with the first and easiest task, which was necessary as a basis for the design; namely, to familiarize myself with the style of architecture and the living habits of New York in 1850 in general, and of Washington Square North in particular.

Armed with sketchbooks and a camera, I roamed the streets of what is now downtown New York. As the spirit of another era slowly took hold of me, Washington Square became an "uptown" district. The skyscrapers disappeared and I realized that with just a little imagination it is even now possible to find in this modern city many treasures of century-old architecture.

I rang the doorbells of those lovely houses with their handsome old stoops in order to acquaint myself with the interiors which have been the landmarks of Washington Square since 1830, when the first families moved "uptown."

As I planned the design for the park, to be filled with romantic trees, I realized that I had to tone down this conception, for early prints showed that Washington Square was a parade ground in those years, with the old Victorian castle-like New York University on one side, and that it consisted of a large lawn with very few trees and very few benches. After I had searched many weeks in the picture collections of all the libraries, and had benefited by the kind help of all the historical societies in New York, a clear picture of life in a city in those past years crystallized in my mind.

Wandering through this early city, I hit upon such lovely museum pieces as the Tredwell house, an example of the typical residence of a rich merchant. I wandered through backyards of houses and saw those gardens and dwellings along the "Mews" which once represented the stables of the elegant places on Washington Square. Here I picked up a detail for an iron fence which would express the wealth of Dr. Sloper, and there a stairway which would help to dramatize Catherine's last climb up the stairs.

Those details were helpful, but ultimately the basic character of the house came from analyzing the past of our doctor. Although the main action of the story is laid in 1850, with a short episode five years later, I traced back the doctor's life from indications in the play and in the novel so that this house would have the atmosphere of having been lived in for many years.

Dr. Sloper, according to my notes, was married to a wealthy New York girl about 1835, and the house was built while they were on their honeymoon in Paris. It was probably designed by him in the currently popular style, the Greek Revival, with its high columns inside and double mahog-

any sliding doors connecting the rooms. It even contained the doctor's office, with direct access from the street.

When the doctor and his bride returned from France, they furnished
the house with delicate pieces in exquisite taste—Duncan Phyfe pieces,
and others which they brought with them from Europe. A French spinet
occupied a special place, and the whole house had an atmosphere of
loveliness.

Then his wife died, and as the doctor's practice improved he enlarged
the house. He kept the old part untouched, giving it the feeling of a shrine.
He moved the spinet into the back parlor near his favorite chair; and he
added, in the now modern Victorian period, a small wing containing a
winter garden and a study.

After having gleaned what I could of what Dr. Sloper must have done
to the house, I proceeded to design it. It was to become not a house of one
period, but of many—it must give the feeling of having gone through
several styles, thus making that first phase of his life which existed only in
his memory stand out and become visible to us.

The ground plan had to conform with the restrictions of those enclosed,
narrow building lots which characterize Washington Square North; entrance in front with a narrow long hall, and garden and stable at the back.
This gave reality and the feeling of enclosure within a city block.

But within this plan many vital elements must be incorporated. There
had to be room for a dramatic staircase which was to play an important
part in the story. One of the old houses of downtown New York gave me
an idea for a staircase which was laid out so that from one vantage point
three flights of stairs could be seen—with the father's bedroom on the
second floor and the girl's bedroom and guest room on the third floor.
There had to be room for an interesting arrangement of hall, dining
room, front parlor, back parlor, study, and so on. All this we built in the
studio, with the sliding doors placed so that certain vistas into rooms
became dramatically important. The father's chair in the back parlor, for
instance, dominated the house, and a direct view to the entrance hall was
possible.

The garden and the stables were planned with flowers and had to work
in different seasons. Trees with foliage and summer flowers were replaced
by bare trees, or by the foliage of spring—all with the careful consideration
of the characteristic vegetation in New York. The grass had patches of bad

growth even in the summer, and anyone who appreciates the difficulty of growing nice grass in New York will know that we were authentic.

Then there was the planning of the period of 1855—five years later. Again careful search into the characters' personalities gave the clue for changes in the house.

The father had died, and now that only women inhabited the house, the elegance and strictness disappeared, and a feeling of less discriminating taste was noticeable. The curtains became softer, more Victorian; certain pieces of furniture were changed, slip covers had been put on others, and we hoped to give the impression that the women in the house were drifting slowly toward a status of unalterable spinsterhood.

The park changed too—fortunately I found that the years around 1850 were full of changes in New York. Gas was introduced on Washington Square; so our audience sees the change from the earlier kerosene lamps to the laying of pipes for the new gaslight. And of course the old "Washington Square Parade Ground" was now really called "Washington Square Park."

One of the more costly problems was to find adequate furniture to match the description of exquisite taste and wealth, both of which were attributes of Dr. Sloper. Our expert on furniture, Emile Kurie, went to New York and bought fine antique furniture, including the spinet, fine paintings, and ornaments, knowing that under the examining camera close-up the standard prop furniture would not convince anyone of the great wealth of the heiress.

Thus the whole house was built, the life and habits of the characters were carefully considered, hundreds of sketches were made to indicate the most effective camera setups, and the director liked and approved it all.

But there was yet an obstacle before those sets could be called ready. This obstacle, so different from those of real life or of the stage, was the camera itself, with the sound boom. Proportions of rooms had to be carefully thought out so that they would photograph: not too high, or too much of the ceiling would be lost outside the range of the lens; and not too low, of course, or there would be lost the typical architectural proportions of elegance and period. And, what was more important, all those walls and ceilings had to be constructed so that they could come apart—they had to be made "wild," as the technical expression goes—to make elbow room for the cameras.

After having seen the house standing on the stage, almost habitable with its main floor, garden, and stables, and the staircase leading up to second and third floors, it was pitiful to see it torn apart again, limb by limb, a windowed wall here, a corridor ceiling there, so that a shot could be taken from behind a column, or so that the sensitive sound boom could reach into a narrow passage without picking up too much echo. It is typical of a movie set that the further the shooting of the picture is advanced, the more the walls of the set are pulled away; but no audience will ever know how little of the house was left, how little of many months of work remained standing when that final scene was taken.

No audience will ever see that last scene the way we saw it, or will ever have to use as much imagination as the actress had to, in order to make herself believe that she was left alone in a big house. This is what they would have seen when Olivia de Havilland played her last scene, the scene in which Catherine ascends the staircase as her lover knocks in vain on the entrance door of the lonely house: Where that lonely and silent house was supposed to be, there was a big boom with the camera on it, there was the camera crew giving orders, there was the man who lifted the high boom arm up to the third floor, and in the midst of all the turmoil was Olivia de Havilland as Catherine, masterfully ascending the steps of an abstract staircase which was completely detached from all the remaining architecture and stood—Daliesque—in the middle of a swirling and active group of men who were trying to direct, to photograph, to light, and to sound-control the scene of a dark and lonely house, deserted and silent.

The Limitations of Television

Rudy Bretz, TV pioneer, entered the television field eleven years ago when CBS formed its original staff. Cameraman, director, and inventor, he later became production manager of station WPIX. He is at present preparing one of the first definitive books on television production facilities and techniques. His article, "Television as an Art Form," appeared in Volume V, Number 2, of the *Hollywood Quarterly.*

. . . . .

AN EXAMINATION OF THE equipment and the methods of operation today in both the production of television programs and their reception reveals a long list of obstacles in the way of full realization of the new medium.

A large deterrent to the full enjoyment of any program is, of course, the small size of the average television screen, for actual physical size has a great deal to do with visual enjoyment. The visual sensation created by a large picture is greater than that created by a small one, since a large picture covers more of the retina with light. This restriction has led to a great concentration on close-ups and a hesitancy in the use of long shots, simply to make sure that the audience is able to see the subject properly. A feeling of claustrophobia, of watching a scene with blinders on, sometimes results from this lack of long shots.

Television receivers are very rarely in perfect working order. One of the most common ailments does not totally impair reception and so goes unnoticed. This is poor centering or overexpansion of the picture on the face of the picture tube. So much of the edges of the picture are lost on most sets that advertisers carefully avoid placing their messages anywhere but in the central 50 per cent of the picture area. Obviously the effectiveness of careful composition is seriously limited when only a small percentage of receivers can show the entire picture.

There are four production obstacles which seem to be prominent throughout the television field. There is never enough space, enough time, enough staff, or enough money for satisfactory production. Creative people working in the small stations, especially, are almost always frustrated. They complain of having to throw together productions, go on the air with them unrehearsed, and work in incredibly cramped quarters.

The average studio is much too small. Most television stations are operated by concerns which previously had operated radio stations. The management is familiar with production problems in radio. The engineering department usually has had contact with no other kind of show production. This is immediately felt in the design and construction of the television studio. It is usually the chief engineer of the radio station who is put in charge, and it is he who advises on the choice of studio locations, orders the equipment, and provides for the production facilities. A typical attitude is that television is the same thing as radio except that pictures are added. (I have actually heard this attitude expressed and been told about many key people, in the small stations, who hold it.) Experience has shown that the operation of a television studio requires many service departments and storage areas. Scenery must be constructed, painted, and stored. Props must also be stored. Provision must be allowed for dressing and make-up rooms. About four or five times the area of the studio itself is desirable for these service functions. Only a very few of the small television stations have made reasonable allowance for any of these functions, and, even more discouraging, a large percentage of small television stations have made no allowance whatever. An engineering maintenance shop is always provided. Dressing rooms are usually thought of. But space to construct, paint, and store scenery is usually lacking. Props are commonly stored along the side of the studio. The same goes for flats, fireplaces, roller drums, and furniture. I have seen studios—pitifully small to begin with—reduced in size by another 20 or 30 per cent because of lack of proper storage. Painting and set construction also must often be done in the studio itself, since no space has been allowed for the purpose elsewhere.

The result of this, in many cases, is to reduce drastically the amount of set construction that is done, and the variety of background sets that the studio keeps on hand. Some studios have given up changing sets entirely and do every show in front of a permanent background which is varied from show to show by the use of drapes, set dressing and the like. Another studio has permanent flats hinged to the studio wall, in order to produce quickly a great variety of simple sets by swinging these flats out in the desired combinations. Another studio uses stage wagons for permanent sets, and mounts a threefold set on either side of a castored wagon eight feet long and two feet wide. After one set is used, the wagon is rolled around, and the set on the reverse side serves as a background. These ingenious methods do not really solve the problem, however; they simply make it possible to do a lot in a small space.

The large network origination studios in New York are faced with the same storage problem as elsewhere. Having no place near the studio to store sets, and finding it would cost too much to truck them across town to a warehouse after each use, one studio chose for a time to destroy everything that was not connected with a permanent show. Thousands of dollars worth of scenery was broken up almost daily.

The small size of the actual television studio is a great deterrent to adequate production. Television studios must be large. Ellwell, art director for NBC television, says, "It has been found impractical to attempt television in a room smaller than thirty feet wide and fifty feet deep." Only 35 per cent of the existing television studios are as large as this. Cramped quarters lead to conditions such as I watched in a Chicago studio where the set for one scene of a dramatic show had to be struck during the show so that cameras could work in this area to shoot a following scene. Fluidity of motion, both of camera and actor, is hampered by small studio size. The result is often static shooting from unvarying positions.

I recall a time at WPIX when the studio was ringed on all sides by the sets for the evening shows, and because there was no time to strike and reset, an afternoon production was set in front of the evening scenery. The total working area was left a space about fifteen feet square. This was crowded with a large Fearless Panoram dolly, two cameras on tripod dollies, a gigantic Mole Richardson microphone boom, and a number of floor lights. Plus personnel, of course—about six or eight crew members. There was very little fluidity of movement or repositioning of cameras under these conditions.

A sometimes serious problem in small studios is background noise. This does not matter particularly during a show which frankly originates in the television studio; but, in the case of dramatic shows, it can be destructive to the story illusion which they attempt to build up. In large studios it is not so much of a problem, since the microphones are farther from the sources of unwanted sound.

The economics of television is based on the sale of time. Time is money in video. It is the commodity which is bought and sold. If time must be devoted to purposes from which revenue cannot be derived, it must be kept to a minimum. Sustaining shows for which rehearsal time is not purchased by a sponsor are cut down to the lowest possible amount—sometimes lower. Network commercial shows with an adequate budget will allow about a 10 or 15 to 1 rehearsal ratio—5 to 7½ hours rehearsal for a half-hour show. (The hours are paid for at the average New York price of approximately $250 apiece.) In a small station, a director who attempts a dramatic show is lucky to get a 3 to 1 rehearsal ratio—an hour and a half of rehearsal for a half-hour show. This refers to "camera rehearsal," the actual use of facilities on the studio floor; rehearsals outside the studio are not so strictly limited. As a result, great value is placed on preplanning since the director must have all his camera positions, angles, and composition planned beforehand, so that he will not have to waste time in the studio through trial-and-error methods. New techniques which the director has observed, but which he himself has not tried before, are very difficult to attempt. Refinements of production, special lighting effects, improved camera shooting, and more carefully rehearsed cutting are not possible with limited camera rehearsal time.

Practically all the television programs in the small stations are format shows for which no rehearsal time is necessary after a series has once been launched. Interviews, guest panels, quiz, charade, and audience-participation shows follow the same pattern every time. Economic necessity determines in large measure the type of programs that are produced. The requirement that programs must be rehearsed and produced on schedule is a limiting factor in itself. So long as television is an advertising medium, operating on the network principle, this will be true. Schedules are immovable. There is no stretching of rehearsal time, postponing of the hour of production, last-minute changing of schedule for any reason. The show absolutely must go on.

Twin obstacle to the lack of time is the lack of personnel. If there were more people in the production and program departments of a station, the lack of time might not be too serious. As things are today, the director in a small station finds himself working in all capacities. This is excellent training for a few months' time, but becomes very frustrating before long. It can prevent his producing even one show of which he can be proud.

Lack of adequate personnel leads also to extremely long hours. When this condition is imposed, creative fire is further dampened. A common complaint is that a man is underpaid. This is almost inevitable, except

where unions are firmly entrenched, because of the large number of professional people who are willing to make great sacrifices to get into the
field. Since it is possible to staff stations with low-paid personnel, and
most stations are operating at a loss anyway, there is no logical purpose,
from management's point of view, in raising the scale of wages.

It is the lack of money, of course, which causes lack of time and personnel. But lack of adequate production budgets is the main point here.
This results in relatively low quality of production, second-class talent,
the use of sets and props that make-do. This again refers to the local program originated at the small station, and bears no application to the commercial network show. Some of the big shows this year have gone on such
a spending jag that it is difficult for many people in the trade to understand where the money goes. High figures run between $30,000 and
$70,000 an hour. The local producer in Toledo, however, must put on
a local show (just following this network extravaganza) at a budget of
$70, instead of $70,000. Of course, people will say his show is worse,
but somehow or other they will watch it. Audience reports in small
towns, where two or three stations compete in local programming, often
show that the station with the smallest program budgets and the poorest
facilities is holding the largest audience. Could it be that lack of enough
money to do things wrong is pushing these harried producers into techniques of pure television which interest the audiences more?

It has often been said that the main thing that has kept radio from really amounting to something has been the domination of the commercial
motive and the business mind. Since the economic basis of television in
America is the same as that of radio—the sale of time for advertising purposes—it seems logical to expect that television will be hampered in the
same way.

Within this commercial framework, however, it is sometimes possible
for art to bloom. There have been cases in radio; history presents many
examples among the other arts. Painting in the Renaissance, in the great
Dutch school, and architecture in almost all ages were completely commercial enterprises. Court painters, musicians, and poet laureates were
just as dependent on the favor and caprice of their lords as we today when
we fawn upon the presidents and vice-presidents of our big sponsoring
companies. Yet these conditions in the past were not exactly death to the
development of art.

Of course, in those examples art was a one-man proposition, whereas today's communication media are coöperative. Creation here is the result of many people working together. It is quite probable that one mind is stronger than many when it comes to the creation of art. Often, a Hollywood film that begins with a long list of writers, producers, and subproducers turns out to be a hodgepodge, whereas a film that starts with the credit "Written, directed and produced by" is likely to be a good film. At least it will have unity.

In television production there is a plethora of agency executives, producers, and subproducers who are the commercial minds. Although they may know showmanship, these people are in a position where they must give prior allegiance to the advertising of their sponsor's product.

This results, first of all, in conservatism. Hollywood production has shown the same tendency and, of course, it has been true of radio for years. An experiment that has been tried and has failed, for whatever reason, is dropped cold by everybody; while a successful show, no matter how ordinary, is copied and recopied as closely as legal restrictions will allow.

The second result of commercialism is a policy of constant surveillance and meddling through all phases of the production. The executive feels he *should* know more than the directors, producers, and other creative minds that he hires, and it is a very rare executive indeed who can admit what he does not know. Since he is boss, his suggestions are followed even though they are destructive to what the director has conceived. Unfortunately there is usually such a long string of bosses. Above each boss is a more powerful boss who knows even less about the creation of a show, and who makes even more captious and even more inviolate decisions. These people are probably acting in complete good faith. Each is held responsible for what is done under him and, particularly in this new medium, he does not feel confidence enough in anyone to leave him strictly alone and stake his own reputation on the result. This hierarchy reaches up to the highest individual in the sponsoring firm, who, when he is unsure of his own judgment, refers the problem back to the audience for its reaction: he asks his wife. It is quite possible that this unscientific kind of audience measurement is behind many of the big decisions with which sponsoring firms and agencies determine the life and death of creative productions.

There is another aspect of group thinking and creating which tends to produce a relatively uninspired and pedestrian result. In order to use a certain technique or device in his show, the director must first convince his various bosses and co-workers of its value. There is a great difference between being able to do a thing, and being able to explain, *before you do it,* why it will be good. An intuitive feeling that a device will work is not enough to convince others in a story conference. The proponent of an idea must prove the idea is good. He must give examples of its successful use. He is limited to what the others have seen and will understand, and limited by what he himself can put across. I know of a writer who can sell an idea in glowing words so that everyone in conference is delighted. Yet, when the idea is given form, it often turns out to be commonplace.

A major problem in television is the advertising message between the acts of a show. This interruption to a show's continuity is analogous to the intermission between reels in the silent picture days, except that those periods were made as pleasant as possible. Candy or cigar vendors didn't plant themselves shouting in front of each member of the audience. Too much creative thought today is directed toward devising new and more powerful sledge hammers to aid in sales persuasion. A few of these commercials have been almost universally pleasing, but studies have shown that it is the commercials with a high score of dislike reactions which bring in the highest percentage of increased sales.

A large number of viewers have discovered a way to outwit the commercial. They simply lean forward and turn off the sound. Immediately the irritation is gone. The televiewer has an advantage over the radio listener in this respect. He is devoting his entire attention to the television set. He is never across the room or involved in some other occupation. He is within easy reach of the tuning dial. (Tuning the television set is a skill of which new owners are proud, and they are anxious to display that skill.)

A certain number of television commercials are rewarding to watch. The classic example is the Sid Stone commercial on the Milton Berle show, which was always one of the top numbers of the program. Most TV commercials are not live television at all, but film productions utilizing production techniques impractical in television. If such commercials rise to the quality of art—and there is indication that this is possible—it will be film art, not television art. But it will be film art that owes its existence to the commercial demands of the television medium.

Fred Killian, program manager of WENR-TV in Chicago, made an interesting point in a conversation with me a few months ago. He said the public will accept and enjoy the educational, the documentary, and other nonfiction programs only if they are well sugared with commercials. His point was that the commercial sponsorship of a program lends dignity and importance to the show in the minds of the viewing audience. I know of no empirical evidence on this point, even in the field of radio, but it is an interesting consideration.

A general obstacle to the best possible production in television is the lack of understanding between engineering and production personnel. Two entirely different points of view are represented in these two departments; entirely different backgrounds are required for the people working in them. It is extremely difficult for a man who measures the quality of a production by its dramatic values, visual interest, and so forth to understand a man who measures a production with another yardstick, who is pleased by such things as "picture quality" and "low signal to noise ratio," and is distressed by a slight indication of "key-stoning" or "streaking." The same thing is true in the other direction. The fault is lack of education on both sides. It is appalling how few production people attempting to work in this highly technical medium have the background of high school or college physics on which to build an understanding of the tools they are using. Engineers, who have worked in radio, do have a general idea of the elements of timing in showmanship, especially if they have been operating engineers. But the straight technician has only the haziest notion of what constitutes a show and no idea at all about artistic merit.

The problem of cameramen is a good example and will serve to illustrate the overall problem. It is generally conceded that in motion pictures the cameraman is a key man, and must be almost as fine an artist as the director. In still photography the cameraman is all; he is the creator by himself. In television this has not entirely carried over. About half the TV stations hire cameramen for their knowledge of showmanship and photographic skill. The other half hire men with technical and engineering background. Of this latter group of stations, about half choose men who also show particular interest in or ability with the camera, train them intensively in their job, and let them slowly forget their technical background. The other half of this group—roughly one quarter of all television cameramen — are rotated from week to week over all the jobs in the engineering department. Technical men at heart, interested primarily in circuits and electronic phenomena, they are out of their element on a camera. The cameraman's job thus becomes the lowest calling. It is sometimes described as "the salt mine," disliked and dreaded by the engineer as a boring assignment calling for none of his intelligence and training. Many an engineer sits morosely on the camera, doing what he is instructed to do and no more. Any unusual angle or effect that a production man may try to get is resented, ridiculed, or apathetically tolerated by the cameraman.

The system of rotating engineers is always maddening to production people. This is made even worse in some stations by the scheduling of engineers to fit work shifts which may not correspond at all with rehearsal schedules. Thus a director sometimes finds his engineers or cameramen changing between rehearsal and air time.

The camera operator is only one of a group of *operating* engineers. As such, their activities are confined to *running* the equipment, not to designing or maintaining it. Other operating engineers are: projectionist, audio operator, switcher, dolly pusher, microphone boom operator, record spinner, and lighting expert. I know of one station, WHEN in Syracuse, which has classified all of these jobs under the program department. I consider this a very significant move. It has made possible the assignment of "showmen" to operating jobs. The job of an operating engineer is definitely a showman's job, the job of putting on a show. It is almost entirely nontechnical. Where some technical understanding does enter in, station WHEN feels, as do WCAU and WPTZ in Philadelphia, that it is easier to teach a showman how to punch buttons and adjust a few dials than it is to teach an engineer showmanship. Furthermore, the fact that all personnel connected with production are in the same group completely eliminates group rivalry. This normal rivalry between human groups accounts for much of the war between engineers and program people.

The creative cameraman is a big factor in production quality. That in itself, however, is not enough. When the cameraman respects the director, he is eager to help him achieve any effect he has in mind. When the director respects the cameraman, he will encourage him to make creative contributions to the increased excellence of the program. Unfortunately, this ideal situation is by no means common. Many directors are unfamiliar with or unable fully to understand the cameraman's job. This is true, to a certain extent, of station staff directors, but is much truer of agency and package firm directors, whose contact with stations is irregular and whose television experience is limited.

WBAD, the Dumont station, was faced with this problem years ago. Its solution was to follow the lead of NBC and separate the director from the cameramen, forcing him to give all his orders to a technical director, who relayed them to the cameramen. Thus the technical director (or TD, as he is usually called) worked with the cameramen as captain of a team. There is no doubt that this protected the cameramen from the aggravations of trying to work with incompetent directors. However, a good director was automatically prevented from doing his best work on the spontaneous type of program. Split seconds of reaction time make the difference between catching an action and missing it. By the time instructions were relayed through a TD to the cameramen, it was often too late to carry them out. NBC early established this "TD system" of television directing, but the shows at this network have almost always been scripted and well rehearsed, so that spontaneous instructions from director to cameraman are rarely necessary.

By far the most common method of operation allows the director to speak to the cameramen, while an engineer—who may be called the "technical director," or more often the "switcher"—operates the switching and fading equipment following the director's cues. In some operations, for the sake of more accurate cutting or merely for the sake of economy, this engineer is dispensed with entirely and the director runs the switching system himself.

The directors at NBC had long been discontented with the "TD" system and wanted to work directly with the cameramen. At one point last year they decided to do something about it. The company backed them up and announced that henceforward the directors, as well as the technical directors, would have intercom connection with the cameramen, and that the directors would be free to give directions to the cameramen at any time. This caused considerable misunderstanding until it was finally straightened out; the union objected strenuously to the reduction in importance of the TD. It was finally agreed that in the unrehearsed show the director would be allowed to speak to the cameraman, but that in the regular rehearsed production the operation would continue in the earlier pattern.

The technical director system is now in force at the ABC network studios, but in a more liberal form that appears to be close to the ideal. Both director and TD talk to the cameramen (at least in the unrehearsed type of show) so there is no artificial limitation on quality, and at the same time the technical director is taking an active hand in helping the director run the show.

Most of television program production is in a first phase of development, which may be called the technical phase. A parallel can be found in the history of motion pictures just after the advent of sound. No one in Hollywood at that time understood audio equipment. Accordingly, experts were summoned from the RCA laboratories in New York, where the sound system was first developed, and were virtually put in charge of production. It was the day of the engineer in Hollywood. Visual quality deteriorated to zero. The camera was frozen in a sound-proof booth; actors were held to static positions under the microphone. It was not until motion picture men, such as Douglas Shearer, were sent to New York to learn sound that the reign of the engineer was broken, and the sound film was free to develop to its natural boundaries.

As long as the technical requirements of television remain a mystery to the station's program personnel, TV will not advance past the first stage in its development. Where creative men are on the cameras, however— where lighting men, for example, are chosen not only for their thorough understanding of the technical peculiarities of the medium, but also for their backgrounds in photographic or theater lighting as well—there television production is beginning to emerge out of the technical stage, and to develop as a medium of creative art.

6 Television

Hollywood in the Television Age

Samuel Goldwyn is a major pioneering figure in the history of the motion picture industry. This article, reprinted from the *New York Times* of February 13, 1949, may be regarded as the first fully developed, authoritative statement on the challenge of television to the industry.

. . . . .

MOTION PICTURES ARE entering their third major era. First there was the silent period. Then the sound era. Now we are on the threshold of the television age.

The thoroughgoing change which sound brought to picture making will be fully matched by the revolutionary effects (if the House Un-American Activities Committee will excuse the expression) of television upon motion pictures. I predict that within just a few years a great many Hollywood producers, directors, writers, and actors who are still coasting on reputations built up in the past are going to wonder what hit them.

The future of motion pictures, conditioned as it will be by the competition of television, is going to have no room for the deadwood of the present or the faded glories of the past. Once again it will be true, as it was in the early days of motion picture history, that it will take brains instead of just money to make pictures. This will be hard on a great many people who have been enjoying a free ride on the Hollywood carrousel, but it will be a fine thing for motion pictures as a whole.

Within a few years the coaxial cable will have provided a complete television network linking the entire country. Whether the expense that is involved in producing full-length feature pictures for television can possibly be borne by advertisers or will be paid for by individual charges upon the set owners, no one can say today. But we do know that with America's tremendous technological capabilities and our ability to adjust to new situations, nothing will stand in the way of full-length feature pictures in the home produced expressly for that purpose.

Even the most backward-looking of the topmost tycoons of our industry cannot now help seeing just around the corner a titanic struggle to retain audiences. The competition we feared in the past—the automobile in early movie days, the radio in the 'twenties and 'thirties, and the developing of night sports quite recently—will fade into insignificance by comparison with the fight we are going to have to keep people patronizing our theaters in preference to sitting at home and watching a program of entertainment. It is a certainty that people will be unwilling to pay to see poor pictures when they can stay home and see something which is, at least, no worse.

We are about to enter what can be the most difficult competition imaginable with a form of entertainment in which all the best features of radio, the theater, and motion pictures may be combined. Today there are fifty-six television stations on the air, with sixty-six additional stations in process of construction. The chairman of the Federal Communications Commission points out that by 1951 there may be 400 stations in operation. There are now 950,000 receiving sets installed, sets are being produced at the rate of 161,000 per month, and next year that rate will be doubled. Soon there will be a potential audience of fifty million people or more.

Here we have the development that will change the whole entertainment business. Fifty million Americans will be able to sit at home and take their choice of visiting the ball park, the prizefight matches, the wrestling bouts, the legitimate theater, and the motion pictures without stirring from their own living rooms. It is going to require something truly superior to cause them not only to leave their homes to be entertained, but to pay for that entertainment.

How can the motion picture industry meet the competition of television? Most certainly the basic business tactics—if you can't lick 'em, join 'em—apply in this case. If the movies try to lick television, it's the movies that will catch the licking. But the two industries can quite naturally join forces for their own profit and the greater entertainment of the public. Instead of any talk about how to lick television, motion picture people now need to discuss how to fit movies into the new world made possible by television. Here are some of the ways in which that tailoring process can be effected:

First, the reality must be faced that if the motion picture industry is to remain a going concern—instead of turning into one that is gone—it will have to turn out pictures several times as good as pictures are, on the average, today. Such recent pictures as *Joan of Arc, The Snake Pit, Portrait of Jennie, Johnny Belinda, The Search,* and *Miss Tatlock's Millions* are proof that Hollywood has creative capacities which are utilized all too rarely. Pictures like these, far above the average today, will have to be the norm in the future.

A factor on our side is that people will always go out to be entertained because human beings are naturally gregarious. But before the moviegoer of the future arranges for a baby sitter, hurries through dinner, drives several miles, and has to find a place to park, just for the pleasure of stepping up to the box office to *buy* a pair of tickets, he will want to be certain that what he pays for is worth that much more than what he could be seeing at home without any inconvenience at all.

Assuming that better pictures will be made, there remains the problem of how the motion picture industry is going to receive financial returns for pictures made for television. The greatest potentialities lie in a device called phonevision.

This device is not yet known to the American public because it has not yet been placed upon the commercial market, but to motion picture producers it may well be the key to full participation in this new, exciting medium of entertainment. Reduced to its simplest terms, it is a system by which any television-set owner will be able to call his telephone operator, tell her that he wishes to see *The Best Years of Our Lives* (if I may be pardoned for thinking of my favorite picture), or any other picture, and then see the picture on his television set. The charge for the showing of the picture will be carried on the regular monthly telephone bill.

Phonevision is normal television with the additional feature that it can be seen on the phonevision-television combination set only when certain electrical signals are fed into the set over telephone wires. No television set without the phonevision addition is capable of picking up phonevision programs, and no phonevision-television set can pick up such programs without those electrical signals supplied over the telephone wires on specific order.

The fee paid by the set owner will presumably be divided between the television transmitter, the picture producer, and the telephone company. The range of possibilities which this prospect opens to motion picture producers is almost limitless, for every television owner becomes just as much a box-office prospect inside his home as outside it.

It must be borne in mind that full-length pictures in the home are not necessarily something which will be realized in the immediate future. Despite the rapid pace at which we hurtle ahead, I am inclined to believe that the production of full-length pictures designed especially for home television will not become a practical reality for at least five to ten years more. Although phonevision seems to be ready for commercial adaptation today, it is obvious that no motion picture producer can risk the huge investment required for a full-length feature picture for television alone unless he has some reasonable assurance of recovering his costs.

In addition to producing for television, motion picture companies will undoubtedly make strenuous efforts to participate in the ownership and operation of television stations themselves. Already several of the larger companies have made extensive plans along these lines. An element which could blight the development of television would be the introduction into that field of monopolistic controls and practices similar to those which, in the motion picture industry, have hurt independent production. But this possibility should be reduced to a minimum by the fact that television-station ownership by theater companies and their affiliated interests, as well as others, will be limited by the Federal Communications Commission rule which provides, in effect, that no single interest can own more than five television licenses.

What effect will the exhibition of films over television have upon the type of films produced? First, one must hedge by saying that until we know whether the use of phonevision can supply sufficient revenue, or until advertisers can bear the cost of such full-length productions—a remote possibility—we will all remain in the dark as to the direction to be taken by pictures produced essentially for that medium. One can venture a few predictions, however, as to the reasonable probabilities.

There is no doubt that in the future a large segment of the talents of the motion picture industry will be devoted to creating motion pictures designed explicitly for this new medium. As today's television novelty wears off, the public is not going to be satisfied to look at the flickering shadows of old films which have reposed in their producers' vaults for many years. Nor will the public be content to spend an evening looking at a series of fifteen-minute shorts such as are now being made for television. There will be a vast demand for new full-length motion picture entertainment brought directly into the home.

I believe that when feature pictures are being made especially for television, they will not differ basically from those made for showing in theaters. The differences will be chiefly variations in techniques. The craving which all of us have to lose ourselves, temporarily at least, in the adventures, romances, joys, trials, and tribulations of characters created by storytellers does not change much, whether those characters are portrayed in a novel, on the stage, or on the screen—or whether that screen is in a theater or in one's own living room.

But in this new medium there will undoubtedly be a greater emphasis on story values than exists today. A person rarely walks out of a theater before he has seen the picture he came to see, regardless of whether it lives up to his expectations. A variety of reasons are behind this—the admission price he paid, the fact that he has no control over the program, the fact that if he leaves it will probably be too late to go to another theater, etc. At most, only one of those factors—the equivalent of an admission price—will be present in the home. The knowledge that the spectator will be able to move from one picture to another by the mere turn of the dial is bound to make those who will produce pictures primarily for television concentrate on keeping the audience vitally interested.

I believe, too, that there will be a reversion, for a time at least, to a lustier, broader type of acting than we have seen since sound changed motion picture acting techniques. Because of the small viewing surface of present-day home television screens, the subtleties of underplaying which can be observed on the large motion picture theater screen are lost to the television viewer. Unless the home screen becomes measurably larger, actors will find that the emotions which they can portray today by nuances will have to be conveyed by much broader expression.

Along the same general line, I am inclined to believe that the pacing of feature pictures designed primarily for television will be found to be more rapid than the normal tempo of motion pictures in the theater. Feature television pictures will probably not run over an hour—a reduction of from thirty to fifty per cent of the running time of present-day features. The need for compressing the essential elements of the story will inevitably result in accelerated tempo.

All of this makes for an exciting and stimulating future even though it is impossible to forecast what the specific nature of the interests of motion picture companies or individual theater owners in television stations will be. Ultimately, a pattern will evolve out of the jumbled jigsaw puzzle of experimentation.

The certainty is that in the future, whether it be five or ten or even more years distant, one segment of our industry will be producing pictures for exhibition in the theaters while another equally large section will be producing them for showing in the homes. The stimulus of this kind of competition should have nothing but good results. The people best fitted to make pictures for television will be those who combine a thorough knowledge of picture-making techniques with a real sense of entertainment values and the imagination to adapt their abilities to a new medium.

The weak sisters in our ranks will fall by the wayside. But no one in our industry who has real talent need fear the effects of television. I welcome it as opening new vistas for the exercise of creative ability, spurred on by intense competition.

I have always been basically optimistic about Hollywood and its potentialities. I see no reason to change my views now. I am convinced that television will cause Hollywood to achieve new heights and that, as time goes on, above these heights new peaks will rise.

FROM VOL. 4, NO. 2, WINTER 1949   Lyman Bryson
Edward R. Murrow

You and Television

Lyman Bryson, educator and CBS counselor on public affairs, was joined by Edward R.
Murrow, CBS news analyst and commentator, in discussing television on CBS's regular fifteen-minute series (6:15 E.S.T.) devoted to topics of popular interest. Edited
excerpts from the ediphone script of the discussion appear below.

. . . . .

BRYSON: Some of my colleagues in the educational world have asked me
recently: What are you going to do with television? What are you going
to do to make the world a more enlightened and pleasant and intelligent
place with this new weapon? If you accept my theory, Ed, that news is one
of the most important branches of education—and you do, I believe . . .
MURROW: Yes, enthusiastically, Lyman.
BRYSON: Then, let's start out with what television is going to do to news
coverage.
MURROW: Well, I have strong opinions on television and news. It seems
to me that finding either pictorial or animated material to support or sustain the news broadcast is emphasized at the expense of sound news judgment and therefore that television is in some danger of failing to present
the news fully and in perspective.
BRYSON: Do you mean that the pictorial devices used to maintain interest will distort the meaning of the news, or that news is more effectively
broadcast without the distraction of visual material, or do you mean both?
MURROW: I mean both. For example, several times at the Philadelphia
conventions of 1948 the television camera suddenly focused on a weary
delegate who was sitting there with his mouth open, sound asleep, while
a speech was being made. This certainly detracted at least somewhat from
the impact of the speech, and although it may not have been deliberate,
it was certainly an editorial distortion.
BRYSON: Does this mean, then, that the cameraman suddenly enters the
news field as a commentator and an analyst, in effect?

MURROW: Well, I think the cameramen must learn news values, and the newsmen, on the other hand, must learn something about pictorial values. How this is to be brought about I don't know, but I am convinced that it is necessary. Basically, however, the news must come first and pictorial support second. I believe in pictures, but they should not be allowed either to dominate or to distort the news content.

BRYSON: You don't expect much help from pictures, then, in trying to tell people what the news means?

MURROW: Oh, yes; certainly. There are whole vast areas of news that cannot be covered effectively in sound broadcasting alone. For example, I doubt that anyone can make a national budget understandable or meaningful through a microphone. I think that with the proper charts and graphs it could be made more meaningful in television. In spot news and eyewitness reports also, certainly, television pictures are a tremendous advantage.

BRYSON: What about television's effect upon politics in general, upon political destinies? Are persons who aren't "telegenic" going to be handicapped politically? You remember when we started saying that no one could be President of the United States again unless he had a good baritone voice.

MURROW: Well, we were wrong there, it seems. I would think, Lyman, that television is not going to change political fortunes, political oratory, or voting very much, although there are many who say that it will. I am not certain that the individual voter will make a better appraisal of a candidate just because he has an opportunity to see him, nor do I believe that the individual viewer will be wiser or better informed just because his eyesight, his vision, is extended so that he can see things the breadth of the country. . . . But you are especially interested in the educational impact of new techniques. What do you think the educational impact of television will be?

BRYSON: I can be a little more optimistic about television in the classroom than you are about its effect upon politics and upon news, Ed. I should think that it is one more device that a good teacher can use to change the pace of the classroom, to interest the students, because, after all, kids that are tied to seats—and they are, more or less, even in the most advanced schools—like something that gives them a new way of getting at information. But television won't make good teachers out of bad, any more than it will make good politicians out of bad, or statesmen out of politicians. It will be subject to exactly the same difficulties that you indicated in talking about news. You can distract a child from the meaning of a lesson by giving him a picture that isn't really relevant to what the lesson is supposed to teach him. I wish I could feel confident that we shall not fumble adult education in television as we have by and large in the other great media of mass communication. One would like to look forward, Ed, to an enlightened and informed American people who had only to sit in their own living rooms and turn on the radio and the television machine and understand the world in which they live!

MURROW: What is going to happen to group relations? Are we all going to sit at home and look at receivers?

BRYSON: I think we will use television as we learned to use radio—as one more extension of our senses. We'll use it to get entertainment. We'll use it to find out what's going on. We'll use it in education, in politics, and for news reporting. But there is a basic problem here that I'd like to ask you about. You know perfectly well that as a reporter you can select a fact which is unquestionably a fact, and you can state it as a fact, and you can completely distort and misrepresent a situation. But with pictures you can do it far more effectively than you can with words; that is, you can completely deceive people about what actually happened or about a condition by publishing a picture that is a camera picture, and you can say, "This is what happened," and it isn't what happened at all. There is no illusion like the illusion that, being an eyewitness, you know everything that happened. Now, do you think there is even more danger of manipulation of the stream of information than there has been?

MURROW: I don't know. I should think that as the power of a medium increases, its possibilities of distortion increase, and that the possibility of distortion in both pictures and the spoken content will have to be watched very carefully in television. But I don't know the relative dangers, Lyman.

BRYSON: Well, isn't it true that the more tools we have, the more possibilities there are for us to misuse them and the easier it is to do so? With television, we have a more delicate and complex tool than we have had before—and therefore a more dangerous one.

MURROW: Unquestionably.

BRYSON: Surely, you have never believed that the microphone in front of you had any wisdom of its own . . .

MURROW: No, I've maintained all along that a speaker whose voice reaches from one end of the country to the other is no wiser or more prescient than he was when his voice would carry only across the living room or from one end of a bar to the other.

BRYSON: It seems to me that at a time like this, when television is beginning to take its place alongside the other great media of mass communication, we have to remind ourselves that wisdom and nonsense are found in human beings and not in the machines that they use.

FROM VOL. 6, NO. 2, WINTER 1951   May V. Seagoe

Children's Television Habits and Preferences

Dr. May Seagoe is professor of education at the University of California at Los Angeles. She is the author of over forty articles and a few research studies of greater length in her own field. Her interest in the field of children's entertainment dates back to one of her earliest studies, before the era of the Payne Fund studies, on "The Child's Reaction to the Movies." She served as leader of the Workshop on Psychological Aspects of the Child Audience of the Children's Theater Convention held on the Los Angeles campus of the University of California in the summer of 1951.

. . . . .

TELEVISION IS THE NEWEST addition to the illustrious family of our mass entertainment enthusiasms. We have had dime novels, movies, radio, comics—and now television. Each time we seem to go through the same stages. We remember the alarm raised soon after the advent of the talking picture, which in time gave rise to the Payne Fund studies, which in turn showed that the same movies might either help or hinder growth, reinforce social standards, or teach the techniques of crime, depending upon the person who saw them and the attitudes he took to the seeing. For a while films seemed designed more for children than adults: then, when we had examined the matter and learned how to use movies, the alarm died away. The same thing happened with the widespread use of radio, leading to the studies of Eisenberger and others. The same thing went on in relation to the comics. Now we are starting that cycle with television. Whenever there is a new social invention, there is a feeling of strangeness and a distrust of the new until it becomes familiar. In television we are rapidly passing from the period of viewing-with-alarm to that of careful investigation.

This is especially true where children are concerned. We have a tendency to think of them as needing protection from an over-demanding and sometimes hostile world. We often think of them, too, as a breed apart, either more or less than human. Actually, of course, their fundamental values are similar to those of adults; the development from child to adult is continuous and our differentiation of "children over eight" from "children under eight" chooses an arbitrary point on a continuum. Such differences as occur (and they are important) are qualitative differences related to mental age, experience level, degree of emotional resilience, and degree of social development. When we talk of criteria for children's programs, then, we are talking of criteria which in many ways apply to adult programs as well, the difference being one of degree of complexity or theme in relation to experience, or to ability to take emotional tension, or to kinds of social interest. Children—and we have defined them as those between four and twelve—are not homogeneous in standards but different points on the scale of growing toward adulthood.

With the newness of television it is easy to see its novelty, less easy to see that it is only one more of a long series of similar inventions. It is actually much like the movies in some ways, the radio in others, the theater in still others. Differences between these media are related, not to basic psychological values, but to the availability of the medium, its intensity of stimulation, its limitations, and the usual viewing conditions. Theater is available to relatively few children, both because of distance and expense; but television is increasingly available in a majority of homes, and radio in nearly all homes. Theater presents more rounded stimulation than television, radio and movies differ in sensory appeal, movies in color attract more than do black-white versions, and the musical drama appeals more than drama alone because of its greater use of movement and sound in addition to dramatic action.

In addition, television is a realistic medium, limited in the space in which action may occur, limited in number of rehearsals and number of showings. Motion pictures have a greater latitude in some ways, though, like television, the mode of appeal is limited to the visual and auditory. Radio has its limitation to the auditory alone, with greater appeal to the imagination and greater mobility and range as a result. And theater has the greatest impact of all because of its completeness of appeal; yet it also has its limitations in time and space. Each medium has its special strengths and weaknesses, but the fundamental psychological principles operating differ in degree rather than in kind. What makes good theater makes good television, and good radio has much in common with good movies.

The matter of viewing conditions has been less recognized as a factor in differential viewing. When the child hears radio or sees television it is with a family group: supervision and postdiscussion are very easily arranged by the careful parent. Yet the older child and the adolescent want to get away from that same supervision; can you imagine a "first date" to sit with the family to watch television? In the theater and movies there is independence, but there is also an impersonal aggregate of individuals, making the audience reaction different. Perhaps that is why television appeals primarily to the preadolescent and movies to the adolescent, though policies in the industries concerned emphasize the trend.

In order to try to get an indication of what television is doing to children, how much time they spend watching, whether television cuts down on time spent listening to radio or going to movies and theater, and what shows children really like, a brief questionnaire was devised. Interested teachers who were also graduate students at UCLA agreed to gather information from their classes, and to enlist the help of other teachers in their schools. The children were chosen so as to include four different school districts in the Los Angeles area, with approximately the same number of children from each grade and from three socioeconomic levels.[1] From kindergarten through grade three questions were answered through interviews; those in grade four and above filled out the questionnaires themselves. All cases above the age of twelve were eliminated. All told, 323 children gave answers. Table 1 gives the distribution of cases by grade and by district.

Turning to the listening and viewing habits of the children, table 2 shows that the average motion picture attendance for all cases in our sample is every other week, that older children go more often, and that those of higher socioeconomic status also attend more frequently. As for radio listening, the average is less than an hour a day, with increasing frequency with age and decreasing frequency with socioeconomic status. In television, more than two thirds of the children in the sample own a set, without regard to age of child or to socioeconomic status. In television time the average for all children is more than two hours daily, increasing

1. The sampling was determined roughly on the basis of type of community and availability of experimental subjects. Results are approximate rather than finely controlled and definitive.

TABLE I

Number of Cases

GRADE LEVEL	SOCIOECONOMIC LEVEL			
	Low	Middle	High	All
Seventh	15	43	—	58
Sixth	26	—	20	46
Fifth	—	25	19	44
Fourth	—	27	21	48
Third	25	—	22	47
Second	—	—	22	22
First	—	27	11	38
Kindergarten	—	—	20	20
Totals	66	122	135	323

slightly with age and decreasing slightly with socioeconomic status. Even those who do not own television sets often view shows at a neighbor's house; very few have no contact with television. Theater is relatively un-developed in this sample, only one in four having seen a stage show, and even that figure including an entire class which was taken to a play. The number attending theater increases slightly with age and socioeconomic status, a reversal of the trend in the other media. In summary, table 2 shows that the average child sees motion pictures every two weeks, listens to the radio an hour a day, has a television set and watches it two or more hours a day, and has had no theater experience. The time spent in all the media increases with age, a phenomenon related to ability to enjoy vicari-ous experience and to give increasing attention. The interesting fact about high as opposed to low socioeconomic status is that those from the "high" areas have more theater experience, and use radio and films and television less than those from depressed areas.

More important in a consideration of television, however, is what own-ing a television set does to children's motion picture and theater atten-dance and radio listening. Table 3 presents these figures, broken down in a different way, from the same questionnaire. Here it is clear that those who own television sets attend motion pictures less often (once in two weeks

TABLE 2

Frequency of Movie Attendance, Radio Listening, and Television Watching

ITEM ON QUESTIONNAIRE	TOTAL RE-SPONSES	GRADE PATTERN								SOCIO-ECONOMIC PATTERN		
		K	1	2	3	4	5	6	7	L	M	H
How often do you go to the movies?												
More than once a week	18	1	—	—	4	4	—	4	5	4	5	9
Once a week	77	2	2	5	7	14	9	13	25	14	34	29
Once in two weeks	39	1	—	2	4	7	6	7	12	9	16	14
Once a month	55	3	1	7	10	7	13	9	5	10	12	33
Less than once a month	73	4	7	8	10	13	9	12	10	15	21	37
How much time do you spend listening to the radio?												
More than two hours a day	60	1	1	1	9	10	14	12	12	15	25	20
One to two hours a day	71	3	1	7	8	7	12	14	19	17	19	35
Less than an hour a day	125	12	8	10	22	21	15	16	21	20	49	56
Do you have a chance to watch television?												
Have a television set at home	200	12	6	15	29	38	30	30	40	47	74	79
Watch at a friend's house	51	3	3	6	9	8	9	6	7	7	11	33
Do not see television often	38	4	—	1	9	2	5	7	10	10	10	18
How much time do you spend watching television?												
More than two hours a day	129	2	1	3	20	31	19	22	31	36	62	31
One or two hours a day	69	6	2	11	13	5	13	7	12	12	16	41
Less than one hour a day	60	6	—	6	10	8	7	11	12	12	14	34
Have you seen a stage play this year other than one put on by children in your school?												
Yes	74	4	1	6	—	21	17	16	9	12	15	47
No	202	15	5	14	46	25	26	25	46	50	76	76

TABLE 3

Owners and Nonowners of Television Sets Compared

ITEM ON QUESTIONNAIRE	TOTAL RESPONSES	OWN TELEVISION	DO NOT OWN TELEVISION
Do you have a chance to watch television?			
Have a television set at home	200	200	—
Watch at a friend's house	51	—	51
Do not see television often	38	—	38
How often do you go to the movies?			
More than once a week	18	12	6
Once a week	77	39	38
Once in two weeks	39	27	12
Once a month	55	38	17
Less than once a month	73	51	22
How much time do you spend listening to the radio?			
More than two hours a day	60	25	35
One to two hours a day	71	42	29
Less than an hour a day	125	101	24
How much time do you spend watching television?			
More than two hours a day	129	121	8
One to two hours a day	69	54	15
Less than one hour a day	60	13	47
Have you seen a stage play this year other than one put on by children in your school?			
Yes	74	41	33
No	202	155	47

instead of once a week), listen to radio less (less than one hour rather than two hours or more a day), spend much more time with television (more than two hours compared to less than one hour a day), and see plays a little more often than those who do not own television sets. One child put the matter succinctly: when asked how often he went to the movies or listened to the radio, he answered, "Only when the television isn't working."

Turning from the amount of time spent with films, radio, television, and theater to what children like, we find some most interesting patterns. Table 4 summarizes the programs to which children in the sample say they

TABLE 4

Shows Seen or Heard

PROGRAM	TOTAL RESPONSES	GRADE PATTERN								SOCIOECONOMIC PATTERN		
		K	1	2	3	4	5	6	7	L	M	H
Radio Programs:												
Lone Ranger	36	1	3	2	14	5	5	4	2	10	6	20
Clyde Beatty	30	—	1	2	10	3	3	6	5	3	6	21
Sky King	23	—	1	2	3	2	5	2	8	3	5	15
Our Miss Brooks	20	—	—	1	—	1	5	9	4	2	12	6
Straight Arrow	20	—	2	3	4	1	5	—	5	2	4	14
Mark Trail	19	—	1	2	4	2	3	2	5	2	13	4
Cisco Kid	19	1	1	1	10	3	1	1	1	6	11	2
Baby Snooks	16	—	—	—	—	3	8	1	4	2	—	14
Tarzan	16	2	—	—	2	1	9	2	—	—	5	11
Aldrich Family	13	—	—	—	—	3	2	7	1	4	9	—
Andrews Family	11	—	—	—	—	4	5	2	—	1	7	3
Gang Busters	11	—	—	—	—	8	2	1	—	1	8	2
Music	11	1	3	—	1	1	—	—	5	1	4	6
Jack Benny	10	—	1	—	—	1	1	5	2	1	5	4
My Friend Irma	10	1	—	—	2	1	2	1	3	—	5	5
Red Skelton	10	—	—	—	—	—	4	2	4	4	4	2
Baseball games	9	—	—	—	1	1	1	—	6	2	7	—
Buster Brown	9	—	—	—	—	8	—	1	—	1	2	6
Charlie McCarthy	9	—	—	2	1	—	1	3	2	1	—	8
Happy Theater	9	—	—	5	4	—	—	—	—	3	4	2
Lux Radio Theater	8	—	—	—	1	1	2	2	2	—	4	4

(continued)

TABLE 4 — *Continued*

PROGRAM	TOTAL RESPONSES	GRADE PATTERN								SOCIOECONOMIC PATTERN		
		K	1	2	3	4	5	6	7	L	M	H
Let's Pretend	7	1	—	—	—	—	—	5	1	2	1	4
Red Ryder	7	—	—	—	—	—	6	1	—	1	4	2
Uncle Whoa Bill	7	4	—	3	—	—	—	—	—	—	—	7
Gene Autry	6	—	3	1	2	—	—	—	—	—	3	3
Father Knows Best	6	1	—	—	—	—	1	2	2	2	—	4
Your FBI	6	—	—	—	3	—	1	2	—	3	—	3
Arthur Godfrey	5	—	—	—	—	4	—	1	—	1	4	—
Bob Hope	5	—	—	—	1	—	—	2	2	1	2	2
Breakfast Club	5	—	—	—	2	1	—	1	1	1	1	3
Cliff Stone	5	—	—	—	—	—	3	2	—	2	3	—
Hopalong Cassidy	5	1	3	—	—	1	—	—	—	—	3	2
Horse Races	5	—	2	—	—	—	3	—	—	—	5	—
Life of Riley	5	—	—	—	1	1	2	—	1	—	3	2
People are Funny	5	—	—	—	—	—	1	3	1	1	—	4
Space Patrol	5	1	—	—	1	1	—	—	2	1	2	2
117 others	190						Not differentiated					
Total	593	14	21	24	67	57	81	70	69	64	152	187
Television:												
Space Patrol	71	2	1	5	9	16	14	12	12	17	27	27
Time for Beany	64	2	11	8	14	10	8	8	3	20	22	22
Crusader Rabbit	37	4	3	4	8	10	3	5	—	7	4	26
Space Cadet	31	1	—	2	1	15	4	4	4	3	13	15
Laurel and Hardy	30	—	7	—	2	9	6	4	2	4	19	7

Milton Berle	29	1	—	2	1	2	12	7	4	4	12	13
The Ruggles	28	—	1	—	1	3	6	6	11	8	14	6
Lone Ranger	27	1	2	2	6	4	6	4	3	2	10	15
Doye O'Dell	25	1	4	2	5	6	—	4	7	9	8	8
Eastside Kids	24	—	—	—	—	9	7	1	3	2	20	2
Comics	18	—	3	—	2	8	2	—	3	1	12	5
Hopalong Cassidy	15	3	3	3	4	2	—	—	—	3	1	11
Howdy Doody	15	5	1	6	1	2	—	—	—	1	—	14
Cisco Kid	13	2	—	2	2	4	—	3	3	1	2	10
Wrestling	13	—	—	—	1	5	2	2	1	3	3	7
Charlie Chase	12	—	3	—	3	3	—	2	4	3	5	4
Comedy Hour	12	3	—	—	2	1	1	1	7	3	3	6
Baseball games	11	—	—	—	1	1	—	2	3	5	4	2
Flash Gordon	11	—	—	—	2	3	2	1	—	1	7	3
Western Films	9	2	—	3	1	—	—	3	6	4	—	5
Spade Cooley	8	—	—	—	1	—	1	—	4	2	6	—
Alan Young	7	—	1	—	1	—	—	1	—	—	4	3
Handy Hints	7	2	—	—	1	2	—	2	—	2	2	3
Hometown Jamboree	7	—	—	—	—	—	—	4	3	5	2	—
Beulah	6	1	—	—	—	—	—	—	1	1	4	1
Big Movie Matinee	6	—	—	—	—	—	4	3	—	2	3	1
Burns and Allen	6	—	1	—	1	1	3	1	3	1	3	2
Gabby Hayes	6	—	—	1	—	3	—	—	—	—	4	2
Movies	6	—	—	—	—	—	1	—	6	—	6	—
Tim McCoy	6	—	—	2	1	2	—	—	1	1	2	3
Hail the Champ	5	—	1	—	2	—	—	1	1	1	1	3

(continued)

TABLE 4 — *Concluded*

PROGRAM	TOTAL RESPONSES	GRADE PATTERN								SOCIOECONOMIC PATTERN		
		K	1	2	3	4	5	6	7	L	M	H
Queen for a Day	5	—	—	—	—	—	1	—	4	1	4	—
Saturday Movie Matinee	5	—	—	—	1	—	—	—	4	1	4	—
Triple Feature Theater	5	—	—	1	—	—	—	2	2	1	2	2
72 others	119				Not differentiated							
Total	699	30	42	43	74	121	83	83	104	119	233	228
Films:												
Bedtime for Bonzo	21	1	1	3	6	3	3	4	—	8	9	4
King Solomon's Mines	16	—	1	1	3	4	4	2	1	1	—	15
Bird of Paradise	13	—	—	—	2	3	3	2	3	1	6	6
Samson and Delilah	13	—	—	—	5	—	—	1	7	—	7	6
You're in the Navy Now	7	1	—	—	2	—	1	2	1	—	1	6
Cinderella	5	2	1	2	—	—	—	—	—	—	—	5
Flying Missile	5	—	—	—	—	—	5	—	—	—	5	—
Meet the Invisible Man	5	—	—	—	—	—	—	—	5	2	3	—
75 others	133				Not differentiated							
Total	218	4	3	6	18	10	16	11	17	12	31	42
Stage:												
In the Month of May	18	—	—	—	—	—	16	—	2	—	1	17
South Pacific	10	—	—	—	—	—	—	5	5	—	1	9
Hansel and Gretel	8	—	—	—	—	—	—	1	7	7	—	1
37 others	43				Not differentiated							
Total	79	—	—	—	—	—	16	6	14	7	2	27

listen regularly (radio and television), and which they have seen lately and liked (motion pictures and plays). The popular programs, together with age trends and socioeconomic patterns, are apparent from the table. Differences in listing in radio and television for programs with the same title may be significant. The results for films and for theater are limited by what has been shown in the neighborhood, and hence constitute a less accurate cross section of preferences. Within each grouping, however, the frequency of seeing or hearing a show is significant. The appeal of adventure (including westerns), family shows, and comedy is clear in both radio and television.

There remains the question, however, whether children see these programs regularly because they really enjoy them or because the shows happen to come at times when the radio or television set is on anyway. Questions on what radio and television shows children in this sample like best are illuminating. Table 5 isolates radio and television shows seen regularly by ten or more children, and gives the proportion for each of the mentions as "liked best" to "seen regularly." The purpose is to see whether intensity of enjoyment is different from frequency of listening. It is clear from table 5 that the radio shows "The Lone Ranger," "Clyde Beatty," and "Sky King" are seen most often, but that "Baby Snooks," "Our Miss Brooks," "Tarzan," and "The Andrews Family" have the highest ratios of mentions as "best liked" to mentions as "seen regularly," that is, they tend to be favorites when opportunity for listening is held constant. Similarly, the television shows "Space Patrol" and "Time for Beany" are seen most often, but "Laurel and Hardy," "Flash Gordon," and "Eastside Kids" have higher ratios as "best liked." Though the method of analysis is relatively untried, there is the suggestion that frequency of listening or viewing is different from intensity of enjoyment.[2]

We have seen, then, that television has a major impact on the child audience. Radio listening and motion picture attendance are partially sacrificed to television viewing. Older children watch television with increasing

2. To test the matter further, coefficients of correlation were computed. *Rho* was used because of the small number of programs included in each group. The coefficients were .07 for radio programs and .08 for television. Since coefficients of correlation vary from .00 or no relationship at all to 1.00 or perfect relationship, it is clear that how regularly a child hears a program has little relationship to how intensely he enjoys it. This warrants further study.

TABLE 5

Intensity of Enjoyment of Certain Shows

SHOW	SEEN OR HEARD BY	BEST LIKED BY	RATIO OF LIKES TO SEEN OR HEARD
Radio:			
Lone Ranger	36	15	.42
Clyde Beatty	30	14	.47
Sky King	23	4	.17
Our Miss Brooks	20	11	.55
Straight Arrow	20	5	.25
Mark Trail	19	4	.21
Cisco Kid	19	2	.11
Baby Snooks	16	12	.75
Tarzan	16	11	.69
Aldrich Family	13	4	.31
Andrews Family	11	6	.55
Gang Busters	11	4	.36
Music	11	4	.36
Jack Benny	10	2	.20
My Friend Irma	10	3	.30
Red Skelton	10	3	.30
Television:			
Space Patrol	71	21	.30
Time for Beany	64	24	.37
Crusader Rabbit	37	16	.43
Space Cadet	31	11	.35
Laurel and Hardy	30	20	.67
Milton Berle	29	8	.28
The Ruggles	28	14	.50
Lone Ranger	27	3	.11
Doye O'Dell	25	7	.28
Eastside Kids	24	14	.58
Comics	18	10	.56
Hopalong Cassidy	15	8	.53
Howdy Doody	15	6	.40
Cisco Kid	13	4	.31
Comedy Hour	13	2	.15
Wrestling	12	2	.17
Charlie Chase	12	5	.42
Baseball	11	2	.18
Flash Gordon	11	7	.64

frequency, at least to the age of twelve. Low socioeconomic status is no handicap in television viewing, but a positive factor instead. Children show distinct preferences for certain programs, especially adventure, family programs, and comedy. However, the favorite program is not always the one seen most often. These results are, of course, based on a limited sample of children in one area only, and the treatment has some of the crudeness characteristic of all pioneering. If the findings stimulate further and more precise investigation, the purpose of this article will have been achieved.

How to Look at Television

Dr. T. W. Adorno, as Research Director during the past year of the Hacker Foundation of Beverly Hills, California, conducted the pilot study which is here published for the first time. Others involved in this study include Mrs. Bernice T. Eiduson, Dr. Merril B. Friend, and George Gerbner. Dr. Adorno has now returned to Germany, where he has resumed his professorship in the Philosophy Department at Frankfurt University and his position as co-director of the Institute of Social Research in Frankfurt.

. . . . .

THE EFFECT OF TELEVISION cannot be adequately expressed in terms of success or failure, likes or dislikes, approval or disapproval. Rather, an attempt should be made, with the aid of depth-psychological categories and previous knowledge of mass media, to crystallize a number of theoretical concepts by which the potential effect of television—its impact upon various layers of the spectator's personality—could be studied. It seems timely to investigate systematically socio-psychological stimuli typical of televised material both on a descriptive and psychodynamic level, to analyze their presuppositions as well as their total pattern, and to evaluate the effect they are likely to produce. This procedure may ultimately bring forth a number of recommendations on how to deal with these stimuli to produce the most desirable effect of television. By exposing the socio-psychological implications and mechanisms of television, often operating under the guise of fake realism, not only may the shows be improved, but, more important possibly, the public at large may be sensitized to the nefarious effect of some of these mechanisms.

We are not concerned with the effectiveness of any particular show or program; but, we are concerned with the nature of present-day television and its imagery. Yet, our approach is practical. The findings should be so close to the material, should rest on such a solid foundation of experience, that they can be translated into precise recommendations and be made convincingly clear to large audiences.

Improvement of television is not conceived primarily on an artistic, purely aesthetic level, extraneous to present customs. This does not mean that we naïvely take for granted the dichotomy between autonomous art and mass media. We all know that their relationship is highly complex. Today's rigid division between what is called "long-haired" and "short-haired" art is the product of a long historical development. It would be romanticizing to assume that formerly art was entirely pure, that the creative artist thought only in terms of the inner consistency of the artifact and not also of its effect upon the spectators. Theatrical art, in particular, cannot be separated from audience reaction. Conversely, vestiges of the aesthetic claim to be something autonomous, a world unto itself, remain even within the most trivial product of mass culture. In fact, the present rigid division of art into autonomous and commercial aspects is itself largely a function of commercialization. It was hardly accidental that the slogan *l'art pour l'art* was coined polemically in the Paris of the first half of the nineteenth century, when literature really became large-scale business for the first time. Many of the cultural products bearing the anti-commercial trademark "art for art's sake" show traces of commercialism in their appeal to the sensational or in the conspicuous display of material wealth and sensuous stimuli at the expense of the meaningfulness of the work. This trend was pronounced in the neo-Romantic theater of the first decades of our century.

Older and Recent Popular Culture

In order to do justice to all such complexities, much closer scrutiny of the background and development of modern mass media is required than communications research, generally limited to present conditions, is aware of. One would have to establish what the output of contemporary cultural industry has in common with older "low" or popular forms of art as well as with autonomous art and where the difference lies. Suffice it here to state that the archetypes of present popular culture were set comparatively early in the development of middle-class society—at about the turn of the seventeenth and the beginning of the eighteenth centuries in England. According to the studies of the English sociologist Ian Watt, the English novels of that period, particularly the works of Defoe and Richardson, marked the beginning of an approach to literary production that consciously created, served, and finally controlled a "market." Today the commercial production of cultural goods has become streamlined, and the impact of popular culture upon the individual has concomitantly increased. This process has not been confined to quantity, but has resulted in new qualities. While recent popular culture has absorbed all the elements and particularly all the "don'ts" of its predecessor, it differs decisively in as much as it has developed into a *system*. Thus, popular culture is no longer confined to certain forms such as novels or dance music, but has seized all media of artistic expression. The structure and meaning of these forms show an amazing parallelism, even when they appear to have little in common on the surface (such as jazz and the detective novel). Their output has increased to such an extent that it is almost impossible for anyone to dodge them; and even those formerly aloof from popular culture—the rural population on one hand and the higher level of education on the other—are somehow affected. The more the system of "merchandising" culture is expanded, the more it tends also to assimilate the "serious" art of the past by adapting this art to the system's own requirements. The control is so extensive that any infraction of its rules is *a priori* stigmatized as "high-brow" and has but little chance to reach the population at large. The system's concerted effort results in what might be called the prevailing ideology of our time.

Certainly, there are many typical changes within today's pattern; e.g., men were formerly presented as erotically aggressive and women on the defensive, whereas this has been largely reversed in modern mass culture, as pointed out particularly by Wolfenstein and Leites. More important, however, is that the pattern itself, dimly perceptible in the early novels and basically preserved today, has by now become congealed and standardized. Above all, this rigid institutionalization transforms modern mass culture into a medium of undreamed-of psychological control. The repetitiveness, the selfsameness, and the ubiquity of modern mass culture tend to make for automatized reactions and to weaken the forces of individual resistance.

When the journalist Defoe and the printer Richardson calculated the effect of their wares upon the audience, they had to speculate, to follow hunches; and therewith, a certain latitude to develop deviations remained. Such deviations have nowadays been reduced to a kind of multiple choice between very few alternatives. The following may serve as an illustration. The popular or semipopular novels of the first half of the nineteenth century, published in large quantities and serving mass consumption, were supposed to arouse tension in the reader. Although the victory of the good over the bad was generally provided for, the meandering and endless plots and subplots hardly allowed the readers of Sue and Dumas to be continuously aware of the moral. Readers could expect anything to happen. This no longer holds true. Every spectator of a television mystery knows with absolute certainty how it is going to end. Tension is but superficially maintained and is unlikely to have a serious effect any more. On the contrary, the spectator feels on safe ground all the time. This longing for "feeling on safe ground"—reflecting an infantile need for protection, rather than his desire for a thrill—is catered to. The element of excitement is preserved only with tongue in cheek. Such changes fall in line with the potential change from a freely competitive to a virtually "closed" society into which one wants to be admitted or from which one fears to be rejected. Everything somehow appears "predestined."

The increasing strength of modern mass culture is further enhanced by changes in the sociological structure of the audience. The old cultured elite does not exist any more; the modern intelligentsia only partially corresponds to it. At the same time, huge strata of the population formerly unacquainted with art have become cultural "consumers." Modern audiences, although probably less capable of the artistic sublimation bred by tradition, have become shrewder in their demands for perfection of technique and for reliability of information, as well as in their desire for "services"; and they have become more convinced of the consumers' potential power over the producer, no matter whether this power is actually wielded.

How changes within the audience have affected the meaning of popular culture may also be illustrated. The element of internalization played a decisive role in early Puritan popular novels of the Richardson type. This element no longer prevails, for it was based on the essential role of "inwardness" in both original Protestantism and earlier middle-class society. As the profound influence of the basic tenets of Protestantism has gradually receded, the cultural pattern has become more and more opposed to the "introvert." As Riesman puts it,

> . . . the conformity of earlier generations of Americans of the type I term "inner-directed" was mainly assured by their internalization of adult authority. The middle-class urban American of today, the "other-directed," is, by contrast, in a characterological sense more the product of his peers—that

is, in sociological terms, his "peer-groups," the other kids at school or in the block.[1]

This is reflected by popular culture. The accents on inwardness, inner conflicts, and psychological ambivalence (which play so large a role in earlier popular novels and on which their originality rests) have given way to complete externalization and consequently to an entirely unproblematic, cliché-like characterization. Yet the code of decency that governed the inner conflicts of the Pamelas, Clarissas, and Lovelaces remains almost literally intact.[2] The middle-class "ontology" is preserved in an almost fossilized way but is severed from the mentality of the middle classes. By being superimposed on people with whose living conditions and mental make-up it is no longer in accordance, this middle-class "ontology" assumes an increasingly authoritarian and at the same time hollow character.

The overt "naïveté" of older popular culture is avoided. Mass culture, if not sophisticated, must at least be up-to-date—that is to say, "realistic," or posing as realistic—in order to meet the expectations of a supposedly disillusioned, alert, and hard-boiled audience. Middle-class requirements bound up with internalization such as concentration, intellectual effort, and erudition have to be continuously lowered. This does not hold only for the United States, where historical memories are scarcer than in Europe; but it is universal, applying to England and Continental Europe as well.[3]

1. David Riesman, *The Lonely Crowd* (New Haven, 1950), p. v.

2. The evolution of the ideology of the extrovert has probably also its long history, particularly in the lower types of popular literature during the nineteenth century when the code of decency became divorced from its religious roots and therewith attained more and more the character of an opaque taboo. It seems likely, however, that in this respect the triumph of the films marked the decisive step. Reading as an act of perception and apperception probably carries with itself a certain kind of internalization; the act of reading a novel comes fairly close to a *monologue intérieur.* Visualization in modern mass media makes for externalization. The idea of inwardness, still maintained in older portrait painting through the expressiveness of the face, gives way to unmistakable optical signals that can be grasped at a glance. Even if a character in a movie or television show is not what he appears to be, his appearance is treated in such a way as to leave no doubt about his true nature. Thus a villain who is not presented as a brute must at least be "suave," and his repulsive slickness and mild manner unambiguously indicate what we are to think of him.

3. It should be noted that the tendency against "erudition" was already present at the very beginning of popular culture, particularly in Defoe who was consciously opposed to the learned literature of his day, and has become famous for having scorned every refinement of style and artistic construction in favor of an apparent faithfulness to "life."

However, this apparent progress of enlightenment is more than coun-
terbalanced by retrogressive traits. The earlier popular culture maintained
a certain equilibrium between its social ideology and the actual social conditions under which its consumers lived. This probably helped to keep
the border line between popular and serious art during the eighteenth
century more fluid than it is today. Abbé Prévost was one of the founding
fathers of French popular literature; but his *Manon Lescaut* is completely
free from clichés, artistic vulgarisms, and calculated effects. Similarly, later
in the eighteenth century, Mozart's *Zauberfloete* struck a balance between
the "high" and the popular style which is almost unthinkable today.

The curse of modern mass culture seems to be its adherence to the almost unchanged ideology of early middle-class society, whereas the lives
of its consumers are completely out of phase with this ideology. This is
probably the reason for the gap between the overt and the hidden "message" of modern popular art. Although on an overt level the traditional
values of English Puritan middle-class society are promulgated, the hidden message aims at a frame of mind which is no longer bound by these
values. Rather, today's frame of mind transforms the traditional values into
the norms of an increasingly hierarchical and authoritarian social structure. Even here it has to be admitted that authoritarian elements were also
present in the older ideology which, of course, never fully expressed the
truth. But the "message" of adjustment and unreflecting obedience seems
to be dominant and all-pervasive today. Whether maintained values derived from religious ideas obtain a different meaning when severed from
their root should be carefully examined. For example, the concept of the
"purity" of women is one of the invariables of popular culture. In the earlier phase this concept is treated in terms of an inner conflict between
concupiscence and the internalized Christian ideal of chastity, whereas in
today's popular culture it is dogmatically posited as a value *per se.* Again,
even the rudiments of this pattern are visible in productions such as *Pam-
ela.* There, however, it seems a by-product; whereas in today's popular
culture the idea that only the "nice girl" gets married and that she must
get married at any price has come to be accepted before Richardson's conflicts even start.[4]

4. One of the significant differences seems to be that in the eighteenth century the
concept of popular culture itself moving toward an emancipation from the absolutistic
and semifeudal tradition had a progressive meaning stressing autonomy of the individ-

The more inarticulate and diffuse the audience of modern mass media seems to be, the more mass media tend to achieve their "*integration.*" The ideals of conformity and conventionalism were inherent in popular novels from the very beginning. Now, however, these ideals have been translated into rather clear-cut prescriptions of what to do and what not to do. The outcome of conflicts is pre-established, and all conflicts are mere sham. Society is always the winner, and the individual is only a puppet manipulated through social rules. True, conflicts of the nineteenth-century type—such as women running away from their husbands, the drabness of provincial life, and daily chores—occur frequently in today's magazine stories. However, with a regularity which challenges quantitative treatment, these conflicts are decided in favor of the very same conditions from which these women want to break away. The stories teach their readers that one has to be "realistic," that one has to give up romantic ideas, that one has to adjust oneself at any price, and that nothing more can be expected of any individual. The perennial middle-class conflict between individuality and society has been reduced to a dim memory, and the message is invariably that of identification with the *status quo*. This theme too is not new, but its unfailing universality invests it with an entirely different meaning. The constant plugging of conventional values seems to mean that these values have lost their substance, and it is feared that people would really follow their instinctual urges and conscious insights unless continuously reassured from outside that they must not do so. The less the message is really believed and the less it is in harmony with the actual existence of the spectators, the more categorically it is maintained in modern popular culture. One may speculate whether its inevitable hypocrisy is concomitant with punitiveness and sadistic sternness.

---

ual as being capable of making his own decisions. This means, among other things, that the early popular literature left space for authors who violently disagreed with the pattern set by Richardson and, nevertheless, obtained popularity of their own. The most prominent case in question is that of Fielding, whose first novel started as a parody of Richardson. It would be interesting to compare the popularity of Richardson and Fielding at that time. Fielding hardly achieved the same success as Richardson. Yet it would be absurd to assume that today's popular culture would allow the equivalent of a *Tom Jones*. This may illustrate the contention of the "rigidity" of today's popular culture. A crucial experiment would be to make an attempt to base a movie on a novel such as Evelyn Waugh's *The Loved One*. It is almost certain that the script would be rewritten and edited so often that nothing remotely similar to the idea of the original would be left.

Multilayered Structure

A depth-psychological approach to television has to be focused on its multilayered structure. Mass media are not simply the sum total of the actions they portray or of the messages that radiate from these actions. Mass media also consist of various layers of meaning superimposed on one another, all of which contribute to the effect. True, due to their calculative nature, these rationalized products seem to be more clear-cut in their meaning than authentic works of art which can never be boiled down to some unmistakable "message." But the heritage of polymorphic meaning has been taken over by cultural industry in as much as what it conveys becomes itself organized in order to enthrall the spectators on various psychological levels simultaneously. As a matter of fact, the hidden message may be more important than the overt since this hidden message will escape the controls of consciousness, will not be "looked through," will not be warded off by sales resistance, but is likely to sink into the spectator's mind.

Probably all the various levels in mass media involve *all* the mechanisms of consciousness and unconsciousness stressed by psychoanalysis. The difference between the surface content, the overt message of televised material, and its hidden meaning is generally marked and rather clear-cut. The rigid superimposition of various layers probably is one of the features by which mass media are distinguishable from the integrated products of autonomous art where the various layers are much more thoroughly fused. The full effect of the material on the spectator cannot be studied without consideration of the hidden meaning in conjunction with the overt one, and it is precisely this interplay of various layers which has hitherto been neglected and which will be our focus. This is in accordance with the assumption shared by numerous social scientists that certain political and social trends of our time, particularly those of a totalitarian nature, feed to a considerable extent on irrational and frequently unconscious motivations. Whether the conscious or the unconscious message of our material is more important is hard to predict and can be evaluated only after careful analysis. We do appreciate, however, that the overt message can be interpreted much more adequately in the light of psychodynamics—i.e., in its relation to instinctual urges as well as control—than by looking at the overt in a naïve way and by ignoring its implications and presuppositions.

The relation between overt and hidden message will prove highly complex in practice. Thus, the hidden message frequently aims at reinforcing conventionally rigid and "pseudorealistic" attitudes similar to the accepted ideas more rationalistically propagated by the surface message. Conversely, a number of repressed gratifications which play a large role on the hidden level are somehow allowed to manifest themselves on the surface in jests, off-color remarks, suggestive situations, and similar devices. All this interaction of various levels, however, points in some definite direction: the tendency to channelize audience reaction. This falls in line with the suspicion widely shared, though hard to corroborate by exact data, that the majority of television shows today aim at producing or at least reproducing the very smugness, intellectual passivity, and gullibility that seem to fit in with totalitarian creeds even if the explicit surface message of the shows may be antitotalitarian.

With the means of modern psychology, we will try to determine the primary prerequisites of shows eliciting mature, adult, and responsible reactions—implying not only in content but in the very way things are being looked at, the idea of autonomous individuals in a free democratic society. We perfectly realize that any definition of such an individual will be hazardous; but we know quite well what a human being deserving of the appellation "autonomous individual" should *not* be, and this "not" is actually the focal point of our consideration.

When we speak of the multilayered structure of television shows, we are thinking of various superimposed layers of different degrees of manifestness or hiddenness that are utilized by mass culture as a technological means of "handling" the audience. This was expressed felicitously by Leo Lowenthal when he coined the term "psychoanalysis in reverse." The implication is that somehow the psychoanalytic concept of a multilayered personality has been taken up by cultural industry, but that the concept is used in order to ensnare the consumer as completely as possible and in order to engage him psychodynamically in the service of premeditated effects. A clear-cut division into allowed gratifications, forbidden gratifications, and recurrence of the forbidden gratification in a somewhat modified and deflected form is carried through.

To illustrate the concept of the multilayered structure: the heroine of an extremely light comedy of pranks is a young schoolteacher who is not only underpaid but is incessantly fined by the caricature of a pompous and authoritarian school principal. Thus, she has no money for her meals and is actually starving. The supposedly funny situations consist mostly of her trying to hustle a meal from various acquaintances, but regularly without success. The mention of food and eating seems to induce laughter—an observation that can frequently be made and invites a study of its own.[5] Overtly, the play is just slight amusement mainly provided by the painful situations into which the heroine and her arch-opponent constantly run. The script does not try to "sell" any idea. The "hidden meaning" emerges simply by the way the story looks at human beings; thus the audience is invited to look at the characters in the same way without being made aware that indoctrination is present. The character of the underpaid, maltreated schoolteacher is an attempt to reach a compromise between prevailing scorn for the intellectual and the equally conventionalized respect for "culture." The heroine shows such an intellectual superiority and high-spiritedness that identification with her is invited, and compensation is offered for the inferiority of her position and that of her ilk in the social setup. Not only is the central character supposed to be very charming, but she wisecracks constantly. In terms of a set pattern of identification, the script implies: "If you are as humorous, good-natured, quick-witted, and charming as she is, do not worry about being paid a starvation wage. You can cope with your frustration in a humorous way; and your superior wit and cleverness put you not only above material privations, but also above the rest of mankind." In other words, the script is a shrewd method of promoting adjustment to humiliating conditions by presenting them as objectively comical and by giving a picture of a person who experiences even her own inadequate position as an object of fun apparently free of any resentment.

Of course, this latent message cannot be considered as unconscious in the strict psychological sense; but rather, as "inobtrusive," this message is hidden only by a style which does not pretend to touch anything serious and expects to be regarded as featherweight. Nevertheless, even such

5. The more rationality (the reality principle) is carried to extremes, the more its ultimate aim (actual gratification) tends, paradoxically, to appear as "immature" and ridiculous. Not only eating, but also uncontrolled manifestations of sexual impulses tend to provoke laughter in audiences—kisses in motion pictures have generally to be led up to, the stage has to be set for them, in order to avoid laughter. Yet mass culture never completely succeeds in wiping out potential laughter. Induced, of course, by the supposed infantilism of sensual pleasures, laughter can largely be accounted for by the mechanism of repression. Laughter is a defense against the forbidden fruit.

amusement tends to set patterns for the members of the audience without their being aware of it.

Another comedy of the same series is reminiscent of the funnies. A cranky old woman sets up the will of her cat (Mr. Casey) and makes as heirs some of the schoolteachers in the permanent cast. Later the actual inheritance is found to consist only of the cat's valueless toys. The plot is so constructed that each heir, at the reading of the will, is tempted to act as if he had known this person (Mr. Casey). The ultimate point is that the cat's owner had placed a hundred-dollar bill inside each of the toys; and the heirs run to the incinerator in order to recover their inheritance.

Some surface teachings are clearly observable. First, everybody is greedy and does not mind a little larceny, if he feels sure that he cannot be discovered—the attitude of the wise and realistic skeptic that is supposed to draw a smile from the audience. Second, the audience is told somewhat inconsistently: "Do not be greedy or you will be cheated." Beyond this, however, a more latent message may again be found. Fun is being poked at the universal daydream of the possibility of coming into an unexpected large inheritance. The audience is given to understand: "Don't expect the impossible, don't daydream, but be realistic." The denunciation of that archetypical daydream is enhanced by the association of the wish for unexpected and irrational blessings with dishonesty, hypocrisy, and a generally undignified attitude. The spectator is given to understand: "Those who dare daydream, who expect that money will fall to them from heaven, and who forget any caution about accepting an absurd will are at the same time those whom you might expect to be capable of cheating."

Here, an objection may be raised: Is such a sinister effect of the hidden message of television known to those who control, plan, write, and direct shows? Or it may even be asked: Are these traits possible projections of the unconscious of the decision-makers' own minds according to the widespread assumption that works of art can be properly understood in terms of psychological projections of their authors? As a matter of fact, it is this kind of reasoning that has led to the suggestion that a special socio-psychological study of decision makers in the field of television be made. We do not think that such a study would lead us very far. Even in the sphere of autonomous art, the idea of projection has been largely overrated. Although the authors' motivations certainly enter the artifact, they are by no means so all-determining as is often assumed. As soon as an artist has set himself his problem, it obtains some kind of impact of its own; and, in most cases, he has to follow the objective requirements of his product much more than his own urges of expression when he translates his primary conception into artistic reality. To be sure, these objective requirements do not play a decisive role in mass media which stress the effect on the spectator far beyond any artistic problem. However, the total setup here tends to limit the chances of the artists' projections utterly. Those who produce the material follow, often grumblingly, innumerable requirements, rules of thumb, set patterns, and mechanisms of controls which by necessity reduce to a minimum the range of any kind of artistic self-expression. The fact that most products of mass media are not produced by one individual but by collective collaboration, as happens to be true also with most of the illustrations so far discussed, is only one contributing factor to this generally prevailing condition. To study television shows in terms of the psychology of the authors would almost be tantamount to studying Ford cars in terms of the psychoanalysis of the late Mr. Ford.

Presumptuousness

The typical psychological mechanisms utilized by television shows and the devices by which they are automatized function only within a small number of given frames of reference operative in television communication, and the socio-psychological effect largely depends on them. We are all familiar with the division of television content into various classes, such as light comedy, westerns, mysteries, so-called sophisticated plays, and others. These types have developed into formulas which, to a certain degree, pre-establish the attitudinal pattern of the spectator before he is confronted with any specific content and which largely determine the way in which any specific content is being perceived.

In order to understand television, it is, therefore, not enough to bring out the implications of various shows and types of shows; but an examination must be made of the presuppositions within which the implications function before a single word is spoken. Most important is that the typing of shows has gone so far that the spectator approaches each one with a set pattern of expectations before he faces the show itself—just as the radio listener who catches the beginning of Tchaikovsky's Piano Concerto as a theme song, knows automatically, "Aha, serious music!" or, when he hears organ music, responds equally automatically, "Aha, religion!" These halo effects of previous experiences may be psychologically as important as the implications of the phenomena themselves for which they have set the stage; and these presuppositions should, therefore, be treated with equal care.

When a television show bears the title "Dante's Inferno," when the first shot is that of a night club by the same name, and when we find sitting at the bar a man with his hat on and at some distance from him a sad-looking, heavily made-up woman ordering another drink, we are almost certain that some murder will shortly be committed. The apparently individualized situation actually works only as a signal that moves our expectations into a definite direction. If we had never seen anything but "Dante's Inferno," we probably would not be sure about what was going to happen; but, as it is, we are actually given to understand by both subtle and not so subtle devices that this is a crime play, that we are entitled to expect some sinister and probably hideous and sadistic deeds of violence, that the hero will be saved from a situation from which he can hardly be expected to be saved, that the woman on the barstool is probably not the main criminal but is likely to lose her life as a gangster's moll, and so on. This conditioning to such universal patterns, however, scarcely stops at the television set.

The way the spectator is made to look at apparently everyday items, such as a night club, and to take as hints of possible crime common settings of his daily life, induces him to look at life itself as though it and its conflicts could generally be understood in such terms.[6] This, convincingly enough, may be the nucleus of truth in the old-fashioned arguments against all kinds of mass media for inciting criminality in the audience. The decisive thing is that this atmosphere of the normality of crime, its

---

6. This relationship again should not be oversimplified. No matter to what extent modern mass media tend to blur the difference between reality and the aesthetic, our realistic spectators are still aware that all is "in fun." It cannot be assumed that the direct primary perception of reality takes place within the television frame of reference, although many movie-goers recall the alienation of familiar sights when leaving the theater: everything still has the appearance of being part of the movie plot. What is more important is the interpretation of reality in terms of psychological carry-overs, the preparedness to see ordinary objects as though some threatening mystery were hidden behind them. Such an attitude seems to be syntonic with mass delusions as suspicion of omnipresent graft, corruption, and conspiracy.

presentation in terms of an average expectation based on life situations, is never expressed in so many words but is established by the overwhelming wealth of material. It may affect certain spectator groups more deeply than the overt moral of crime and punishment regularly derived from such shows. What matters is not the importance of crime as a symbolic expression of otherwise controlled sexual or aggressive impulses, but the confusion of this symbolism with a pedantically maintained realism in all matters of direct sense perception. Thus, empirical life becomes infused with a kind of meaning that virtually excludes adequate experience no matter how obstinately the veneer of such "realism" is built up. This affects the social and psychological function of drama.

It is hard to establish whether the spectators of Greek tragedy really experienced the catharsis Aristotle described—in fact this theory, evolved after the age of tragedy was over, seems to have been a rationalization itself, an attempt to state the purpose of tragedy in pragmatic, quasi-scientific terms. Whatever the case, it seems pretty certain that those who saw the *Oresteia* of Aeschylus or Sophocles' *Oedipus* were not likely to translate these tragedies (the subject matter of which was known to everyone, and the interest in which was centered in artistic treatment) directly into everyday terms. This audience did not expect that on the next corner of Athens similar things would go on. Actually, pseudo-realism allows for the direct and extremely primitive identifications achieved by popular culture; and it presents a façade of trivial buildings, rooms, dresses, and faces as though they were the promise of something thrilling and exciting taking place at any moment.

In order to establish this socio-psychological frame of reference, one would have to follow up systematically categories—such as the normality of crime or pseudo-realism and many others—to determine their structural unity and to interpret the specific devices, symbols, and stereotypes in relation to this frame of reference. We hypothesize at this phase that the frames of reference and the individual devices will tend in the same direction.

Only against psychological backdrops such as pseudo realism and against implicit assumptions like the normality of crime can the specific stereotypes of television plays be interpreted. The very standardization indicated by the set frames of reference automatically produces a number of stereotypes. Also, the technology of television production makes stereotypy almost inevitable. The short time available for the preparation of scripts and the vast material continuously to be produced call for certain formulas. Moreover, in plays lasting only a quarter to half an hour each, it appears inevitable that the kind of person the audience faces each time should be indicated drastically through red and green lights. We are not dealing with the problem of the existence of stereotypes. Since stereotypes are an indispensable element of the organization and anticipation of experience, preventing us from falling into mental disorganization and chaos, no art can entirely dispense with them. Again, the functional change is what concerns us. The more stereotypes become reified and rigid in the present setup of cultural industry, the less people are likely to change their preconceived ideas with the progress of their experience. The more opaque and complicated modern life becomes, the more people are tempted to cling desperately to clichés which seem to bring some order into the otherwise un-understandable. Thus, people may not only lose true insight into reality, but ultimately their very capacity for life experience may be dulled by the constant wearing of blue and pink spectacles.

Stereotyping

In coping with this danger, we may not do full justice to the meaning of some of the stereotypes which are to be dealt with. We should never forget that there are two sides to every psychodynamic phenomenon, the unconscious or *id* element and the rationalization. Although the latter is psychologically defined as a defense mechanism, it may very well contain some nonpsychological, objective truth which cannot simply be pushed aside on account of the psychological function of the rationalization. Thus some of the stereotypical messages, directed toward particularly weak spots in the mentality of large sectors of the population, may prove to be quite legitimate. However, it may be said with fairness that the questionable blessings of morals, such as "one should not chase after rainbows," are largely overshadowed by the threat of inducing people to mechanical simplifications by ways of distorting the world in such a way that it seems to fit into pre-established pigeonholes.

The example here selected, however, should indicate rather drastically the danger of stereotypy. A television play concerning a fascist dictator, a kind of hybrid between Mussolini and Peron, shows the dictator in a moment of crisis; and the content of the play is his inner and outer collapse. Whether the cause of his collapse is a popular upheaval or a military revolt is never made clear. But neither this issue nor any other of a social or political nature enters the plot itself. The course of events takes place exclusively on a private level. The dictator is just a heel who treats sadistically both his secretary and his "lovely and warm-hearted" wife. His antagonist, a general, was formerly in love with the wife; and they both still love each other, although the wife sticks loyally to her husband. Forced by her husband's brutality, she attempts flight, and is intercepted by the general who wants to save her. The turning point occurs when the guards surround the palace to defend the dictator's popular wife. As soon as they learn that she has departed, the guards quit; and the dictator, whose "inflated ego" explodes at the same time, gives up. The dictator is nothing but a bad, pompous, and cowardly man. He seems to act with extreme stupidity; nothing of the objective dynamics of dictatorship comes out. The impression is created that totalitarianism grows out of character disorders of ambitious politicians, and is overthrown by the honesty, courage, and warmth of those figures with whom the audience is supposed to identify. The standard device employed is that of the spurious personalization of objective issues. The representatives of ideas under attack, as in the case of the fascists here, are presented as villains in a ludicrous cloak-and-dagger fashion; whereas, those who fight for the "right cause" are personally idealized. This not only distracts from any real social issues but also enforces the psychologically extremely dangerous division of the world into black (the outgroup) and white (we, the ingroup). Certainly, no artistic production can deal with ideas or political creeds *in abstracto* but has to present them in terms of their concrete impact upon human beings; yet it would be utterly futile to present individuals as mere specimens of an abstraction, as puppets expressive of an idea. In order to deal with the concrete impact of totalitarian systems, it would be more commendable to show how the life of ordinary people is affected by terror and impotence than to cope with the phony psychology of the big shots, whose heroic role is silently endorsed by such a treatment even if they are pictured as villains. There seems to be hardly any question of the importance of an analysis of pseudo-personalization and its effect, by no means limited to television.

Although pseudo-personalization denotes the stereotyped way of "looking at things" in television, we should also point out certain stereotypes in the narrower sense. Many television plays could be characterized by the sobriquet "a pretty girl can do no wrong." The heroine of a light comedy is, to use George Legman's term, "a bitch heroine." She behaves toward her father in an incredibly inhuman and cruel manner only slightly rationalized as "merry pranks." But she is punished very slightly, if at all. True, in real life bad deeds are rarely punished at all, but this cannot be applied to television. Here, those who have developed the production code for the movies seem right: What matters in mass media is not what happens in real life, but rather the positive and negative "messages," prescriptions, and taboos that the spectator absorbs by means of identification with the material he is looking at. The punishment given to the pretty heroine only nominally fulfills the conventional requirements of the conscience for a second. But the spectator is given to understand that the heroine really gets away with everything just because she is pretty.

The attitude in question seems to be indicative of a universal penchant. In another sketch that belongs to a series dealing with the confidence racket, the attractive girl who is an active participant in the racket not only is paroled after having been sentenced to a long term, but also seems to have a good chance of marrying her victim. Her sex morality, of course, is unimpeachable. The spectator is supposed to like her at first sight as a modest and self-effacing character, and he must not be disappointed. Although it is discovered that she is a crook, the original identification must be restored, or rather maintained. The stereotype of the nice girl is so strong that not even the proof of her delinquency can destroy it; and, by hook or by crook, she must be what she appears to be. It goes without saying that such psychological models tend to confirm exploitative, demanding, and aggressive attitudes on the part of young girls—a character structure which has come to be known in psychoanalysis under the name of oral aggressiveness.

Sometimes such stereotypes are disguised as national American traits, a part of the American scene where the image of the haughty, egoistic, yet irresistible girl who plays havoc with poor dad has come to be a public institution. This way of reasoning is an insult to the American spirit. High-pressure publicity and continuous plugging to institutionalize some obnoxious type does not make the type a sacred symbol of folklore. Many considerations of an apparently anthropological nature today tend only to veil objectionable trends, as though they were of an ethnological,

quasi-natural character. Incidentally, it is amazing to what degree television material even on superficial examination brings to mind psychoanalytic concepts with the qualification of being a psychoanalysis in reverse.
Psychoanalysis has described the oral syndrome combining the antago-
nistic trends of aggressive and dependent traits. This character syndrome
is closely indicated by the pretty girl that can do no wrong, who, while
being aggressive against her father exploits him at the same time, depending on him as much as on the surface level she is set against him. The difference between the sketch and psychoanalysis is simply that the sketch
exalts the very same syndrome which is treated by psychoanalysis as a reversion to infantile developmental phases and which the psychoanalyst
tries to dissolve. It remains to be seen whether something similar applies
as well to some types of male heroes, particularly the super-he-man. It
may well be that he too can do no wrong.

Finally, we should deal with a rather widespread stereotype which, in
as much as it is taken for granted by television, is further enhanced. At
the same time, the example may serve to show that certain psychoanalytic
interpretations of cultural stereotypes are not really too farfetched. The
latent ideas that psychoanalysis attributes to certain stereotypes come to
the surface. There is the extremely popular idea that the artist is not only
maladjusted, introverted, and *a priori* somewhat funny; but that he is really an "aesthete," a weakling, and a "sissy." In other words, modern synthetic folklore tends to identify the artist with the homosexual and to respect only the "man of action" as a real, strong man. This idea is expressed
in a surprisingly direct manner in one of the comedy scripts at our disposal. It portrays a young man who is not only the "dope" who appears
so often on television but is also a shy, retiring, and accordingly untal-
ented poet, whose moronic poems are ridiculed.[7] He is in love with a girl
but is too weak and insecure to indulge in the necking practices she rather

---

7. It could be argued that this very ridicule expresses that this boy is not meant to
represent the artist but just the "dope." But this is probably too rationalistic. Again, as
in the case of the schoolteacher, official respect for culture prevents caricaturing the
artist as such. However, by characterizing the boy, among other things by his writing
poetry, it is indirectly achieved that artistic activities and silliness are associated with
each other. In many respects mass culture is organized much more by way of such associations than in strict logical terms. It may be added that quite frequently attacks on
any social type seek protection by apparently presenting the object of the attack as an
exception while it is understood by innuendo that he is considered as a specimen of the
whole concept.

crudely suggests; the girl, on her part, is caricatured as a boychaser. As happens frequently in mass culture, the roles of the sexes are reversed—the girl is utterly aggressive, and the boy, utterly afraid of her, describes himself as "woman-handled" when she manages to kiss him. There are vulgar innuendos of homosexuality of which one may be quoted: The heroine tells her boyfriend that another boy is in love with someone, and the boyfriend asks, "What's he in love with?" She answers, "A girl, of course," and her boyfriend replies, "Why, of course? Once before it was a neighbor's turtle, and what's more its name was Sam." This interpretation of the artist as innately incompetent and a social outcast (by the innuendo of sexual inversion) is worthy of examination.

We do not pretend that the individual illustrations and examples, or the theories by which they are interpreted, are basically new. But in view of the cultural and pedagogical problem presented by television, we do not think that the novelty of the specific findings should be a primary concern. We know from psychoanalysis that the reasoning "But we know all this!" is not infrequently a defense. This defense is made in order to dismiss insights as irrelevant because they are actually uncomfortable and make life more difficult for us than it already is by shaking our conscience when we are supposed to enjoy the "simple pleasures of life." The investigation of the television problems we have here indicated and illustrated by a few examples selected at random demands, most of all, taking seriously notions dimly familiar to most of us by putting them into their proper context and perspective and by checking them by pertinent material. We propose to concentrate on issues of which we are vaguely but uncomfortably aware, even at the expense of our discomfort's mounting, the further and the more systematically our studies proceed. The effort here required is of a moral nature itself: knowingly to face psychological mechanisms operating on various levels in order not to become blind and passive victims. We can change this medium of far-reaching potentialities only if we look at it in the same spirit which we hope will one day be expressed by its imagery.

7 The Hollywood Picture

Why Wait for Posterity?

Iris Barry is one of the founders of the London Film Society. She is also one of the founders of the Museum of Modern Art Film Library, where she is now curator. In addition to being a regular reviewer for the New York Herald Tribune *Books,* she is the translator of Bardèche and Brasillach's *History of the Film,* the author of several novels, and has written widely on the motion picture.

. . . . .

SINCE THE COBBLER'S CHILDREN are always the worst shod, it is natural enough that Hollywood should be almost the last place in the world where the films of the past are esteemed seriously. Film executives have been known to speak rather grandly now and then about preserving films for posterity, in the spirit, presumably, of those who seal up cans of Spam, phonograph records, and newspapers in the foundations of new buildings. For, though the producing companies all scrupulously preserve their negatives, since in their physical possession and through the copyright act the legal ownership of story rights is thus assured, nothing has ever been done by the industry itself to make it possible to *see* the screen classics of the past. It would probably be absurd to expect it to do so, for several reasons. First, it could not possibly be profitable. Second, the problem of selection might be an embarrassing one. But chiefly such an undertaking would run counter to the main impulse of the film community. The men who finance and produce motion pictures, as well as the men and women who make them, are inevitably and primarily concerned, not with history or the films of the past, but with the films they are planning for tomorrow or making today. It is, likewise, not painters or sculptors who establish museums or become art historians!

Yet the film companies have made one great concession in this direction. To make it possible for outstanding films of the past to be seen and studied they have permitted, under necessarily severe restrictions and for strictly noncommercial purposes, an educational institution to obtain prints of important older films at the cost of making the prints, and to circulate these to other nonprofit organizations. The institution that does this is the Museum of Modern Art in New York. Its exhibitions of painting, sculpture, architecture and housing, primitive and folk art, industrial design and the like are nationally famous. Its exhibitions of films are becoming so, for in the course of a year, at daily showings in the Museum auditorium, a series of sixty-eight American and thirty-six foreign motion picture programs now runs the gamut of international film history from Louis Lumière and Edison's films of 1895 to John Huston's *Maltese Falcon* and Capra's *Why We Fight* series. Extensive series of these same "old" films are also given regularly, among other places, at the Art Institute of Chicago, the Philadelphia Museum of Art, the San Francisco Museum, Vassar College, Cornell University, and the University of Texas. The audience is a considerable one, and it is growing.

Founded in 1935, with John Hay Whitney as its president, and financed by subscriptions from patrons of the Museum and a three-year grant from the Rockefeller Foundation, the Museum of Modern Art Film Library was originally launched auspiciously in Hollywood, and its plans were warmly approved at a party which, with Mary Pickford's permission, the officers of the organization held at Pickfair in August, 1935. Louella Parsons even went to town about it twice that very week! At the party, Will Hays extended his favor to the enterprise before a distinguished group of guests. Sam Goldwyn, Harold Lloyd, and Walt Disney, as well as Miss Pickford herself, promised to contribute to the collection of outstanding films of the past which the Museum planned to amass, "so that the films may be studied and enjoyed as any one of the other arts is studied and enjoyed." Prints of the Lloyd comedies, incidentally, were the first to arrive, which is why the work of that admirable comedian, his ageless *The Freshman* and inimitable *Grandma's Boy,* were the first to be familiar to a whole new generation.

The problem of obtaining prints from the big producer-distributor companies was necessarily more complex. Terms were finally worked out that proved acceptable to the legal departments of Paramount, Loew's, Twentieth Century–Fox, Warners and Universal, so that early in 1936 the Film Library had actually begun to rent out its first series of programs [1] to colleges, museums, and other nonprofit organizations, which were thus

---

1. Entitled "A Short Survey of the Film in America" and including *The Great Train Robbery,* Sarah Bernhardt's *Queen Elizabeth, Sunrise, All Quiet on the Western Front,* and Disney's *Steamboat Willie.*

for the first time able to institute a study of the growth, technique, aesthetics, and sociological content of the most popular and liveliest of the arts. Gradually the Museum's collection grew. Between 1936 and 1939 a selection of French, German, Russian, and Swedish pictures was obtained direct from negatives in Europe, so that epochmaking productions such as *The Cabinet of Dr. Caligari* and *Potemkin* could be seen once more in uncut versions. In view of what was to happen shortly afterward in Europe this was particularly fortunate, for much has since been destroyed there. Public-spirited individuals like Mrs. Edwin Knopf, who donated a print of the Eleanore Duse *Cenere* of 1916; Mrs. Philip Manson, who contributed the Asta Nielsen *Hamlet* of 1920; and Messrs. Krimsky and Cochran, from whom *Maedchen in Uniform* was obtained, all added to the muster. In 1939 the late Douglas Fairbanks placed all his own negatives, as well as prints of some of his earlier pictures, in the Film Library's safekeeping. William S. Hart was next to follow suit, and recently Colleen Moore contributed prints of many of the pictures she had starred in. In 1939 all that remained of the old Biograph Company negatives were acquired from R. H. Hammer (and what a problem they constituted, with their single perforations!). In 1940 there was added what remained of the Edison Company's material. Most important and most complex, the post-Biograph films of D. W. Griffith had already been secured.

Since so little of the work of the Film Library is known to the body of filmmakers, it will perhaps be useful to elaborate somewhat upon the many technical and financial obstacles that were encountered.

The Museum of Modern Art, unlike most other famous museums, has no endowment and is in receipt of no public funds. Established in 1929, exactly nine days after the stock market crash, it has nevertheless developed steadily through depression and war. In 1939 it acquired its own building, and raised the money to pay for it in full. But its ever-increasing annual budget has never been met by its income[2] from a growing attendance, phe-

---

2. Income of the Museum of Modern Art for 1943–1944:

Earnings	$284,226.39
Contributions	280,305.81
Memberships	61,513.90
	$626,046.10
Government contracts	394,676.60
	$1,020,722.70
Expenditures	$1,099,805.45

nomenal sales of publications, rentals of exhibitions and film programs, and the annual dues from memberships, which now exceed 8,000. Nor have the extremely generous contributions of its trustees and supporters always entirely covered the resulting annual deficit. As one of its largest and costliest departments, the Film Library has therefore, save for the first years, also continually been short of funds. No gift of money has ever been made, nor has even one $1,000 life membership ever been subscribed by anyone in films, and in ten years only two contributions have been received from any film organization.

It is hardly necessary to explain how costly a medium celluloid is. The storage and insurance charges for the Film Library's 18,000,000 feet of film are alone a large item. When the American producer-distributors permitted the organization to obtain prints from the negatives which they themselves preserve, it was on condition that the cost of the prints and of print replacements be met by the Museum. Only to *look* at a film costs money when it is necessary to pay to have a print made before even an exploratory look can be given to it! Furthermore, the Museum was faced with the even heavier expense of making duplicate negatives from foreign films of which prints had been obtained abroad, because it was the only way both to insure preservation and to make certain of a supply of further prints as they should be needed in the future.

Beyond these financial problems lay graver ones of a technical nature. We might assume, and almost everyone will agree, that such landmarks of the cinema as *Tol'able David, It Happened One Night, Male and Female, Greed,* and *The Black Pirate*—to take but a few titles almost at random—are among the "musts" in any retrospective of film history. Let us see what even so brief a list has entailed.

To begin with *The Black Pirate:* One Technicolor print of this was turned over to the Museum by the actor-producer himself, along with the rest of the Fairbanks material. His estate now owns everything, but the Film Library holds the material and has the right to use it noncommercially. A second print had been acquired, with much else, when the Harvard University Film Foundation transferred its collection to the Museum in 1936. The Harvard print dated from 1926, the print from Fairbanks was by no means new, and Fairbanks had made *The Black Pirate* in two-color Technicolor, which has long been obsolete. No new color prints can be made. As there was obviously no advantage in letting the

Male and Female (1919), by Cecil B. DeMille,
with Gloria Swanson (center)

two original prints deteriorate unseen in a vault, they have been occasionally projected with special care at the Museum, where they have given
delight to a few thousand people. But they are now (as they would equally
have been had they remained in the vault) at the point of final deteriora-
tion. The only way to salvage something of this splendid film, either for
living students or for posterity, is therefore to make a duplicate black-and-
white negative from which future prints—still in black-and-white, of
course—can be made. The Museum's annual appropriation for this kind
of work is inadequate to its needs, and there is other and equally vital material that calls for urgent attention. But *The Black Pirate* has been dupli-
cated and will be preserved, even though not, alas, in its original form.

Happily, the films *Male and Female* and *It Happened One Night*
presented no difficulties except for an allocation of money for future replacement of existing prints and the obtaining of permission—not yet
forthcoming—to circulate the latter. Such permission is often delayed, or
subsequently withdrawn temporarily, because a remake is due or because
the 16-mm. or 35-mm. rights have been leased to a distributor.

The case of *Tol'able David* was a grave one. The film was remade in 1930, and apparently the original negative no longer exists; certainly it has not been traced. Fortunately, Richard Barthelmess himself had kept a good print in his possession. This he recently presented to the Film Library, and so, now that consent has been obtained from its legal owners, a duplicate negative and positive prints have been made.

The story of *Greed* has always been an unhappy one, as with many of von Stroheim's films. The Museum obtained both 16-mm. and 35-mm. prints, which were made, of course, by the owner-producer company from its negative, though paid for by the Film Library. No one regrets more than the staff of the Library that these prints are not the equivalent of the film as von Stroheim finished it; but I am among those who would far rather see the briefer (and magnificent) version that does exist than nothing at all, and it does seem a little odd that the Film Library should be abused, as it has been, because someone else had cut the Von Stroheim picture!

The Film Library has faced another kind of problem with certain early talking pictures. In some, the negative sound track has shrunk, so that even with special laboratory work it is difficult to get satisfactory results. There were also early Vitaphone sound-on-disk subjects, like *The Lights of New York,* which seemed to possess historical interest, so that the Film Library had to have a special re-recording job done, again at the Museum's expense, with Warners' consent. It would be only fair to add here that, friendly and coöperative as all the major companies have been, Warners has from the beginning been the most coöperative of all.

I have already referred to the technical difficulties which the old Biograph negatives presented. Thanks to the wonderful craftsmanship that characterized that firm's work, they were found to be in prime shape although they had been stored in a tumbledown building, with broken windows, which the Fire Department had condemned as a menace. Incidentally, the quality of the original laboratory work on negatives proves to be the most important factor in determining the life of any film. Film rushed through the laboratory carelessly and in haste will deteriorate in less than a decade. Careful workmanship has kept other negatives sound for fifty years.

But when the Film Library was founded it was not the Biograph films only that had been lost to view. Most of D. W. Griffith's major productions were inaccessible even to him, for unhappily he had been a creative

genius but not a businessman. Some of his most famous pictures were being held against unpaid storage bills; others were afterward included in a
receivership sale; and the Film Library made it its first obligation to rescue as much as possible of this material. When recovered, by no means all
of it was in good shape. The holding laboratory had already reported some
of the negatives in "very bad condition," and not all prints were complete.
The negative of *Intolerance,* for example, that was finally obtained measured 10,872 feet, although two positive prints measured approximately
11,000 feet each and one acquired earlier measured 11,446 feet. Footage
missing from the negative was consequently duped from the prints and
cut in to provide the most complete record of this superb film that it was
possible to make. Only lack of adequate funds has prevented the Museum
from taking heroic measures with all the Griffith material. I am of the opinion that new dupe negatives of his films should, ideally, have been made
up immediately; but the Museum had, even in its first years, spent close
upon $10,000 in laboratory work on Griffith pictures alone. Therefore
we can only hope to continue this work of restoration gradually, year by
year. On the other hand, if D. W.'s memorable contributions to Biograph
and thereafter are visible at all, it is due solely to the efforts of the Film
Library. And, if the Museum has rather noticeably not been besieged by
present-day directors, editors, or cameramen wishing to study the work
of Griffith, and of Bitzer, his master cameraman, thousands of students
and admirers outside the industry have during the past ten years been able
to enjoy it again.

Unfortunately, in many places the programs of the Film Library are
shown only through 16-mm. prints. Everyone knows that 16-mm. projection frequently leaves much to be desired, not only because of the small-
ness of the screen and the length of the throw, but because all too often
the prints are of inferior quality. This may be because they have been
made up from dupe negatives, themselves made from worn or incomplete
prints. As I have said earlier, sometimes *this is all that remains.* In art museums we are forced to content ourselves with casts made from broken
sculptures; yet these are esteemed highly. It is also unfortunate that the
making of 16-mm. prints, particularly since the war, is often rushed and
poor work. Poor visibility on the screen is just as likely, or more likely,
to come from poor projection—inadequate illumination, dirty aperture,
inaccurate focusing, or sound adjustment. It is a pity, then, that all too

many colleges, museums, or film societies where the Museum's film programs are shown are equipped with 16-mm. projectors only. But in view
of the high cost of 35-mm. equipment and of employing a licensed operator to run it we must expect this situation to persist. Even in Hollywood,
for many years past, *the only showings of films from the Museum's collection
have been confined to the 16-mm. ones.* This, too, is a surprising and regret-
table circumstance, which one earnestly hopes that the Guilds will ultimately remedy.

Whatever the cost, the difficulties, and the shortcomings in the presentation of the Film Library's programs, the basic question is whether the
project was worthwhile. What, really, is the point in dragging old films
back to light?

First, I believe that it benefits the general esteem and standing of the
motion picture industry as a whole; for if the great films of the past are
not worth taking seriously and are not worth reëxamination, then presumably neither are the "great films" of today. It would be unthinkable
that the only books available to literary men and women should be no
more than those published in the past year or so. And what critical judgment could then be exercised? The opportunity to refer again to the more
important films of the past must surely serve the same purpose as a library
of books serves a writer. Then too, there is of course the simple question
of pleasure: films like the brief *Uncle Tom's Cabin* which Edwin S. Porter
made in 1903, or Ince's *The Italian* (of which only one 16-mm. print is
known to exist), or Flaherty's *Moana,* Dreyer's *Passion of Joan of Arc,* the
early Seastrom pictures, *Million Dollar Legs,* or Keaton's *The Navigator* are
a delight to look upon, besides being packed with ideas and ingenuity. Do
you want to see Billy Sunday or Caruso, the Czar, Pavlova, or Bernhardt?
Are you curious to know what the original "vamps," "flappers," or "bright
young people" looked like? Only the films of the period—*A Fool There
Was, Our Dancing Daughters, Flaming Youth*—can accurately and fully
serve as documentation. Finally, there is the value that the older films may
have to technicians of today. Was there not something about the cutting
of *Intolerance* or *Potemkin* or *Public Enemy,* something about the camerawork in *The Last Laugh* or that romantic early Garbo picture *The Atonement of Gösta Berling,* that it might be profitable to recall?

It is upon the last question that Hollywood as a whole might perhaps
most usefully linger. The Museum of Modern Art has collected the ma-

terial, but, beyond a certain point, only Hollywood can help the Museum to use it fully and profitably. To be specific, one of the next tasks that faces the Museum's Film Library is the preparation and compilation of programs that will illustrate and analyze film technique. There should obviously be available studies of the work of cameramen, and of editors, a comparison of the work of directors in handling similar dramatic situations, an inquiry into the past use of sound and music. This can be best done by a careful selection of sequences and scenes from films, rather than by whole films. It will be a long and complex job, and an expensive one.

Now is the time for Hollywood and its technicians to join with the Film Library in a collaboration that would once and for all give precise information to students everywhere about the styles and innovations, the creative contributions, of the men and women working in motion pictures everywhere in the world for the past fifty years—the achievements that have carried the motion picture from its celebrated infancy to near-maturity and made it indeed an art (as well as an industry) with which one can truly be proud to be connected.

The Atonement of Gösta Berling. (The Story of Gösta Berling.) Svenska-Biograf, 1923. Director, Mauritz Stiller. Novel, Selma Lagerlof. Scenario, Mauritz Stiller and Ragnar Hylten-Cavallius.

The Black Pirate. Allied Artists, 1926. Director, Alfred Parker. Adapted by Jack Cunningham from a story by Elton Thomas (Douglas Fairbanks).

The Cabinet of Doctor Caligari. Decla-Bioscop, 1919. Director, Robert Wiene. Scenario, Carl Mayer and Hans Janowitz.

Cenere. Ambrosio-Caesar-Film, 1916.

Flaming Youth. First Nat'l, 1923. Director, John F. Dillon. Novel, Warner Fabian. Scenario, Harry O. Hoyt.

A Fool There Was. Fox, 1914. Director, Frank Powell. From the play based on Rudyard Kipling's poem *The Vampire.*

The Freshman. Pathé, 1925. Directors, Fred Newmeyer and Sam Taylor. Story, Sam Taylor, John Gray, Ted Wilde, and Tim Whelan.

Grandma's Boy. Pathé, 1922. Director, Fred Newmeyer. Screenplay, Hal Roach, Sam Taylor, and Jean Havez.

Greed. MGM, 1923. Director, Erich von Stroheim. Novel, *McTeague,* by Frank Norris. Scenario, Erich von Stroheim.

Hamlet. Art-Film, 1920. Director, Svend Gade. Scenario, Erwin Gepard.

Intolerance. Wark Prod. Corp., 1916. Director, D. W. Griffith.

It Happened One Night. Col., 1934. Director, Frank Capra. Short story, *Night Bus,* by Samuel Hopkins Adams. Screenplay, Robert Riskin.

The Italian. 1915. Director, Thomas Ince.

The Lights of New York. WB, 1928. Director, Bryan Foy. Story and scenario, Hugh Herbert and Murray Roth.

Maedchen in Uniform. Deutsche Film, 1931. Director, Leontine Sagan. Play, *Yesterday and Today,* by Christa Winsloe. English text, Donald Freeman.

Male and Female. Par., 1919. Director, C. B. DeMille. Play, Sir James Barrie. Scenario, Jeanie Macpherson.

The Maltese Falcon. WB, 1941. Director, John Huston. Novel, Dashiell Hammett. Screenplay, John Huston.

Million Dollar Legs. Par., 1932. Director, Edward Cline. Adapted by Henry Myers and Nick Barrows from story by Joseph L. Mankiewicz.

Moana. Famous Players–Lasky, 1920. Written and directed by Robert J. Flaherty.

The Navigator. MGM, 1924. Directors, Donald Crisp and Buster Keaton. Story, Jean Havez, Clyde Bruckman, and Jo Mitchell.

Our Dancing Daughters. MGM, 1928. Director, Harry Beaumont. Screenplay and story, Josephine Lovett.

The Passion of Joan of Arc. La Société Générale des Films and L'Alliance Cinématographique Européenne. 1928. Director, Carl Theodor Dreyer. Sources, trial records. Scenario, Carl Theodor Dreyer, in collaboration with Joseph Delteil.

Potemkin. First Studio of Goskino, Moscow, 1925. Director and writer, S. M. Eisenstein.

Tol'able David. First Nat'l, 1922. Director, Henry King. Screenplay, Henry King and Edmund Goulding.

Uncle Tom's Cabin. 1903. Edwin S. Porter.

Why We Fight. U.S. Signal Corps. (All under supervision of Col. Frank Capra.) No. 1: *Prelude to War.* Narration, Maj. Eric Knight and Capt. Anthony Veiller. No. 2: *The Nazis Strike.* Narration, Maj. Eric Knight and Capt. Anthony Veiller. No. 3: *Divide and Conquer.* Narration, Maj. Eric Knight and Capt. Anthony Veiller. No. 4: *The Battle of Britain.* Narration, Capt. Anthony Veiller, Maj. Eric Knight, and S. K. Lauren. No. 5: *The Battle of Russia.* Narration, Capt. Anthony Veiller.

Hollywood—Illusion and Reality*

HOLLYWOOD IS CONSISTENTLY, relentlessly publicized; yet most of the people who know the motion picture industry as their means of live-lihood and the focus of their lives will agree that the general public is uninformed, or blatantly misinformed, even by well-intentioned commentators, concerning the realities of motion picture production, the problems that face the craftsmen in the industry, and the community in which they live. I am not referring primarily to the expensive foolishness about the stars that fills the fan magazines—a comparatively unimportant by-product of the system of stereotypes and illusions which creates a false perspective concerning everything pertaining to the production of pictures.

Let us consider, as an example, an article by Raymond Chandler on "Writers in Hollywood" in the November *Atlantic*. Chandler has much that is pertinent, and indeed imperative, to say about the importance of the script as the key to the process of picturemaking, the failure to make effective use of writing talent, and the straitjacketing of creative freedom under the present studio system. But Chandler's useful comments on the underestimation of the writer are invalidated by his own underestimation of everything that concerns Hollywood. He begins by observing that "Hollywood is easy to hate, easy to sneer at, easy to lampoon." He notes the danger of exaggeration, citing a critic's casual reference to "run-of-the-mill $3,000-a-week writers." He very properly stresses the fact that "50 per cent of the screen writers of Hollywood made less than $10,000 last year."

Having set himself the task of describing the real Hollywood, the author finds himself drawn irresistibly within the gates of the illusory Hol-

*[No biography was provided for the author in the original publication. This piece was taken from a section called "Notes and Communications," which consisted of shorter and less formal pieces for which author bios were not always considered necessary.]

lywood, the never-never-land of spendthrift zanies and comical incompetents. Having warned against the danger of economic exaggeration, he proceeds to walk into the trap: "There are writers in Hollywood making two thousand a week who never had an idea in their lives, who have never written a photographable scene, who could not make two cents a word in the pulp market if their lives depended on it." The actors are also easy to lampoon. Hollywood makes "historical epics in which the male actors look like female impersonators, and the lovely feminine star looks just a little too starry-eyed for a babe who has spent half her life swapping husbands." As for the producers, "Some are able and humane men and some are low-grade individuals with the morals of a goat, the artistic integrity of a slot machine, and the manners of a floor-walker with delusions of grandeur."

It is not my purpose to argue about these characterizations. Every community has its quota of frivolous, ill-mannered and evil persons. The point I wish to make relates to the repetition of clichés; Chandler even uses the old one that "nearly every sleeve conceals a knife"; the repetition creates a cumulative distortion. Since screen writers are "a pretty dreary lot of hacks," and since they are content to live in an "atmosphere of intellectual squalor," it seems fatuous to suggest that they be granted greater artistic freedom. There is no indication that they would know how to use this freedom if they had it.

Writers may derive some comfort from the fact that they are becoming increasingly prominent in the strange hierarchy that is supposed to inhabit the Hollywood wonderland. Emil Ludwig describes the makers of screen plays in a recent issue of a French newspaper; the article is translated from the German, but it may be permissible to quote a passage as it appears in French, in order to preserve its Gallic flavor. The writers, according to the eminent historian, "ont la taille svelte, portent volontiers des chandails bariolés, changent de maîtresses plus souvent encore que de studios." Perhaps none of us in Hollywood have seen these "svelte" writers, wearing their gaudy sweaters and changing mistresses more frequently than they change studios, but we can welcome them without rancor as additions to the interminable gallery of fictitious Hollywood portraits.

The Hollywood stereotype, like other stereotypes, has not been manufactured accidentally. It is a significant social phenomenon. Those who perpetuate the myth may have diverse purposes and viewpoints. But the cliché retains its power, whether it appears as an unabashed harlequinade of the *Once in a Lifetime* sort, or under the guise of sober "scientific" investigation with appropriate statistical tables as in Leo Rosten's *Hollywood,* or in the subtleties of Christopher Isherwood's *Prater Violet.* The net result is the building of an ungainly Rube-Goldberg-cartoon edifice, which stands between the serious craftsmen who are the majority of the industry's workers and the audience they seek to serve. It is probable that most of the members of that audience—which covers the world—know nothing of the problems of the industry or of the social awareness and invigorating concern with the creative potentialities of the medium that are characteristic of the real Hollywood.

An analysis of the mythology that has grown up around the American picture industry would involve a difficult research job, but it is to be hoped that some scholar will undertake the task. It would be an invaluable contribution to our understanding of social attitudes toward the motion picture. It might also reveal the underlying forces and pressures that shape these attitudes. At a time when the freedom of the screen is under attack by powerful political and economic interests, it may not be amiss to note that mockery and illusion can cushion the attack and divert attention from the issues of public policy that are involved. As long as the average citizen thinks of Hollywood as a glamorous funnyhouse, he cannot think of it as a place where a public trust is fulfilled, and where the most sacred of our traditional liberties—freedom of thought and freedom of communication—must be preserved.

Negro Stereotypes on the Screen*

TYPE CASTING IS A COMMON curse in Hollywood. Possibly the most unjust example of this practice is the persistent typing of the entire Negro race as menials and buffoons, a tradition that has been followed ever since the establishment of the American film industry. Now, after many years, a protest is beginning to be heard. The change in attitude is traceable to the growing social consciousness that has developed in this country in the last few years. Nowhere has this increased awareness become more noticeable than among Negroes themselves.

The most forceful protests have come from Negro servicemen who have served overseas. These men have seen the astonishment of people in Asia, Africa, and Europe at discovering that the average American Negro soldier is a normally intelligent and self-assured individual rather than the ignorant and illiterate buffoon habitually portrayed in our films.

Among the civilian population, too, there have been objections to this stereotype. Negro newspapers, civic and political organizations, and ministers and teachers are opposing this harmful distortion. As succinct proof that the Afro-American group is not composed exclusively of illiterate menials, they point to the 1940 Bureau of Census statistics. These figures show that at that time there were in this country some 3,524 Negro physicians and surgeons; 2,339 college presidents and professors; 1,052 lawyers and judges; 132,110 craftsmen and foremen in industries; and 6,801 trained nurses.[1]

---

*[No biography was provided for the author in the original publication. This piece was taken from a section called "Notes and Communications," which consisted of shorter and less formal pieces for which author bios were not always considered necessary.]

1. The Census further indicates how widely Negroes are represented among the professions and skilled trades. There are 17,102 clergymen; 1,463 dentists; 6,943 musicians and music teachers; 63,697 school teachers; 1,231 electricians; 20,798 carpenters; 3,965 tailors and furriers; 11,000 dressmakers and seamstresses; 28,229 barbers, beauticians,

What has been the colored American's relationship to the film industry in all these years? Negroes entered Hollywood motion pictures as early as 1915 as "atmosphere" and "extra" players. Among the most popular of the early actors was Noble Johnson, who played innumerable non-Negroid feature roles. Perhaps the earliest protests from colored moviegoers were lodged against D. W. Griffith's *Birth of a Nation,* on the grounds that the picture harmed good race relations by depicting Negroes as rapists and slaves.

About fifteen years ago Clarence Brooks portrayed the role of an educated West Indian doctor in *Arrowsmith,* in which Ronald Colman was starred. In 1932, Hazel Jones played a beautiful Burmese siren whose wiles ensnared the late Lon Chaney in *West of Singapore.* About the same time, Etta Moten was cast as a South American singer in *Flying Down to Rio.* These performances, however, were never very loudly acclaimed because the parts represented groups other than American Negroes.

From 1941 to 1944 there was a decided improvement in Hollywood's treatment of the American of color. The emphasis on morale-building entertainment as part of the war effort resulted in an increased employment of Negro players. They took part in entertaining members of the armed forces at various camps and recreational centers and in bond-selling drives and other war-related activities.

During the same period the Negro public displayed a growing interest in colored players and in the types of roles assigned to them. Most of the studios answered affirmatively the demand for better and more dignified roles for colored artists. Ernest Anderson played the ambitious youth in *In This Our Life,* in which Bette Davis was starred. Kenneth Spencer appeared as a Negro war hero in *Bataan.* Rex Ingram played an important role in *Sahara.* Ben Carter was seen in a dignified part in *Crash Dive.* Dooley Wilson received much favorable comment for his work in *Casablanca.*

Three years ago, two all-colored films opened new avenues. The cast of *Stormy Weather* included Lena Horne, Bill Robinson, Cab Calloway, and many other Negro artists. *Cabin in the Sky* featured Ethel Waters, Roch-

---

and manicurists; 5,000 stenographers and secretaries; more than 100,000 clerical workers; 1,210 real-estate brokers; and 48,614 college students. Moreover, there are six Negro-owned and operated banks with aggregate deposits of $9,914,290; and approximately 200 Negro-controlled insurance companies.

ester, and Lena Horne. The latter picture was criticized for its stereotyped theme of the Negro's conception of God.

In the past year or so there has been a decided drop in the employment of Negro actors and actresses. It is said that orders have been given to "write out" Negro characterizations in story scripts, for fear of giving offense. But Negro leaders contend that the fight against the stereotype cannot be solved by the expedient of eliminating the Negro from pictures. They say that the problem of readjustment of values between the makers of motion pictures and the Negro public involves the creation of more understanding and a clearer conception of issues. A recognition of these factors will bring about a change in racial conception as interpreted in our domestic movies.

I have already pointed out that the war has brought about a deep sense of racial consciousness within the Afro-American group. Indeed, the Negro recognizes that he has a large stake in the current struggle to highlight the importance of the social responsibility of motion pictures in the creation of new patterns of universal understanding and interracial adjustment.

Arrowsmith. Goldwyn-UA, 1931. Director, John Ford. Novel, Sinclair Lewis. Screenplay, Sidney Howard.

Bataan. MGM, 1943. Director, Tay Garnett. Original screenplay, Robert D. Andrews.

The Birth of a Nation. Director, D. W. Griffith. Novel, *The Clansman,* with supplementary material from *The Leopard's Spots,* by the Rev. Thomas Dixon, Jr. Screenplay, D. W. Griffith and Frank Woods.

Cabin in the Sky. MGM, 1942. Director, Vincente Minnelli. Musical play book, Lynn Root. Screenplay, Joseph Schrank.

Casablanca. WB, 1942. Director, Michael Curtiz. Play, *Everybody Comes to Rick's,* by Murray Burnett and Joan Alison. Screenplay, Julius T. Epstein, Philip G. Epstein, and Howard Koch.

Crash Dive. Fox, 1943. Director, Archie Mayo. Original screen story, W. R. Burnett. Screenplay, Jo Swerling.

Flying Down to Rio. RKO, 1933. Director, Thornton Freeland. Story, Louis Brock.

In This Our Life. WB–First Nat'l, 1941. Director, John Huston. Novel, Ellen Glasgow. Screenplay, Howard Koch.

Sahara. Col., 1943. Director, Zoltan Korda. Story, Philip MacDonald. Screenplay, John Howard Lawson and Zoltan Korda.

Stormy Weather. Fox, 1943. Director, Andrew Stone. Unpublished story, Jerry Horwin and Seymour E. Robinson. Screenplay, Frederick Jackson and Ted Koehler.

West of Singapore. Mono., 1933. Director, Al Ray. Author, Huston Branch. Adaptation, Adele Buffington.

FROM VOL. 2, NO. 2, JANUARY 1947 | John Houseman

Today's Hero: A Review

John Houseman, co-founder with Orson Welles of the Mercury Theater, divides his
time between producing and directing motion pictures in Hollywood and plays on
Broadway. His last picture was *The Blue Dahlia*. He is currently directing a modern
version of *The Beggar's Opera* with Duke Ellington's music.

. . . . .

EVERY GENERATION HAS ITS MYTH—its own particular dream in which
are mirrored the preoccupations of its waking hours. In years of rich artistic activity the myth becomes absorbed into the intellectual and emotional
life of its time. In a period of general anxiety and low cultural energy like
the present the dream reveals itself naked and clear. Then we witness the
fascinating and shocking spectacle of a nation's most pressing fears and secret desires publicly exhibited in whatever art form happens, at the moment, to be the most immediately accessible to the largest mass of its
people. Today this art form is the Hollywood-made motion picture.

I have argued elsewhere against the notion that Hollywood enjoys any
real free-will in the choice of its subjects. The best it can do, in the general run of its product, is to reflect as honestly and competently as it can
the interests and anxieties of its hundred million customers. That this reflection is at the moment a rather frightening one can hardly be blamed
on the entertainment industry. The current "tough" movie is no lurid
Hollywood invention; its pattern and its characteristics coincide too
closely with other symptoms of our national life. A quick examination of
our daily and weekly press proves quite conclusively, whether we like it or
not, that the "tough" movie, currently projected on the seventeen thousand screens of this country, presents a fairly accurate reflection of the
neurotic personality of the United States of America in the year 1947.

The current American Legend, like all such myths, assumes varying
forms. It shifts, changes, and feeds upon itself, grows more outrageous
and fanciful, until finally it bursts of its own absurdity. Since this might

be happening any day now, I believe this is the proper time to analyze the "tough" movie at the moment of its fullest and ripest development. From among the motion picture advertisements of any current big-city newspaper, a perfect specimen at once presents itself.

The Big Sleep is based on a not very recent detective story by Raymond Chandler. Its plot is complex—too complex to be understood by most of its audiences, and far too complex to be related here. In one essential respect the picture differs from the book. The latter is a narration, the unraveling of an elaborate tangle of interrelated events. The movie by its very nature is a *dramatization*. Thus its values are automatically changed. The book was cynical, hardboiled, and quick-moving—a slick, atmospheric job of detective fiction written by Chandler with a fine contempt for his characters and the sordid world they inhabit. Marlowe, in the book, is an instrument of the plot; the other characters are colorful signposts in a complicated maze. In the movie the approach is basically *romantic*. Marlowe is played by an important male star. He makes love to a rising and very lovely female star. To a hundred thousand paid customers this spells Romance, and Marlowe's exploits become the stuff of contemporary American Legend.

So let us examine him, today's Hero, this fellow who follows Heathcliffe, Mr. Rochester, Buffalo Bill, Horatio Alger, and Little Caesar into the romantic dreams of the English-speaking world. He is not young; he is somewhere in his middle thirties. He is unattached, uncared-for, and irregularly shaved. His dress is slovenly. His home is a hall bedroom, and his place of business is a hole in the wall in a rundown office building. He makes a meager living doing perilous and unpleasant work which condemns him to a solitary life. The love of women and the companionship of men are denied him. He has no discernable ideal to sustain him—neither ambition, nor loyalty, nor even a lust for wealth. His aim in life, the goal toward which he moves and the hope which sustains him, is the unraveling of obscure crimes, the final solution of which affords him little or no satisfaction. For this he receives twenty-five dollars a day (plus expenses), and he certainly earns it. His missions carry him into situations of extreme danger. He is subject to terrible physical outrages, which he suffers with dreary fortitude. He holds human life cheap, including his own. The sum of his desires appears to be a skinful of whiskey and a good sleep. In all history I doubt there has been a hero whose life was so unenviable and whose aspirations had so low a ceiling.

In the Heroine he has a worthy mate. She is by Arlen out of Heming-
way, a sister under the skin to Iris March and Brett Ashley. Like those
heroines of the First World Peace, she drifts through life in a hopeless,
smoldering kind of way. Some obscurely disgraceful event in her past
overshadows her present and inhibits her from intelligent behavior. Unlike her more vital sisters, who swept glamorously up and down the conti-
nent of Europe in Blue Trains and Hispanos, she sits moping discontent-
edly in her father's house. Her shady entanglements are not with members
of the international fast set, but with an obscure and melancholy gangster
operating in the San Fernando Valley. Like the Hero, she is utterly lacking in ideals and ambition.

At certain intervals throughout the picture, Hero and Heroine are
left alone together to conduct their joyless and ill-mannered courtship.
When, in the end, they get together, one wonders whether they do so under some mysterious working of the laws of natural selection or whether
their merging is simply due to the fact that everyone else in the movie is
dead, in irons, or on the lam.

These, then, are our protagonists. Surrounding them is a whining herd
of petty chiselers, perverts, halfwits, and nymphomaniacs—poor, aimless creatures without brains, without skill, without character, without
strength, without courage, without hope. Not only are they totally lacking in moral sense; they seem to have no sense of anything at all—except
fear. From first to last they move through the story with one single desire—to be left alone. "We know we are no good," they seem to say, "we
are sad, futile, foolish people. But our crimes are petty. We do not really
hurt anybody much except ourselves and each other. After all, this is a
free country. Let us be."

In one of the current "tough" pictures, technically one of the best, the
Hero, finding himself spotted by his enemies, lies in bed waiting for them
to come and finish him off under the blankets. And here, I think, is the
key to the nature of the present American Legend. The howls of certain
critics and ladies' organizations notwithstanding, it is *not* violence and
spasmodic savagery that are the outstanding features of the "tough"
movie. Violence is a basic element in American life and has always been
an important element in American entertainment. What is significant
and repugnant about our contemporary "tough" films is their absolute
lack of moral energy, their listless, fatalistic despair. In this respect they
are in direct contrast to the gangster film of the 'thirties, which was char-

acterized by a very high vitality and a strong moral sense. The vitality may
have been antisocial, the moral tone may have stemmed from a false morality bred of power-hunger, lust, and greed, but at least the energy and the
morality were always present; and so, consequently, was the tragic sense.
The Hero (*Little Caesar, Scarface,* et al.), misguided, arrogant, and brutal
though he may have been, rose triumphant, by his own will, against fearful odds. When he finally fell, he did so with a sort of tragic grandeur,
paying the price of his sin. The inevitable and deeply moral lesson of the
gangster picture was: crime may be profitable, glamorous, and lots of fun,
but in the end you pay the price with your life! The moral of our present
"tough" picture, if any can be discerned, is that life in the United States
of America in the year 1947 is hardly worth living at all.

It is not by chance that so many of the successful pictures of our time,
those which attract our highest professional talent and technical skill, are
"Whodunits" and thrillers in which the tension is entirely external and
mechanical, never organic. The "tough" movie, generally speaking, is
without personal drama and therefore without personal solution or catharsis of any kind. It almost looks as if the American people, turning
from the anxiety and shock of war, were afraid to face their personal problems and the painful situations of their national life.

One final, technical observation. For some years now the "Whodunit"
has achieved a special kind of quality in its preoccupation with genuine
atmosphere and realistic detail. Hitchcock started it with his English chase
pictures. Since then, the tradition of carefully selected, significant realism
has lent distinction to many of our American suspense pictures, e.g., *Double Indemnity, Murder, My Sweet, The House on 92nd Street,* and the Third
Avenue scenes of *Lost Weekend.* In this respect, *The Big Sleep* marks a violent and deplorable retrogression. Its southern California characters wan-
der through a fairyland of studio back lots and sound-stage exteriors as
unreal as the squares and mansions inhabited by the gentry in Metro-
Goldwyn-Mayer's British upper-class romances.

An Exhibitor Begs for "B's"

Arthur L. Mayer, for twenty years a theater exhibitor, both circuit and independent, owns the Rialto Theater in New York, which has recently terminated a long-time policy of exhibiting blood-and-thunder films exclusively, in order to show foreign films instead. With his partner, Joseph Burstyn, he has imported many memorable foreign films, among them *Open City*. Also active in documentary production, Mr. Mayer is a director of World Today, Inc., founded by John Grierson, as well as supervisor of Pilot Films, the Motion Picture Association's experimental educational project. During the war he served as Assistant Coördinator of the War Activities Committee of the Motion Picture Industry, as Film Consultant to the Secretary of War, and as Assistant to the Chairman of the American Red Cross.

. . . . .

FOR YEARS THE SELF-APPOINTED custodians of our morals—economic as well as social—have accused the motion picture industry of being a monopoly dominated by the producers and the distributors, who, by means of a nefarious device known as block booking, have compelled exhibitors, and therefore audiences, to consume bad films along with the good. Bad and good, in this kind of thinking, were synonymous respectively with cheap and expensive. If exhibitors were no longer compelled to book "B" pictures in order to obtain "A's"—so went the argument—the artistic and intellectual standards of the screen, now depressed by greedy movie magnates, could soar to rarified levels. Through a system of trial and error—government trials, and the errors of all concerned—this Utopia has at length been achieved. It now appears, however, that in destroying block booking our blockheaded reformers have also undermined the industry's primary expedient for progress—a fumbling, crawling expedient, but better than none. I refer to those "B" pictures which used to be produced, without stars, at costs of from $100,000 to $300,000. Untrammeled by either huge costs or the necessity of "protecting" an investment in a featured player, they provided a field for occasional experiments in thematic material, and a testing and training ground for new directors, writers, cameramen, and actors. Out of these "B's" came much that was appalling, but a saving fraction that made for progress and higher standards.

Even a spokespaper for the industry, the *Motion Picture Herald,* refers to the "necessity of stemming the current declining tide in quality." A reliable survey indicates that although 85,000,000 persons in the United States are in a financial position to go to the movies at least once a week, only 60,000,000 are regularly doing so. A potential audience of 25,000,000 is apparently so cold to the current movie merchandise that it has developed an immunity to advertising superlatives and all the ballyhoo of exploitation. This situation deeply disturbs the studio executives and they proceed to lose their heads completely. They cut their advertising budgets, reorganize their executive staffs, retaining the institutionalized dead weight, and discharge young employees with young ideas. Obviously, if moving pictures, both as commerce and as art, are to prosper, and if in spite of tripled production costs they are to meet successfully the challenge of the rapidly rising tide of television, outdoor night entertainment, and foreign film production, some new means for encouraging the spirit of innovation and initiative which dominated their early days must be devised.

It must be emphasized that the pioneers of the picture industry were experimentally minded. "Pants pressers," I have heard them derisively designated. If that were true—and it is not—they would have creased trousers horizontally, diagonally, or in any other unprecedented fashion calculated to excite public comment and to enhance private profit. To the casual observer they appeared mild, meek men. But in the spirit they were wild-eyed, irrepressible rebels. Their lofty ambitions were matched by their lively imaginations. They looked at a small animated picture in a box and saw the germ of the greatest mass medium of entertainment, art, and communication that man has ever known. They took the shadows of which Edison thought so slightingly that he declined to invest $150 in an application for foreign patents, and transformed them into the substance of a two-billion-dollar industry. They haunted nickelodeons and dreamed of marble palaces with regimented ushers, luxurious lounges, rising orchestra pits, and rising admission prices. The three-minute, jerky snatches of battleships and of girls climbing apple trees blossomed before their eyes into three-hour reconstructions of the classics, technically impeccable though slightly altered in content for mass consumption.

The legitimate theater from which at first they drew a sustenance of hack performers and creaky dramas faded into a satellite stage. Adolph Zukor would introduce Sarah Bernhardt in *Queen Elizabeth* to Main Street; Jesse Lasky bring Geraldine Farrar from the Diamond Horseshoe to the Bijou; Samuel Goldwyn cultivate Mary Garden; Carl Laemmle dream of the star system, which, in the hands of Metro and Paramount, would eventually darken his small Universal.

The unique nature of the new medium was explored by its exploiters. There were no shackling traditions. No one maintained that he knew exactly what the public wanted. No themes were too high-brow or radical; no actors too unknown, too passé, or too subversive; no technical difficulties insurmountable. Pictures ceased to be made in the streets (now, with critical acclaim, they are returning to them) and were staged on studio sets. Writers, cameramen, directors, actors, laboratory technicians—frequently one and the same—learned the rudiments of their trade. The director discovered how to guide the seeing eye of a mobile camera, and the cameraman how to manipulate it so as to intensify audience participation. Together, they explored a new world of double exposures, dissolves, strange camera angles, and pictorial composition to create mood and emphasis. Shamefaced actors, condescending between theatrical engagements to appear on the screen, acquired new techniques more realistic and more akin to pantomime than anything that had been required of them on the stage. The art of editing was discovered, with its fluid manipulation and interplay of sequences.

The story of how the experimental screen of thirty years ago was converted into the assembly-line production methods of today is far too long to recount here. Nonetheless—occasionally by intent, sometimes by accident, and frequently with considerable stealth on the part of all participants—pictures continued to emerge which strayed from the well-worn familiar paths and tried, in content or mechanics, to tell a new story, or to tell the old story in new terms. They cost little, as compared with present standards, and consequently a producer could afford now and then to give his craftsmen some leeway for innovation. He used them also to introduce and to train new writers, new directors, new actors, new cameramen, new editors, new musical directors. Occasionally, one of these experimental "B" pictures boomed into a box-office bonanza. *Hitler's Children,* which cost less than $150,000, proved a gold mine for Edward

Golden, its producer, and brought to its adaptor, Emmet Lavery, and its director, Edward Dmytryk, the mingled joys and tribulations of national reputations.

On the whole, guided not unnaturally by considerations of immediate income rather than cinematic progress, the exhibitors are little inclined to experiment with experimental pictures. They have found the moviegoing public pathetically apathetic to art and readier to spend its hard-earned cash for escapist entertainment than for significant studies of controversial issues or the miseries of mankind. Their zeal for the development of new screen personalities is tempered by the sad experiences of seeing their protégés of yesterday adorning the marquees and screens of their competitors.

Under the much-abused block-booking system the exhibitor had little choice. To get the good pictures he had to play the bad, or at any rate what he considered the bad. It cannot be denied that this system of buying films like fruit in a basket, good on top, bad at the bottom, encouraged the production and consumption of as vast an avalanche of triviality as has ever been inflicted upon a public, inoffensive or otherwise. With rare exceptions, producers, authors, directors, and performers of "B" pictures seemed to consider the assignment a chore below their personal dignity, to be performed perfunctorily, carelessly, and ineptly. They regarded themselves as copycats following the path of least resistance, rather than as bloodhounds on the trail of thrilling new audience scents or, more accurately, cents.

Block booking, however, served as a vehicle for a substantial amount of dramatic and technical innovation that proved of great value to subsequent "A" productions, and for the schooling and introduction to the public of many of the present brightest luminaries of the film firmament. It is doubtful if any five-million-dollar specials did more to advance the cause of good pictures than such comparatively inexpensive films as Von Sternberg's *Salvation Hunters,* Flaherty's *Moana,* Mamoulian's *Applause,* Vidor's *Our Daily Bread,* Dieterle's *Fog over Frisco,* Capra's *Flight,* Hecht and MacArthur's *The Scoundrel,* John Ford's *Lost Patrol,* Leo McCarey's *Make Way for Tomorrow,* Preston Sturges' *The Great McGinty,* Garson Kanin's *A Man to Remember,* Val Lewton's *The Curse of the Cat People,* and Adrian Scott and Edward Dmytryk's *Crossfire.*

It could be argued that a system of distribution which encouraged such provocative productions will be judged to have more than atoned for its sins. Certainly, no large industry can continue to prosper, no art to flourish, which fails to assure progress through constant experimentation and the encouragement of innovations. The majority of our leading directors and stars, from Porter and Pickford to Wyler and Van Johnson, were trained in the hard school of inexpensive films. Samuel Goldwyn, over the years the most consistent producer of high-class, high-cost pictures, cut his eye teeth on program features. Great cameramen like Gregg Toland, James Wong Howe, and Karl Freund had years of experimental work behind them before they achieved their present mastery of their art.

Nevertheless, the opponents of block booking, unmindful of such considerations, arose in their righteous wrath. Smiting right and left, they have felled that innocent bystander, the experimental picture. Under the recent court decree, block booking is banned. All pictures must be sold individually. Every film must stand or fall on its potential box-office merits. There must be competitive bidding by exhibitors for each production. Such an auction-block system can only increase the present pressure for star values, elaborate production, and huge advertising campaigns. The learned judges can now repair to their homes and over the teacups bewail the immaturity of the films and their lack of social content. They have devised a scheme not even dreamt of by government prosecutors or ladies' club lecturers, guaranteed temporarily to increase producers' profits and permanently to impede cinematic progress. Some new performers may be developed in limited numbers on the legitimate stage, or imported from abroad. Some competent authors, albeit untrained in the mysteries of film adaptation, may be tempted from the less lush fields of fiction and drama. But where or how shall we develop the directors, cameramen, and technicians of the future? How many producers will dare to experiment with new personalities, much less new themes, new backgrounds, and new techniques in pictures costing two million dollars and more?

The elimination of "B's" is not solely attributable to the ban on block booking. Hollywood, always prone to excess, has inflated even the inflation. In the past four years the prices of stories and materials, the remuneration of labor from the most expert to the least skilled, has risen so much that the cost of producing anything from a short to a super-duper has almost tripled. While expenses mounted and war prosperity brought longer runs, the studios produced fewer and fewer films. In 1941–1942 American movie companies made 534 pictures. In 1946–1947 there were approximately 375. Warner, Metro, Paramount, Universal have for the past few years shunned "B's" like the plague and associated themselves exclusively with high-budget pictures. They have indicated no change in their production plans for the immediate future. With declining production, employment fell during the past year alone from 30,000 to 21,000. For the first time in many years, 20th Century–Fox and several other major companies report that in a period longer than six months they have not signed a single actor or entertainer from Broadway. The men and women thrown out of work, the returning veterans who cannot find jobs, the newcomers who cannot even find a place to sleep, are in large measure young people vibrant with old visions now discarded by their disillusioned elders and with new ideas of how to achieve them. If the motion picture industry neglects to train these boys and girls, if it denies them an opportunity to develop and perfect their skills, it is ruining not only their futures but its own.

During the last year there have been, as there always will be, a few exceptions to the rule that experimentation and expensive pictures do not go hand in hand. MGM's *The Beginning or the End* represented a huge investment in an effort to dramatize, so that all who sit can see, the dangers inherent in atomic-bomb warfare. Its good intent was of the highest order, but it was soon playing on double features with a Skelton comedy billed above it. Eugene O'Neill's *Mourning Becomes Electra,* although its artistic merits may be the subject of acrimonious debate and its box-office fate the subject of universal agreement, is a lavish and laudable adventure on the part of RKO. Louis de Rochemont's *Boomerang,* like its predecessors *The House on 92nd Street* and *13 rue Madeleine,* proved a noteworthy effort to utilize documentary techniques, which made such rapid strides during the war, as a medium for exciting tales of current events. It was of such pictures that Michael Curtiz once said, "They make your hair stand on the edge of your seat." They discard the shackles of formal studio sets and go to the city streets for their backgrounds and even for nonprofessional players in minor roles. They may well serve to stimulate the long-sought production of pictures in areas remote from the Hollywood scene, particularly New York City, where the ferment of an international capital, combined with the presence of talented authors and actors, laboratory and studio facilities, make such ventures in independent production particularly propitious. Cost, however, as well as exclusively high-brow appeal, must be cautiously pruned. In the entire United States there are fewer than 100 theaters catering primarily to sophisticated, novelty-seeking audiences—"sure seaters," we used to call them because seats were always available. Foreign films, even those of merit, have seldom in the past grossed more than $50,000. A technically satisfactory two-reeler costs more than that today.

For many years, unit production, as opposed to the mass methods of major companies, has been the white hope of the intellectuals. The comparatively high standards of the Goldwyn, Selznick, and Disney organizations have in a measure justified faith in independent production. During the war, motivated more by the burden of high taxes than by a desire for freedom of self-expression, many directors and performers seceded from the major companies and formed their own producing units. Thus far they have done nothing to prove that their standards of skill and taste are superior to those of their former employers. Now, with the increased pressure of inflated costs and deflated loans, it would be unreasonably optimistic to expect them to venture far in experimental fields.

This is even truer of independents, like Monogram for example, which specialize primarily in inexpensive action pictures, westerns, and reproductions on a modest scale of major-company successes. A notable recent exception by a company which never before dallied with novelty was Republic's *Specter of the Rose*. Ben Hecht was given a free hand as writer, producer, and director to forage in new pastures. The verdict at the box office was negative, but it is reassuring to know that his sponsors are financing Orson Welles in the production of *Macbeth* on a short shooting schedule.

All in all, however, a dark cloud obscures the American silver screen. English, French, Italian, and Scandinavian pictures are surging forward, vibrating with new aspirations and newly acquired skills. Film lovers who have not yet seen the Italian picture *Paisan,* the French *Battle of the Rails,* or the Danish *Day of Wrath* have a treat in store for them. Unless domestic producers are prepared to return to the eager experimentalism of their early days, their leadership in the cinema world is threatened. Other industries spend millions in their research laboratories. General Electric and Standard Oil know that these millions are not wasted. Comparatively speaking, through renewed production of "B's," the motion picture industry could finance its research with little loss and with occasional surprising profits.

But the "B's" of the future cannot be the "B's" of the past. Like *Crossfire,* they must be formative rather than formula. They must experiment with new subjects, new attitudes, new locales. They must make no assumptions about public taste except that, like the tide, it flows and ebbs even when it is least apparent. They must welcome new talents and new faces, some of which will eventually become the best-loved talents and faces in the world. Above all, they must be made by men—and there are hundreds of them in Hollywood and elsewhere—who are proud to prove that, although handicapped by small budgets, they have the instinct and the craftsmanship and, above all, the passion, to illuminate the road to the future.

A Word of Caution for the Intelligent Consumer of Motion Pictures

Franklin Fearing, professor of psychology at the University of California at Los Angeles, is a member of the editorial board of the *Quarterly of Film, Radio, and Television*. He is directing the research of graduate students in the fields of social psychology and the problems of human communication. During the summer of 1951 he conducted graduate courses at Columbia University, and spoke at the Consumer's Union Conference at Vassar College. The following article is based on the talk Dr. Fearing delivered at the conference. Both his address and one given at the same meeting by Dallas W. Smythe will be published in a forthcoming volume, *Consumer Problems in a Period of International Tension,* Consumer's Union of the United States.

. . . . .

DALLAS W. SMYTHE has discussed in some detail the problems relating to the consumer's interest in television and radio sets and in programming. While I am assigned the topic of films, I think almost everything I have to say holds with equal force for radio and television. There are differences, but from the point of view of the social scientist, these are the mass media of communication, and the factors we are interested in are found in all of these media.

Dr. Smythe has implied that you are interested, as intelligent consumers, in better programs. I want to say something about some of the problems that come up in trying to decide what precisely we mean by the term "better programs" or "better films." I can't offer you any criteria so that you will know whether you are going to like the next movie that you go to see. The testing that researchers do in this area is quite different from the kind of testing that Consumer's Union does with respect to tomato juice or vacuum cleaners. It has a different implication. It is called effects analysis and is mainly concerned with the *impact* of films and radio programs on people. What effects, if any, do the contents of these programs have on human beings, on their attitudes, their beliefs, and more con-

cretely on their behavior? How do people react to films and the other
mass media? What role do these media play in their lives? What purposes
do they serve in society?

The answers to these questions so far as systematic research at present
can answer them will not tell us directly the differences between "good"
and "bad" films, nor will they give us anything in the nature of a list of
the Best Buys, so familiar to Consumer's Union subscribers, in films and
TV programs. I think we should be clear on one point. The questions
with which we are here concerned can only be answered, even tentatively,
by carefully designed research conducted by trained investigators. Social
causation is always complex. A seemingly unimpeachable connection between stimulus A and social effect B may turn out to be only apparent.
The armchair *dicta* of even the most intelligent and sophisticated observers can only give us hypotheses which carefully planned research may endeavor to test. This research is quite tedious and undramatic, but as the
results accumulate, they may give us a basis for understanding the role,
and hence a policy regarding the control of the great mass media of communication in our society.

Many people have strong feelings and beliefs about these problems. It is
here that the professional and amateur viewers-with-alarm, good people
all of them surely, tend to get high blood pressure. They witness a film,
for example, which has a great deal of violence in it, or which depicts
crime, or they listen to a radio program which is filled with violence, or
crude slapstick, and vulgarity, or they watch Johnny listening, and they
get dreadfully alarmed about the effects *on Johnny*. And the people who
are more vocal in this matter tend to implement their alarm. They set up
campaigns to do something about it. Currently a favorite target for such
activities in many communities has been the comic strip. It is another
mass medium of communication, and what I have to say will apply equally
well to it. Periodically there is a wave of interest in the supposed evil effects of comic strips, and good people form committees to do something
about them.

I am sure you are familiar with this kind of attitude, and probably most
of us one time or another have shared this concern, and a feeling that
something ought to be done. We don't like what we hear or see on radio
or TV programs and we feel that their effects must be bad, that they are
probably responsible for the increase in juvenile deliquency or the divorce

rate, or whatever social ill about which at the moment we happen to be concerned. And if we are vocal and articulate, we find it very easy to set in motion the machinery of reform.

Back of these attitudes and activities are some interesting assumptions, assumptions which need careful analysis, and assumptions about which we need to have a considerable body of data before we are ready to organize a committee or try to pass a law or try to get the local police force on the job. Let us examine some of them.

The basic assumption seems to be that there is a simple causal connection between the content of a film or TV program and human behavior and attitudes. In other words, Johnny might become a delinquent or do something very, very bad after seeing a similar act on the TV screen.

The assumption that there is a simple relationship between the mass media and the behavior and attitudes and beliefs of human beings needs careful testing. It is here that we confront a paradoxical situation.

On the one hand, on general grounds, it seems that films, for example, have had a tremendous impact on human culture all over the world. It is almost trite to say that the content of films, as determined in a very small area in Los Angeles County, in one way or another has affected people all over the world, has changed their interests, habits, and even moral standards. If it is true that films can have such far-reaching effects, surely they could also cause Johnny to become a drug addict or to commit a crime, or, at the very least, put wrong ideas in his head.

On the other hand—and here is the seeming paradox that I want to explore with you this evening—research, conducted as carefully as we now know how to conduct it, reveals that the effects of these media—films and radio, especially films—on human attitudes and behavior is unexpectedly slight.

I want to proceed cautiously here because I am very conscious of the difficulties of conducting rigorous research in this area. It may be that our inability to demonstrate clear-cut effects of films or radio means that our methods of investigation need to be sharpened, and that with better procedures we might find more effects than now appear to be the case. This important qualification underlies all that I have to say.

Let us look at some of these researches. I think they might interest you from the point of view of their methods as well as their results. Perhaps the most elaborate study of the impact of films on human beings yet undertaken is the investigation of the effects of films used by the army in World War II. The film program of the army probably represents the most extensive use of films for concrete educational purposes yet attempted. Films were used by both the army and navy at every step in their training program as educational devices.

There were two types of films. One group was called "nuts and bolts" films, and the other "orientation" films. The nuts and bolts films were concerned with teaching specific skills. There were films on the thousand-and-one specialized activities which men in service had to learn.

The orientation films, on the other hand, are of special interest to us, because they resemble the Hollywood commercial product a little more closely. As the term implies, the orientation films used in the army were concerned with modifying the attitudes, beliefs, and motives of the individuals who were exposed to them. The best example of the orientation films, some of which you may have seen, were the "Why We Fight" series. "The Battle of Britain," "The Battle of Russia," and "The Battle of China" are three notable examples.

These films were magnificently done. They were made by the best-trained film people, writers and directors and so on, in Hollywood, and that means from the technical point of view probably the best that can be found anywhere. These are magnificent documentaries, interesting, dramatic, exciting.

The general intent of these films was to interpret the goals of the war to the soldier, to increase his confidence in our allies, and to intensify his hostility toward the enemy—in a word to strengthen his motivation to fight. The general method was to marshal the facts in the most cinematically effective and dramatic form, and allow the soldier to draw his own conclusions. This is, of course, a widely accepted method and is the basis of much educational procedure.

The analysis of the effects of these films has recently been published in one of the four volumes called *Studies in Social Psychology in World War II.*[1] Volume III, called "Experiments on Mass Communication," reports the results of all the tests of the effects of these films.

Now what are the results?

1. C. I. Hovland, A. Lunsdaine, and F. D. Sheffield, *Experiments on Mass Communications,* Vol. III (Princeton University Press, 1949).

In the first place, the nuts and bolts films, the ones designed to teach skills, as tested in this and similar investigations, showed up very well; they were successful as adjuncts in the process of training soldiers in these various specific skills and imparting specific information. But, when the test results of the effects of the orientation films on general attitudes and motivations were carefully analyzed they were found, on the whole, not very great. That is to say, when opinions and beliefs were tested in various ways before exposure to the film, and then retested afterward, there was surprisingly little change in the direction intended by the makers of the film. The most definite effects were on the amount of factual knowledge and on opinions specifically covered by the film. The films had very little effect on opinions or attitudes of a more general nature. In the matter of the men's motivation to serve as soldiers—one of the primary objectives of the orientation film program—the tests showed no effects.

An interesting exception to these general results was the so-called sleeper effect. It was found that in some groups, although there was no detectable effect on opinions and presumably on behavior, immediately after the film, there were effects that could be detected some nine weeks later, especially in individuals shown by tests to be already predisposed to accept a particular opinion.

If you are concerned with carrying the torch for films as a means of affecting people's opinions and motivations, the sleeper effect should give you some support. If it turns out that this delayed effect is especially marked on the individual's generalized attitudes rather than on specific attitudes, it will be an important finding indeed. This will be true even if this effect is restricted to individuals already predisposed in the direction of the film content.

I have briefly, much too briefly, summarized some of the results of a very extensive research on the effects of films, especially on attitudes and opinions. And bear in mind that it is with regard to this area that many people are most nervous. They fear that a film showing violence, as I have said, may make people tolerant of violence. In other words, they assume that people, or at least certain people, passively accept whatever is presented to them on the screen or in the TV and radio program. While it is true that we cannot translate directly to the Hollywood commercial product the results of these investigations on a particular kind of film shown under the conditions that existed in the war situation, nevertheless they do have some bearing on our problem. They suggest that people do not come to any kind of communication situation with blank minds, and that attitudes and opinions are perhaps more resistant than we had thought.

There are other researches that bear on this last point. I will describe very briefly an investigation of a more specific sort which was undertaken at the University of California by Dr. Daniel Wilner working as a graduate student under my direction.[2]

You may have seen the film called *Home of the Brave*. It is an excellent film, and is, in fact, the first film which broke the taboo that had existed for a long time in Hollywood regarding films in which the problem of the Negro and Negro-white relations was the central theme. It is a dramatic, even a melodramatic film, the protagonist of which is a Negro soldier.

We were interested in finding out how individuals who by various tests are known to be highly prejudiced against Negroes react to this film, as contrasted with individuals at the other end of the scale who have very little or no prejudice. In other words, in this type of experiment we deliberately selected individuals who have known but differing attitudes toward the major themes of the communication content, and we asked ourselves the question: How do they handle communicated material which is contrary to their already-accepted beliefs?

In viewing this film the high-prejudice people are put, psychologically speaking, on a spot because its basic theme is, from their point of view, an affront. It exposes frankly and dramatically many of the stereotypes and beliefs about Negroes which they have accepted and now hold very close to their hearts. So you might expect—well, what would you expect?

We found that to an amazing degree the high-prejudice individuals were enabled in terms of their patterns of belief and stereotypes to revise the content of the film and see in it or select from it that which they wanted to see. That is, if the film may be said to have a "message" or basic theme, these people did not get it, or got it in a distorted form. For example, some might have found, in the collapse of the Negro soldier, reaffirmation of their belief in the inferiority of the Negro race.

2. Daniel Wilner, "Attitude as a Determinant of Perception in the Mass Media of Communications: Reactions to the Motion Picture *Home of the Brave*" (unpublished Ph.D. diss., 1950, on file in the library of the University of California, Los Angeles campus).

This is probably not true of all the high-prejudice people. There is undoubtedly a very small hard-core group that are intellectually aware of their prejudice, and are able to watch a film of this type with a superior smile; they reject it *in toto*.

Findings of this sort mean that people can modify, or, to use our psychological jargon, restructure material of this type to suit their needs and beliefs. This perhaps explains why this film, in spite of its supposedly "controversial" character, was a box-office success in the South as well as in other parts of the country.

From this we cannot conclude with certainty what its effects have been on attitudes about Negros or Negro-white relations. It may be that people can see this film, and come out with their prejudices intact, or, perhaps, actually strengthened. These patterns of evasion, as they are called, are numerous and subtle and undoubtedly have nullified many a well-intended program of social reëducation.

Let us look at another investigation, again of the effects of a Hollywood film.[3] During the war a film called *Tomorrow the World* was produced. It was based on the successful Broadway play of the same name. *Tomorrow the World* is the story of a dreadful teenage Nazi boy who is brought to this country and to the home of an American college professor. Here he endeavors to Nazify his companions, upsets the whole household of the college professor, and even tries to wreck the latter's approaching marriage with a Jewish girl. At the end we find this boy, Emil, in the hands of the police.

The question posed by the film is what can you do with Emil? Can he be reëducated? Can German youth be reëducated? In 1942 these were, as they still are, pressing questions.

This film was shown by Doctors Wiese and Cole to about 4,000 children ranging from the fourth grade to the eighth grade. Some of the children were from very superior homes. Others came from a very depressed or semislum area. And the third group were several hundred children from middle-class homes in Salt Lake City. I haven't space to describe the details of the methods used by Doctors Wiese and Cole. In general their purpose was to give the children an opportunity to tell what they got out

3. M. Wiese and S. Cole, "A Study of Children's Attitudes and the Influence of a Commercial Motion Picture," *Journal of Psychology*, XXI (1946), 151–171.

of the film and especially to answer such questions as "What would *you* do with Emil?" "Do you think Emil should be punished?" (Remember this film is about a boy and his relations with other children as well as with adults.)

So these children had a chance to react to a number of questions before and after seeing the film. There were some very striking differences among the different social groups. The children from the depressed area in Los Angeles—a large proportion of whom were Negroes as well as representatives of other ethnic groups—were much more punitive and realistic in their attitude toward Emil. Also, they were not shocked by his ruthless and gangster-like behavior as were the children from the middle- and upper-class homes. It is a type of behavior with which they had some familiarity.

The children coming from socially and economically superior homes had a more detached, almost philosophic attitude. They—especially the children from middle-class homes—tended to see Emil and his problem in terms of the stereotyped, idealized formulas regarding democracy and the American way of life which they had learned in school. The upper-class children were especially reactive to Emil's anti-Semitism, which the film brought out very strongly. A considerable proportion of the children in this group came from Jewish homes.

Other findings of the study bear out these trends. The point is that there was much variation in what this film meant to groups of children coming from differing social and economic backgrounds. What they got from the film was in part conditioned by their socioeconomic background.

Similar findings were obtained in a recently reported study of the effects of a non-Hollywood film called *Don't Be a Sucker*.[4] This film was made by the Army Signal Corps during World War II and was specifically designed to reduce intergroup prejudice. In fictional form it endeavors to expose the dangerous and anti-democratic purposes of rabble rousers who try to stimulate hatred toward various minority groups. The investigators, Eunice Cooper and Helen Dinerman, planned a research designed to discover the extent to which the "messages" of the film came through to audiences of high school students and adults. Briefly summarized, they

4. E. Cooper and H. Dinerman, "Analysis of the Film 'Don't Be a Sucker': A Study in Communication," *Public Opinion Quarterly,* XV (1951), 243–264.

found that selective perception operated: that is, that individuals reacted in terms of their predispositions. Those whose attitudes favored the messages of the film accepted them, those whose attitudes did not were able to evade or misperceive them. These misinterpretations, or "boomerang" effects, frequently mean that a basic message planned by the makers of the film is completely nullified.

Again, these results seem to document the notion that the impact of the mass media of communication cannot be conceived in simple cause-and-effect terms. We must revise our view that whatever is "in" a film or radio program will somehow inevitably come through and have a predetermined effect on those exposed to it.

There is one other type of research that I want to refer to, and this gets us over into radio. These are investigations concerned with the soap opera. Most people, especially "intelligent consumers," never listen to them. They seem trivial and trite. But they do have a large listening audience among housewives. The researcher asks the question: What function do these programs have for their listeners? The investigations on this problem indicate that soap operas serve a variety of socially meaningful functions for the housewives who listen. Broadly speaking, they furnish her with vicarious experience. This may seem strange to sophisticated people, but, strange or not, the housewife sees in the soap opera some reflection of her own problems, and she gets some assistance on her own problems in the solutions or the attempts at solution which are presented in the soap opera itself.

This is a kind of finding about the effects which has a slightly more, shall we say, positive tone than the findings that I have been describing. But, even here the relationship between program content and response is not a simple one; it is not an effect in which the ideas that are presented via the program are projected in some direct way on people's minds with direct effects on attitudes and behavior. The effects are selective, and are dependent on already existing needs.

This, then, is roughly and sketchily the picture of some of the research results to date on this enormously complicated problem of effects of the mass media of communication.

What can we say about them? What does this add up to? Well, it is very hard to formulate any broad generalization that will make all of this rather contradictory material fall into place. We still have the fact—if it is a fact—that Hollywood films have an enormous social impact on people all over the world. I sometimes wonder if these alleged world-wide effects have not been exaggerated. The fact that millions of people all over the world go to these films, and that their culture and way of living is changing or seems to be changing in the direction of being more like us—at least as we are represented in films—does not demonstrate a simple causal relation. Other factors may be operating.

In any event the exact nature of this impact is not clear. It may on occasion be highly specific. If shiny motor cars are driven by glamorous males or females in movies, it may well increase the demand for American automobiles in Calcutta but not necessarily in Timbuktu. In Timbuktu they may believe motor cars are inhabited by evil spirits. In many oriental countries public embracing and kissing is regarded as indecent and such scenes have to be deleted from our films. But if this taboo is disappearing, it does not necessarily mean that Hollywood films alone are responsible. My point is that because the audience for the mass media is large it is not amorphous and faceless, ready to accept anything projected on it.

The researches I have reviewed here in general support this. The viewer and listener are dynamic participants in the situation. They react *on* the content presented rather than reacting *to* it. *How* they react is determined by many factors *only one of which is the content of the film itself.* This is not equivalent to saying that film and radio have no effects. Rather, it raises the much more complicated question of what effects under what conditions.

What does this mean so far as the intelligent consumer is concerned? What should he do?

I think we ought to see, if the results of these investigations have any meaning, that a certain note of caution has been sounded. Certain caution is called for before we launch ourselves on a program of immediate change of film and radio content or TV content because we are fearful that it is going to have certain effects, presumably effects which we disapprove.

I should point out that once you launch yourself along the path of regulating the content of films or other mass media, you are, if you do not watch out, going directly toward some form of censorship, some form of continuous and permanent control. This may, of course, be what you intend. If so it raises a number of thorny and very complicated problems, the chief of which is: Who is to decide what the "good" content is? Who is to be the censor?

We say we want "good" films, and "good" radio programs, but we are pretty vague as to what we mean by "good." Sometimes I think we mean by "good," films and radio programs which are *not disturbing to us.*

I have been impressed by the fact that people who are shocked by the radio programs or the films or the comic strips, never seem to be afraid that they themselves are going to be harmed. It is always somebody else who is in danger; it is Johnny, or the people on the other side of the tracks, about whose morals they are fearful. I wonder if they are not projecting their own disturbance with the problems that are sometimes raised in these films.

Take the matter of violence. It is the depiction of violence, I find, that is upsetting to many of my friends who go to movies occasionally. They think there is "too much" violence in films and radio programs. They think this has bad effects, not on them of course, but on children or other people whose moral fiber is presumably weaker than theirs. We live in a world in which violence, both individual and mass, is the rule and not the exception. In fact, the amount of real violence in the world is considerably greater than all the violence that will ever be shown in films. It may be that violence in films is actually a rather pale reflection of the violence in the real world. It may be, also, that people who are upset by it are really suffering from certain guilt feelings. They are uneasily aware of this violent world and perhaps, in some degree, of their own responsibility for it. It is easy to reduce the uneasiness which we all feel in the present turbulent world by blaming films. This is a scapegoating mechanism with which social psychologists are already familiar.

But to come back to the problem of improving films and the other mass media. I do not wish to be understood as saying that films should not be better than they are, or that it is impossible to have critical standards for evaluating them. I am convinced that most intelligent consumers of films could play a more effective role in this matter if, in addition to moral indignation, they had a clearer understanding of what they have a right to expect from films, radio, and TV. Conceivably this might be achieved by a course on how to evaluate motion pictures. Such a course would sketch the historical development of the film and present information about the more important technical devices which distinguish the films from other media of communication. Here the intelligent consumer would learn something about the styles and methods of different directors and screen writers. These differ as do the methods of creative artists working in other media. If we wish to make our approvals and disapprovals effective, we should be able to recognize and reward those who do a good job.

Most important, such a course should include something about the psychological and social role of drama and storytelling in human society. We should understand some of the human needs which are served by these agencies. Such a course should give the intelligent consumer a basis for demanding not just "better" films, but films which deal significantly with significant problems, and with no loss of their entertainment quality. It is not a question of eliminating a particular kind of action in a film that happens to disturb us, but a question of whether the disturbing action is placed in some sort of meaningful context so that we have a better understanding that makes a movie or story or play exciting and hence, in the real sense of a much-overworked word, entertaining. In this sense, if motion pictures are to achieve their full potential, they will be more rather than less disturbing because they will deal with disturbing problems. This will be achieved not by emasculating films through hampering restrictions, but by demanding that they deal honestly with every kind of human problem.

But with or without special courses, I have indicated some of the reasons why I think the intelligent consumer should proceed with caution over a terrain which is full of unsuspected pitfalls and much of which isn't even mapped. I don't believe the great mass media stand so much in need of policing as they do of intelligent analysis, and moral indignation is not enough.

There's Really No Business Like Show Business

Jay E. Gordon is a former associate editor of the *Hollywood Spectator,* a position he left at the beginning of World War II to become director of the Army Training Film Center in San Francisco. He had previously been active in the exhibition and distribution of motion pictures, but is at present a free-lance motion picture critic.

.....

MORE AND MORE THESE DAYS, we read that to improve the motion picture business we have only to produce better pictures. A good show can't miss, we are assured. This is the opinion of the majority of theater operators, who, unfortunately, are sufficiently preoccupied with taxes, labor contracts, real estate values, and popcorn consumption to find themselves lacking the time for study necessary to provide a genuine understanding of the reasons behind the failing box office. Having no control over the content of the pictures he plays, the theater operator is loath to accept any responsibility for low grosses; all the services he provides and the methods he employs to sell them are uniform throughout the year; therefore he can deduce only that money-making pictures are good pictures, and money-losing pictures are bad pictures. If his theater consistently loses money, he believes that he has been subjected to a series of particularly bad pictures. If the pictures could improve, he insists, he would make more money.

I submit that the motion picture industry is failing to observe in full one of the basic precepts of modern business—specialization.

When a producer wants to show a scene involving the interior of a submarine, does he merely ask his cast and crew if anyone knows how the interior of a submarine should look? He does not. He asks the navy to send him a submarine specialist to advise on the matter—and he usually takes the expert's advice. When the producer wants to show an English courtroom, he calls in an expert consultant. When he wants to show an Egyptian tomb, he call for an Egyptologist. But when he is finished with his film and is ready to sell it, does he call in a specialist? No. He goes to the publicity department, and instructs them as to methods he wants employed in promoting the film. From this misguidance, together with instructions from the home office, the exploitation and publicity departments set to work fabricating an advertising campaign for the film. Right there, the ball is dropped, and a touchdown is left to pure chance.

From this stamping press, whose dies never change, comes the showman's guide, the pressbook. From lack of time or courage, most theater operators look no further than the pages of this hackneyed handbook, and thus individual initiative in showmanship never gets a try. The pressbook is full of words and various sizes of the two or more thematic illustrations. It has ideas on tying the picture to the brands of sport shirt sold locally, and contains a dozen or so publicity stories to be handed out to the local papers. These stories strike the editors with much the same effect as a damp flapjack in the face. If the editor does not print one of these literary gems once a week, the theaterman tells him that the paper is not being fair. So there it rests. The publicity and advertising men of the film company, if they have any talent, are frustrated by insistent directions from both the artistic and the business sides of the company to the point where they merely turn out one more pressbook, just like the last one— just like the last thousand. On the other end, the theaterman relies on only this factory-stamped pressbook and his conscience, neither of which seems to be a ticket seller.

In this country we have a good many business pursuits. One of these is known fondly as "the advertising game." Just as successful businessmen turn to tax consultants, accountants, and lawyers for specialized services, so do they turn to advertising agencies to provide the machinery of selling. Advertising agencies have but one mission: to disseminate carefully prepared information to the general public through tested media in a manner conducive to action. The *Encyclopaedia Britannica,* in defining the functions of an advertising agency, lists market research, indoctrination of salesmen, preparation of written and pictorial matter, liaison between the advertiser and the media, and assistance to the advertiser in cultivation of the good will of the trade and of the public. The efforts of the advertising agency spell the success of many a business enterprise. A motion picture production company—including the studios, the home office, and the board of directors—surely qualifies as a business enterprise.

But show business is different! True, at the present writing and for most of the past, it can be agreed that there is really no business quite like show business. Basically, however, the film industry is trying to sell a commodity to the public. And, in its attempt to do so, it is passing over one of the most potent forces in modern business—the advertising agency.

There is a little business in all arts, but little art in business, it has been said. Occasionally there appears a businessman of whom many say: "Now, there is an artist." Such a man is Henry J. Kaiser, whose business operations are conducted with such skill and finesse that he has been described as a true business artist. When Mr. Kaiser sets out to sell a commodity, he gathers around him the advisers and specialists on his staff, then calls in representatives of the advertising agency he has selected. They discuss the product and they discuss objectives. The producers offer whatever ideas or limitations they have in mind concerning media, emphasis, or theme, then decide upon and allocate a budget. From that point on, the method of attaining objectives with the product is left to the specialized skills, arts, and experiences of the advertising agency.

Now let us take an example. Suppose one of Mr. Kaiser's engineers says, "Mr. Kaiser, every auto made these days is identical with every other one of the same make and model, except for minor differences in color or accessories; therefore no one can say his Kaiser sedan is really tailored to suit him and him alone. Now, Mr. Kaiser, I suggest we tailor the steering wheel to each owner's preference. People's hands are of different size and shape. Half the people who drive find the feel of the steering wheel awkward. So if we ship our cars to the dealers minus the steering wheels, then give each dealer a kit for molding the wheel in plastic to fit the owner's hands, we can truthfully say each car is form-fitted, tailor-made. When the car changes hands, a new owner can get a new fitting for a couple of dollars. It will be revolutionary." After a meeting of minds among engineers and stylists, and a "dry run" test at two or three locations ("sneak previews"), Mr. Kaiser will call together the group mentioned above and the advertising agency will go to work.

The agency will have to sell something old, transportation; something already widely advertised, the current-model Kaisers; plus something new, the hand-molded steering wheel. They will have tradition to buck, will have to disprove in advance the skeptics who are confident that such an idea is impossible or at least unnatural. The advertising campaign will have to sell a product, an idea, yet with it a basic service. They will be successful, of course, and after that all cars will have form-fitted steering wheels.

The film industry has a basic service to sell—entertainment. It has the latest models to show—current themes, popular stars, and noted directors. It also has something special each time—a specific story to tell. The film company may be said to be highly skilled in the business of putting a specific story on celluloid, but, when it comes to selling the product, can it honestly claim to be more efficient and qualified in the advertising game than the advertising professionals? Not unless it wishes to claim more business acumen than is possessed by Henry J. Kaiser.

Advertising in show business has not come along very far since the advent of the walking billboard. Originally the advertisement of a show consisted of a poster on the wall beside the door to the theater. Then someone put a poster on each side of the door. Later a man was hired to carry a sandwich sign back and forth in front of the theater; then he ventured all over the neighborhood. Still later, the same format as the poster beside the theater door appeared in the newspapers. Outdoor advertising, in terms of posters at conspicuous locations over the town, expanded the original poster idea. This is in terms of live theater. Only in recent years have magazine or radio advertisements been employed for specific attractions.

Naturally, motion picture advertisements followed the format employed by theaters. Some fifty years before the birth of the movies, a man with the gift for what we call showmanship came along and added flamboyance to advertising in the form of the brass band, the parade, and general noise making. The influence of Barnum on advertising in show business cannot be overlooked. "Give them a free sample," Barnum said, "and they will flock to pay for more." His circus parade stopped at intervals to permit acrobats, clowns, and elephants to perform in the street. Here was the beginning of our "preview trailers."

Somewhere along the line of evolution from the single poster beside the theater door to the four-color spread in today's multi-million circulation weekly, the showman-advertiser has dropped the ball. He has retained the ridiculous "full list of credits" but he has forgotten the basic qualities a good advertisement must possess. The good advertisement should be honest, direct, attractive, should arouse interest, and should compel action.

Let us take a film and examine its advertising—a hypothetical film—in order that everyone can say: "I know whom he means."

Our film is called "The Jungle and Mr. Smith." It is a cavalcade of action involving the Smith family in the Philippines from the time of Dewey's capture of Manila until the date of Philippine independence. It is a patriotic story of American aid to a backward Oriental colony culminating in the latter's rise to the stature of a nation among nations, told as a background to a human story of an American family who helped make it possible. The story has romance, children growing up, humor, action in the forms of typhoons, earthquakes, volcanic eruptions, floods, life, death, all the elements necessary to make a fascinating two hours. The film has been made by a top studio, in color, with a top producer, director, and writer, three top stars, and good supporting cast. Incidental to plot there is some crime, punishment, adultery, disloyalty, and divorce in the picture. All in all, however, it is a film to make Americans proud they are Americans, and to make Filipinos grateful to the Americans for their help. Yes, it could be called propaganda. Russian critics would attack it. The *Daily Worker* would warn against it. It would have all the elements for success.

Now, let us look at the pressbook. Most prominent in the pressbook, of course, is a reproduction of the 24-sheet, the highway billboard poster. In full colors, the poster would feature a native girl, scantily clad, lying in a rice field, looking up at a bare-chested American, a pistol strapped to his side. He would be appraising her. In the middleground a water buffalo and a nipa hut on stilts, with a volcano erupting in the background. Across the top would be the caption: "Tropical passion in the torrid Philippines!" Small letters: "Tantamount Pictures present." . . . Big letters: "The Jungle and Mr. Smith" . . . "starring Gary Potter . . . Helen Doyle . . . Ben Sutton." Small letters: "Color by Talknocolor . . . a John Eastman production . . . with George Gillette . . . Dorothy Funk . . . Mark Fowler . . . Edwin Carton . . . Mary Douglass. . . . Produced by Henry Wadsworth . . . directed by John Eastman . . . written for the screen by James Collins . . . from an original story by Carlos Felipe Rodriguez."

Yes, that is a highway poster. Even at twenty-five miles per hour, a person riding past such a poster could have it in view for no more than one or two seconds. The driver of a car could hazard no more than a half-second glance away from his driving vigil. Obviously the last 50 words of that 62-word poster are wasted.

Traditionally, the 24-sheet sets the style of the advertising prepared for a film. All newspaper and magazine advertisements are merely variations of the format and content of the 24-sheet. So it is that everything that follows is based on a poster that is basically wrong in the first place.

Now, let us look at the five qualities of a good advertisement. Honesty comes first. The minor incident of infidelity referred to in the film has no place in its advertising, not in honest advertising, at any rate. Instead of "Tropical passion in the torrid Philippines," the catch line should be "See a nation rise from the jungle," or a similarly significant comment. The illustration should show a white man helping a faltering native to his feet. The title and two or three names could be added, but no more wordage. That would help in being direct. As to being attractive, this can come only by the employment of art. Art is created by an artist. Posters designed for 99 per cent of our films are not artistic, they are merely trite rearrangements of type surrounded by pictorial illustration. How many posters created for films have been reproduced in the *Commercial Art Annual*, published by the trade to honor distinguished commercial art? I counted only a handful since 1932. And in the book, *The One Hundred Greatest Advertisements—Who Wrote Them and What They Did*, by Julian Lewis Watkins (1949), the only advertisement even remotely connected with the entertainment industry was one for Lucky Strike cigarettes featuring Constance Talmadge, and that appeared in 1929. It might be pointed out also that in the *Commercial Art Annual*, practically all the film posters shown were foreign-created. The only American picture advertisement was a newspaper layout for Warner's *The Story of Louis Pasteur*, which cannot exactly be called a current release.

In simple language, motion picture advertising is dishonest. Batten, Barton, Durstine, and Osborne do not make dishonest claims for products they promote. Neither do Young and Rubicam. Advertising agencies, for all their high-tension, super-vitaminized campaigns, have perhaps surprisingly high ethical standards. For instance, if the Motion Picture Association wished to engage Young and Rubicam to conduct a campaign promoting motion pictures to the detriment of television, a war of one medium against the other, the agency would either refuse to accept the motion picture account or it would withdraw from all contracts now held with television accounts. This is known as unilateral representation, a basic principle in advertising.

Under the general heading of dishonest advertising, there should be placed the almost universal inclination to drape every film poster with the female bosom or the unclad limb. Obviously if every film had these members as its major motivating factors and most significant theme material, the blue laws soon would put the cinema in the Smithsonian Institution along with the stocks, the Iron Maiden, and other immoral machinery.

A classic of advertising stupidity was the particularly sad experience of the British Technicolor film *Colonel Blimp,* a warm, humorous, human story of an externally stuffy old man. Instead of leaning heavily on the art of David Low, the cartoonist who created Colonel Blimp and made him Britain's favorite, those responsible for advertising this picture in America chose to highlight all the posters and mats with a bosomy girl in a suggestive pose. The people who paid to see what was advertised were disappointed, for many were not of a temperament to enjoy the good colonel; but, more's the pity, the people who could have enjoyed Colonel Blimp were repelled by the advertising, and did not venture into the theater. Yes, it was a flop over here, but the picture was a success at home where more sensible and honest advertising was employed.

"Replacement or Refund of Money Guaranteed by Good Housekeeping if Not as Advertised Therein," proclaims a seal common to all sorts of products. Would anyone dare to make such a claim in reference to motion picture advertising?

An almost frightening spectacle is a high motion picture official stating: "We must get back to good, old-time, loud, slam-bang, ballyhoo showmanship." He goes on to insist that Barnum was right, and all that. He means that in the old days many films so promoted were huge successes. What he forgets is that in most cases success came when that kind of advertising was appropriate to the attraction, and people found themselves receiving the goods as advertised. Barnum was right to offer a free show in the streets with his circus parade when advertising "the greatest show on earth," but Mr. Barnum handled Jenny Lind in a somewhat different manner.

Every motion picture produced is a thing apart, a separate and distinguishable entity, an isolated artistic creation, related to others only by virtue of the medium it employs. Each motion picture should be sold as a separate article of commerce, advertised in accordance with its own merits and within the bounds of established rules of salesmanship pertinent to creations of art. If this appears to be difficult in these days of double bills, my answer is the same as it was the first time I ever heard of double bills: "To the devil with the practice!" People go to the theater to see a particular film, not two particular films. With television time gobbling up celluloid by the supersonic mile, producing companies now can afford to concentrate on making fewer pictures without contributing to the unemployment rolls. People can stay at home and see a "second feature," so it will become increasingly fruitless to try to sell a "second feature" away from home.

To set forth some courses of action which would improve the box office financially, I submit the following to the industry.

Place basic motion picture advertising in the hands of people who know advertising, markets, media, sales techniques—the American advertising agencies whose efforts have made the world conscious of Coca-Cola, Chesterfields, Ivory Soap, and the beer that made Milwaukee famous.

Permit only honest advertising. If bare legs and a plunging neckline are motivating factors in a film, employ them in the advertising. If not, employ whatever really represents the film honestly. Permit genuine graphic artists to create poster art, with a minimum of restriction from either studio or home office.

Advertise each film in a manner harmonious with its singular character, plot, intent, and action. If the film was made to appeal to the hundred million Americans who love dogs, it should be sold to those people to the exclusion, if necessary, of those who despise dogs.

In coöperation with all studios, theater chains, and distributors, advertise the lasting values of motion pictures by constant, consistent, institutional advertising.

Advertise not only the stars—who come and go too fast to have any lasting value—but the producers, directors, writers, and the production companies themselves. Identify the executives as capable businessmen. Promote the producers as experienced, well-educated, sensitive creative artists. Promote the directors who have been performing with distinction for twenty and thirty years (while top stars have come and gone by the hundreds), and promote the writers who have been at it all their lives. Rid the public of the notion that anyone can produce or direct or write a motion picture. Promote the fact that competence in these arts and sciences comes just as hard as competence in engineering, surgery, finance, law. Put a solid foundation under the motion picture industry.

There is no "lost audience," there is only a lost habit. Employ every medium to sell motion pictures as "the place to go." Institutional advertising should be aimed at the reëstablishment of the movie-going habit. Place full-page advertisements in newspapers and magazines with messages of the character placed by the Association of American Railroads, the Dairy Industry, the American Meat Institute, and the United States Brewers Foundation. Place advertisements in journals of all trades and crafts. A slogan could be adopted if it embodied the full message. "Movies Are Better Than Ever" won't do; it is a flat and debatable statement. "Let's Go to the Movies Tonight" would do, because it arouses the gregarious instincts in all of us, it urges action, and it urges action tonight. Billboards facing the homeward-bound traffic leading from all metropolitan centers should carry this message. Coca-Cola is a success partly because of its "Let's have a Coke" posters, each with a fresh illustration, but all with the message repeated over and over. The film industry could do no better than repeat "Let's Go to the Movies Tonight."

"Movietime, U.S.A.," a campaign originated, in part, from the clamor of exhibitors who wanted the industry to stage a fall film festival at a time when football, television, and the warm hearth are strong competition, was switched to a full year campaign. The idea sounded logical to the typical Hollywood promotion man. If a picture about ice skating makes money, why not make six more, and make six times as much money? That is called the film cycle technique, or the film cycle scourge. But a year's campaign is too much . . . it will die on the vine. The Democrats and Republicans would not dare to wage a campaign longer than five months to elect a president. Crosley, manufacturer of television and home appliances, is spending nine million dollars this fall on a sixty-day campaign. A campaign is an entity, too, but the Crosley people know sales will not cease at the end of their sixty-day promotion.

Another form of institutional advertising is the forum. The industry should encourage the establishment of civic and cultural movie forums, and should support them by sending out directors, producers, writers, executives, cinematographers, sound engineers, and costume designers all over the country, to lecture or to participate in forums.

Discourage movie gossip columns both in the public prints and on radio and television. Encourage programs of the character of *Invitation to Learning* discussing motion pictures instead of books.

Encourage the publication of books, serious books and otherwise, telling the story of motion pictures. There is a dearth of literature devoted to the motion picture. Of a half-dozen serious efforts in the past few years, those of Schary and Spottiswoode come first to mind. A recent biography of Charlie Chaplin was little more than the enumeration of films produced by him, but it has its place in the literature of the screen. A similar, more exciting book could be written of a dozen other leaders in the industry. Promote books on film music, cinematography, art and set design, film editing, organization and conduct of a location trip, or the accomplishments of sound engineers. Publish the twenty best motion picture scripts every year. Publish a symposium of critical analyses of films each year. The publishers who sell properties to Hollywood for millions of dollars each year certainly could be interested in publishing books that would aid in the public relations of the film industry. The literature of the motion picture industry should be expanded greatly. It is appallingly barren.

Accompany the films edited down from features for free loan to schools with trailers selling the motion picture medium in theaters as a desirable form of entertainment.

Create and maintain in Hollywood an adequate motion picture museum. The properties in custody of educational institutions should be brought out into the open where Mr. and Mrs. John Q. Public, visiting from all over America, could inspect them. Working sets, regular screenings, and lectures in such a museum would save studios time and money now lost conducting tours through working sets. Most major industries have museums for just this purpose. This, too, is public relations.

Use television. Television is not to be feared. It is an advertising medium, and a potent one; therefore a percentage of every film advertising budget should be allocated to television advertising. Positive selling can be more profitable than negative selling in the form of deriding television's shortcomings, therefore industry personnel and particularly comedians should be invited to promote motion pictures positively, consistently.

Motion pictures are not dead, not dying. Modern merchandising methods can still save motion pictures if given a chance. To paraphrase a famous quotation: "This above all, to thine own industry be true."

There's Still No Business Like It

In the fall, 1951, issue, the Quarterly *printed an article by Jay Gordon, "There's Really No Business Like Show Business," which questioned the effectiveness of motion picture advertising practices. Among other things, Mr. Gordon criticized the tendency to overlook advertising professionals, to play up sex and violence even if neither has much to do with the film, and to crowd billboards with full lists of credits lost to the passing motorist. Mr. Gordon suggested that larger audiences might result from better advertising, based on honest presentation of the content of films and on methods proved successful for other types of products.*

Reactions from Hollywood's writers, producers, and others have been curiously mixed. The following are excerpts from some of the letters received in reply to a request for comments.

It is an interesting and helpful piece. —JEAN HERSHOLT

I think Mr. Gordon has a fine and unusual understanding of the subject, and, for the most part, I couldn't agree with him more. My slight differences with him have to do with his advocacy of institutional advertising, which I think is meaningless in our industry—that is, if I understand his use of the words "institutional advertising" correctly. . . . Each picture is a new product and, roughly, Hollywood has to sell something over four hundred new products a year—and herein lies the difficulty. Lucky Strike, Kaiser-Frazer cars, or Coca-Cola can plug away at the one trade name day in and day out for fifty-two weeks a year, and these products are available day in and day out fifty-two weeks a year which makes for a different proposition than selling a picture which is available for a very limited time in any given area.

Again I congratulate Mr. Gordon on his fine piece and hope it receives wide circulation in our industry. —WILLIAM PERLBERG

I quite agree with the author that there is evidence that the motion picture industry's advertising policies could well be re-examined and modernized. Personally, however, I should go further—much further. I believe that the various units of the industry should combine their resources to effectuate a large-scale, amply financed, public relations campaign, embracing not only ideas such as those advanced by Mr. Gordon, but all phases of public relations in as many fields as practicable, including the political. I think it is time that the motion picture industry stopped dodging and ducking, with an occasional counterpunch. I think we should get off the defensive and hit out in a forthright and positive and big campaign to tell the story of an industry that is the greatest medium of mass entertainment the world has ever known, and certainly need not be ashamed of saying so. —WILLIAM H. WRIGHT

I was fascinated by Jay Gordon's article. . . . I am asking our Publicity Department and Sales Department to read this and to give me some indication of the impression it made on them. —SOL LESSER

I think it is an excellent article and I couldn't agree with Mr. Gordon more heartily. —VALENTINE DAVIES

Mr. Gordon's comments on the absurdity of film advertising are completely sound in my view. I have had my eye on these ads since 1931 and can see no difference in the dishonesty and vulgarity of the average ad and indeed no difference in its content during a period in which the *medium,* the film, changed so radically. Of course each film should be advertised "in a manner harmonious to plot, content, and action." Where I disagree is with Mr. Gordon's plea for not advertising the star but the directors, producers, and companies. This seems to me sheer madness. These are businessmen, the least glamorous hence least "saleable" of all God's creatures. And why advertise screen writers? Can we not humble ourselves, not before outsiders but before ourselves, and admit that we are hacks because we have no control over our work and are bossed about and put up with it?

So there I would part company with your author excepting for one important new phenomenon arisen in the industry in the last few years, the producer-director-writer. Such a man need not be a hack. He can be a creative artist. He may even be worth advertising. You are familiar with the

early Shakespeare quartos, in some of which the writer was not even ac-
corded his initials on the title page, let alone the use of his name, that is
to say, "screen credit." It is obvious from these first quartos that whatever
this beginner wrote, the men who corresponded to our producers and directors pulled it about and changed it about. Later on, however, the title
pages and texts show Shakespeare becoming what corresponds to a triple-
threat man in Hollywood—producer-writer-director—and as such he
deserved advertising, if there were any advertising. But was his name ever
box-office, as that of Burbage was? Perhaps. —JOHN L. BALDERSON

Gordon complains at great length that the industry doesn't rely on "advertising professionals." A phone call or two would have acquainted him
with the fact that all of the industry's national advertising (and a great deal
of the regional-exhibitor advertising) is worked out by and placed through
the nation's top advertising agencies, including firms like J. Walter Thompson and Buchanan and Company. Either he didn't make his point clear
—or he has egg all over his face. . . .

I agree with the comment about "honesty" and even the over-emphasis
on the "female bosom and the unclad limb." But flip through any magazine, scan the ads prepared by advertising agencies for the widest range of
products and note how many other industries use sex for selling. . . . I
could go through the article paragraph by paragraph. But, in sum, I
found this a poor advertisement for the *Quarterly* because of error and ignorance in unhappy combination. —INDUSTRY OBSERVER

I found Mr. Gordon's article very absorbing reading. Much, if not all that
he says, merits serious consideration by the industry. —SAM ENGEL

You are right as rain in thinking that I would be interested in Mr. Gordon's article and I filed it under the economics of the movies in preparation for a brief chapter in the new and still untitled Lively Arts which I
am doing for Knopf for 1953. As for comment, I think Mr. Gordon exposes the weaknesses of movie promotion, but his imaginary film about
the Philippines is the pay-off. The poster he describes is exactly right and
I am afraid will keep the audience away so that in the end it would be said
either that the picture should never have been made at all, or should have
been publicized for elements it did not contain.

On a smaller scale *Streetcar* and *A Place in the Sun* and *The Marry-*

ing Kind are all being publicized slightly off the exact beam and while this may cause a little resentment, a lot of people are seeing good pictures. —GILBERT SELDES

Thank you very much for letting me see Jay Gordon's piece. It makes sense to me. As you yourself know, studio people argue about this all the time, but the answer from the exploitation and advertising departments is that we don't know what we're talking about. How would we like it, they demand, if they tried to tell us how to make pictures? This is a line that so far we have found no answer to.

I'm sure that nine-tenths of moving picture advertising is utterly useless, except in the actual printing of the name of the picture on a piece of white paper, and that probably half of it discourages people who might want to see that particular picture. I don't suppose anybody in the world has a higher respect for sex than I have, but I still don't believe it is the solution to every picture that is offered to the public. But the faith that those advertising fellows have in it awes even me. You may remember the story of the rube character in the olden days who was supposed to have gone back again and again to look at one of the first of the silents showing an automobile beating an express train across the tracks in the confident expectation that some day that train was going to smack that car. It's the same still with the advertising boys. They are confident that this entire country is made up of rube characters who are going to go back again and again with the expectation of some day seeing a man and a woman actually in bed together, a spectacle that I do not anticipate seeing in our lifetime. Sometimes I wish that the people of this country had as much faith in and devotion to our flag as our advertising departments have in their belief in this possibility.

I agree almost one hundred per cent with what Mr. Gordon says on this subject, but I'm not the head of a studio and I have no authority to alter this approach to advertising. And in addition to that, I am too old and tired to become a reformer of any kind. —NUNNALLY JOHNSON

I've read "There's Really No Business Like Show Business." The article written by Jay E. Gordon, who describes himself as "a freelance move critic," (!) is a revealing one. It largely reveals, however, that the author has only the sketchiest knowledge of his subject. Mr. Gordon's approach to the problems of selling a motion picture, as well as his apparent ignorance

of present-day methods of so doing hardly entitle him to a reply, except
that his off-base arguments have been given some circulation and therefore might create serious misapprehensions among others whose knowledge of show business is equally incomplete.

In the first place, Mr. Gordon takes the producers to task for relying
on studio publicity departments in promoting films. This is an argument
that is hard to analyze, since these same studio publicity departments
have, over the comparatively short period of twenty-five years, completely
revolutionized the general concept of publicity and public relations and
have paved the path toward bringing glamour to industry and individuals and products—a path that has since been well traveled by almost
every exploiter of services or products in every field.

These selfsame studio publicity departments, dismissed by Mr. Gordon in one sentence, have made pictures and people famed the world over
on a scale never before accomplished by any advertising agency or public
relations firm in the whole history of exploitation.

The men and women employed in the studio publicity departments
are experts—that's why they're hired and that's why studios pay them salaries considerably in excess of those paid people in similar positions in advertising agencies. The fact that American motion pictures are famous the
world over is due in no small part to the efforts and ideas of these same
experts, whom Mr. Gordon dismisses so lightly.

He also seems completely unaware of the fact that advertising agencies—the biggest and best in the business—*are* employed by the motion
picture studios to prepare the advertising campaigns on each motion picture. Therefore, the faults found in motion picture advertising by Mr. Gordon can be traced directly to the advertising agencies which he proclaims
as a cure-all!

He claims that movie advertising is dishonest and that advertising
agencies do not create dishonest ads. How does this jibe with the fact that
every advertisement prepared for a major motion picture for the past
fifteen years has been prepared by an advertising agency?

The remainder of his ideas are equally naïve and unsupported by fact.
He seems to suffer under the delusion that a "pressbook" is the sole contribution made by a publicity department to the sale of a motion picture.
How wrong he is! In actuality, a pressbook is merely a printed guide sent
to exhibitors showing them how to sell the picture, and including a num-

ber of stock stories which they can give to the newspapers along with their advertisements, which also are included in the pressbook.

To use the pressbook as a sole example of the work done by a publicity department is about as sensible as using a visitor's guide to Washington as an example of all the work done by the United States government.

Furthermore, far from being "hackneyed handbooks," many of these pressbooks represent dynamic and original approaches to the problems of selling motion pictures. I can only assume that Mr. Gordon has read few pressbooks lately on major motion pictures. If he cares to read some, I have a few handy that would provide considerable inspiration for some of the "experts" from eastern advertising agencies.

Mr. Gordon's ideas on how to sell a movie are too ridiculous to deserve comment. Suffice to say that if any producer were foolish enough to follow his advice, he would suffer the financial disaster his folly would deserve.

Mr. Gordon points out that no motion picture advertisements are included in the *Commercial Art Annual* as proof of his contention that picture advertisements are insufficient. These annuals, made up by arty eastern advertising men, wouldn't admit a motion picture advertisement on general principles, no matter how effective it was. Let me point out the advertisements on *The Champion,* on *Bend of the River,* those that Foote, Cone, and Belding did on *The Blue Veil* and *Clash by Night* for us, the advertisements on *The Greatest Show on Earth, David and Bathsheba, An American in Paris, A Streetcar Named Desire,* and *A Place in the Sun* as advertisements which, dollar for dollar, outdrew probably any contained in the *Commercial Art Annual.*

I'll not argue that there aren't motion picture advertisements which are gross, stupid, in bad taste, misleading, and downright untrue. But these are not the majority. The faults of these advertisements lie largely with the advertising agencies which prepared them, the selfsame experts lauded as infallible by Mr. Gordon.

Mr. Gordon seemingly looks upon the motion picture business as a decaying enterprise that is doddering toward its grave. Nothing could be farther from the truth. In fact, good pictures today are doing better business than ever before in the history of show business. The pictures doing the best business are those which are properly sold.

In every case, the pictures getting the greatest sales campaigns—*The Greatest Show on Earth, An American in Paris, The Pride of St. Louis,* and

Singin' in the Rain—are ones where the campaigns have been carefully planned by coöperative meetings between a creative producer, studio publicity and advertising men, and the advertising agency. All three intellects are needed to create a good sales campaign on a motion picture.

In Hollywood today, ballyhoo doesn't mean circus parades and hairbrained stunts—necessarily. On *Clash by Night* the publicity campaign has been aimed at all levels, from the intellectual to the pure entertainment seeker. The personal appearance tours planned for the stars, the producers, the writer, and the director will hit every walk of life—and every section of the country's newspapers.

Hollywood is alive and receptive to the problems of selling a picture today, against the increased competition of television. Our experience shows one fact predominant: a good picture, properly sold, will return its makers more profit than ever before thought possible; a bad picture, no matter how well it is sold, will not return a penny. —JERRY WALD

Hollywood's Foreign Correspondents

Harva Kaaren Sprager is instructor in journalism in the Graduate Department of Journalism at the University of California at Los Angeles. She has been a member of the staff of radio station WQXR, New York, the San Francisco *Chronicle,* and the Los Angeles *Daily News,* and is now serving as one of the Los Angeles editors of a new quarterly publication, *Idea and Experiment.*

. . . . .

MORE THAN 70 FOREIGN CORRESPONDENTS in the Los Angeles area devote full or part time to reporting news and gossip of Hollywood for almost 2,000 newspapers and magazines and 600 radio stations in 70 foreign countries. In the summer of 1951, almost half of these correspondents filled out an 8-page questionnaire planned to reveal something of their backgrounds, and a good deal about what their problems are and how they handle the job of picturing Hollywood for readers thousands of miles away. The results of the survey indicate that the portrait which these Hollywood foreign correspondents send abroad is not different from the one painted by United States newspapers, magazines, and networks. Both are rather like an outdoor movie set—the part that shows gets the most attention.

The survey[1] of the foreign correspondents shows that 81 per cent[2] do interviews with stars and actors. Talks with writers and directors provide material for 61 per cent while executives are interviewed by 56 per cent. Movie reviews are written by 74 per cent, and 56 per cent handle gossip and chit-chat.

Mere scandal, however, is not popular. Forty-three per cent used the story of Judy Garland's suicide attempt in June, 1950, but of that group, one third mentioned the incident in passing, one third handled the story

1. Conducted by mail questionnaire with a 41 per cent response.
2. The foreign correspondents, of course, do not specialize in just one sort of story. They were asked to indicate in this category, what sort of stories they handle. Since all of them listed more than one, the percentages in this paragraph will total more than 100.

as straight news, and the final third tried to explain the tragedy from a sociological and psychological point of view. The story was ignored by 57 per cent. One correspondent said: "I did not even mention this attempt (if there was one) in my articles. This is the kind of 'malheurs' that I leave to the scandal hunters."

Seventy-two per cent reported that they also write about sociological aspects and problems of the motion picture industry. There are indications, however, that this percentage may reflect a misunderstanding of the term "sociological." The correspondents were asked to list the stories they had written during the previous two months. The number of articles concerned with the sociological phases of Hollywood were no more than 10 per cent of the total.

Of all the various commentators in Hollywood, the foreign correspondents are probably the only ones who are not excited about television as a source of material. Sixty-six per cent have not written anything about the young medium. Thirteen per cent—all reporters for countries which do not have or will not have television in the near future—have discussed television, but only as a curiosity. A growing interest in television was noted by 21 per cent. Canadians, who will soon have television, and Mexicans, who have it now, are particularly eager to read about the subject. Swiss and Swedish editors are also greatly interested, even though their countries have not as yet been invaded by this new form of communication.

Studio and personal publicity handouts are extremely useful to the foreign correspondents. Eighty-one per cent make use of them. Of this group, 21 per cent mentioned that they use handouts only occasionally and 17 per cent reported that the material is culled for ideas.

"I may be one of the few, but I consider studio material excellent and very useful," one writer stated. "Most of the correspondents throw press releases in the wastepaper basket because it is too much trouble to read them. But if you are patient enough to go through them, you will find good ideas. In this way I have made feature articles from simple notices, because three good lines can give you the subject of a real good column. And, as a rule, the publicists of the studios are first class newspapermen themselves."

Nineteen per cent reported, some of them emphatically, that they do not use handouts at all.

Of course, not all of the material that the foreign correspondent gathers comes from studio handouts. Eighty-three per cent get most of their news through personal contacts and interviews. Twenty-six per cent reported they get some of their material by seining the Los Angeles metropolitan papers, the trade papers, or the New York dailies for news items.

While some eschew the studio handout, almost all of them rely on the studios for the still pictures that the large majority (87 per cent) send abroad. The studios supply 83 per cent of this group with pictures whereas 17 per cent make their own arrangements for photographs.

The motion picture industry is not the sole concern of these writers. In addition to Hollywood, news of general interest is covered by 56 per cent.

The Hollywood foreign correspondents are as varied in background and training as are the many countries for which they write. Professionally, 35 per cent had previous experience in newspaper work before beginning to chronicle the cinema. Another 17 per cent listed creative writing as a previous vocation while 21 per cent have worked in various capacities in the theater and motion pictures abroad. Other past occupations include those of sculptress, model, translator, consular official, clerk, telephone operator, and teacher. In all, 35 per cent have sampled two or more careers.

Their educational histories are equally diverse. Eighty-seven per cent attended college or university. Of the 30 percent who took graduate work, less than 1 per cent received doctor of philosophy degrees. Their specializations in college read like a university catalogue—journalism, psychology, political science, engineering, commerce, humanities, medicine, literature, history, sociology, philosophy, languages.

At first glance, it would seem impossible that a few more than 70 people could adequately supply 2,000 newspapers and magazines and 600 radio stations with publishable material, even from such a news-laden spot as Hollywood. However, it must be remembered that some of the Hollywood foreign correspondents work for wire services whose widespread, duplicating coverage raises the total considerably. In addition, with one or two exceptions, all of them write for more than one publication and for more than one medium. The most frequent combination of media is newspaper and magazine with 35 per cent. Twenty-one per cent of the correspondents write for newspapers, magazines, and radio, while a negligible per cent write only for radio or magazines. Another 17 per cent write for newspapers only.

While the foreign correspondents frequently mix their media, they rarely cross linguistic lines. Ninety-five per cent write in only one language. English and German are most frequently used (26 per cent each), followed by Spanish (17 per cent) and French (13 per cent).

In view of the large number of outlets for Hollywood material abroad, even subtracting the number covered by wire services, it is surprising that so few in this press corps derive their entire income from their Hollywood writing. Only 17 per cent fully support themselves as foreign correspondents. Thirty-eight per cent earn 20 to 25 per cent of their income and another 21 per cent a quarter to a half of their income from this source.

Although the reason that the majority of the accredited foreign correspondents do not or cannot derive all their income from motion picture reporting is not entirely clear, one may make certain surmises. Some, obviously, consider Hollywood reporting merely a sideline. Other contributing factors involve foreign exchange difficulties as well as the fact that free-lancing for newsprint-poor and dollar-short newspapers is not too lucrative.

The difference between the professional and semiprofessional Hollywood foreign correspondent is more than economic. It is the basis for the difference between the two foreign correspondent groups in Los Angeles—the Hollywood Foreign Correspondents Association and the Foreign Press Association of Hollywood.

The Hollywood Foreign Correspondents Association is the older and the larger of the two groups, with a membership of 58. It was founded in 1941 and admits to membership any accredited professional[3] correspondent of any newspaper or magazine published abroad, of any foreign language publication circulated in the United States, or of any radio station outside the United States or broadcasting shortwave abroad. According to the by-laws, the group was organized to promote coöperation among reporters covering motion pictures for the foreign press and radio.

In June, 1950, a group within the Hollywood Foreign Correspondents Association formed the Foreign Press Association of Hollywood. Membership qualifications are based on whether the writer derives the *major* portion of his regular income from journalism and at the same time is a paid correspondent for foreign publications. Membership now numbers

3. Professional in the sense that the writer is paid for his writing.

between 12 and 18 (the exact number is not divulged, curiously enough). The secessionists believed that the position of the professional foreign press correspondent was being weakened because they claimed the older organization had been "taken over" by the semiprofessionals and had become too much of a social club.[4]

The problems involved in covering Hollywood for the foreign press are varied and of different intensity from those that beset reporters for the United States press. Generally they fall into three categories: competition, getting and presenting usable news, and lack of coöperation on the part of the studios.

Competition among the foreign correspondents is extremely keen, and 13 per cent noted that it was one of their special problems. In this regard, language is a determining factor. Spanish language correspondents, for instance, have much more competition than Swedish reporters. First of all, many more Hollywood correspondents write in Spanish than in Swedish. Then, too, a story in Spanish—the same story—can be sold in all but one of the Latin and South American countries as well as in Spain. The only additional effort involved is making a copy of the article and mailing it. Consequently, Spanish language reporters try to sell to all possible outlets. Swedish correspondents, on the other hand, are limited to communication media in only one country.[5]

Some correspondents also claim there is unfair competition from studio personnel. A few mentioned that some of the studio publicists write for foreign newspapers "on the side," and since they are closer to the source of the news, they enjoy an advantage over the foreign representative.

4. The feeling about the professional-semiprofessional issue is strong on the part of the Foreign Press Association. According to the vice-president, Nora Laing, the president Henry Gris, of the United Press, refused to permit his group to coöperate officially in this survey when he discovered the members of the Hollywood Foreign Correspondents Association were also being polled. Members were not, however, prohibited from participating on an individual basis.

5. Article 12 of the Hollywood Foreign Correspondents Association Code of Ethics, however, states: "It is considered unethical for any correspondent seeking new outlets for his material to try and take over space allotted to another member of our association. Before accepting a new publication, a correspondent must check with the Association to make sure that the said publication is not already represented. If the publication is being represented, then the correspondent must obtain permission from the publication's present correspondent before taking further action."

In addition, the correspondents complain that the studios and their re-leasing agencies abroad will by-pass the Hollywood correspondent and supply their newspapers with special articles and pictures if their editor requests. This procedure diminishes their chances of selling articles. The two correspondents' associations have been trying to solve this problem, and the Foreign Press Association has worked out a tentative plan with the major studios whereby a studio will refuse a request for a special story if the paper has a correspondent in Hollywood.

Thirty-five per cent reported problems in the getting and presentation of news appropriate for their audience. Foreign movie-goers apparently prefer to read about their favorites—personalities not always of similar newsworthiness in the United States. Foreign releasing schedules are an-other complicating factor. As one correspondent put it: "The main prob-lem seems to be to find material of special interest to European readers, to pick the stars they like and the pictures they are going to see, as quite a few of the American movies are not shown in Europe."

As for the presentation of the material, a few correspondents feel that they have difficulty in creating a true picture of the film capital. Specifi-cally, one said his problem is "to avoid picturing Hollywood as a 'glam-our place.'" Another listed "trying to make European people see Holly-wood people as Hollywood people see themselves." The main problem of another is "to write about movies without becoming an unpaid pub-licity agent of the studios." Still another said his predicament is "avoid-ing anything in the sexy angle and yet getting something interesting to write about."

Charges of a lack of coöperation on the part of the studios were made by 26 per cent, emphatically and sometimes bitterly. A correspondent for the Spanish-speaking areas complained: "In spite of the fact that Mexico City, for instance, contributes far more money than does Los Angeles to the American movie industry, the local columnist is treated with more consideration than the representative of the Mexican press, who besides being a correspondent, could also be considered a diplomatic representa-tive in a sense. He interprets not only the words of the movie stars, but their actions, so that when told to the reading public, across the borders of the various lands, a wrong impression is not created. A newspaperman from Cucamonga, let us say, if he writes in English, is considered more important to the studios and its artists as a general rule, than the representatives of publications of the Spanish reading public, not taking into consideration the fact that, in the entire world, there are over 178 million persons who speak Spanish."

The scheduling of previews is also criticized by some. "Previews are only too often 'afterviews.' Some studios make it a habit to show movies some days after they can be seen in any Hollywood theater and sometimes weeks after the first showing in New York City." A correspondent for Turkish publications commented: "There is not sufficient coöperation from the studios. We are often invited to preview movies after they have already been released locally. We are not being given enough of an opportunity to meet the directors and watch the movies in the making."

This charge of lack of opportunity was explored further by another writer who reported that although he had never been refused a favor when he asked, little is volunteered by the studio. "All the initiative had to come from my side. Very little guidance and real help was offered by the initiative of the studios. I have found it much easier to collaborate on assignments with such industries as the aircraft industry. Even government bureaus are nowadays much more helpful towards the foreign correspondent than the publicity offices in Hollywood." [6]

Actually, from an American newspaperman's point of view, the complaint that the studios are uncoöperative because they do not take the initiative points up the fact that the majority of the Hollywood foreign correspondents do not have a newspaper background.

Again from the American standpoint, the admission that some of the correspondents get their news from trade papers and Los Angeles and New York dailies is interesting. American newspaper tradition and training requires that a newspaperman gather facts himself and the opposite practice is a reflection in part of the European newsman's attitude that the facts and how they are obtained are not as important as the use made of them.

6. The studios apparently also make a distinction between the professional and semi-professional correspondent. The director of the foreign department of one of the major studios said that some of the professional foreign correspondents enjoy the same privileges and receive the same consideration as the domestic correspondents. He admitted that scheduling and space problems force the showing of many of the newest pictures to the foreign reporters after they have been released locally. Because pictures are exhibited so much later abroad, the foreign correspondents, he explained, do not have to see them as soon as does the local press.

On the whole, the foreign readers are getting the same star-dusted image of the Hollywood scene as does the American public. The foreign correspondents, because most of them are not under the pressure of turning out daily pieces, have an opportunity to approach their subject with depth and perception. This survey indicates that they are ignoring their opportunities—the majority of exported Hollywood news deals in interviews, reviews, and chit-chat.

Critics and commentators of Hollywood, including the foreign correspondents, often criticize the industry for making pictures which give foreign countries a distorted impression of Hollywood and American life. As a group, the foreign correspondents are in no position to join in the criticism, for their writings do very little to place the American motion picture industry in proper perspective.

8 Scenes from Abroad

Advanced Training for Film Workers: Russia

Jay Leyda is the translator of *Film Sense*, by Sergei Eisenstein.

. . . . .

AMONG THE MANY UNANSWERED QUESTIONS in the film business there is one of apparently small importance to its present but of gigantic importance to its future: Can you teach people how to make films?

This question recently came into particularly sharp focus for me when I received a cable from the Soviet film journal, *Iskusstvo Kino,* requesting me to prepare an article for them on "film schools, training, and libraries in the United States." Soviet film education has been conducted for so long on such a broad scale, both in technical and in audience training, that the editors of *Iskusstvo Kino* naturally assume that the great American film industry must be doing at least as much in this field as the far smaller Soviet film industry. I have not yet had the courage to tell them that the American film industry does nothing of the sort.

For, in combing the thorough historical survey prepared by the National Board of Review, *The Motion Picture in Colleges and Universities,*[1] as well as the hopefully entitled article by Paul Perez in *Boxoffice,* "College Training for Film Jobs,"[2] I have found no evidence that any connection or mutual responsibility exists between the film teachers and the film industry. The National Board's survey recorded many words of good will spoken by both bodies, and even a few benevolent gestures, but no sign of realization that each needed the other—badly. The lack shows up even more strikingly when one notices in the survey that it is *not* the educational institutions of Los Angeles, "film center of the world," that are

1. Paper 8 in a series of study outlines, Facts and Opinions about the Motion Picture (New York, The National Board of Review of Motion Pictures, 1943).
2. *Boxoffice,* November 17, 1945.

conducting the most interesting or energetic courses in film, and that the "film jobs" about which Mr. Perez writes may place the graduate student anywhere in the film business *except* in a Hollywood studio.

This would sound fantastic and even incredible to film workers within an industry that has pursued a quite different policy for twenty-five years. Since the first months after the nationalization of the private Russian film studios and theaters, the planners of the Soviet film industry have persistently developed two types of film education, since from the first they knew that without audience training there would not be constantly elevated demands by the audience on the film makers, and that without the organized schooling of future film makers there could not be a constant supply of fresh talents and trained artists to respond to the audience's demands. Any other course of procedure would have had to rely on chance and economic pressure to effect a change in the backward Russian film industry of 1919, and it was clear that such a lack of instructional method would never develop a Soviet cinema of artistic and social power.

But apparently the American film industry has always felt so confident of its world leadership that it has been content to let both its audience and its personnel learn in the school of hard knocks. This contentment has produced the whole rationale of "It can't be done" so often heard in Hollywood and most recently expressed by Raymond Chandler in a blistering but aimless denunciation of film-writing methods: "There is no teaching, because there is no one to teach. If you do not know how pictures are made, you cannot speak with any authority on how they should be constructed; if you do, you are busy enough trying to do it." [3] Another writer, of longer residence in the film community, Howard Estabrook, has dismissed at least one discussion of film education with the remark, "The best place to learn to swim is in the water." And of the many expressions of direct opposition, among the other artists of American films, to the whole idea of teaching about films, Paul Muni's is typical: "There is no textbook, no school of acting I can recommend. I believe that an actor can really place himself in a part, relying on instinct and experience to guide him, without depending on academic formulas." [4] The faint touch of demagogy in "academic formulas" is characteristic of this argument.

3. "Writers in Hollywood," *Atlantic Monthly*, November, 1945.
4. "The Actor Plays His Part," in *We Make the Movies* (New York, Norton, 1937). A similar dismissal of film education was made ten years earlier by Osbert Burdett, in an

Yet we regularly admit surprise at the expressiveness and originality of Soviet films: not only do new works by recognized masters of long experience such as Eisenstein, Pudovkin, Dovzhenko, Kozintzev, or Trauberg thus delight us; lesser and as yet unfamiliar Russian, White Russian, Georgian, or Urkrainian names, we find, are often attached to the most unexpected pleasures in our filmgoing: of Donskoy, who made *The Childhood of Maxim Gorky* trilogy and *The Rainbow;* Pyriev, who has given us two of the best film operettas, *The Country Bride* and *They Met in Moscow;* Eisemont of *The Girl from Leningrad;* Raizman of *Mashenka;* Lukov of *Two Soldiers;* Arnstam of *Zoya.* These and many other young directors of equal importance, along with more than half of the Soviet actors we see in films, as well as almost all the cameramen who have recorded the war's tragedy so thoroughly, and a great many of the film writers who are too often neglected in our admiration of Soviet films, not to mention the innumerable administrators in the studios and film theaters who bring an enviable imagination to their work—all are graduates of one of the several film institutes in the U.S.S.R. Even one of the "masters," Pudovkin, had no film experience before joining a class in the first film school organized; and he still has duties in its successor, the All-Union State Institute of Cinematography in Moscow, as a teacher. I feel sure that neither his director-pupils nor his actor-pupils are instructed by "academic formulas."

It may be of value to learn more about the one film institute in the world that has successfully functioned in close relationship with its country's film industry for twenty-five years. A quantity of information on the All-Union State Institute of Cinematography (V.G.I.K.) is available for American inspection, and I hope that this article may lead to more detailed inspection of that body of film-teaching experience.

Here is a clear and authoritative statement on the whole field of Soviet film education as of 1939:

"The state is interested in developing new masters of the cinema art and provides liberally for such training. Children who show aptitude and

---

essay, "The Art of Mr. Chaplin": "An American producer of films [Robert T. Kane] has lately offered to establish and endow a Chair of Cinema Research at one of the eight principal universities of his country. . . . How pathetic is the belief in the power of money; how ineradicable the faith in professors! All the previous art in the world has sprung from illiterate and unsophisticated people. . . . It is wiser, then, not to look to academies when we are considering the possibilities of the youngest of the arts." *Critical Essays* (New York, 1926).

The Childhood of Maxim Gorky (1938), by Mark Donskoy

desire for work in film may, upon graduation from high school, enter one of the state technical schools or colleges in this field. Like all Soviet students in such institutions, they not only get their tuition free, but are paid state stipends for their support while learning.

"There are three higher educational establishments in the cinema field: the Kiev and Leningrad Institutes for Cinema Engineers and the All-Union State Institute of Cinematography in Moscow for the education of directors, scenario writers, cameramen, and designers. Besides this the big studios in Moscow, Leningrad, Erivan, and Tpilisi have actors' schools. Students of the State Cinema Institute get a broad general education in addition to their specialized training. . . .

"For cameramen, special disciplines include photography, electrical technique, apparatus, lighting technique, composition, and the technique of filming. Designers study costumes and manners of the past, drawing, painting, architecture, lighting, anatomy, and stage designing. Directors occupy themselves with the theory and practice of their art, cutting, acting, speech technique, make-up, and the organization and accounting of film production. It is interesting to note that the program of the directors includes a course in camera technique and art, while the cameramen similarly study the problems of directing. Among the faculty are such famous figures as Sergei Eisenstein, Lev Kuleshov, Vsevolod Pudovkin, and Mikhail Romm; such cameramen as Edward Tisse, Anatoli Golovnya, and others.

"The school turns out research workers as well as practicing personnel. It is equipped with laboratories, an experimental studio for student productions, a library of Russian and foreign works, and a large library of films. Among the 3,000 films here preserved, about half are foreign. They include Lumière's first films . . . some of Chaplin's early comedies, a number of films by D. W. Griffith, Cecil B. DeMille, Thomas Ince, and French and German masters. The collection is invaluable for a study of the world history of the cinema.[5]

"To graduate, the student must present, in lieu of a thesis, a plan for the production of a full-length film, he must take a sequence of the picture in the studio, and spend a certain period in practice work. Then, whether he be director or cameraman, he usually goes to work as assistant to one of the famous masters of the Soviet cinema, although the more talented students sometimes are set to work independently on certain films. The many graduates who come from the national peoples usually go home to work in the studios of their own nationality."[6]

The course at the Institute that has naturally received most attention in the rest of the world has been the course in film direction, both because Soviet film achievements have usually been regarded abroad as exclusively directorial triumphs and because film direction has seemed the most unteachable of film crafts.

Two recent textbooks[7] used in this course have come to this country, and in their different ways they are models that can be followed in any serious attempt to teach this subject. They are quite distinct from each other in form and tone, but they both possess two elements in common with all good textbooks, namely, usefulness and stimulation.

Film Direction: An Anthology (1939) was compiled by Yuri Genika un-

5. This collection was used last year in celebrating the fiftieth anniversary of the Lumière first public performance in 1895, in the compilation of three instructional films on the history of cinematography.

6. From *Soviet Films, 1938–1939* (Moscow, State Publishing House for Cinema Literature, 1939). (In English.)

7. Both are published by Goskinoizdat (State Cinema Publishing House) for the All-Union State Institute of Cinematography: Chair of Film Direction.

der the supervision of Yefim Dzigan (the director of *We Are from Kronstadt*). The editor assembled an enormous quantity of documents relating to the director's job generally, and specifically as he moves from stage to stage of the production process. Both Soviet and foreign materials have been drawn upon, and I imagine the chief reason for the predominance of the former is that Soviet film artists have chosen to be more articulate and frank than other artists. Perhaps all our own need is encouragement?

Principles of Film Direction (1941), by Lev Kuleshov, is a more immediately attractive work, being completely personal, and even humorous, as it goes systematically about its job of leading the student director from one fascinating problem to the next. This admirable artist, a veteran film teacher, has generously turned over his years of experience as well as most of his working hours to the large responsibility of training the next generation of film directors. On May 10, 1944, Kuleshov was appointed Director of the Institute.

Kuleshov's most famous pupil, Vsevolod Pudovkin, has felt his responsibilities, too, to the younger generation of film directors. As far back as 1926 he published two popular handbooks, *The Film Scenario* and *The Film Director and Film Material*, for use in and out of the Institute. Ivor Montagu's translation of these two pamphlets as *Film Technique* (1929 and 1933) has become a classic of world film literature, along with Pudovkin's *Film Acting* (1935), which is actually a course of lectures delivered at the Institute.

The best known of the Institute's teachers is Sergei Eisenstein. Visual evidence of his students' tasks can be found in two works in English: *Soviet Films, 1938–1939*, and Vladimir Nilsen's *The Cinema as a Graphic Art* (1936); both contain illustrations of student classroom work in composition, production design, and mise-en-scène. Eisenstein's own book, *The Film Sense* (1942), was based on a group of lectures given by him at the Institute. An important document in studying the teaching methods of the Institute is Eisenstein's published "Programme for Teaching the Theory and Practice of Film Direction."[8] Its scope, as well as its depth of treatment, will impress every pedagogue and every film maker, although its

---

8. Translated by Stephen Garry and Ivor Montagu in *Life and Letters To-day*, Nos. 6 and 7, 1936, 1937. Reprinted by the Larry Edmunds Bookshop (Hollywood, 1944), together with Eisenstein's descriptions of work at GIK, originally published in *Close Up*.

thoroughness may irritate advocates of the unprepared and "instinctive." Eisenstein has outlined in staggering detail a four-year course built on this general method (in his Introduction to the "Programme"):

". . . an approach from the simplest and most obvious forms and manifestations . . . is the only one that will ensure conscious orientation in the more complicated problems of film directorial knowledge and craftsmanship.

"Only such an approach will ensure a single theoretical embrace of all the more complex varieties of the subject of film direction, whilst thoroughly characterising the specific quality of each individual section of it. . . .

"At every stage of its course the subject of film direction organically impinges upon and in a planned manner grows into neighboring disciplines, where each branch is at the same time thoroughly studied under the guidance of specialists."

There is by no means unanimity among Soviet film makers with respect to film education. One man who thinks the Institute goes too far in its training is no less an artist than Alexander Dovzhenko, who in 1936 proposed a new schedule for the film director's course:

"It does not take a long period of study to make a film director. Five years would be harmful. One year of study—and then to work. Otherwise the student dries up, becomes 'wise.' He knows everything, including the peculiar mistakes of each director, and becomes a mediocre average of them all. . . . I shall organize a studio in the Ukraine. I have promised the Government to train at least four new directors during the next two years. In doing this, I shall combine study with practice to the maximum degree, endeavoring not to make 'little Dovzhenkos' of my pupils, but to develop rather the individual talents which they may possess."[9]

I have not tried to be too oblique in demonstrating the fallacy in Mr. Chandler's proposition. The Soviet director-teachers I have mentioned *do* know how pictures are made, *can* speak with authority on how they should be constructed, and are never too busy ("trying to do it") to pass on their experience and knowledge to others. If anyone should reply, "Oh, *that's* Moscow; *this* is *Hollywood;* you can't do that sort of thing *here*," I can point to a successful experiment being conducted at the Ac-

9. A speech reported in *Moscow Daily News,* March 6, 1936.

tors' Laboratory Theater, where some of the best film actors in this community are frankly and helpfully discussing methods and experiences in their profession for the benefit of the actor-students in the Laboratory Workshop.

Though Soviet film artists and administrators may not be in complete accord on professional film-training requirements, there is unanimity among them on another group of film students—the audience. Aside from a great deal of direct activity, such as lectures by film makers at factories, clubs, and even film theaters (!), and, in reverse, visits by groups of workers and students to film studios (all of which enjoy the practice of *shefstvo,* or "mutual patronage" with some school, factory, or military unit), the major work in this field is managed by the printed word.

The astonishing quantity of popular film literature published in the Soviet Union is all adapted to the program of audience education—hundreds of books and pamphlets from the first Russian volume on film aesthetics, *Kinematograph* (1919), a collection of essays (including ones by Lunacharsky and Kommissarzhevsky), to the latest wartime pocket-size editions of current film scripts (including translations of the Lamar Trotti–Sonya Levien script of *In Old Chicago* and the Hellman-Parker film treatment of *The Little Foxes!*). The rich variety of film knowledge thus placed in the public domain makes English and American film books seem very meager indeed.

Both Harcourt, Brace and W. W. Norton can be proud of the *quality* of their respective film-book lists (each has contributed four in the past nine years!), but the separation between film books and film makers is what is most deplorable in this field. For example, Dudley Nichols is the single American film maker of top importance who in the past ten years has volunteered the time and the will to provide such assistance to the American film audience—in his collaboration with John Gassner in editing two volumes of modern American scripts.[10] The rest of our best film people hesitate before print as before a taboo, doling out little more than a preface or an interview once every year or so. Has this curse been placed on the printed word by its exclusive film employment in publicity? Hasn't D. W. Griffith as much to tell us as Lev Kuleshov, Chaplin as much as Eisenstein, Capra as much as Pudovkin? American film makers, film critics,

10. *Twenty Best Film Plays* (New York, Crown Publishers, 1943) and *Best Film Plays of 1943–1944* (same publishers, 1945).

and film audiences need these words as badly as the Soviet public does; perhaps more, by this time.

Of all Soviet film literature, there are two volumes that should shame us into action. They stem from the serious interest among Soviet film people in all American film activity, an interest that has often embarrassed me when in Soviet newspapers I have come upon grave discussions of *The Great Waltz* or *Sun Valley Serenade!* In the midst of war, and in spite of paper shortages and more obviously urgent tasks, the State Cinema Publishing House planned and began an ambitious series, Materials on the History of World Cinema Art, under the editorship of Eisenstein and Yutkevich. The first two volumes, which deal with American cinematography and were compiled by Pera Attasheva and the late S. Akhushkov, have already appeared, offering to American eyes concrete evidence of Soviet film scholarship.

Volume I contains three essays about an American master, all his random published personal statements, contemporary accounts of him, the chief critical studies about him, a list of his films, biographical sketches of all his co-workers; and the sun around whom this whole system circles is David Wark Griffith. The essays are apparently the major feature of the volume (an important and original piece of historical criticism by Eisenstein, studies by Mikhail Bleiman the screen writer, and Sergei Yutkevich, on Griffith's relation to film writing and film acting, respectively); but the character and purpose of this and the following volume seem more important to me. They show a consuming eagerness to know, and a willingness to put the maximum effort into communicating that knowledge.

The subject of Volume II is Charles Chaplin.[11] The form of the Griffith volume is followed: four essays—by Bleiman, Kozintzev, Yutkevich ("Sir John Falstaff and Mr. Charles Chaplin"), and Eisenstein—plus a compilation of everything (far too little) that could be found in print by Chaplin himself. Although American film publishing can wave, in reply to Volume I of this historical series, Iris Barry's valuable monograph on Griffith (New York, Museum of Modern Art, 1940), Volume II has not yet been equaled by us, notwithstanding the handful of Chaplin "biographies."

Soviet film literature has developed its specialists, also. The film critic

---

11. This is at least the third work on Chaplin written and published in the Soviet Union. Both his twenty-fifth anniversary in films (in 1938) and his fiftieth birthday (in 1939) were celebrated in Russia, as was also the publication of this volume in 1945.

occupies a place on the staff of every newspaper, as he does in this country. And Soviet film historians work continuously in their field, uncover-
ing new material and revealing new historical analysis. The conditions
that discourage continuity and second works by our historians, such as
Terry Ramsaye and Lewis Jacobs, would not be understood by Nikolai
Iezuitov and Venyamin Vishnevsky, the two most active Soviet film historians. But judged on a basis of the Griffith and Chaplin volumes, the
film artists themselves bear the heaviest responsibility of establishing critical tastes and standards—and we are brought back abruptly to the question of professional Soviet film education.

It has aim, but no end. It goes on after you leave the Institute. You
actually "graduate" from one degree of schooling to the next degree. An
example of this eternal postgraduate work is the Film Actors' Theater,
formed on September 28, 1944:

"The company of this new theater is to be drawn from actors in the
film studios and will also include a number of stage actors willing to appear regularly in films. . . .

"One of its tasks is to train actors for films. The theater will recommend to film directors actors for film rôles after having trained them in
the stage performance of fragments from scenarios.

"The new technical method of filming now being experimentally introduced at the Mosfilm Studio demands thorough preliminary preparation of the whole cast. . . . This work will consist of preparations for actual filming, with rehearsals, preliminary work on make-up, settings and
costume sketches, the composer's work on the film score, etc." [12]

One explanation for the double phenomenon of self-education and ed-
ucating younger people in one's own profession may be that fear of the
young and the cultivation of professional selfishness have been weeded
out and outlawed as thoroughly in the Soviet scene as has anti-Semitism.

These principles of film education are not unattainable in our own industry. We have a *Hollywood Quarterly* to prove that the most logical developments open up only if someone pushes hard enough. If a university
can push a respectable film magazine, perhaps the same university can
pull out of our film people a film institute and related film literature. It
took a war to make American film talents like Anatole Litvak speak pub-

12. *Soviet Film Chronicle,* October, 1944.

licly about their profession at the G.I. University in Biarritz. Shall we need another war to make them teach in Hollywood?

Other institutions for professional film education are being projected or beginning in various parts of the world, notably the new Institut des Hautes Etudes Cinématographiques which the most ambitious and restless members of the French film industry have organized—in spite of the pleasingly worn ruts offered to them by a postwar industry based on prewar thinking. There have been other institutions: for four summers, from 1935 to 1938, the Educational Handwork Association, in conjunction with the British Film Institute, held a London Film School;[13] Los Angeles itself once looked upon the promising opening of a Cinema Workshop at the University of Southern California. And the soundest American program for a film institute has not yet been tried, thirteen years after its formulation by Harry Alan Potamkin. His "Proposal for a School of the Motion Picture,"[14] though little more than a sketch, has a balance and emphasis, based on American film needs, that any planner would do well to consult.

There will be other programs, other schools—even in Hollywood. But, to maintain its leading position in the film world, the American film industry must see, and soon, the necessity of a film school, a school in which the industry's best people will be the teachers, a school from which the industry will regularly absorb the best-trained talents in all film crafts, a school whose standards will be established by more than commercial needs. The initiative may be taken by a university, by the producing companies, or by the combined guilds and unions of the industry, but before the school is fully satisfactory and workable all three bodies will have to be participants in it. Time passes, and the more we lose of the present, the more we lose of the future.

13. This school, concentrating on instructional and documentary films, has at least two American equivalents at present: the Institute of Film Techniques at the College of the City of New York, and Sawyer Falk's course at the University of Syracuse.

14. Published four months after his death, in *Hound and Horn,* October, 1933.

Advanced Training for Film Workers: France

Since 1934, Charles Boyer has appeared mainly in American motion pictures. During the war he was active on behalf of American-French Relief organizations and the Free French Movement in the United States. He is the founder of the French Research Foundation, a nonprofit organization dedicated to the strengthening of Franco-American friendship. His most recent pictures include *Gaslight, Confidential Agent,* and *Cluny Brown.*

. . . . .

EVEN THOSE OF US WHOSE confidence and admiration for France lead us to expect miracles of her look with amazement on her actual achievements since the liberation. After four years of simmering under the Occupation's fire and pressure, the lid has been removed once more from the nation's cauldron of intellectual and artistic endeavor. And instead of finding its contents evaporated and shrunken, we discover the pot still full and bubbling with vigor! Literary reviews and magazines devoted to art and fashion which have reached us from Paris since V-E Day maintain and even surpass their traditional standards of creative originality and artistic presentation. The world of letters and the theater are intensely busy. And France's music makers have contrived to turn the very echoes of misery and defeat into inspiring melodies for tomorrow.

Into this atmosphere—and perhaps, to some extent, out of it—has been born a new Paris conservatory. It is fitting that this "Institute of Advanced Film Studies" (Institut des Hautes Etudes Cinématographiques), the first school of its kind, should be established in France, the birthplace of motion pictures. Indeed, French motion picture men, admittedly foremost in the field, feel that their medium, after fifty years' existence, should no longer be regarded as a commercial enterprise, nor as a stepchild of the arts, but should be recognized for what it is already, and for what it is destined to become: a high creative art of incalculable social import.

With rare common sense these men have taken practical steps toward the achievement of this recognition. They have founded a school of motion pictures where young people of talent can learn the theory and practical application of the many arts and techniques that go to make up a good film.

The Institute of Advanced Film Studies, which is actually functioning at 6 Rue de Penthièvre in Paris, is conceived along ultramodern and far-reaching lines. It boasts a library entirely devoted to the film and its ramifications, already containing some 12,000 volumes. The founders of the Institute look upon this library as a mere nucleus for the comprehensive Office of Film Documentation which they expect to assemble.

IDHEC is already gaining public recognition through its magazine, *Cinéma*, which carries in its initial issues some of the lectures and texts offered to students at the Institute. This material, as indicated by a few sample titles from *Cinéma*, is highly worthwhile. Louis Taquin discusses "Direction and Script"; Pierre Blanchar shares his professional knowledge and experience in an article on "The Technique of Motion Picture Acting"—fascinating reading for the layman, "must" reading for future stars; Marcel L'Herbier outlines the latest developments in television and its relationship to motion pictures; Jean Vivie traces the invention and history of the cinema.

The Institute itself, staffed by such motion picture veterans or members of the advance guard as L'Herbier, Gremillon, Carne, Taquin, Becker, Spaak, Moussinac, Mitry, Vivie, Gerin, Lods, etc., enjoys the support of Professors Jasinski, Aymand, Touchard, and Rousseau, to name but a few, and has aroused the interest of France's foremost writers, painters, musicians, and men of science.

IDHEC operates on the theory that the chief deficiency in motion pictures today arises from the fact that the majority of men and women in the industry entered this field by chance or through some fortuitous connection, without previous thought or preparation for the jobs they are called upon to fill. Up to now the only school for motion pictures has been the school of experience, attended to the detriment of quality in general film production and, often enough, with little profit to the individual because he is not suited to the type of work he finally learns to perform. Furthermore, old hands in the business seldom have either the time or the patience to train unpromising apprentices to their own levels of achievement, reached the hard way over long years of trial and error. The Institute feels that the chief need, then, is for a channelization of talent and the systematic direction of effort and instruction from the outset.

If progress in films is to be made, the "know how" so painfully acquired by the motion picture masters of today must be passed along without the loss of years to producers, directors, actors, and technicians of the future. However, the Institute recognizes the need for practical experience to supplement academic instruction. As soon as the student in a given branch of picture making has received the necessary background and fundamental training, he is provided with opportunity to practice the rudiments of his craft under the actual conditions he will meet later in the studios when he is on his own.

Subjects covered in the Institute's curriculum include production, direction, acting, film writing, sound and lighting techniques, special effects, costume design, keeping script, animation, the history and development of motion pictures and allied arts, and courses in the domain of general culture—the background indispensable to worthy film creation. If any phase in the broad scope of motion picture art has been overlooked by the Institute, its directors are eager to have such omissions brought to their attention. The organization's guiding spirit seems to be one of open-minded receptivity and a keen desire for renewal and improvement.

This all sounds ideal. But where, one is inclined to wonder, shall young people capable of profiting from such instruction be recruited? It is well known that talent or even aptitude in motion pictures is a rare composite in which character and temperament are important factors. The answer is that the Institute recruits its students from all walks of life. Their abilities and leanings are as numerous and varied as the techniques contributing to a harmonious finished product on the screen. They have but one thing in common: a love of the motion picture, a burning desire to elevate the medium to new artistic heights, and a sincere wish to contribute their share to its social and aesthetic progress.

It goes without saying that the mystery and glamour attached in the public mind to motion pictures attracts young people in droves to studio gates and, more recently, to IDHEC's doors. It is equally obvious that a large majority of these young hopefuls are eminently unsuited to picture making. For this reason the Institute has spent months of intensive research in the fields of psychology and psychoanalysis, to devise examinations accurately evaluating motion picture ability.

Systems of grading heretofore employed have been abandoned as useless in selecting candidates for film careers. For if a student graduates from school with a mathematics rating of 80, language 50, and natural sciences 90, his average standing of 70 tells us nothing of his capability as an artist, his adaptability to constantly varying circumstances, nor his ingenuity in meeting the hundreds of unforeseen technical problems he would encounter on a movie set.

IDHEC's entrance examinations for film candidates are competitive — and they are stiff. Proofs of facility, gifts of imagination, an inventive spirit, and visual aptitudes are determined by all sorts of tests, ranging from written composition to psychological aptitude examinations. Oral questioning, done by competent film critics, brings the imponderables of personality to light. The Institute's tests are not infallible, naturally. But the experimental work it has already done and continues to carry forward in connection with the intelligent selection of its students is, in itself, an important contribution to the science of education in general.

The school realizes that it cannot create film artists overnight, any more than a painter, a musician, or a great writer can be solely the product of training. Its aim, therefore, is to direct and expand talent where it is latent, and to develop personalities fitted to meet the constant demand for renewal inherent in motion picture creation. It does not expect that its diploma will represent a guarantee of extraordinary skill or talent. But it feels that producers of films on the lookout for new artists and technicians will accept IDHEC graduates, confident in the solidity of their basic training, and with reasonable hopes for their future achievements.

IDHEC is soliciting correspondents, both professional and nonprofessional, throughout the world. The organization's purpose is to arouse wider and more intelligent interest in motion pictures, and to stimulate exchanges of data and suggestions mutually advantageous to all who are engaged in the cinematographic arts. If IDHEC receives support in the pursuit of this disinterested policy, the results may eventually prove to be a long step forward on the path of international cooperation and good will.

IDHEC, a French University of Motion Pictures, furthers the French pioneering tradition — a pioneering of the intellect. Since it is the first institution of its kind, it is unfettered by the rules and customs governing most establishments of learning. The Institute makes good use of all that has been proved most effective and best in conservatories and educational foundations already in existence, but it is unhampered in its choices, free in the creation of new methods to meet new problems, awake to the necessities of the present and the challenge of the future.

The Institute of Advanced Film Studies has a sense of profound responsibility in the training of actors and technicians who will contribute to the shaping of the films of tomorrow—films certainly destined, in turn, to shape and influence world opinion and world events. The founders of the Institute are not concerned with politics. They feel that if their graduates remain loyal to the high artistic and technical integrity demanded of them during their formative period, they will automatically strive to uphold beauty and truth, thus serving the best interests of mankind.

FROM VOL. 2, NO. 4, JULY 1947 Vsevolod Pudovkin

Translated by Jay Leyda

The Global Film

Vsevolod Pudovkin, the Russian director, is best known for his early films, *Mother,
The End of St. Petersburg,* and *Storm Over Asia.* His latest films, *The Russian People,*
based on Simonov's play, and *Admiral Nakhimov,* have not yet been seen in this
country.

. . . . .

I AM PROFOUNDLY CONVINCED that the film, an art of quite recent appearance, possesses exceptionally great potentialities for the expression of
man's broadest thoughts and ideas. Film history gives us a concrete example of the potentialities that distinguish the film from the other arts. We
clearly remember those days in which our Soviet film was born and ma-
tured, a period which at the same time was the formative period of our
Soviet state. The enormous struggle within this period was nourished by
the highest ideas of human significance. Our best films, linked to this
time, are familiar to all. All of them, no matter how various were the styles
of their individual authors, were alike in one respect: they strove to unite
in a persuasive visual form events widely separated in time as well as events
spread over the farthest reaches of the earth. Giving substance to the largest ideas of humanity, they did not so much aim to tell about as to *show*
the connection between phenomena, with the conviction which sight
alone can provide and which only the film can provide fully.

The creative study of a montage of visual fragments, established in this
period, revealed the true meaning of this fundamental and mighty
method in film art. By montage an artist could communicate to the spectator in simple, graphic, and sharply expressive means what would seem
to be the most complex and abstract generalizations. The artists of that
day tried to keep pace with the flashing succession of new, vital, and significant ideas, and sought new forms of art in which they could be embodied, but it was the film in particular that proved the most powerful
means for the expression of those ideas, and undoubtedly influenced both
the theater and the literature of the time.

Then, too, it was suddenly realized by all that the motion picture camera was a new sort of instrument, allowing the human eye to penetrate into regions hitherto closed to it. The motion picture camera was regarded as a telescope that could take the human eye into cosmic space, or as a microscope that could bring into the field of vision the world of infinitesimal organisms. Actually, the camera lens never saw more than did the human eye; it was the creative unification on the screen of all that the camera could see in many scattered places—throughout the world, if you wished, and at any time—constructed into a vision as single and convincing as a landscape or portrait, that gave this picture of the true relationships of phenomena. Before film existed no eye could see this, just as without the telescope no one saw the satellites of Jupiter, or as no one saw living cells before the existence of the electronic microscope.

Films, moreover, were still "silent," which gave them one more important capacity: an unlimited audience. The silent film was visually international in the fullest sense of the word. Its only words appeared in subtitles that could be replaced in any language without harming the artistic integrity or the organic elements of the work.

And then what happened?

In the silent films we artists constantly overcame huge difficulties. Each step required effort; it was necessary to invent perpetually. The silent film was full of creative inventions without which it could not have progressed. It was precisely in the period of the silent film that the film scenario represented a specific literary genre, one so individual that it quickly filtered into other literary forms, including playwriting.

But when sound came, and the screen actor began to speak, film workers encountered a new kind of actor, already experienced, and armed with theater culture. They also encountered a new kind of writer, armed with the experience of writing for the theater. Influences turned abruptly in the opposite direction: literature and the theater began to rule the film with their traditions more and more. One could watch the gradually lessening efforts of the film artist to show everything, to help the spectator see everything with his own eyes, and to rouse and convince him by the immediacy of his perception.

Films began to tell of things more and more in words. It was no longer necessary to send out the motion picture camera in search of the realities of truth. The desire of a director to film a London street in London itself, with all its inimitable peculiarities and subtle detail, which would make this London street valuable in the spectator's knowledge of real life—this desire also faded. Now the London street was quietly built in the studio, for the director had begun to acquire a theatricalized relation to the film, and was becoming content with an abstract treatment and conventional depiction of the street, which was needed, after all, only as a background for spoken dialogue, itself the point of the film. Imperceptibly, all the vast significance of unimpeded vision and the examination of life which the motion picture camera had given us was replaced by verbal narrative, as it naturally has always existed and exists today in the theater. Spectators were gradually deprived of that wonderful possibility of witnessing real life with their own eyes, a possibility that had been realized so generously and fruitfully in the days of the silent film. Like some cheated prize-winner, the spectator was offered a magic-lantern lecture about Africa in place of the plane trip that would have allowed him to see Africa with his own eyes.

Along with many of my comrades in art, I still feel sad to see the latest films using the most modern technical devices for the imitation of living nature—putting lifeless settings before the cameras. Location trips to distant points are avoided as unprofitable. Hollywood, the world's center of technical film organization, is quite satisfied with its back lots full of used and reused sets for all the cities of the world. The few pitiful rivers, sandy places, and hills that happen to be near the great film city have long since grown accustomed to being made up as the Ganges, as the Sahara, as Mont Blanc. If everything can be told in words, as in the theater, why give yourself the extra trouble of showing anything? *Showing* costs more than *telling*, just as a trip costs more than a lecture. So, for purely commercial considerations, because production costs could be cut and because the craft required for the adaptation to films of methods already evolved in the theater and literature was easier and more convenient, the modern film was impoverished; motion pictures now bear a closer resemblance to recordings of performances on a stage than they do to the magnificent, original, and powerful films that were once given us.

Sound films also completely lost their international character. Pictures produced in one country were nearly destroyed as works of art when they were exhibited in other countries. Since the spectator has to read, almost without pause, the translated words of the film's dialogue, idiotically printed on the picture itself, he cannot be expected to gain any impression from the pictorial composition of the original film. Furthermore, the spectator—for he is no longer an auditor, but only a spectator—can only be distracted by the unknown language coming from the loud-speaker; this has no more meaning for him than the static in poor radio reception. His attention, instead of being attracted to the direct perception of the work of art, is broken up; his impressions are scattered in all directions, and he is not fully moved, as one should be by a work of art. Our contemporary film with its superimposed subtitles gives me the impression of an entertaining bus excursion that has been arranged by removing tires, muffler, and springs from our vehicle. Such excursions give me nothing but nervous indigestion. Attempts at dubbing the translated dialogue in the mouths of the original actors have been little more successful.

If you agree with me that modern methods of producing a sound film narrow the audience for it, as a complete art experience, to a single country and a single language group, then you, too, must come to the unavoidable conclusion that the problem of creating a film comprehensible to all peoples must be taken up with far more conviction and strength than we have hitherto applied to solving it. I repeat: the world-wide comprehension of the film is a goal that must be identified with the all-embracing goal, imperatively required today, of a direct exchange of ideas of general human significance.

For this reason I am sincerely convinced that our foremost talents, chiefly the younger ones, or those that are young enough to be daring and decisive, must be newly directed to the rough and difficult road of creative invention. Where is this road? Are there no artists who have already attempted to travel it?

Here I want to draw attention to one sort of film that has acquired particularly clear definition during the war. This is the feature-length documentary film, which uses the facts of living actuality as filmed by the motion picture camera, but which unites them in montage with the aim of communicating to the spectator certain, sometimes quite general and abstract, ideas. Such a documentary film is not merely informational. It differs from the newsreel in the same way that an editorial or article in a newspaper differs from the news item in the next column. Thanks to those properties of films which I mentioned above, we have the right to look upon such documentary films as a phenomenon of high art.

I have been able to see several of these documentary feature films, all created while the war was being fought. There is, for example, the American film, *Prelude to War*. One of its striking characteristics is its direct, bold, and broad use of montage methods that were discovered in the period of the silent film. *Prelude to War* conducts its function of communicating with the spectator along three correctly distinct and separated paths—the word, the picture, and the music. The voice of the commentator leads the work of formulating and summarizing the abstract propositions. Visual fragments, fixing factual material that was photographed in Germany, Italy, and Japan—material originally scattered over half the globe—are linked together and organized for the express purpose of persistently persuading the spectator of three basic assertions:

1) Fascism is blind discipline, reducing the human being to the condition of a slave (ceaseless mechanically moving cohorts of the fascist organizations in Germany, Italy, and Japan).

2) Fascism is an organized deception of the people (persistently repeated shots of thousands of people at a peak of hysterical ecstasy, surging heads, waving arms, filmed in such a way that you cannot make out human faces, and you get an impression of a disturbed anthill; similar shots from Germany, Italy, and Japan are shown repeatedly).

3) Fascism is domination by a handful of worthless men, deliberately exploiting the darker instincts of mankind (regularly persistent display, in close-up, of the fascist leaders, chiefly in moments of oratorical exaltation, smacking of something very close to idiocy).

These three basic assertions are pursued in a montage of various combinations with invariably repeated persistence. United with the abstractions of the commentator's speech, the visually perceived facts produce an unusually powerful impression. Personally, I do not agree with the primitive treatment of fascism presented by this film, but the powerful impression made by such an organized film production on the spectators is indubitable. Such a film is fully international, and can be fully understood anywhere. The commentator's voice may be translated into any language without disturbing the integrity of impression. The montage of visual images does not require translation. I shall leave open the question of the music in this film, because the musical element here is used in the usual cliché manner.

I am convinced that this form of the documentary feature film will gain ever-increasing significance in the post-war period, first, because we need no longer doubt that it can be understood by all the peoples of the world, and second, because, thanks to this advantage, it can be widely used for fully and profoundly acquainting peoples with one another and can serve to a very considerable degree in expressing universal ideas in a graphic and striking way. The task of the artist working in this form is to find more subtle means for artistic communication of simple propositions, as well as of their profound development on the philosophic and pictorial planes.

I must again stress the tremendous significance of the documentary film in achieving the desired goal of bringing peoples together. Real truth about a people cannot be shown in separated and partial examples, localized to one or another place. It must be allowed to tell itself on a broad scale, revealing, as a principle, the historical essence of each phenomenon.

I want to draw attention to one other path along which we can conduct our search for new forms. We all know that human speech is not the first, but the last, culminating, moment in the expression of the inner state of man. Figuratively speaking, the word may be thought of as the foam rising to the crest of an emotional wave as it reaches its height. The word was organically preceded by that vast wealth of mimic expression which man possesses and which we were able to read so easily and accurately in the close-ups of actors in the silent films. There are words so immediately linked with mimed actions that their meaning is already read on the speaker's face before the word has been fully articulated. Their intonations take on almost purely musical functions. In these words may be revealed the secret of the musical phrase that can be sensed not only as a formal combination of sounds but also as a kind of composer's speech giving clear expression to feelings and thoughts. Such a word can be almost completely comprehended by any person, regardless of the language in which it is spoken.

We were once very close, in film art, to the discovery of such a film vocabulary. It often appeared in the subtitles of silent films, and even these mute letters had the cogency of spoken words. I do not consider that the speech we had in the silent film, in the form of subtitles, was artistically destitute. Its words were carefully chosen and appeared only when necessity flung them to the crest of a wave of feelings and thoughts that had already been read by the spectator in the mimed performance of the actor.

Such words are really universally understood and may well serve as a lead in our search for a new film form comprehensible to all. This would be a task well worth all the creative strength spent on it.

Music stands in direct relation to such words and cannot be questioned as an organically necessary element within any film. The relation between music and cinema is not accidental. The profound rhythmic structure of every film is musical by nature. Silent films could not exist, nor did they ever exist, without music, even though sound was not recorded on the film itself at that time. But the fact cannot be overemphasized that music has not *yet* been utilized in film making to the full extent of its possibilities. There are, of course, many pictures known as "musical films," filled and running over with music, but these are, with rare exceptions, no more than screen translations of musical plays or shows that could be just as well produced on any stage. The mighty capacity offered by music to bear profound meanings, approaching heroic speech, has scarcely been touched by film artists. It is to musical thought of this kind that creative film attention must be directed.

It would be absurd to interpret what I have said as a recommendation to abolish the sound film or even as a recommendation to erase all dialogue from future films, replacing it with laconicism and music. These thoughts have been merely an attempt to put into words a task which, I feel, all responsible film artists must face: to find and develop new film forms which will answer the universal desire for unity that has arisen among all the peoples of the world. Alongside the sound film, which has achieved so much in so brief a time, a new kind of film is waiting to be born. Now it is time to gather together all the scattered attempts and experiments made by artists in an instinctive expression of this need, to revive the vast opportunities left latent in our silent film experience, and to begin work on this new film for all the world.

The Postwar French Cinema

Georges Sadoul is a widely known film historian and critic. Two of his studies of pioneers in film have appeared in the *Hollywood Quarterly*.

.....

THE IMPORTANCE OF THE current crisis in French cinema should not be exaggerated, although its effect on the quality of production is undeniable. The truth is that the French cinema has been in a state of chronic crisis for the last thirty years.

The industry operates on a very narrow basis in France. In a country where half the population lives in the country or in small villages, there are relatively few motion picture theaters, and attendance is limited. For every Frenchman buying one movie ticket, an Englishman buys five or six, an American eight or ten; moreover, the price of admission is three to five times greater in England and America than it is in France.

Before 1914, in spite of its undeveloped home market, France had a quasi-monopoly of international film trade. In 1908, according to George Eastman, founder of the Kodak enterprises, the Pathé Company alone was selling twice as many films in the United States as all the American producers put together. But the young American industry soon dominated its home market, and then eliminated French competition in nearly all foreign countries. In 1920 the big companies in Paris, playing a losing game, liquidated their agencies and studios abroad, and relied on importing American, German, and Swedish films for part of their French revenue.

French production, which had been foremost in quantity and to a certain extent in quality, collapsed after 1914, systematically discouraged by these big firms. By 1928 France was producing only fifty films a year. The industrial policy of the interests that monopolized the industry discouraged the directors grouped around Louis Delluc who wanted to make French cinema an art. At the end of the silent-film period most of them renounced their ambitions and resigned themselves to producing commercial films. Aside from the efforts of the avant-garde, reserved to a very limited élite, there was no longer a French School, but only individual creators, the most important of whom were Jacques Feyder and René Clair.

The introduction of sound film and the resulting public demand for French-language films stimulated production. It grew in two years from fifty to two hundred films a year, a certain number of them being products of German and American companies. But, aside from those made by René Clair, they remained for the most part wholly mediocre and very much inferior to German and American productions of the same period.

In 1934, René Clair, discouraged by the difficulties he encountered, settled down in England. Jacques Feyder had been in the United States since 1929. The brightest hope of the younger generation, Jean Vigo, died at twenty-nine, exhausted by the struggle he had led. The two largest French firms, Pathé and Gaumont, closed down, and Paramount interrupted its enormous production program in Paris. The depth of the depression had been reached. One might well have believed that the French cinema was doomed. Happily, this was far from true.

The downfall of the big companies had to a certain extent reëstablished free competition. Smaller studios gave opportunities to talents that were still unknown or had been blacklisted by the larger studios. The absence of René Clair was compensated for by the return of Jacques Feyder. The much-criticized efforts of Marcel Pagnol now began to bear fruit. In 1935 a French School was born, grouped around Jacques Feyder, Jean Renoir, Marcel Carné, and Julien Duvivier. In foreign capitals it regained for France the artistic position lost twenty years earlier.

The second World War brutally interrupted the renaissance. Renoir, René Clair, and Duvivier were able to reach Hollywood. Feyder had to take refuge in Switzerland. The *Propaganda Staffel*, organ of Nazi censorship, kept French cinema under rigid control. As an art it was threatened with eclipse. But a certain number of directors emerged who effectively took the place of those who were missing. Discovered or rediscovered were Jean Grémillon, Jacques Becker, Louis Daquin, Robert Bresson, Jean Delannoy, and H. G. Clouzot. Marcel Carné directed *Les Visiteurs du soir* and *Les Enfants du Paradis*. In all occupied Europe there was no better cinema than that of France, almost all of whose personnel were active in organizations of the Resistance.

Certain economic factors favored the pursuit of the renaissance of

French cinema. Before 1939, 35 to 40 per cent of receipts had gone to American and German firms. Under the occupation, American films were banned and the Germans tried to monopolize the screen, but the mediocrity of their production and its propagandist content provoked a spontaneous popular boycott of Doctor Goebbels' films.

The foreign share in receipts fell below 10 per cent, and French production, sharply favored, in spite of all the difficulties born of the war, was able to release a total of seventy-five films in 1942, as compared with an average annual output of a hundred and twenty in the years preceding the outbreak of the war.

The Liberation, the fighting, and the heavy bombardment that led up to it, brought film making almost to a standstill in 1944. In a country still virtually without communication and electricity, the studios resumed production with the greatest difficulty in 1945. Nevertheless, they soon had to their credit important artistic achievements and were honored at international festivals in Brussels, Cannes, Venice, and elsewhere.

With the reëstablishment of normal international exchange, foreign competition on the economic plane reappeared. In June, 1946, in Washington, Blum and Byrnes signed motion picture agreements between France and the United States. The prewar film import system—that of "contingency"—limiting to one hundred and twenty the number of American films to be imported each year was replaced by the "quota" system. French theater programs were now to include at least 31 per cent of domestic films, but no limitation was placed on the number of foreign films to be imported. As a result of the agreements the share of the domestic income reserved for French producers, which had been more than 90 per cent during the war, fell below 40 per cent in the first quarter of 1947. Before 1939 it had comprised between 60 and 70 per cent. A wave of panic began to spread. In the winter of 1947–48, eight out of thirteen studios closed their doors. Unemployment mounted to 80 per cent in some branches of the industry. The number of feature films, which had reached ninety-four in 1946, fell back to seventy-four in 1947.

The strong feeling among technicians, artists, and studio workers was shared by a large body of public opinion. Hundreds of thousands of moviegoers joined Committees for the Defense of French Cinema. As early as the first months of 1948, Parliament concerned itself with the problem, and the French government denounced the Washington agreements.

They were replaced in October, 1948, by arrangements more favorable to French cinema. The "quota" was increased from 31 to 40 per cent; the number of dubbed films to be imported was reduced to the level of 1938. Finally, a special assistance act was passed which gave the various branches of the industry a subsidy of 2,000,000,000 francs.

These measures, foreshadowed from the beginning of 1948, stimulated French production: ninety-six films were made in 1948, the highest production figure since 1938. However, although new circumstances had been established, new dangers appeared. Since the beginning of 1949 the country has been in a threatening economic crisis. Unemployment and bankruptcies have multiplied. The standard of living, already very low at the time of the Liberation in comparison with that of 1938, continued to decline rapidly from 1946 on. Although the price of admission has increased much less than the general cost of living, theater attendance has fallen sharply. In 1948, attendance in industrial areas fell 25 to 30 per cent from the levels of the preceding year. The first figures reported in 1949 showed a further decline of 20 to 25 per cent from the already very unsatisfactory totals of 1948, when attendance was actually poorer than it was in 1944, a year of bombardments, battles, and shortages of electricity.

Under such conditions, French producers—who are almost always independents without large capital resources—hesitate to undertake films that risk not being able to repay production costs on the domestic market. Yet French films cost little. The average budget for a picture was about 40,000,000 francs, or $100,000 in 1948. A superproduction might cost as much as 80,000,000 francs, but a budget greater than 100,000,000 francs, or $250,000, is considered a real extravagance. In 1948 only two films exceeded, by an insignificant margin, the $250,000 limit. The tendency of French producers to plan in terms of low budgets is not always shrewdly calculated. One of the two films budgeted at more than $250,000 in 1948, H. G. Clouzot's *Manon,* will very quickly earn large profits for its producer by virtue of its great success in France and abroad, whereas *Monsieur de Falindor,* a film budgeted at less than $50,000, is likely to lose half the meager capital invested in it.

One of the characteristics of the present situation in the French industry is that the differences in the profitability of films, formerly narrow, are now very considerable, and may vary for films made on identical budgets in a ratio of 1 to 20, and even more. This phenomenon is due to the economic crisis, but also to a change in the audience. More and more French people go to see movies selectively, choosing films in whose quality they have confidence. They are losing the habit of attending the theater closest to their homes without considering the program, and they are becoming increasingly exacting about what is offered to them.

The French producers who pursue a policy of mediocre production at bottom prices will eventually be proved wrong, but their attitude has had a most undesirable effect on quality. Since the Liberation most of the directors of outstanding talent have made few films, or none, for it was feared that their demands on the budget would be excessive. Jacques Feyder, who returned to France in 1944, had not been assigned one film to direct up to the time of his death in 1948. In five years, Jean Grémillon, author of *Lumière d'été* and *Le Ciel est à vous*, directed only one film. The same was true of Jacques Becker, who made *Goupi Mains Rouges,* Marcel Carné, in spite of the great success of *Les Enfants du Paradis* and *Les Visiteurs du soir,* René Clair, and Claude Autant-Lara.

Nevertheless, the development of French cinema continues and its achievements are far from negligible. In the following survey it will not be possible, unfortunately, to take into account whether a given film is already known to the American public.

The absence of Jean Renoir and the loss of Jacques Feyder are deeply felt. But the prewar masters René Clair, Julien Duvivier, Marcel Carné, and Marcel Pagnol have each produced a film in France since 1945.

René Clair was abroad for more than twelve years. *Air pur,* the film he started in 1939, was interrupted by the declaration of war and will never be finished. *Le Silence est d'or* was an opportunity for him to rediscover, in the atmosphere of Paris, some of the avant-garde traditions with which he grew up and, more especially, the beloved French cinema before 1914 to which his art owes so much. In *Le Silence est d'or,* without losing any of his smiling optimism, he shows a certain melancholy, almost bitterness; but the lightness of his touch and the swift precision of his art swept away, at least outwardly, the seriousness that might have clouded the comedy and transformed into querulousness the grumbling charm of this "journal of a fifty-year-old man." The success of *Le Silence est d'or* was considerable in France and in Europe. But for three years René Clair did not work on another film. In collaboration with the dramatist Armand

Salacrou he is now preparing *La Beauté du diable,* a free adaptation of Goethe's *Faust.* It is being shot outside of France, in Rome. . . .

After the triumph of his elaborate *Les Enfants du Paradis,* Marcel Carné had exceptional means at his disposal for *Portes de la nuit.* The film was to be a fantasy and its hero was a personification of "destiny" as a vagabond. But it was also to be a study of the hard winter that followed the Liberation. The Barbès-Rochechouart metro in Montmartre, the sorry working-class districts on the north side of Paris, the dismal Saint-Martin canal, demolished areas, the main railroad yards, were the locales in which the protagonists, conceived for Carné by his regular screenwriter, Jacques Prevert, moved. Reality, too minutely elaborated, seemed a studio set, especially when the new Italian films were being shown triumphantly on French screens at the same time. In addition, a false poetry, in the manner of the 'twenties and 'thirties, marred the scenes of fantasy. The almost total failure of the film was not its just due, however, for it did contain admirable sections.

Subsequently, Carné began to work on *La Fleur de l'âge,* a film about penitentiaries for children, written by Jacques Prevert. Shooting was far from complete when the film was abandoned. Carné then spent long months in Italy preparing, from a script by dramatist Jean Anouilh, a modern version of *Euridyce,* to be played by Michèle Morgan. The project failed. It seems that Carné, whose *Quai des Brumes* and *Le Jour se lève* place him among the world's greatest directors, will not soon have a chance to make another film.

Marcel Pagnol, who is very popular in the United States, is far less so in France, for reasons that are not immediately apparent. But the fact is that Pagnol has always mixed the best with the worst in his films, even at the peak of his fame before the war. In comparison with the works of his best period—*Angèle, Jofroi, La Femme du boulanger*—his *La Fille du puisatier* (1940) represents a definite decline. His film *Naïs,* an adaptation from Zola released after the Liberation, was below average in quality.

His last work, *La Belle Meunière,* is a fictional version of the life of Schubert, interesting only because it experimented with the new, still imperfect, French color process, *routcolor.* About the film itself the less said the better, for it is totally without merit.

Julien Duvivier reopened his French career with *Panique,* which was well performed by the excellent actors Michel Simon and Viviane Romance. But the script, the story of a man unjustly accused of murder and lynched, is conventional. It would be difficult, indeed, to count such a film among the achievements of the maker of *Pépé le Moko, La belle équipe,* and *Un Carnet de bal.*

Among those who proved themselves during the Occupation, Jean Grémillon is certainly one of the most effective and talented. He first appeared in the ranks of the avant-garde soon after 1925, but after one or two commercial failures he was constrained to direct films unworthy of his considerable ability.

On the eve of the war, Jean Grémillon again attracted attention with his *L'Etrange Monsieur Victor,* magnificently played by Raimu, and *Remorques,* a film that was to star Jean Gabin and Michèle Morgan. He was prevented from completing the latter by the opening of hostilities.

After the success he achieved under the Occupation with *Lumière d'été* and *Le Ciel est à vous,* Jean Grémillon undertook a project with a wide social canvas: *Le Massacre des innocents,* a story of France between 1935 and 1945. The plans did not go through. He then prepared, under the sponsorship of the French government, *Le Printemps de la liberté,* in commemoration of the Revolution of 1848. Just as the shooting was about to start, the government withdrew its promised support and the film could not be made. This is to be much regretted, for the script, which has been published, proves that *Le Printemps de la liberté* would certainly have been one of the best postwar French films.

After this setback, Jean Grémillon directed a script by the dramatist Jean Anouilh, *Pattes blanches,* which was released in France in April, 1949. Here, Grémillon demonstrated full mastery of his talents. He was able to give vivid reality to a story set in a small town in Brittany which opposes a ruined young man, a fishmonger in love, a forlorn girl, a disinherited bastard, and a hunchbacked inn servant. Thanks to Grémillon and his actors, these characters became believable and gripping. But inadequacies in the screenplay are evident, despite the dramatic talent of Jean Anouilh.

Jacques Becker, who became famous with *Goupi Mains Rouges,* was for many years Jean Renoir's assistant. But the disciple has shown great individuality. *Falbalas,* which he directed in the last months of the Occupation, is a brilliant painting of the milieu of Parisian *haute-couture.* But *Falbalas* did not reach the high perfection of *Antoine et Antoinette,* a chronicle of the everyday life of Parisian workmen, whose simplicity of tone and uncompromising rejection of customary dramatic devices cannot but bring to mind the best films of the young Italian school. Jean Grémillon and Jacques Becker are among the best representatives of the realistic French school, along with Georges Rouquier, René Clément, and Louis Daquin.

Georges Rouquier presented in *Farrebique* a picture, at once homely and lyrical, of the daily life of peasants in southern France. This full-length film owes much to *Nanook* and *Moana*, but Georges Rouquier's special merit consists in having portrayed men in their everyday struggle with nature not under exotic skies but in the setting he knows most intimately. The inhabitants of the farm seen in *Farrebique*, acted by themselves, are close relatives of Rouquier.

René Clément, who worked as a technical director on Cocteau's fantasy, *La Belle et la bête*, and on Noël-Noël's comedy, *Le Père tranquille*, worked independently as the director of *Les Maudits*, a story of a group of Nazis and collaborationists who take refuge in a submarine and roam all over the world in search of a safe place to land. In spite of the somewhat awkward, melodramatic plot, the direction and the performances were outstanding. Clément has not directed another film since *Les Maudits*, nor has Georges Rouquier since *Farrebique*, completed in 1946.

Louis Daquin's career began under the Occupation with a picture full of charm and freshness, *Nous les gosses*, but his following films were disappointing. He has recently reaffirmed a real mastery of the medium in *Le Point du jour*, which is a picture of a miner's life in the collieries of northern France. Vladimir Pozner wrote a simple and straightforward script for this striking film, the outstanding French production of the 1948–49 season.

Because of Becker, Rouquier, Clément, and Daquin, one may speak of a realistic French school. Following the tradition created before the war by Jean Renoir, in particular, it might rival the new Italian school, if its representatives had more frequent opportunities to direct films.

H. G. Clouzot is one of the figures in French cinema upon whom the highest hopes are based. His talent proved itself under the Occupation with *Le Corbeau*. The sharp controversy stimulated by the film was constructive rather than destructive to a director of such great talent as Clouzot. In 1947 he won great success with *Quai des Orfèvres*, a trite enough detective story which was invested with unquestionable value by the remarkable performance of Jouvet and the great plastic sense of the director. *Manon*, which Clouzot finished early in 1949, was awaited hopefully. The script of the film, written by Clouzot himself, was a free transposition in modern terms of the well-known eighteenth-century novel by the Abbé Prévost.

Excellent performances were given by Michel Auclair and Cecile Aubry, a young actress whose talent has earned her a contract in Hollywood.

Unhappily, Clouzot demonstrated in *Manon* that he was not able to cope with large-scale social problems as Renoir did before the war and as the new Italian school does today. A certain extreme romanticism, a complacence with abstractions at points where representing reality directly was called for, a misuse of borrowings from the great film classics, numerous improbabilities, and errors in taste disappointed the most faithful of Clouzot's admirers. Nevertheless the film was well received and has become a popular success.

In the naturalistic and readily pessimistic genre, which Clouzot favors, Yves Allégret, brother of the already well-known Marc Allegret, has directed *Dédée d'Anvers* and *Une si jolie petite plage*. This skillful and talented director makes the mistake of basing his work too faithfully on the themes, the characters, and even the bad habits of the prewar French school. One is still waiting for him to produce a truly original work that will go beyond the average successful film.

The work of Claude Autant-Lara also belongs in the category of naturalistic films. Like Grémillon, he is an old member of the avant-garde of 1925 who was restricted for a long time to directing films unworthy of his talent. He was recognized under the Occupation with the release of *Le Mariage de chiffon* and, especially, *Douce,* a conventional enough novel out of which Pierre Bost and Jean Aurenche developed an excellent script.

In 1947, with the same collaborators, Claude Autant-Lara adapted a novel by Raymond Radiguet, *Le Diable au corps,* which had been popular during the First World War. This was a polished work in which Autant-Lara ably directed his talented young actors, one of whom, Gérard Philipe, became a new European sensation. The superior quality and values of *Le Diable au corps* are beyond question.

During the Occupation, poetic and fantastic films had been almost obligatory for directors who did not want to deal with reality as it existed

Devil in the Flesh/Le Diable au corps (1947), by Claude
Autant-Lara, with Gérard Philipe and Micheline Presle

under German control. This genre now seems to be disappearing. Its last
expression was Jean Cocteau's brilliant, glacial *La Belle et la bête.* He tried
vainly to repeat its success with *Ruy Blas* and *L'Aigle à deux têtes.* However,
by filming his best stage play, *Les Parents terribles,* Cocteau accomplished
a remarkable technical feat and produced his best film.

To make our enumeration exhaustive we shall name the often uneven
work of talented and prolific directors such as Jean Delannoy *(La Symphonie pastorale, Aux yeux du souvenir)* and Christian Jaque *(Boule de suif,
D'homme à hommes).*

The French documentary school, in spite of serious difficulties, continues to produce interesting films, among which have been *Van Gogh* by
Alain Resnais, *Goemons* by Anik Bellon, and *Naissance du cinéma* by Roger
Leenhardt, who produced the wholly fresh and commendable film, *Les
dernières vacances.* To the French documentary school may be added the
poetic *Noces de sable* made in Morocco by Andrès Zvoboda, and *Paris 1900*
by Nicole Vedres, who succeeded in arranging scattered pieces of pre-1914
film into a sly and charming montage.

Talent is not scarce in the French cinema. Perhaps the assessment must be that the school, in spite of its numerous and brilliant successes, has remained on a plateau for several years and no longer has the richness and youth that it had before 1940. Perhaps the judgment will be that the direct and poetic contact with reality that earlier French films always had has been replaced by a complacent self-indulgence in old formulas and a certain academicism.

Nevertheless, we do not believe that the slight hesitation that marks the French school today is due basically to lack of initiative or talent among its film makers. It is, in large measure, the present economic difficulties that limit initiative and narrow the choice of subjects and oblige film makers to return to old subjects rather than seek new and original themes in the life around them.

The vitality of French cinema is incontestable. For fifteen years it has managed to keep alive in spite of the deaths, absences, departures, or exile, of its best practitioners. We believe that, thanks to its rich resources of talent, the French school will continue to be one of the foremost among the various national cinemas for a very long time to come.

FROM VOL. 10, NO. 3, SPRING 1956   Hugh Gray

When in Rome . . .

Hugh Gray is a screen, radio, and television writer. His connections abroad have included working with Korda, Cavalcanti, and the B.B.C. As a screen writer in Hollywood
since 1944, his credits include *Quo Vadis?, Ulysses, Helen of Troy,* and *The Prince
and the Pauper.* Mr. Gray was recently appointed an assistant professor in the Motion Picture Division of the Department of Theater Arts, University of California, Los
Angeles.

. . . . .

THE INDISPENSABLE Paul Rotha, writing in 1930 of the movie of 1913, re-
called that it was out of Italy that there came the first

> big productions or "feature films" as they were known, including a version of
> Homer's *Odyssey, The Fall of Troy* . . . but greatest of all, the forerunner of every
> spectacle film since, was *Quo Vadis?,* a veritable mammoth production of 1913,
> eight thousand feet in length. This was bought and shown by George Kleine
> in America where, to that date, the most pretentious effort had been *The Life
> of Buffalo Bill.* Since the day when American producers first saw *Quo Vadis?*
> cinema audiences of the world have been presented with super-spectacle after
> super-spectacle. From *The Birth of a Nation,* Griffith's reply to the Italian pic-
> ture at the end of 1914, through the years of *The Ten Commandments* . . . *Ben-
> Hur* . . . super-films abounded, developing today into . . . the singing, danc-
> ing and talking variety. In the few years just before the war the feature film
> sufficed to build up the industry (increased audiences meant bigger film stu-
> dios and larger cinema theaters), and in 1914 the opening of the Strand The-
> ater on Broadway marked a new era in the history of the cinema. The way was
> open for the position as it is today.

As we read, we cannot help feeling a haunting sense that we are round
again at the place where we came in; and that the student of the cinema
in the year 2000, when all the prints will have presumably perished, will
have to look very closely at the dates in order to find some way to distinguish the two periods 1913 and 1950. Certainly, it is where *we* came in—

we, that is, who have been involved during the past few years in the re-making of *Quo Vadis?*, of *The Odyssey,* and of *The Fall of Troy,* though we have called the latter *Helen of Troy* and have given to Odysseus his Latin name, Ulysses.

Now that the last of this trio, *Helen of Troy,* has finally been presented to the world in a simultaneous global première, some recollections of the days of their remaking, mellowed a little by retrospect, may be worth re-cording. But first, in order to complete our sense of historical perspective, let me quote again from the same context of Rotha's *Film Till Now:*

> With the outbreak of war in 1914, film production naturally came to an end in Europe. The road was left clear for America to secure for herself the su-preme commercial control which she still holds. It was simply a matter of cir-cumstance of which the Americans were quick to take full advantage. That they made the best of their opportunity is only to their credit.

So much indeed had the United States made of her opportunity that five years after World War II the first-generation, American descendant, so to speak, of the Italian spectacle-film maker was back in the "old coun-try" with seven million dollars in his pocket, or at least to his credit in blocked lire, to give his native city a boost and at the same time—since pure altruism is not apparently a feature of business—to do himself a bit of good by using up the blocked lire to make a super-spectacle for half price. He was also prepared, like so many who return to the country of their parents' origins, to challenge the old saying about teaching one's grandmother to suck eggs.

For ten years or more, L. B. Mayer, whose debut in the motion-picture world was as a successful exhibitor of religious movies, had been planning to make *Quo Vadis?* at some favorable moment. Nineteen forty-nine was the silver-jubilee year both of his taking over at Culver City and of the making of the fabulously successful *Ben-Hur.* This twofold silver jubilee was to be celebrated by an even more successful picture, a version of *Quo Vadis?* that would be made with all of MGM's wonderful resources, which were only a dream in the Rome of thirty-five years ago. Circumstances of one kind and another, however, delayed the proposed 1949 start; and it was not until the spring of 1950 that the production was ready to roll. In preparation for this event, multitudinous personnel winged above The City to land at Ciampino Airport. Two thousand years previously, Horace, on the eve of Rome's Augustan surge, had expressed the pious hope that never in all its travels would the sun set eyes on a city greater than Rome. Whether or not this hope was justified in the Phoebus-eye view of the Trans-World Apollos arriving from Culver City, I cannot say. It is more than likely that the majority were preoccupied with the thought that never would this City of Rome below them, nor indeed all the world, see a spectacle to equal the one in which they were about to take their share.

As for me, I do not recall that my thoughts during these moments of arrival were of either of these things. I remember now—as I was being driven from Ciampino to the nearby studios of Cine Città, my eyes delighting in the cypresses that mark the line of the Appian Way—only the German-accented voice of the studio emissary dutifully reciting, like a Cook's guide, a thoughtfully prepared recitative of advice for travellers innocently abroad in Italy and the regulations I would be expected to observe during the making of the picture. For everything was very efficiently organized, as it had to be if the picture was to be completed as planned.

The "old country" over the centuries had had her ups and downs and the present was one of her downs. Or was it? And in what sense? Had not *Open City* and *Paisan, Shoe Shine, Bicycle Thieves,* and a host of other pictures come out of her during the five glorious years preceding our arrival? Which way, indeed, is up; and which, down? This was a question which increasingly presented itself to thoughtful minds in the company during this time in Rome, not only in reflecting on the kind of movies a studio makes (we were back where Rome began thirty years ago) or on the way people made them, but also when pondering subjects without any relation to movies at all, such as the way other peoples think and live. It was difficult for the thoughtful, for example, to understand how it was possible at one and the same time for them to be so exasperated by and yet so completely in love with a place and a people.

Some of the company, of course, increasingly saw only inefficiency, stupidity, and incorrigible rascality. In others, love prevailed; and what at first had seemed to be conservative prejudices were revealed to be in reality ancient traditions to be respected as a part of a different, well-tried way of life. At one end of this line, then, was the overworked executive who collapsed on the set one night before my astonished and horrified eyes, as if poleaxed. The "inefficiency" of the Romans and their "incomprehensible way of life" had been too much for him; and when, a few weeks later, he began to show signs of recovering from his nervous breakdown he declared that this was the first and the last time he would leave home, and that, once back, he would never move outside the city limits of Beverly Hills. At the other end of the line was the lady from the MGM wardrobe department who found her man and her home among the Romans.

Of course, the situation originally confronting the advanced guard that came from Culver City to study the terrain at Cine Città presented a powerful challenge to that organizing ability, that energetic drive, that capacity to get things done, which have characterized the American in developing his own country and in opening up industry in others. But the fact was that *Quo Vadis?* was to be made on what had been a battlefield, and the battle scars were still very much in evidence.

Cine Città had been built by Mussolini to house the Italian motion-picture industry in a way worthy of the future that he had planned for it. Across the Via Toscolana from it, he had built the Centro Sperimentale where Italian youths would learn to become film makers. Italian troops who had gone over to the Allies had fought the Germans for possession of these sites during the struggle for Rome. Long before abandoning the studios, the Germans had stripped them of every piece of portable cinematic equipment. Some of the buildings were still in ruins, and the largest stage of all was roofless long after *Quo Vadis?* was completed. The studios had long served as a camp for displaced persons, and several hundreds were still there when we arrived. They were a sign and a remembrance to us of the terrible years just passed, these men and women, penniless and homeless, with their children who whiled away the time playing, of all things, at war! To add to our difficulties, under the conditions then prevailing in Rome, sufficient electricity could not be generated locally to supply the needs of a Technicolor production of the scope of *Quo Vadis?*. Thus, at any hour of the night—usually at the most inconvenient—the light would suddenly go out in one or other section of the city. Clearly, the "old country" was in a bad way.

And yet, in the end, out of Cine Città there came a negative as technically first-class as any that Hollywood could produce; and it was shot on schedule. Only long planning and the vast resources of MGM admirably organized and oriented by the determination to do, when in Rome, as Hollywood does when at home, made this achievement possible. For to have done in Rome as the Roman industry did seemed to the executives of MGM to be the sure road to a debacle, not because of inherent defects in the methods of the Roman film makers working toward their own ends, but because the men from Culver City could not work that way. After all, between the man from Culver City and the Roman there are many differences. These derived not only from their respective societies, so differently constituted, but also from a different sense of time. How truly different the latter is I was to grasp more fully later, during the making of *Ulysses*.

In Culver City, then, as elsewhere in Hollywood, shooting starts at nine and continues till six o'clock with an hour's break for lunch. So was it to be at Cine Città even through the rising heat of June on into the terrible dog days of August when every man, woman, and child even if they have to beg, borrow, or steal their fares, leaves Rome for the beaches of the Lido di Roma, Fregene, and elsewhere. Under the Hollywood rule, too, the siesta—that centuries old and wise period of repose and recollection that follows lunch—was abolished. However, it was by no means easy to secure the observance of this rule by a people firmly set in a habit so admirably part of their way of life and in view of which they start the working day far earlier than we do.

Equally revolutionary was the edict that no *festa*—no public holiday, that is—would be observed in the studios. The fourth of July was transferred to the Saturday following, thus giving the only full week-end holiday during the entire period of production. Now, in Italy the *festa* is a frequent occurrence—less frequent than in the days of the Emperors when there were something like 120 public holidays—and in the peak period of the production, from April through August, there should normally have been eight of them. Seven of these, the Romans might reluctantly have foregone, but not the eighth. This, the dearest of all to the Roman heart, is the Ferragosto, the age-old commemoration of the triumph of Augustus on his return from his victory over Anthony and Cleopatra, a holiday later taken over by the Christian Church and dedicated to the Blessed Virgin's Assumption into heaven. None of the Romans could believe, up to the very last, that on this day of all days the cameras would turn, and the memory of Augustus would be ignored in the spurning of a deeply rooted custom. But Augustus would not allow himself to be completely ignored. Indeed, in the circumstances, what happened is the kind of thing that makes it easy for superstition to survive everywhere in the world.

This day that is Ferragosto had been set for the beginning of the shooting of the great banquet scene in Nero's palace; and, of course for so large a set, the largest stage—the roofless one—was to be used, tarpaulined over against the unlikely arrival of rain. Then, in the small hours of the morning of his flouted feast day, the divine Augustus opened the flood gates of heaven and set the rains pouring down upon the magnificent set—all elaborately ready for the traditional Roman orgy that might, likewise, have offended Augustus' deeply ascetic soul. Telephones rang urgently, and the night was suddenly full of the hurrying feet of men summoned to save the dazzling furnishings and to mop up the flooded floors. Thus, unofficially, the feast of Ferragosto was observed. Nothing so startling had happened on the production since the first day of shooting.

For this great inauguration, the Roman press and all the resident correspondents had been gathered together. The brief and breathless moment passed. But a second take, for safety, was naturally called for. The bells rang, the instructions were shouted, and the company waited in hushed expectancy for the cameras to roll. But they did not roll. The electric power had suddenly and inexplicably failed. How could this be? Had not equipment been shipped by the holdful from the United States and dynamos removed from Italian destroyers and installed at Cine Città to generate the needed current? There was one ready answer that sprang to mind, and men looked uneasily at one another. Sabotage! Would this set a pattern? Was the hidden red hand poised to wreck and ruin all that had been planned? For some little while, it looked more and more as if this dark suspicion were true. But experience in handling the power and in nursing the equipment finally provided the true explanation, and sanity was again restored.

Perhaps the most daring decision of all was to record the definitive sound track at the time of shooting. Such a procedure is still virtually unknown in Italian production, where dubbing is the order of the day. In actual production, only a guide track is made; and this, for a number of reasons. One of these may very well be the difficulty of getting anything like adequate silence on the stages, not only because many of them are not soundproof, but also perhaps because so voluble a people are apt to interpret a plea for absolute silence as merely a request to talk only in a stage whisper. Another reason may derive from the fact that certain actresses, and even some actors, can be admired only for their beauty, since their power to charm the ear is something less than their power to fill the eye. With all this practice in dubbing their own films and with the vast consumption of dubbed American pictures by a people who are among the most ardent movie-goers, the Italian industry has reached a high level in a technique, to which the current version of *Ulysses* is a puzzling exception. But more of that later.

It is, of course, sometimes said that the Italians operate in this way from inefficiency, or because they are lazy. The record of Italy in engineering in general and in the electrical field in particular gives this the lie. And as for laziness, this is a judgment that should not be made without a clear understanding of what a man's neighbor considers to be truly important in life as well as in movies.

Indeed, precisely because of these standards of value, which gave the organizers and the engineers such headaches, the Romans were able to contribute so much to the color and atmosphere of *Quo Vadis?*. For every Italian is an actor, and at least every other Italian is an artist or an imaginative artisan. Further, history is in every Roman's blood; and those who built the sets for *Quo Vadis?* and made the dressings for them had a passionate love of beautiful detail that flowed over into their work even though there was not the slightest likelihood of much of it being seen. The over-all effect, however, would not have been the same without it.

Each man, likewise, felt himself a qualified critic of the script and its production, for the story was out of the Romans' past that still lives so vividly about them. They were tolerant of us for the most part and ready with ideas and advice—even the humblest extra—but there were limits to what they could accept. In Italian, for example, as some of the members of the crowd explained to me, the very word for a well-shaped woman derives somehow from the name of Nero's mother. Such a woman is *una Poppaea,* and the use of the name in description is accompanied always by a gesture indicative of liberal curves. That an actress with less than generous curves had been cast for such a part remained a source of unhappiness to them and offended without possibility of forgiveness the whole sense of historical association contained for them in the name *Poppaea.*

It was, however, as actors that the Romans were mostly with us—on several days, as many as nine thousand of them. And how they gave of their wonderful best! The first time that I was fully aware of their desire to give of this best in the spirit of the true artist was during the shooting

of the first crowd scene, at the opening of the picture when the victorious
Roman General Marcus Vinicius (Robert Taylor) is shown returning from
his campaign, bringing booty and countless prisoners. In our story, the
good guys were the Christians; and the bad guys were the pagan Romans.
And, as every child knows from the irrefutable evidence of history down
the centuries, Christians are mild and gentle; and pagans are brutal. It was
in the course of setting this note for the rest of the movie that the Roman
masters were to be shown lashing their prisoners along the Appian Way
as the hapless creatures struggled to haul the battering rams and towers
that had reduced their cities. During this scene, a certain number of the
prisoners had to collapse and even die under the relentless brutality of the
lash. Now every extra in Rome is a star, at least in the measure of his devotion to his art; and such was each man's determination to give of his
best that the advancing army was constantly halted by bodies piled in
front at the exact places where the cameras were set up. There, the ground
was as littered with corpses as if the prisoners had been moving forward
not under the lash but against a stronghold of machine guns. Each man
felt it incumbent upon him, for the good of the picture, to die in agony,
imperially, as Caesar might have died, right into the lenses.

Perhaps the strongest indication, however, of their devotion to the arts
of the theater, and a clue for those seeking to understand another people
was given at a later moment. It was one of those occasions when the production was interrupted by what we usually called labor disputes. The details of these incidents were complicated and not at all as politically inspired as some—the sabotage school—wished to believe. Mostly, indeed,
they were not even matters of money, but of human dignity and working
conditions. A common trade-union weapon throughout Italy is the lightning strike, that may last from a few minutes to several hours. Indeed in
Rome, it is not uncommon to find the streetcars suddenly halted for a few
minutes and then, as suddenly, moving on. The value or ultimate effect
of these maneuvers is not at once evident. There were occasions, however,
when the crowds on the set felt called to adopt them; and after a fair
warning, a mob of eight or nine thousand men and women who had been
roaring and yelling as they knew the crowd had roared and yelled in the
Circus Maximus, was all of a sudden seated and as silent as a Roman
crowd can be. Then, the protest made and honor satisfied, at the end of
the stipulated period of fifteen or thirty minutes, they would rise to their

feet; and the only malice they showed thereafter was in their countenances, as the part required from good actors asked to vent their fury on the Christians in the arena. What simple pride they have in their work!

The name *Quo Vadis?* was spoken everywhere all over Rome. It was like the opening up of a new industry in a hard-hit town. When a man told his neighbors, "I'm working in *Quo Vadis?*" they nodded in appreciation; and they knew that he would give of his best, as they would, even if it were only as a super carrying a spear, while dressed in hot metal under a scorching sun. Difficult and wearing though this might be, it had to be done. After all, in those moments was one not an artist? *Pazienza! Pazienza.*

Indeed, there are two words, although superficially contradictory, that a man must learn to understand; and then he will survive, happily, any Roman film adventure, even though he is the most efficient, pampered Hollywood tycoon. One is *subito* (right away!), the misleading automatic response to any command; and the other is *pazienza,* the literal meaning of which is at once evident, but the full rich meaning of which is learned only after a long while. To understand it fully is to know in some measure why hypertension and sudden death do not haunt the Roman studios as they haunt the stages of multi-million dollar, super-efficient Hollywood. Indeed, something of the full and living sense of this word *pazienza,* and something of the peace that comes with knowing how much faith to attach to the warm, cheerfully deceptive answer *"Subito, signore!"* only truly dawned on me when I returned to work on the production of *Ulysses.*

9 Notes and Communications

| Pierre Descaves

J'Accuse*

Sacha Guitry, who has been summoned to appear before the "Chambre Ci-vique," and to whom the Minister of the Interior has refused an exit permit for Hollywood, has had his "defense" proclaimed and published in an evening paper. Captain Pierre Descaves, son of the famous writer Lucien Descaves, Guitry's colleague at the Académie Goncourt before its recent purge, answers him as follows:

SACHA GUITRY HAS CHARGED in a publication that the discredit from which he is suffering is based on spite. He claims that this discredit is due to the machinations of his "antagonists" and to the malignity of his ene-mies. At his instigation and by way of provocation, the newspaper heads the list of these "enemies" with my name. *I*, the enemy of Guitry? It is an honor which I would not reject had I not, painfully, earned the right to be his judge. For the present, I shall limit my role to that of prosecutor.

Until 1939, after well-deserved successes, the worth and inspiration of which were continuously diminishing, Guitry enjoyed an honorable place in the theater. In 1939, by forcing himself into a literary society heretofore limited to professional writers, he could lay claim to an intel-lectual grasp and to moral responsibilities inherent in his title of member of the Académie Goncourt.

Because, during the dark years of occupation, Guitry did not show himself worthy of these responsibilities, committed errors, was guilty of breach of faith, and failed as a Frenchman,

I ACCUSE Sacha Guitry of having been from 1940 to 1944, at a time when his wealth and expectations gave him ample breathing space, an ac-commodating spectator of the traitorous collaborationist policy by very quickly reopening his theater and by staging his productions;

---

*This article was first published in *France-Amérique,* issue of February 17, 1946.

I ACCUSE Sacha Guitry of having acquiesced, by his attitude of the worldly man of the theater and by his solicitude that everything should go on "as before," in the abdication of those who no longer believed in France;

I ACCUSE Sacha Guitry of having deadened public opinion by his ostentation and by giving the conqueror, at the expense of bleeding France, the proof that among us there were men interested in encouraging laughter in the midst of charnel houses;

I ACCUSE Sacha Guitry of having, like a make-up artist, disguised the misery that was crushing us and of having attempted to transform it into a make-believe happiness;

I ACCUSE Sacha Guitry of having been one of the inspirers of all the cozy surrenders, of all the soft compliances, and of having contributed to the perversion of a confused public opinion; of having encouraged the idea that nothing more could happen, that everything had been gained, that it was easy to breathe on one's knees, even on one's stomach, and that the light of freedom came not from the resistance of the *maquis,* but from a prompter's box;

I ACCUSE Sacha Guitry of having made witticisms when we were preparing passwords and watchwords and to have seen, as freedom's flame, in our dark night, only his floodlights;

I ACCUSE Sacha Guitry, who during happier days had placed himself at the service of the nation to amuse friendly visiting sovereigns, of having without hesitation made, from his stage, friendly overtures to booted ruffians and of having sought their applause, repeating his bows even in the wings;

I ACCUSE Sacha Guitry of having taken advantage of his position as director of a theater and of his privilege as member of the Académie Goncourt to seek and to accumulate innumerable material advantages; of having insulted the misery of the people by his well-fed, satisfied, and selfish way of life;

I ACCUSE Sacha Guitry of having advised the Académie Goncourt to follow a defeatist policy by demanding that the prizes continue to be awarded, that vacancies be filled, that all privileges be maintained;

I ACCUSE Sacha Guitry of having been false to his promises in not resigning from the Académie Goncourt;

I ACCUSE Sacha Guitry of having been the confidant, the guest, the friend of the unspeakable Alain Laubreaux;

I ACCUSE Sacha Guitry not only because he never attempted to pronounce the word "refusal," but because he did not, even once, formulate a word of hope;

I ACCUSE Sacha Guitry of having been one of the earliest collaborators (see the testimony of General De la Laurencie);

I ACCUSE Sacha Guitry of having collaborated in the publication of *Aujourd'hui, Petit Parisien,* and *Paris Soir* (Paris edition);

I ACCUSE Sacha Guitry of having given an enthusiastic interview to the paper of Dr. Ley, "Strength through Joy";

I ACCUSE Sacha Guitry, who before the liberation knew of the fate meted out in Germany to thousands of great Frenchmen, of never having expressed a regret or attempted a protest;

I ACCUSE Sacha Guitry of having played cynically with justice;

I ACCUSE Sacha Guitry of having in him so little of the Frenchman;

I ACCUSE Sacha Guitry of being too cowardly to understand the indignity of his behavior and too flabby to comprehend the indignation of those who have resisted, suffered, and fought.

Je Confirme

September 16, 1946

GENTLEMEN:

I read "J'Accuse" in the July issue of the *Quarterly* [pp. 357–59, this volume] with great interest. In the course of my work with the Information Control Division, I had discussed the question of collaboration with one of the French Film Officers in Berlin. He thought that Sacha Guitry and Danielle Darrieux were classic examples of film actors who had collaborated with the Germans. Danielle Darrieux, for example, went to Berlin to make a picture which showed, among other things, the "benevolence" of the German occupation of France.

I am enclosing the newspaper reproduction of a letter written by Sacha Guitry in 1938 to the editor of the Berlin *Film Kurier,* a leading German trade paper. Herewith my own translation of it:

"Dear Editor:

"It has come to me from many sides that those in Germany and elsewhere who wish to do me harm have called me a Jew.

"I want to make it emphatically clear that this offensive story is no way true.

"I am a Catholic, as were my grandparents. My great-uncle on my father's side was the Comte de Châtre, and my great-uncle on my mother's side was Monsignor de Bonfils, Bishop of Le Mans.

"I was baptized at birth and went to school at the Holy Cross Lycée. I was given my first communion by the Dominican Friars.

"As far back as I can trace I have found it impossible to find anything in my family blood that is Jewish.

"My three marriages also confirm this declaration, which I beseech you, Sir, to make public.

"With thanks in advance, I remain,

"Sincerely

(Signed) *Sacha Guitry*"

The editors of *Film Kurier* headed Guitry's letter "Sacha Guitry Defends Himself" and prefaced it with the following introduction:

"We asked Sacha Guitry to write us a piece for the annual edition of the *Film Kurier* in time for the German opening of his latest picture, *Champs Elysées*. Instead of the article, we received the following communication."

It seems to me that any man who goes to such lengths to deny something about his creed or ancestry gratuitously deserves the closest inspection, and that his letter is an exquisite textbook illustration of its kind.

Sincerely yours,

ROBERT JOSEPH

The Cinémathèque Française*

THE PURPOSE OF THE Cinémathèque Française (The French Film Library) is to establish, in the interests of film art and film history, a museum and archives which shall have the widest possible utilization. It was founded in 1936 by the principal nontheatrical motion picture producers. Others interested in preserving a film repertory joined them to take the necessary steps for the conservation of prints and documents relating to films and for the replacement of prints which have disappeared.

As a library, the Cinémathèque collects and preserves documents relating to films, and purchases or receives, on loan or as gifts, positive and negative prints of films. Films and documents placed in the Cinémathèque remain the property of their owners and cannot be used commercially without their express permission. It goes without saying that in practice permission to use the films is rarely refused. Usually the films handled by the Cinémathèque are old ones; as a rule, in order to avoid commercial problems, recent films are accepted only for preservation and not for circulation.

As a museum, it assumes responsibility for exhibiting film documents and for exhibiting and distributing films which have artistic or pedagogic value. As a research center, the Cinémathèque undertakes historical research programs and provides for the publication of the results.

Although the Cinémathèque receives a subvention from the state and serves somewhat as an official film library, it is, by its constitution and by-laws, a private enterprise developed by its membership. Administered by a board of directors elected by the membership at large at a general meeting, it works for its membership both in the national and international fields. In its international program the Cinémathèque has coöperated

*[No biography was provided for the author in the original publication. This piece was taken from a section called "Notes and Communications," which consisted of shorter and less formal pieces for which author bios were not always considered necessary.]

with the Film Library of the Museum of Modern Art in New York, the British Film Institute, and the Reichfilmarchive—the only prewar film libraries which sought to develop international film collections. At the same time the Cinémathèque has encouraged the formation of national film libraries in other countries.

Between 1936 and 1940 the Cinémathèque participated in numerous international gatherings. The most important were the Méliès Exposition in London, the "French Retrospective" in Venice, and the "Triennial" in Milan. Under its auspices, conversations were held in Paris in 1938 with representatives of the Film Library of the Museum of Modern Art, which led to the creation of the International Federation of Film Archives with headquarters in Paris. At its last meeting in New York before the war, the Federation elected Lamarique chairman, and agreed upon Paris as headquarters of the secretariat.

The Cinémathèque managed to bring together a collection of important silent films which includes work by Zecca, Linder, René Clair, Jean Renoir, and Duvivier. Owing to the disorganization of the film industry at that time, negatives had been forgotten. The Cinémathèque purchased its old prints of the Eclair productions from a chemical laboratory where they were about to be melted down. *Protea,* the first film with sequences, was one of the films thus rescued. During this period the Cinémathèque exhibited or sponsored the exhibition of such films as *La Fête espagnole,* by Germaine Dulac, *Un Chien Andalou,* by Buñuel, *Le Ballet mécanique,* by Léger, *La Terre,* by Dovzhenko, *La Nuit du saint Sylvestre,* by Lupu Pick, *La Symphonie nuptiale,* by Stroheim. It was able to buy and preserve *L'Ange bleu* (German version), *Loulou,* by Pabst, *La Rue sans joie, L'Image,* by Feyder, *Les Mystères de New York, La Passion de Jeanne d'Arc,* and *Homunculus.*

The entire program was achieved without a regular staff. With only 3,000 francs from membership dues and 20,000 to 25,000 from all other sources, the Cinémathèque was forced to rely on the assistance of volunteers.

In June, 1940, the Cinémathèque entrusted its collection to the motion picture section of the French army, and eventually saw it disappear into the service of the Germans. It then faced another sort of difficulty. Some of the membership became collaborationists and wished to use the Cinémathèque for collaborationist purposes. This situation was overcome by

the loyalty of the great majority of the membership and by the courage of
the directorate, which adopted the following tactics in July, 1940, which
prevailed throughout the occupation:

1) Save the greatest amount of film possible.

2) Reconstruct the collection.

3) Recover the lost stocks.

4) Assume the role of protector and conservator, giving up all public
manifestations, projections, or exhibitions which, in the opinion of the
directorate, might be considered treasonable. (To maintain this attitude
during four years under watchful enemy eyes, never to submit to pressure
of any sort, would have been relatively easy if the Cinémathèque, in order to preserve its custodianship, had not been forced to maintain some
semblance of being a functioning public-service organization.)

During the German occupation, the Cinémathèque's warnings of the
danger of destruction by the Germans went unheeded. All plans, all requests by the Cinémathèque, to deposit its films in safety in Algiers in
order to prevent the destruction of the inventory in the northern zone,
were systematically rejected under the pretext that the Cinémathèque was
viewed favorably by the occupying authorities, wherefore the archives
would remain intact.

Eventually, in spite of obstruction, the Cinémathèque was able to save
almost all of its inventory, including the entire American stock in the
south zone and a considerable number of the films in the north. (This fact
permitted the Americans to resume their motion picture activities in
France shortly after the Liberation.)

At the end of the occupation, the Cinémathèque, though not in a position immediately to resume all its activities, was so popular that it obtained adequate funds from local town governments while waiting for the
resumption of subvention by the state. During its reorganization, it encouraged the formation of film clubs throughout France, patterned after
the English film societies. United into the French Federation of Cinema
Clubs, they reached masses of people, guided their taste, and led to further organization of clubs throughout France. For a while, confusion,
conflicts, and errors in planning made coöperation between the Cinémathèque and the cinema clubs difficult; but finally, the Federation developed a policy which made effective coöperation possible.

In February, 1945, the Cinémathèque held its first postwar exhibition, "Images du Cinéma Français." This was followed by the Cinémathèque's publication of a book, *Images du Cinéma Français,* by Nicole Vedres. Other projects have included an exhibition of French films in Lausanne, an exhibition of animated cartoons by Paul Reynard and Ferdinand Zecca, and posters for exhibitions in Brussels, Basle, Warsaw, and London.

The Cinémathèque was officially reopened, and is today the most complete of the film libraries in continental Europe. Contacts with foreign countries were reëstablished in October. Exchanges have been made with London, New York, and the film centers in Switzerland and Belgium, which the Cinémathèque prides itself in having helped to found. Understandings have been reached with Swedish, Danish, Czech, and Polish film centers. An Italian film center was created by uniting the previously existing centers in Rome and Milan. A film center has recently been established in Austria.

Since the occupation, there has been no artistic film activity in Europe in which the Cinémathèque has not participated. At the same time, its full program in Paris has been maintained, including courses on motion picture history at the University of Paris.

In March, 1946, under the auspices of the Cinémathèque, delegates from all European film centers, with observers from the United States and the Soviet Union, met in Paris to codify the by-laws of all film libraries into a system of standard practice, particularly as affecting noncommercial distribution. The importance of the noncommercial film to public education and to technology was emphasized. It is hoped that such agreement on standard practices will lead to the rapid expansion of cinema clubs throughout Europe.

Siegfried Kracauer | FROM VOL. 2, NO. 3, APRIL 1947

Translated by William Melnitz

Jean Vigo*

Siegfried Kracauer, literary editor of the *Frankfurter Zeitung* from 1920 to 1933, writing extensively on cultural affairs including cinema, came from Paris to the United States in 1941 and is now an American citizen. He has worked on the staff of the Modern Art Film Library and has received two Rockefeller grants and two Guggenheim fellowships to further his research in the history and political significance of the German film. His book *From Caligari to Hitler: A Psychological History of the German Film* has just been published by the Princeton University Press. His other works include a novel, *Ginfest,* and a biography of Offenbach in the Second Empire, *Orpheus in Paris.*

.....

Introductory Note | Vladimir Pozner

I SAW JEAN VIGO for the last time in the summer of 1934. He looked even younger than he was—an adolescent with a pointed face, about to die from tuberculosis. Very few people knew his name then, or his work. *A propos de Nice* had been shown in a few theaters only, *Zéro de conduite* had been considered too "harsh" for general release, and, if I am not mistaken, *L'Atalante* had not yet been released. As a rule, rebels are not popular, and in the motion picture industry probably less so than anywhere else. And Vigo was a rebel, on two counts: against the screen formulas and, even more intensely, against the established order of things. He used the camera as a weapon, not as an anesthetic.

In today's France, Vigo's pictures are shown in the neighborhood theaters.

Jean Vigo

JEAN VIGO—who died before he was thirty, in the autumn of 1934— left only a few films. His first film, *A propos de Nice,* can only be men-

---

*This article was first published in the *National Zeitung,* Basel (Switzerland), February 1, 1940.

[366]

tioned here, since for years it has been inaccessible. In 1933, this satirical documentary was followed by *Zéro de conduite,* a film influenced by René Clair and the French avant-garde, depicting a students' revolt in a boarding school. The brief series ends with *L'Atalante* (1934), a masterpiece that brought Vigo to the forefront of French motion picture directors. Among them, perhaps only Vigo and the René Clair of the great Parisian films have been able to discover and conquer territories reserved exclusively to the film. And although Vigo lacks Clair's wonderful lightness, he surpasses him in his profound concern with truth.

His very method of composition reveals an original relation to the screen. Vigo's plots are not the classic, hermetically sealed constructions designed to produce suspense by themselves alone; rather, they are slight, very loosely knit, and not at all purposeful. The plot of *L'Atalante* could not be simpler: Jean, the young master of the river steamer "Atalante," has married Juliette, who soon longs for Paris, away from the monotony of cabin, water, and landscape. She deserts her husband, who, jealous of Paris and the whole world, would be lost in the city if it were not for Père Jules, his old factotum: Père Jules brings Juliette back to poor Jean. The emphasis is on the numerous little single episodes, each more pregnant with suspense than the commonplace story itself. These little episodes compose the plot without, however, depending on it for structure and meaning. The opening passage, in which Jean and Juliette in festive attire proceed like strangers, silently, side by side, through the forest across the field to the beach, far ahead of the wedding party, is a perfect piece of poetry. By stringing his episodes like pearls, Vigo endows a technical fact with aesthetic significance—the fact that the celluloid strip is virtually endless and can be interrupted at any time.

More important are the conclusions Vigo draws from the fact that the camera does not discriminate between human beings and objects, animate and inanimate nature. As if led by the meandering camera, he exhibits the material components of mental processes. In *L'Atalante* we experience with all our senses how strongly the fogs of the river, the avenues of trees, and the isolated farms affect the mind, and how the sailor's relationship to the city is determined by the fact that he looks at the lodgings perched on the quay from sea level. Other film directors, too, have identified objects as silent accomplices of our thoughts and feelings. But Vigo goes still further. Instead of simply revealing the role objects may play in conditioning the mind, he dwells upon situations in which their influence predominates, thus exploring camera possibilities to the full. And since increasing intellectual awareness tends to reduce the power of objects over the mind, he logically chooses people who are deeply rooted in the material world as leading characters of his two full-length films.

Immature boys are the heroes of *Zéro de conduite*. Early in this film two of them ride to school at night in a third-class railroad compartment; it is as if they were left to themselves in a wigwam that imperceptibly fuses with their dreams. We see a man's legs on one of the benches, and then, on the other bench, we see the upper half of a sleeping traveler. This halving of the sleeper, marking him as an inanimate being, increases the impression of isolation from the world, an impression already aroused by the smoke which shuts out the world behind the car window. The partition of the compartment lies somewhat obliquely in the picture, an angle which points to the fact that this entire sequence cannot be located within real space and time. Their adventurous ride stimulates the two boys to pranks. From unfathomable pockets they produce alternately a spiral with a little ball springing out of it, a flute, shriveled toy balloons blown up by the younger boy, a bunch of goose quills with which the older one adorns himself, and finally cigars a yard long. Photographed from below, they squat exaltedly as the smoke of the locomotive mingles with the smoke of the cigars, and in the haze the round balloons float to and fro in front of their pale faces. It is exactly as if the two in their magic wigwam were riding through air. With a jerk, the sleeper falls. "Il est mort!" one of the boys cries, frightened. With the balloons hovering around them, they get off the train; outside we read the sign: "Non Fumeurs," and immediately the wigwam is retransformed into an ordinary railroad compartment.

While the objects in *Zéro de conduite* participate in childish play or occasionally frighten the boys, they become fetishes in *L'Atalante*. As such, they possess Père Jules. Michel Simon's Père Jules ranks among the greatest characters ever created on the screen by any actor or director. The old man, a former sailor, takes care of the "Atalante" in company with his accordion, innumerable cats, and a feeble-minded boy. Grumbling to himself inarticulately, he walks up and down between the steering wheel and the cabin in a sort of daze—so much one with the "Atalante" that he seems carved out of its planks. All that affects him is physical actions, which he, however, does not experience consciously, but immediately translates into similar actions. Jean lifts Juliette with whom he stands back to back: witnessing this amorous scene, Père Jules begins to shadow box. Juliette tries on him the coat she is sewing: the coat induces him to imitate an African belly dancer, and since Africa to him is not far from San Sebastian, he avails himself of the same coat, as he would of a red cloth, to irritate an imaginary bull. He does not remember the events, but reproduces them following certain signals.

Instead of using the objects at his disposal, he has become their property. The magic spell they cast over him is revealed in a unique episode in which Père Jules shows Juliette all the mementos he has brought home from his voyages. The piled-up treasures which crowd his cabin are depicted in such a manner that we feel they have literally grown together over him. To evoke this impression Vigo focuses on the objects from various sides and on many levels without ever clarifying their spatial interrelationship—using nothing but the medium shots and close-ups made necessary by the narrowness of the cabin. The alarm clock, the musical box, the photograph portraying Jules as a young man between two women in glittering dresses, the tusk, and all the bric-à-brac emerging little by little form an impenetrable wickerwork constantly interspersed with fragments of the old man himself: his arm, his tattooed back, his face. How accurately this piecemeal presentation renders his complete submission to the rarities around him can also be inferred from the fact that he preserves in alcohol the hands of a decreased comrade. The idols, on their part, display triumphantly their inherent powers. At the head of their great défilé Vigo marches a doll which, when set into motion by Père Jules, conducts mechanical music from a puppet show like a bandmaster. The magical life of the doll is transmitted to the curiosities that follow in the parade.

". . . un documentaire bien romantique," Brasillach writes in his *Histoire du cinéma* about *A propos de Nice,* "mais d'une belle cruauté, où les ridicules des dames vieilles et amoureuses, des gigolos et de la bourgeoisie décadente étaient férocement stigmatisés." Responding to the overwhelming appeal of material phenomena, Vigo, however, more and more withdrew from social criticism. In *L'Atalante* it appears, indeed, as if he actually had wanted to affirm an attitude hostile to intellectual awareness. Could it be, then, that Vigo's career had taken a retrogressive course? But in *Zéro de conduite* satire still manifested itself, and perhaps he indulged in the magic of mute objects and dark instincts only in order, some day, to pursue more thoroughly and knowingly the task of disenchantment.

Two Views of a Director— Billy Wilder

Herbert G. Luft has been active in Hollywood since 1943 as a film editor, translator, and in studio research and production departments. He is an associate member of the Screen Writers Guild, drama editor and book reviewer for the Los Angeles B'nai B'rith *Messenger*, and West Coast correspondent for the *National Jewish
Post*. Currently he is engaged in the production of television films.

Charles Brackett, formerly a novelist and drama critic of the *New Yorker*, has written
and produced many notable films, often in association with Billy Wilder. Among their
pictures were *Ninotchka, Hold Back the Dawn, The Major and the Minor, The Lost
Weekend, A Foreign Affair*, and *Sunset Boulevard*. Mr. Brackett is president of the
Academy of Motion Picture Arts and Sciences.

. . . . .

*The editors wish from time to time to publish appraisals of the work of
important American film directors. They recognize, in printing Mr. Luft's
article about Billy Wilder, that the author's viewpoint is not a wholly objective one but has been formed by his bitter personal experience. For this reason they asked Mr. Wilder's friend and one-time collaborator, Mr. Charles
Brackett, for the comment which follows Mr. Luft's article. The two pieces
certainly do not say the last word about Mr. Wilder's work, but they point up
one distinction he shares with few of his contemporaries—he is one of the rare
directors of this cautious day whose work may be called controversial.*

I. A Matter of Decadence | Herbert G. Luft

EARLY IN 1929, IN BERLIN, just before the close of the silent era, a group
of motion picture students discovered an outlet for their youthful enthusiasm—away from the theatrical setting of studio-made film. Nothing
much happened in the little opus they called *Menschen am Sonntag*, a
semidocumentary made for producer Moritz Seeler, but for the first time
the camera looked upon real people.

Four middle-class citizens, worn from the week's drab routine, go out to spend a Sunday at Wannsee beach! This bit of simple, rather melancholy reportage became Robert Siodmak's initial chore as director, his assistants being Edgar Ulmer and Fred Zinnemann, with pioneer Eugene Schuftan handling the camera. The screen story was conceived by twenty-three-year-old Billy Wilder, a journalist from Vienna who had started as a copy boy, then graduated to sports writer before leaving for Berlin to become crime reporter on the *Nachtausgabe.*

Even today, *People on Sunday* still is regarded as one of the finest examples of screen art.

Wilder's career is one of the most fascinating success stories of the cinema. With the rise of Nazism, the young writer goes to Paris where he becomes a full-fledged film director *(Mauvaiso graine).* Thus, with an actual directing credit to his name, he arrives at the Hollywood scene in 1935. Today, he amuses himself by relating his earlier experience: "I dragged my carcass up and down Hollywood Boulevard, and starved around for a year and a half before I sold two original stories."

In 1938, Wilder collaborated for the first time with Charles Brackett on the screen play of *Bluebeard's Eighth Wife.* He kept on writing with an ever-increasing speed, turning out *Rhythm on the River, Midnight,* and *What a Life!,* the latter based on the Henry Aldrich character. In 1939, Wilder joined Ernst Lubitsch, working with Brackett and Walter Reisch on the screen play of the Greta Garbo picture *Ninotchka,* which became a sensational success. Then followed a series of craftsmanlike Brackett and Wilder scenarios such as *Arise My Love* (Ray Milland and Claudette Colbert), *Hold Back the Dawn* (Charles Boyer), and *Ball of Fire* (Barbara Stanwyck), all of them dated 1940 to 1941. As a director, Wilder came into his own with *The Major and the Minor* (1942), a mildly amusing comedy with Ginger Rogers.

Still collaborating with Brackett and now functioning as a triple producer-writer-director team, Wilder next presented *Five Graves to Cairo* (1943), a war yarn with Erich von Stroheim portraying Marshal Rommel. It was not until 1944 that Wilder, with *Double Indemnity,* his only co-authorship with Raymond Chandler, established himself as a truly unorthodox film maker.

Between film assignments, Wilder went to Berlin for six months as chief of the motion picture division for the American Information Control. In

November, 1945, back in Hollywood, Wilder hit the peak with *The Lost Weekend*. This film brought him recognition as one of our foremost directors. Next on his schedule was the Austrian monarchy—plus Bing Crosby—in *Emperor Waltz*, a lavish Technicolor spectacle.

After his initial prewar films, something changed Wilder's trend. Though he had watched the pulse of Hollywood and had learned the mechanics of successful motion picture making, seemingly without regret he turned from the media of his much hailed Academy Award winner to more and more controversial subjects such as *A Foreign Affair* and *Sunset Boulevard*. It was as if an impetus that could not be restrained was forcing him on and on.

Twenty-two years have passed since Wilder, having discovered the common man on the streets of Berlin, comes forward with another reportage, an item about a fellow newspaperman (which could have had an affinity with his own life?). *Ace in the Hole*[1] unravels the tragedy of an unscrupulous reporter who has skidded to the bottom of the ladder into complete moral and physical disintegration. Given a slight chance to rise once more, this newshound frantically pursues a story to the point of killing a man buried in an underground cave-in. He deliberately delays rescue by bribing the authorities to use outmoded methods simply because it makes better copy and sells more papers while the victim suffers longer. To this end the reporter lies, cheats, and misleads the public, all to build up an unfortunate accident into the day's headline. Here Wilder has conceived a set of characters who appear totally repulsive and whose reactions are never normal. He has accentuated it all by adding a punch-drunk mob, the mere sight of which makes you hate the whole human race. He has lampooned yellow journalism, but has failed to attack the metropolitan scandal sheets who balloon murder cases and obscene bedroom yarns and actually have created an inexhaustible market for low, gutter reportage. The slant of the theme is worlds apart from the unpretentious approach of *People on Sunday* of 1929.

In an interview, during the production of *Ace in the Hole*, in August, 1950, Wilder stated: "All I try to do is get myself a story, splash it on the screen and get it over with. And I try, for God's sake, to have news in every

---

1. After a few weeks of showing, Paramount renamed the film *The Big Carnival*.

picture I make! To open up, to unroll a problem is interesting enough. We don't have to know the answer, too." Can it be that Wilder thinks to jar the public loose from its inertia and force it to work out its own problems with something of the fervor of our local tabloid editors?

There's no doubt about it, Wilder makes news in every picture, yet, paradoxically, employs the same technique of ruthless exploitation that he castigates so often on the screen, oversimplifying complex human emotions in order to bring out his utterly cynical viewpoint. One can also note his peculiar flair for a high-pitched, spectacular finish. The hero-villain of *Ace in the Hole*, dying, stabbed with a pair of scissors, pays his debt to society by assuming a self-righteous pose and angrily shouting his confession down from a mountaintop to a throng of thousands. Drama, yes! But an easy deathbed repentance for misdeeds mere confession cannot wipe out.

Another vital parallel is the pronounced kinship of Wilder's characters. The obsessed reporter shows a striking resemblance to Walter Neff, the insurance agent from *Double Indemnity*, who is also killed by his partner in crime, the wife of his victim.

Wilder lashes indifference, yet has displayed the same indifference to enliven his own films. Survivors of Nazi concentration camps whose bones were broken in the dungeons must have been just as deeply hurt by the happy-go-lucky treatment of postwar Germany in *A Foreign Affair*, as Papa Minosa is now in *Ace in the Hole*, discovering that his own son, doomed to suffocate in a mountain trap, has become the involuntary object of a noisily staged fairground merriment.

A Foreign Affair has deserved the distinction of presenting one of the most revolting episodes ever projected onto the screen, namely a love idyl, a rather harmless one on the surface, yet by implication more cruel than a picture showing the furnaces of an extermination center with human ashes still smoldering. The fiendishly devised contrast, a "catch-and-get-me" game played against a room filled with archives of war-crime trials, makes the scene, to people with memories, loathsome. It is in even worse taste than if our screen lovers were to go into a final clinch over the still warm body of a slain rival, because the incident offends not only the sentiments of a few but mocks the torture of untold millions.

While the earlier Wilder in *Arise My Love* castigates the isolationism at the beginning of the European conflict, the later Wilder deals with the aftermath of war with the luxurious cynicism of a sophisticate who has acclimatized himself to the ivory tower of Beverly Hills. Even if Europe's surface looked to him in 1947 as he shows it in *A Foreign Affair,* it is a superficial viewpoint bound to mislead an uncertain public.

There are those who would scold us, saying that we shouldn't take motion pictures too seriously. They forget that films have become the universal language of our age, and that nowadays the screen is accepted as an image of life. I recall that in 1945 a friend (a woman who had just returned from a German concentration camp) wrote me about her most heartbreaking experience. She had wept for the first time in six years, wept when she saw her first movie, a superficial picture others devised while she had been undergoing unspeakable sufferings. To her, the callousness of the world at large seemed more cruel than the atrocities of the enemy.

There is a distinct pattern in the work of Billy Wilder that leads us to conclude that he undoubtedly is amused by the callousness of our time. In *Ninotchka,* the character Bulgaroff asks, "How are things in Moscow?" and Ninotchka answers, "Very good. The last mass trials were a great success. There are going to be fewer but better Russians."

The Lost Weekend, the odyssey of a drunk by Charles Jackson, attributes the hero's alcoholism to his sex frustration. Wilder, who, of course, couldn't touch upon the homosexual angle, seems to be rather amused by the plight of the alcoholic. He portrays him as a gentleman lush who sees himself in a third person and comments with a nasty sense of humor. The director inserts deliberate touches, such as the bat scene, for the mere shock effect. Here as in *Ace in the Hole,* he treats his characters with an obscene, obnoxious witticism, which to a lesser extent is apparent even in the harmless *Emperor Waltz,* a travesty on a bygone world of phony grandeur.

Wilder not only creates news in every picture, but also is on the lookout for off-the-beaten-track titles. *Ace in the Hole* happened to be the title of a novel by Jackson Gregory (Dodd, Mead & Company, 1941) which has no connection with his story. The title of *Five Graves to Cairo* is a hoax in itself. The picture opens by showing us a map revealing that the German Africa Corps in 1945 had five secret ammunition dumps throughout Egypt spelling out the five letters of "Egypt." Wilder, of course, knew that the equivalent German word would make eight letters or eight graves.

A Foreign Affair, an original, clearly mirrors the mark of his unhealthy boulevard witticism. The camera focus on a pile of rubble was not exactly a fitting place for wholesome comedy. There are the ruins of Berlin, but not one word to explain why the city had to be utterly destroyed before the spirit of oppression could be broken. The Nazis are seen as double-crossers, yet drawn with much charm and *noblesse,* living in an atmosphere of comparative ease, with a romantic façade covering up a decade of mass murders. Those praising the guts of the story didn't see the malefic travesty. Our occupation forces appear undisciplined and ill-behaved. It is not funny to see Berlin's citizenry tyrannized by the same clique of Nazis whom we have cursed so often, or to view *frauleins* complacently ruling the destiny of American officers, or to realize that a huge black-market exists under the very eye of the military government. Undoubtedly, the frivolous slant of the picture helped to increase animosity against America among those who have lived under the yoke of the Nazis.

Sunset Boulevard sets another bad example for this country. It presents a distorted Hollywood setting centering around a secluded mansion wherein it unravels the tragedy of a love-hungry actress who refuses to admit that she has grown old. The heroine is just as superficial as the congresswoman in *A Foreign Affair,* and just as exceptional. The story is that of the melodramatic cliché of silent movies, a paraphrase on the pathos of an era it went out to ridicule, except that *Sunset Boulevard* takes its own pathos seriously. Here, as in the flickers of the Pola Negri variety, the aging woman buys herself a lover. This time the gigolo comes in the disguise of a film writer. Only once in a blue moon, if ever, do we find such a scribe.

Wilder's "Hollywood" is ice-cold, calculated theater, far from the American way of thinking, and out of step with the real worries and ideals of the film industry which is still bubbling over with the growing pains and vitality of youth. The decadent atmosphere of *Sunset Boulevard* is only matched by the endless narration of a dead man floating in a swimming pool. The picture flays some of the finest creators of the silent screen, such as Erich von Stroheim, Buster Keaton, and H. B. Warner, who in their days showed a more intelligent approach in creating well-rounded characters than do some of today's top-notch boys. As in *Ace in the Hole,* Wilder, master of systematically developed sensationalism, again tops everything with his bombastic finish. The murderess of *Sunset Boule-*

vard walks into the spotlights for a final close-up, with the camera grinding on, Hedda Hopper reporting—and the story ending in repulsive pandemonium.

All in all, Billy Wilder's later pictures are of a shockingly deteriorating nature. Other film makers have portrayed mass hysteria in *Fury, Ox-Bow Incident,* and *The Well* more honestly and more realistically, yet with a deeper belief in the innate decency of man. But Wilder has picked out exceptional characters with no redeeming features whatsoever and presents them to us as average Americans. His heroes have no integrity and expect none from anyone else. Like many Germans, Wilder depicts only the weaknesses and shortcomings of the American people, ridicules their habits, but never senses the strikingly salubrious strength of this vibrantly young republic. He says in an interview on the *Ace in the Hole* set: "We are a nation of hecklers, the most hard-boiled, undisciplined people in the world." Is he referring to his particular Hollywood?

Wilder, who has spent his years in America in a metropolitan atmosphere and, according to his own humorous account, sold his first two stories to a producer in Lucey's restroom, has evidently never been in touch with the "average" American, nor met those who create the physical and cultural wealth of this country. He hasn't seen Americans as they are, or as they should be, but as he—perhaps against his will—was indoctrinated to conceive the "Yankee" when he was still abroad. Subconsciously, he has accepted the cartoon characterization of the uncivilized, unconcerned weakling, the savage of the Wild West who loves only money and owes allegiance to none. To him, evidently, as with the philosophers of the Third Reich, Americans are a frightening array of ruthless, perverse, and criminal elements.

The America of Billy Wilder is not the America I found when I came to this country after having lived in Nazi Germany for six years. I had gone through the concentration camp of Dachau and through the earlier phase of World War II in England. For me—as for the vast majority of newcomers—America has meant a symbol of freedom, not a hoax. If these United States were as decadent and corrupt as Wilder would lead us to believe they are, this country never could have risen to such a position of strength and moral leadership in the world of today.

One can only conclude that Wilder's world is more continental than American. He portrays Americans as if they were demoralized Europeans uprooted between two world wars. The earlier German-made films *(Caligari, Mabuse, Waxworks)*, masterpieces as such, dealt with the same mixture of Old World fears and arrogance, with violence and the sickness of the mind.

Somewhere, somehow, like so many other Hollywoodians, Wilder seems to have lost his human heart on the way to the top. Billy Wilder, a man of original ideas, has the makings of a great film writer and director, if he would lift his talents into a higher sphere of truthful interpretation and moral responsibility. But what he seems to want is sensationalism at any price. Perhaps he will give us a different answer with *Stalag 17*.

II. A Matter of Humor | Charles Brackett

I read Mr. Herbert G. Luft's article about Billy Wilder with a certain fascination. It is like reading an essay about Van Gogh by someone who is color blind. No, more than that—this appraiser of Van Gogh is made actively ill by the painter's favorite color.

Mr. Luft not only doesn't like a joke, he *detests* a joke. This is a limitation of nature to which one should be charitable. Certainly Mr. Luft's tragic experience in a concentration camp should cause one to overlook it. But in choosing Wilder for his subject, Mr. Luft has thrust his deficiency on the reader in a way that cannot be ignored.

Predominant among Billy Wilder's qualities is humor—a fantastically American sense of humor. It was the outstanding trait of the young man with whom I started to work some seventeen years ago. He was sassy and brash and often unwise, but he had a fine, salutary laugh. Also, he was in love with America as I have seen few people in love with it. I mention this because one of Mr. Luft's theses is a belief that Wilder fails to appreciate, and dislikes, America.

Now let us observe the conduct of Mr. Luft when he happens on a joke. He shudders first, then he begins to weigh it on sociological and ethical scales—and, alas, those scales aren't working very well. Take, for instance, the line from *Ninotchka* which he views with horror.

Ninotchka, reporting solemnly on her native land, says, "The mass trials have been a great success. In future there will be fewer but better Russians." This happens to be a line tossed into the script by Ernst Lubitsch, but I spring to its defense with ardor, as would Billy Wilder. Could a single sentence better compress the inhuman Russian point of view? Could that point of view be held up to ridicule in a healthier way?

The indifference-to-America thesis runs into some difficulty when our essayist reviews *Arise My Love* and *Hold Back the Dawn*.

Arise My Love was a comedy with serious undertones and was decried by every America-Firster as warmongering and jingoistic. In it there were tender and adoring references to America—and I can testify that they were put in by Billy Wilder. In those simpler days I took my country's virtues very much for granted.

Hold Back the Dawn, which came a year or two later, was certainly a bouquet laid at the feet of America by two people who loved it dearly.

Mr. Luft brushes aside *The Major and the Minor* as inconsiderable (though I can assure him it filled countless theaters with the lovely and important sound of laughter), and comes to *The Lost Weekend*. Here, for Pete's sake, he finds Wilder at the peak of comicality—poking fun at the infirmities of a hopeless alcoholic! This interpretation defeats me. The very core of *The Lost Weekend* was its insistence that a drunk is not the comedy figure he had usually been on the screen, but a tragically sick man. Throughout the script, Don Birnam, the protagonist, was treated with the compassionate respect any sick man commands. Mr. Luft seems to think the bat-mouse hallucination was interjected by us, or rather by Wilder, as a prize boff. If he will glance at Charles Jackson's novel, he will find it exactly as it was played—a scene of utter terror. Incidentally, the Freudian significance of the scene is that the mouse (representing man himself) is being destroyed by the bat (the winged mouse—man with imagination; in Don Birnam's case, the frustrated writer).

Now we come to *A Foreign Affair*, which, according to Mr. Luft, "clearly mirrors the mark of Billy Wilder's unhealthy boulevard wit." That picture played in the great rubble pile of Berlin. It is a city which most of us in America had regarded with loathing, horror, and dread for the ten preceding years. The war is concluded, and now over its debris are swarming exuberant young Americans—young men whose desires and delights are strong in them, thank God. There's larceny in their hearts, and fun in them and health in them. Does Mr. Luft want a glimpse of the truth about those young men? No. It evokes that horrid sound of laughter. He wants an explanation of why the city had had to be utterly destroyed. That was something the audience knew, and we saw no point in boring them with it again.

The Berlin woman, played by Marlene Dietrich, was such a complete heavy that some humanization of her character became necessary. Therefore she was given a scene which explained what made her tick. I suppose that is what makes Mr. Luft describe her as "drawn with much charm and *noblesse.*" About the audience's reaction to her, I can only report that she ended by going to a labor camp, amid the delighted laughter of American audiences. Apparently to Mr. Luft it was a wistful and romantic exit.

In his criticism of *Sunset Boulevard,* Mr. Luft points out that the heroine was "exceptional." Really? Wasn't she just the average woman who once earned fifteen thousand dollars a week and had thirty million fans in love with her? Of course she was exceptional! She was also tragic. Perhaps we should have told about her with a more audible lump in our throats. We thought it effective to suppress the pitying sounds and let the audience find the pity for themselves.

Now in Mr. Luft's article comes a sentence which I have to quote and analyze. "Wilder's Hollywood is ice-cold, calculated theater, out of step with the real ideals of the film industry, which is still bubbling over with the growing pains of vitality and youth." Is that true? Even if you block that metaphor, is it true? The exact purpose of the young girl in the picture—the sympathetic character—was to embody the ideals of the town, the passion for truth on the screen, the passion for good pictures.

Again I quote: "The picture flays some of the finest creators of the silent screen—Erich von Stroheim, Buster Keaton, H. B. Warner. . . ." Flays them? It merely records that time, which flays us all mercilessly, has not spared them. If they had not been great, that fact would have had no dramatic significance.

To answer another charge of Mr. Luft's, certainly there was sensationalism in the ending of the picture. People like Norma Desmond fade out with a bang, not a whimper.

I come to *Ace in the Hole,* a picture with which I had no connection. It told the story of a ruthless heel. No one was asked to like or admire him. The story of his using the victim of an accident to rebuild his shattered career was not a pretty one, nor was it presented as what *any* newspaper man would do under the circumstances, but it did point up certain cynical qualities in the press and certain appalling habits of behavior in crowds who gather to watch events charged with misery. It was in the vein of American self-criticism which has been a major current in our national literature since the days of *The Octopus* and *The Pit* and *The Jungle*. Because he was born in Austria, is Billy Wilder to be excluded from that vigorous and important trend? I don't think so.

FROM VOL. 10, NO. 2, WINTER 1955 Raymond Jean

Dialogue Between the Moviegoing Public and a Witness for Jean Cocteau

Raymond Jean was an assistant professor of French Literature in France, and is currently an associate professor of Romance Languages at the University of Pennsylvania. His publications include articles in les *Cahiers du Sud, Mercure de France,* and *Cahiers du cinéma* and a booklet of poetry by the Editions P. Seghers in Paris. The following article is a part of a short essay resulting from a conversation between the author and Jean Cocteau.

. . . . .

PUBLIC: May I let you in on a secret? I have an awful feeling that Jean Cocteau, in his recent works, is complaining more and more about us.
WITNESS: Yes, his complaints are coming more frequently nowadays. He seems to be suffering.
PUBLIC: Do you think he's really suffering, I mean in a sincere way?
WITNESS: I do.
PUBLIC: But from what?
WITNESS: It's hard to say.
PUBLIC: From not being understood?
WITNESS: Probably.
PUBLIC: Do you mean in regard to his work for the films?
WITNESS: That in particular.
PUBLIC: You will admit that he's largely responsible. When you want to be understood, you must express yourself clearly. His films are beyond me sometimes.
WITNESS: Do you mean that they're over your head?
PUBLIC: How do you mean?
WITNESS: Do they leave you indifferent? Or do they annoy you?
PUBLIC: Eh . . . eh . . . Well . . .
WITNESS: Sometimes, maybe?

[381]

PUBLIC: Sometimes . . . yes . . . but . . . it's something else.

WITNESS: What?

PUBLIC: Well, I don't understand the obscure allusions in his films.

WITNESS: What obscure allusions?

PUBLIC: What he's trying to say.

WITNESS: But he's not *trying* to say something. He just *says* it.

PUBLIC: I know that story, too. You're going to tell me I have only to look at the film without looking for hidden meanings in it. But that's asking too much of me.

WITNESS: Your symbols and your logic lead you astray. You are looking, at any cost, for a meaning in those things which have other values than meaning alone. You reason too much about these things, as you always will. And how you distort them!

PUBLIC: What else should we do?

WITNESS: You are trying to understand, you say. Are you sure you are trying to see what is going on in front of you? What Cocteau is reproaching you for is your inattention, your lack of eagerness to look closely at what took months of meticulous work to prepare. In his films, the least image missed, he says, ruins the whole. But when it comes to knowing what the film means as a whole, you're at a loss because you have missed that single image. You don't understand, and you are dissatisfied because you don't understand. But while the film is going on you are talking, laughing when you shouldn't be, passing around popcorn or candy and crumpling paper, or getting affectionate with your date. (He—Cocteau—is still speaking.)

PUBLIC: Does he reproach us for all that?

WITNESS: He reproaches the French film-going public—little given to granting a film its complete attention—for behaving in that way and considering itself authorized at the same time to pass flippant judgment on works which take much time and work to produce.

PUBLIC: Well, I pay for my seat to enjoy myself.

WITNESS: That's exactly what you don't do.

PUBLIC: What's that?

WITNESS: Enjoy yourself. I am speaking of course of that false élite of the big premières who claim to be the only ones who ever think, who make comments and judge the value of the film, who think they know it all and can say in two words what they think they understand.

PUBLIC: You mean the intellectual snobs.

WITNESS: Yes, and the other imbeciles. They are the people who revolt Cocteau. He told me that the people with nothing to do, the idlers, are the most dangerous people in the world; for having nothing better to do with their time, they are always prepared to speak ill about anything, spread wrong impressions, criticize, and falsify.

PUBLIC: That's right. But I thought nevertheless that our man Cocteau depended on these same intellectual snobs for a lot of free publicity.

WITNESS: Of course, he does benefit by the support of those people who, dazzled by the brilliance of his works, acclaim them without understanding them.

PUBLIC: But who does understand them, then? That's what I'm waiting for you to tell me. I can see you are going to end by telling me that Cocteau's real audience is the popular audience.

WITNESS: No, but the members of that audience have ideas of their own. They want you to tell a story, and to plunge right away into the narrative; they want to identify themselves with the hero and the heroine, and are delighted to see how good-looking they are at such close range, to take part in their journeys and adventures, to share in their love affairs. All this, they do quite simply and honestly.

PUBLIC: And what do they think about the ideas in these films of Cocteau?

WITNESS: Since they are concerned only with the form of the picture and not with the content, they don't care about the ideas. They are interested only in what they see. They like to be transported to another land, of the marvelous, the supernatural, fairy tales. That's all they look for in the sumptuous and facile productions of American westerns and musicals. They're not at all interested in quality and technique.

PUBLIC: Then our poet Cocteau is the poet of the crowd.

WITNESS: I don't mean that. But from the crowd he gets the most favorable reactions, those which he wants the most. The studio sceneshifters disappoint him less than the critics. And then we have the facts . . .

PUBLIC: What facts?

WITNESS: The facts of his success. You seem to forget that Cocteau has succeeded—and this is something without precedent—in reconciling artistic success with commercial success. This has amazed even his producers. You can see for yourself the general success that *L'eternel retour* and *Orphée* have had. They have been playing for long runs even in neighborhood theaters.

PUBLIC: Yes, because of the infatuation of working girls.

WITNESS: I believe rather because he pleases the young. That puts things in their proper place. And then perhaps Cocteau appreciates more the active interest of the working girl than that of the girls from a Catholic psychoanalytic center who persisted in seeing a phallic symbol in the smokestack of a factory in *Sang d'un Poète*.

PUBLIC: You can't be serious.

WITNESS: I certainly am.

PUBLIC: Didn't this also fool the young people who support him?

WITNESS: That's not very probable. For Cocteau has never stopped being young himself. His secret? He belongs to no school (schools can become hard and dry up) but rather to a movement. From one movement to another, he goes beyond the avant-garde and always comes out in front of these movements with something completely new and different. He never sits idle.

PUBLIC: And what about the place his films have in all that you've said?

WITNESS: They have their place. Many young people who are interested and stimulated by them turn to Cocteau.

PUBLIC: What is his opinion of these young people?

WITNESS: He thinks that our modern cities are stifling them, preventing them from working and from expressing themselves.

PUBLIC: Is he ever severe with them?

WITNESS: No. He only reproaches them for letting themselves be led astray by passing fashions, for making decisions without consulting any authority, for remaining obstinate in their opinions, and for not working.

PUBLIC: How are they supposed to work?

WITNESS: It's true that the doors of the jungle that is the movie business are closed to them. And also, they would rather hope to get a few million from some Aga Khan than to have to work.

PUBLIC: So Cocteau is not optimistic about them.

WITNESS: No, that's not it. He thinks rather that those of them who have anything to say will say it in the end.

PUBLIC: Oh!

WITNESS: And then he knows quite well that among these young people he has a chance of not remaining unknown.

PUBLIC: Unknown! You must be joking!

WITNESS: No. Already too often photographed and interviewed and too much adapted to the public's idea of him, he no longer resembles himself.

PUBLIC: That's because of the legend which surrounds all artists.

WITNESS: Why are you smiling? Do you think that the idea of a legend is the same thing as the legend itself?

PUBLIC: Somewhat.

WITNESS: You're wrong. The poet himself has probably helped to contribute to the false picture which surrounds him. But only in order to protect himself. What you know is only an effigy, a Cocteau of straw which you think is the real Cocteau. The other Cocteau, the true Cocteau, remains intact.

PUBLIC: Is that why he attacks this day and age so freely?

WITNESS: He has not himself been spared insults.

PUBLIC: Why not?

WITNESS: Probably because he is a man who has chosen to remain free and has not allowed himself to become occupied with any work other than his own. And also because he is of an extreme nobility and refinement— qualities not easily tolerated today.

PUBLIC: Do you really think so?

WITNESS: Yes. And what's more, people refuse to believe that these qualities of his can be reconciled with his *avant-garde* spirit, with his aesthetic originality, and with his love for the beautiful. Clown or serious artist, only you can make the distinction.

PUBLIC: Many people also feel uneasy and uncomfortable before his films and his other works.

WITNESS: That's another matter. He always goes *too far*. Rare are the people who like anyone who goes *too far*. Certain everyday realities are just not tolerated; even more, certain plays and films are not tolerated. People have their teeth set on edge when they are presented with the shrill, the violent, the virulent. Take Buñuel, for example. People prefer to close their eyes. If they are compelled to look at these films, any injury done to them serves as a cure, an exorcism.

PUBLIC: Don't you recognize in that something harmful?

WITNESS: That's just one of the many aspects of poetry and art.

PUBLIC: That's true.

WITNESS: Cocteau knows this. Not long ago, he organized with *Objec-*

tif 49 the "Festival du Film Maudit" in Biarritz where they were to show some of these films, "exorcised" by the exploiters from the big motion-picture theaters, by the jury, and by the regular moviegoing public.

PUBLIC: And if the regular moviegoers were to walk out suddenly, who could stop them?

WITNESS: The others.

PUBLIC: What? Whom do you mean?

WITNESS: I mean those young people intensely interested in the film as an art; those old people, curious about something new and different; the intellectual snobs; the affected people. I mean all those people who go to the cinema clubs everywhere to see these films which the big theaters never present. Fortunately, those people still exist!

PUBLIC: But they are definitely in the minority!

WITNESS: As a matter of fact, you start out making these films for only a handful of friends.

PUBLIC: That's admirable!

WITNESS: And, by your leave, you sometimes make them even for yourself. That's the best way to go about it for that is an end in itself. "The more we become advanced in age, the more our work should enrich and reflect us as if they were a child who resembles us." [1]

1. Jean Cocteau, *Journal de la Belle et la Bête* (Paris: J. B. Janin, 1946), 57.

Selected Names Index

Adorno, Theodor, xx, xxiii
Allegret, Marc, 342
Allegret, Yves, 342
Anderson, Ernest, 257
Anger, Kenneth, 32–34
Anouilh, Jean, 339, 340
Apollinaire, Guillaume, 7
Arledge, Sara, 37, 47
Arnstam, Alexandre, 313
Aubrey, Cecile, 342
Auclair, Michel, 342
Aurenche, Jean, 342
Autant-Lara, Claude, 338, 342, 343

Balderson, John L., 295
Barry, Iris, xxiii, 319
Barthelmess, Richard, 248
Becker, Jacques, 335, 338, 340, 341
Bellon, Anik, 343
Berne, Joseph, 24
Bernhardt, Sarah, 244, 250, 265
Bitzer, Billy, 249
Bleiman, Mikhail, 319
Bost, Pierre, 342
Bouchard, Thomas, 46–47
Boyer, Charles, 371
Brackett, Leigh, 262
Bresson, Robert, 335
Brooks, Clarence, 257
Broughton, James, 33
Buñuel, Luis, 363
Burnford, Paul, 43
Bute, Mary Ellen, 25–27

Callenbach, Ernest, xxi
Calloway, Cab, 257

Capra, Frank, xiv, 102, 244, 251, 252, 266, 318
Carné, Marcel, 335, 338, 339
Carter, Ben, 257
Chandler, Raymond, 253, 254, 260, 312, 317, 371
Chaney, Lon, 257
Chaplin, Charles, 85, 315, 318, 319, 320
Chase, Charlie, 85
Clair, René, 335, 338, 363, 367
Clément, René, 341
Clouzot, Henri-Georges, 335, 337, 341, 342
Cocteau, Jean, 54, 341, 343, 381–386
Colbert, Claudette, 371
Collier, John, xviii
Colman, Ronald, 257
Corwin, Norman, 120
Crockwell, Douglas, 36–37, 58
Crosby, Bing, 372
Crowther, Bosley, 109–110
Curry, Finlay, 176
Curtiz, Michael, 258, 268

Daquin, Louis, 335, 341
Darrieux, Danielle, 360
Davies, Valentine, 294
Davis, Bette, 257
Delannoy, Jean, 335, 343
DeMille, Cecil B., 247, 251, 252, 315
Deren, Maya, 29–31, 33–34, 47, 49, 54
De Rochemont, Louis, 112, 114, 268
Dieterle, William, 266
Dietrich, Marlene, 379
Disney, Walt, xvii, 35, 53, 87, 244, 269
Dmytryk, Edward, 266

Donat, Robert, 175
Donskoy, Mark, 313, 314
Dovzhenko, Alexander, 313, 317, 363
Dulac, Germaine, 54, 363
Duse, Eleanor, 245
Duvivier, Julien, 335, 338, 339, 363
Dzigan, Yefim, 316

Eastman, George, 334
Edison, Thomas, 244
Eisenhower, Dwight, 152, 156–157,
Eisenstein, Sergei 20, 252, 313, 315–319
Engel, Sam 295
Estabrook, Howard, 312

Fairbanks, Douglas, 245, 246, 251
Farquhar, Samuel, xviii
Farrar, Geraldine, 265
Faulkner, William, 262
Fearing, Franklin, xvi, xviii
Fejos, Paul, 10
Feyder, Jacques, 335, 338, 363
Fields, W. C., 85
Fischinger, Oscar, 26, 35, 53
Flaherty, Robert, 7–8, 93–95, 98, 250,
   252, 266
Florey, Robert, 9–10
Flory, John, 22
Ford, John, 258, 266
Forster, E. M., 168
Freleng, Friz, 73–74
Freund, Karl, 267
Frugé, August, xvii–xxi
Furthman, Jules, 262

Gabin, Jean, 340
Garbo, Greta, 250, 371
Garden, Mary, 265
Garland, Judy, 300
Gassner, John, 318
Genika, Yuri, 315
Gercon, Jo, 19–20
Golden, Edward, 265–266
Goldwyn, Samuel, xxiii, 244, 265, 267,
   269
Golovnya, Anatoli, 315
Gray, Hugh, xxiii
Grémillon, Jean, 335, 338, 340, 341,
   342
Grierson, John, 112–113

Griffith, D. W., 245, 248, 249, 257, 258,
   315, 318–320, 345
Guitry, Sacha, 357–359, 360, 361

Hackenschmied, Alexander, 102
Hammid, Alexander, 29
Harrington, Curtis, 32–34, 58
Hart, William S., 245
Hawks, Howard, 262
Hays, Will, 244
Head, Edith, xxii
Hecht, Ben, 266, 269
Hilton, James, xvii
Horne, Lena, 257
Howe, James Wong, 267
Huff, Theodore, 22
Huston, John, 106, 244, 252, 258

Iezuitov, Nikolai, 320
Ince, Thomas, 250, 251, 315
Ingram, Rex, 257
Isherwood, Christopher, 254
Ivens, Joris, 95

Jacobs, Lewis, xxii, 19, 44–45, 320
Jaque, Christian, 343
Jarrico, Sylvia, xviii
Johnson, Noble, 257
Johnson, Nunnally, 296
Johnson, Van, 267
Johnston, Eric, 178
Jones, Chuck, xxii
Jones, Hazel, 257
Jouvet, Louis, 342

Kanin, Garson, 266
Kazan, Elia, 22–23
Keaton, Buster, 250, 252, 375, 379
Kessler, Charles, 47, 49
Klein, Charles, 16
Kline, Herbert, 102
Kozintzev, Grigori, 313, 319
Kuleshov, Lev, 315, 316, 318

Laemmle, Carl, 265
Lasky, Jesse, 265
Lavery, Emmet, 266
Lawson, John Howard, xvi, xviii, xxiii
Leenhardt, Roger, 343
Léger, Fernand, 363

Lerner, Irving, 22
Lesser, Sol, 294
Lewton, Val, 266
Leyda, Jay, 327
Litvak, Anatole, 320
Lloyd, Harold, 85, 244
Lorentz, Pare, 101
Louis, Hershell, 19–20
Lubitsch, Ernst, 371, 377
Ludwig, Emil, 254
Lukov, Leonid, 313
Lumière, Louis, 244, 315
Lye, Len, 53

MacArthur, Charles, 266
MacGowan, Kenneth, xvi, xviii, xx
Mamoulian, Rouben, 266
Matiesen, Otto, 10
Mayer, Louis B., 346
McCarey, Leo, 266
McLaren, Norman, 53
Melnitz, William, 366
Milland, Ray, 371
Montagu, Ivor, 316
Moore, Colleen, 245
Morgan, Michèle, 339, 340
Moten, Etta, 257
Muni, Paul, 312
Murrow, Edward R., 115

Nemeth, Ted, 26–27
Nichols, Dudley, 318
Nielsen, Asta, 245
Noël-Noël, 341

Pabst, G. W., 363
Pagnol, Maurice, 335, 338, 339
Painlevé, Jean, 95
Parsons, Louella, 244
Perlberg, William, 293
Peterson, Sidney, 33, 58
Philipe, Gérard, 342, 343
Pichel, Irving, xviii
Pick, Lupu, 363
Pickford, Mary, 244, 267
Polonsky, Abraham, xviii, xxii–xxiii
Porter, Edwin S., 250, 252, 267
Potamkin, Harry Alan, 18, 20, 321
Pozner, Vladimir, 341, 366
Presle, Micheline, 343

Prevert, Jacques, 339
Pudovkin, Vsevolod, xxiii, 20, 313, 315,
    316, 318

Radiguet, Raymond, 342
Raizman, Yuli, 313
Ramsaye, Terry, 320
Ray, Man, 53–54
Reisch, Walter, 371
Renoir, Jean, 335, 338, 340–342, 363
Resnais, Alain, 343
Reynard, Paul, 364
Richter, Hans, 47–48
Riefenstahl, Leni, 102
Robinson, Bill, 257
Rogers, Ginger, 371
Rolfe, Franklin, xviii
Romance, Viviane, 340
Romm, Mikhail, 315
Rosten, Leo, 254
Rotha, Paul, 345, 346
Rouquier, Georges, 341
Ruttman, Walter, 35, 53

Salacrou, Armand, 338–339
Satie, Erik, 7, 72
Schuftan, Eugene, 371
Scott, Adrian, 266
Seacoat, Ellen, xix–xx
Seastrom, Victor, 250
Seeler, Moritz, 370
Seldes, Gilbert, 9, 296
Selznick, David, 269
Shamroy, Leon, 10, 16
Sheeler, Charles, 7–8
Simon, Michel, 340, 368
Siodmak, Robert, 371
Smythe, Dallas W., 271
Spencer, Kenneth, 257
Stanwyck, Barbara, 371
Steiner, Ralph, 18–19, 22
Stern, Seymour, 24
Strand, Paul, 7–8
Sturges, Preston, 266
Swanson, Gloria, 247

Taylor, Robert, 352
Thatcher, Molly Day, 22
Tisse, Edward, 315

Toland, Greg, 42n2, 267
Trauberg, Ilya, 313

Ulmer, Edgar, 371

Van Voorhis, Westbrook, 109, 115
Vedres, Nicole, 343, 364
Vertov, Dziga, 20–21
Vidor, Charles, 20
Vidor, King, 266
Vigo, Jean, 335, 366–369
Vishnevsky, Venyamin, 320
Vogel, Joseph, 47–49, 58
Von Sternberg, Joseph, 266
Von Stroheim, Erich, 248, 251, 363, 371, 375, 379
Vorkapich, Slavko, 9–10, 42–43

Wald, Jerry, 299
Warner, H. B., 375, 379

Warshow, Robert, 85
Waters, Ethel, 257
Watson, James Sibley, 17, 23–24
Webber, Melville, 17, 23–24
Weinberg, Herman, 10, 24
Whitney, James, 35–36, 49, 53, 58
Whitney, John, 35–36, 49, 53, 58
Wilder, Billy, 370–380
Wilson, Dooley, 257
Wright, Basil, 95
Wright, William H., 294
Wyler, William, 180–181, 267

Yutkevich, Sergei, 319

Zecca, Ferdinand, 363, 364
Zinnemann, Fred, 371
Zukor, Adolph, 265
Zvoboda, Andrès, 343

Selected Titles Index

Note: Film titles in italic; radio and television programs in roman and quotes.

Ace in the Hole, 372–374, 376, 378
Age d'or, L' (Golden Age, The), 54
Aigle à deux têtes, L', 343
All Quiet on the Western Front, 175, 244
American in Paris, An, 298
Andalusian Dog, An (Chien andalou, Un), 54, 58
"Andrews Family, The," 219
Angèle, 339
Antoine et Antoinette, 340
Applause, 266
A propos de Nice, 366, 369
Arise My Love, 371, 373, 378
Arrowsmith, 257, 258
Atalante, L', 366–369
At Land, 29–30
Aux yeux du souvenir, 343

"Baby Snooks," 219
Ball of Fire, 371
Band Concert, The, 73
Bataan, 257, 258
Battle of Britain, The (from *Why We Fight*), 252, 274
Battle of China, The (from *Why We Fight*), 274
Battle of Russia, The (from *Why We Fight*), 252, 274
Battle of San Pietro, The, 106
Battle of the Rails, 269
Beauté du diable, La, 339
Beginning or the End, The, 268
Belle équipe, La, 340

Belle et la bête, La, 341, 343, 386
Belle meunière, La, 339
Bend of the River, 298
Ben-Hur, 345, 346
Best Years of Our Lives, The, 85, 19, 201
Bicycle Thieves, 347
Big Carnival, The (aka *Ace in the Hole*), 372
Big Sleep, The, 260, 262
Birth of a Nation, The, 257, 258, 345
Black Pirate, The, 246, 247, 251
Blood of a Poet (Sang d'un poète), 54, 384
Bluebeard's Eighth Wife, 371
Blue Veil, The, 298
Boomerang, 268
Boule de suif, 343
Brief Encounter, 175

Cabinet of Dr. Caligari, The, 6, 8–10, 16–17, 245, 251, 377
Cabin in the Sky, 257, 258
Carnet de bal, Un, 340
Casablanca, 257, 258
Champion, The, 298
Champs Elysées, 361
Chase, The, 36–37
Chien andalou, Un (Andalusian Dog, An), 54, 58
Childhood of Maxim Gorky, The, 313, 314
Ciel est à vous, Le, 338, 340
Citizen Kane, 107
Clash by Night, 298, 299
"Clyde Beatty," 219
Colonel Blimp, 289
Country Bride, The, 313
Courbeau, Le, 341

Crash Dive, 257, 258
Crisis, 102
Crossfire, 266, 269
Curse of the Cat People, The, 266

"Dante's Inferno," 234
Dawn to Dawn, 24–25
Day of Wrath, 269
Dédée d'Anvers, 342
Dernières vacances, Les, 343
Devil in the Flesh, 342, 343
D'homme à hommes, 343
Diable au corps, Le (Devil in the Flesh), 342, 343
Don't Be a Sucker, 278
Double Indemnity, 262, 371, 373
Douce, 342
Dreams That Money Can Buy, 47–48, 54
Dr. Mabuse, 377

"Eastside Kids," 219
Emak Bakia, 54
Emperor Waltz, 372, 374
Enfants du Paradis, Les, 335, 338, 339
Escape Episode, 32
Eternel Retour, L', 383
Etrange Monsieur Victor, L', 340
Euridyce, 339

Falbalas, 340
Fall of the House of Usher, The, 17, 23–24
Fall of Troy, The, 345, 346
Fantasia, 35, 70–71, 74
Fantasmagoria, 36–37
Farrebique, 341
Femme du boulanger, La, 339
Fighting Lady, The, 106
Fille du puisatier, La, 339
Fingal's Cave, 42
Fireworks, 32
Five Graves to Cairo, 371, 374
"Flash Gordon," 219
Fleur de l'age, La, 339
Flight, 266
Flying Down to Rio, 257, 258
Fog over Frisco, 266
Foreign Affair, A, 372–375, 378
Forest Murmurs, 42–43
Fragment of Seeking, 32–33, 58
Fury, 107

Girl from Leningrad, The, 313
Glenn Falls Sequence, 36–37
Goemons, 343
Golden Age, The (Age d'or, L'), 54
Goupi Mains Rouges, 340
Grapes of Wrath, The, 91–92, 107
Greatest Show on Earth, The, 298
Great Expectations, 175
Great McGinty, The, 266
Great Train Robbery, The, 244
Greed, 246, 248, 251

Heiress, The, 180–185
Helen of Troy, 346
Henry V, 175
Hitler's Children, 265
Hold Back the Dawn, 371, 378
Home of the Brave, 276
H_2O, 18–19
House of Cards, 48, 58
House on 92nd Street, The, 262, 268

Informer, The, 175
In This Our Life, 257, 258
Intolerance, 249, 250, 251
Introspection, 37, 42, 47
It Happened One Night, 246, 247, 251

Jean Helion—One Artist at Work, 47
Joan of Arc, 201
Jofroi, 339
Johann the Coffin Maker, 10
Johnny Belinda, 201
Jour se lève, Le, 339
Juarez, 107

Last Laugh, The, 250
Last Moment, The, 10, 15–16, 20
"Laurel and Hardy," 219
Life and Death of 9413—A Hollywood Extra, The, 9–10, 42
Life of Emile Zola, The, 107
Little Caesar, 262
"Lone Ranger, The," 219
Lost Patrol, 266
Lost Weekend, The, 262, 372, 374, 378
Lot in Sodom, 23–24
Loved One, The, 228
Loves of Zero, The, 10

Love Your Neighbor, 79, 81
Lumière d'été, 338, 340

Macbeth, 269
Major and the Minor, The, 371, 378
Make Way for Tomorrow, 266
Male and Female, 246, 247, 252
Mannahatta, 6–7
Manon, 337, 342
Man to Remember, A, 266
Mariage de chiffon, Le, 342
Marrying Kind, The, 295
Mashenka, 313
Massacre des innocents, Le, 340
Maudits, Les, 341
Mauvaise graine, 371
Mechanical Principles, 18–19
Memphis Belle, 97
Menschen am Sonntag (People on Sunday),
   370, 371, 372
Meshes of the Afternoon, 29
Midnight, 371
Miss Tatlock's Millions, 201
Moana, 7, 93, 250, 252, 266, 341
Mobile Composition, 19–20
Monsieur de Falindor, 337
Mourning Becomes Electra, 268
Mr. Motorboat's Last Stand, 22
Murder, My Sweet, 262

Naissance du cinéma, La, 343
Nanook of the North 7, 93, 341
New Realism of Fernand Léger, The, 47
Ninotchka, 371, 374, 377
Noces de sable, 343
Nous les gosses, 341

Odd Man Out, 175–176
Odyssey, The, 345
Open City, 347
Orphée, 383
Our Daily Bread, 266
"Our Miss Brooks," 219

Paisan, 269, 347
Panique, 339
Parents terrible, Les, 343
Paris 1900, 343
Passion of Joan of Arc, The (Passion de
   Jeanne d'Arc, La), 250, 252

Pattes blanches, 340
People on Sunday (Menschen am Sonntag),
   370, 371, 372
Pépé le Moko, 340
Père tranquille, Le 341
Pie in the Sky, 22–23
Place in the Sun, A, 295
Plague Summer, 49
Point du jour, Le, 341
Portes de la nuit, Les, 339
Portrait of Jenny, 201
Potemkin, 245, 250, 252
Potted Psalm, The, 33, 58
Prelude to War (from Why We Fight), 252,
   331
Pride of St. Louis, The, 298
Printemps de la liberté, Le, 340
Public Enemy, 250

Quai des Brumes, 339
Quai des Orfèvres, 341
Queen Elizabeth, 244, 265
Que viva México, 8
Quo Vadis?, 345, 346, 348, 351, 353

Rainbow, The, 313
Remorques, 340
"Reunion, U.S.A.," 119–122
Rhapsody in Rivets, 73–74
Rhythm on the River, 371
Ritual in Transfigured Time, 31
River, The, 101
Ruy Blas, 343

Sahara, 257, 258
Salvation Hunters, 266
Sang d'un poète (Blood of a Poet), 54, 384
Scarface, 262
Scoundrel, The, 266
Search, The, 201
Seashell and the Clergyman, The, 54
Shoe Shine, 347
Silence est d'or, Le, 338
Singin' in the Rain, 299
"Sky King," 219
Snake Pit, The, 201
"Space Patrol," 219
Specter of the Rose, 269
Spy, The, 20–21
Stagecoach, 175

Stalag 17, 377
Steamboat Willie, 244
Storm Warning, 43–44
Stormy Weather, 257, 258
Story of a Nobody, The, 20
Story of Louis Pasteur, The, 288
Streetcar Named Desire, A, 295
Study in Choreography for the Camera, A, 30–31
Sunday Beach, 45–46
Sunrise, 244
Sunset Boulevard, 372, 375, 378
Surf and Seaweed, 18–19
Symphonie pastorale, La 343

Target for Tonight, 97, 106
"Tarzan," 219
Tell-tale Heart, The, 16–17
Ten Commandments, The, 345
They Also Serve, 106
They Met in Moscow, 313
13 Rue Madeleine, 268
Thunder Rock, 175
"Time for Beany," 219
Tol'able David, 246, 248, 252

Tomorrow the World, 277
Tree Trunk to Head, 44–45
Triumph of the Will, 102
Twenty-four Dollar Island, 6–8
Two Soldiers, 313

Ulysses, 349, 351, 353
Une si jolie petite plage, 342

Valley of the Tennessee, 106
Van Gogh, 343
Visiteurs du soir, Les, 335, 338
"Voice of America, The," 152–156

Waxworks, 377
We Are from Kronstadt, 316
West of Singapore, 257, 258
What a Life!, 371
Why We Fight, xiv, 102, 244, 252, 274
Wilson, 107
Wuthering Heights, 175, 180

Zéro de conduite, 366–369
Zoya, 313

DESIGNER Nola Burger
COMPOSITOR G & S Typesetters, Inc.
TEXT 11/13.75 Adobe Garamond
DISPLAY Franklin Gothic